Growth
Volume 1: Econometric General
Equilibrium Modeling

Growth
Volume 1: Econometric General
Equilibrium Modeling

Dale W. Jorgenson

The MIT Press
Cambridge, Massachusetts
London, England

This book was printed and bound in the United States of America.

Library of Congress Cataloging-in-Publication Data

Jorgenson, Dale Weldeau, 1933–
 Growth / Dale W. Jorgenson.
  p. cm.
 Includes bibliographical references and indexes.
 Contents: v. 1. Econometric general equilibrium modeling — v. 2. Energy, the environment, and economic growth.
 ISBN 0–262–10073–8 (v. 1: alk. paper). — ISBN 0–262–10074–6 (v. 2: alk. paper)
 1. Economic development — Econometric models. 2. Equilibrium (Economics).
 3. United States — Economic conditions — Econometric models. I. Title.
 HD75.J67 1998   98–28689
 338.9—dc21   CIP

Contents

List of Tables

Preface

Dale W. Jorgenson

This volume is the first of two volumes devoted to empirical modeling of economic growth and includes papers on linear growth models, the neoclassical model of development of a dual economy, and my initial econometric studies of energy policy and economic growth. The second volume, entitled *Energy, the Environment, and Economic Growth*, is devoted to the more detailed studies of energy policy as well as environmental, trade, and tax policies. The organizing principle for this research is the concept of an intertemporal price system.

An intertemporal price system balances demands and supplies for products and factors of production at each point of time. In addition, prices of assets are linked to the present values of prices of future capital services. This forward-looking feature of an intertemporal price system is combined with backward linkages among investment, capital stock, and capital services in modeling the long-run dynamics of economic growth. A complete theory of economic growth must encompass both forward and backward linkages.

My research on economic growth was initiated in my doctoral dissertation at Harvard University, "Duality and Stability in Dynamic Input-Output Analysis," completed in 1959 under the supervision of Wassily W. Leontief. Leontief (1941) is the founder of empirical general equilibrium modeling, beginning with implementation of the static input-output model. Leontief (1953) gave further impetus to the development of empirical general equilibrium modeling by introducing the dynamic input-output model that was the subject of my thesis. The Swedish Royal Academy of Sciences awarded him the Alfred Nobel Memorial Prize in Economic Sciences in 1973 for "the development of the input-output method and its application to important economic problems."

Leontief's dynamic input-output model is a multi-sectoral model of economic growth, formulated as a system of linear differential equations. This model has a unique, balanced growth equilibrium with a constant growth rate and non-negative output levels in every sector. However, this solution of the model is not necessarily stable. Stability in this context refers to convergence of an economy described by the model to the balanced growth equilibrium from non-negative initial outputs. In the absence of stability, the model would violate the economic requirement that output levels must be non-negative at all points of time.

Michio Morishima (1958) and Robert M. Solow (1959) provided a dual interpretation to the dynamic input-output model. In this interpretation sectoral prices are dual to the outputs of Leontief's model, while the interest rate corresponds to the growth rate of the economy. A solution to the dual to the dynamic input-output model is an intertemporal price system that balances demands and supplies, assures that profits in each sector are non-positive, and has the forward-looking feature that asset prices are equal to present values of future capital service prices. There is a unique, stationary intertemporal price system with a constant interest rate and non-negative prices in every sector, but this solution of the model is not necessarily stable.

In chapter 1, a summary of my Ph.D. thesis published in 1960, I show that the dynamic input-output model is stable if and only if the dual price model is unstable and vice versa. This implies that the models of prices and outputs, taken together, cannot provide a complete theory of economic growth. In chapter 3, I extend this analysis to a number of other models formulated as linear difference or differential equations. My conclusion is that these models are not an appropriate starting point for empirical modeling of economic growth.

Chapter 2 presents a neoclassical theory of a dual economy taking Solow's (1956) neoclassical model of economic growth, rather than Leontief's dynamic input-output model, as a point of departure. My objective is to unify the theory of economic growth for advanced economies, exemplified by Solow's neoclassical growth model, with theories of economic development. My specific focus is the economic-demographic theory of development propounded by Harvey Leibenstein (1957).

The accumulation of capital is endogenous in Solow's growth model, while growth of population and changes in technology are exogenous. In Leibenstein's theory of development population growth and capital accumulation are determined simultaneously. I consider a model of a dual economy with an advanced or modern sector, identified with industry, and a backward or traditional sector, identified with agriculture. I make population growth a function of the food supply; capital accumulation is financed through saving in the industrial sector.

I show that a dual economy can give rise to a low-level equilibrium trap. Leibenstein had introduced this concept to describe an economy with a stationary population and no economic growth. I extend the concept to a Malthusian equilibrium with population and sustenance growing at equal rates. I show that viability of the industrial sector depends on the emergence of an agricultural surplus. With a growing surplus more and more of the agricultural labor force can be transferred to industry. Under these conditions the economy will industrialize and take on the characteristics identified by Solow.

My research on a neoclassical model of the development of a dual economy paralleled work on the classical approach to economic development originated by W. Arthur Lewis (1955). Lewis emphasizes the concept of disguised unemployment in the backward sector, rather than the possibility of a Malthusian equilibrium. He identifies this concept with a condition of zero marginal productivity of labor in agriculture, making available unlimited supplies of labor to the industrial sector without sacrificing agricultural output. The disappearance of disguised unemployment constitutes a "turning point" with continuing growth under the conditions envisioned by Solow. The influential 1964 book by John C. Fei and Gustav Ranis formalizes these ideas and presents considerable empirical evidence in support of them.

The policy implications of the two theories of economic development are radically different. The classical model prescribes forced industrialization along Soviet lines with agriculture as a reservoir of labor waiting to be tapped. The neoclassical model implies that agriculture and industry must be developed in tandem. One strategy is to increase productivity growth in agriculture as a necessary prerequisite for industrial growth. An alternative strategy is to reduce population growth in rural areas in order to create the conditions for development of an agricultural surplus.

In chapter 4, I compare the classical and neoclassical approaches to economic development, focusing on the relationship between the degree of industrialization and the level of development. I derive a series of contrasting implications of the two models of a dual economy. For example, in a regime of disguised unemployment labor productivity in industry is constant and the capital-output ratio declining, while rates of growth of output, employment, and capital are increasing. By contrast the capital-output ratio converges to a constant in the neoclassical model of a dual economy, while labor productivity rose and growth rates are declining.

In chapter 5, I test the two alternative theories of economic development, using direct evidence on disguised unemployment in the agricultural sector assembled by agricultural economists and anthropologists and considered, for example, by T. W. Schultz (1964). I also review indirect evidence from the quantitative economic history of Japan during the late nineteenth and twentieth centuries compiled by Kazushi Ohkawa (1957) and his associates at Hitotsubashi University. Fei and Ranis (1964) cite evidence from this period of Japanese economic history in support of their classical model of a dual economy. I argue that both forms of empirical evidence are consistent with the neoclassical approach.

I initiated research on econometric general equilibrium modeling under the auspices of the Energy Policy Project in 1972. The purpose of the Energy Policy Project was to study alternative policies for stimulating energy conservation. By 1974 Edward A. Hudson and I constructed an econometric general equilibrium model that captures the inter-relationships between energy policies and economic growth. This model incorporates econometric representations of technology and preferences as basic building blocks. We assign a key role to energy taxes in promoting conservation and show how to employ the price system in adapting to changes in the availability of energy resources.

In 1973 Ernst R. Berndt and I constructed econometric models of production in each of nine industrial sectors making up the U.S. economy, including five industries that comprised the energy sector. The non-energy sectors were agriculture, manufacturing, transportation, and services, while the energy sectors were crude petroleum and natural gas mining, coal mining, petroleum refining, electric utilities, and gas utilities. This breakdown of the energy sector made it possible to identify the production and consumption of coal, oil, and natural gas, as well as conversion of these primary energy sources into electricity.

Berndt and I divided inputs in each sector among capital (K), labor (L), energy (E), and materials (M). We expressed shares of these inputs in the value of output as functions of the input prices. We then decomposed energy and materials into components corresponding to the outputs of the energy and non-energy sectors, respectively. I surveyed empirical research on general equilibrium models of production in my paper, "Econometric Modeling of Producer Behavior," published in the volume, *Econometrics and Producer Behavior*. Berndt (1990) provided an exposition of the econometrics of production in his textbook, *The Practice of Econometrics*.

In chapter 6, Hudson and I incorporate the econometric models of producer behavior I developed with Berndt into a nine-sector general equilibrium model of production. We employ this representation of technology to determine intermediate demands for outputs of the nine industries, including demands for the five types of energy. Energy policies require changing energy-output ratios in order to achieve energy conservation. Our key innovation is to determine the input-output coefficients as functions of the prices of the inputs. In Leontief's static and dynamic input-output models these coefficients are exogenous.

Hudson and I combine our model of production with an econometric model of consumer behavior. This representation of preferences is based on the transcendental logarithmic indirect utility function, introduced in my 1975 paper with Laurits Christensen and Lawrence Lau and included in the volume *Aggregate Consumer Behavior*. This model determines the shares of goods and services in personal consumption expenditures as functions of prices and total spending. The responses of these budget shares to changes in energy prices provide an additional channel for energy conservation. Our general equilibrium model is closed by balance equations between demands and supplies for the products of each of the nine sectors and the primary factors of production.

Since prices are endogenous variables in an econometric general equilibrium model, methods for estimation of non-linear systems of simultaneous equations are required for modeling producer and consumer behavior. I present methods appropriate for this purpose in my 1974 paper with Jean-Jacques Laffont, included in the volume, *Econometrics and Producer Behavior*. I developed the corresponding methods for statistical inference in my 1979 paper with A. Ronald Gallant, also included in *Econometrics and Producer Behavior*. These methods were greatly extended by Lars Hansen in 1982 and became the basis for the Generalized Method of Moments. This is now the standard approach to estimation and inference in macro-econometric modeling.

The starting point for my research on econometric general equilibrium modeling is the model of capital as a factor of production I introduced in 1963 in a paper included as chapter 1 of the volume, *Capital Theory and Investment Behavior*. The key innovation of this model is a concept of the cost of capital incorporating tax policy for capital income as a determinant of the demand for capital services. I had employed the cost of capital in modeling the short-run dynamics of investment spending in macro-econometric forecasting models in papers included in the volume, *Tax Policy and the Cost of Capital*. My 1974 paper with Hudson is the first application of this concept in modeling the long-run dynamics of economic growth.

In 1973, Laurits Christensen and I incorporated the cost of capital into a complete system of national accounts for the United States in our paper included in the volume, *Postwar U.S. Economic Growth*. The main innovation in this accounting system is the integration of accounts for investment, capital stock, and capital services into production and income and expenditure accounts. The key to this innovation is a system of vintage accounts for prices and quantities of investment goods. This system includes the prices for investment goods, capital assets, and capital services that comprise an intertemporal price system.

A feature of the Christensen–Jorgenson accounting system essential for econometric general equilibrium modeling is that all accounts are presented in current and constant prices. In conventional national accounting systems, such as the United Nations System of National Accounts (1968) and the U.S. National Income and Product Accounts (1977), the production account provides output, but not input, in current and constant prices. Both are required for econometric modeling of production. Similarly, for econometric modeling of consumer behavior the income and expenditure account must include the flow of capital services from consumers' durables as well as housing. Conventional systems give only purchases of durables, which represent investment rather than consumption.

Hudson and I construct a macro-econometric growth model in order to complete our framework for energy policy analysis. This implements a two-sector neoclassical growth model econometrically and integrates demands and supplies for consumption and investment goods and for capital and labor services. We link the output of consumption goods to personal consumption expenditures and the output of investment goods to the accumulation of capital. The inputs of capital and labor services become the supply side of markets for these factors of production.

Our macro-econometric growth model incorporates an econometric model of producer behavior based on the transcendental logarithmic production frontier introduced in my 1973 paper with Christensen and Lau, included in the volume, *Econometrics and Producer Behavior*. The econometric model of consumer behavior includes the demand for leisure as well as goods and services. Both models are estimated econometrically from time series data from the system of national accounts for the U.S. that I developed with Christensen. The methods of estimation are those presented in my paper with Laffont.

The primary objective of the econometric general equilibrium model I constructed with Hudson was to model the long-run dynamics of U.S. economic growth. This required innovations in econometric methodology and novel methods for data construction. The innovations in econometrics included the development of new techniques for estimation and inference, as well as a new approach for representing technology and preferences as the basic building blocks of an econometric general equilibrium model. The new methods for data construction required the solution of long-standing problems in national accounting in order to integrate income and product accounts with accounts for capital. However, this initial effort fell short of my ultimate goal of modeling the intertemporal price system empirically.

The macro-econometric growth model I constructed with Hudson became the progenitor of a more detailed econometric model for the analysis of tax policy presented in my 1986 papers with Kun-Young Yun and included in the volume, *Tax Policy and the Cost of Capital*. The first innovation in my model with Yun is a forward-looking econometric model of aggregate consumer behavior, based on the "Euler equation" approach originated by Robert E. Hall in 1978. The second innovation is an intertemporal price system with asset prices equal to present values of future prices of capital services. The multi-sectoral model I developed with Peter Wilcoxen in 1990, included in the volume, *Energy, the Environment, and Economic Growth*, retains both features.

In chapter 6 Hudson and I present detailed projections of U.S. economic growth and the demands and supplies for all forms of energy and energy prices for the period, 1970–2000. We show that these projections are in line with alternative projections prepared before the Oil Crisis of 1973. We also show how our projections can be modified to reflect higher prices of imported petroleum. Finally, we consider the imposition of energy taxes in order to promote conservation. We consider a Btu tax, levied on each form of energy in proportion to energy content, an *ad valorem* tax proportional to the market value of each form of energy, and, finally, a petroleum tax. We conclude that economic incentives would make it possible to achieve substantial energy conservation without major economic losses.

In chapter 7, Hudson and I analyze alternative "scenarios" for the future development of energy markets presented by the Energy Policy Project. We first project energy utilization and economic growth under a continuation of historical trends, referring to this scenario as Historical Growth. We next consider a Technical Fix scenario resulting from higher energy prices and the introduction of better practices for energy conservation. The Technical Fix alternative is consistent with energy price increases like those resulting from Oil Crisis of 1973. Wilcoxen and I have analyzed the response of the U.S. economy to these price increases, as well as the further increases associated with the Iranian Revolution of 1979, in our 1993 survey paper, included as chapter 1 in *Energy, the Environment, and Economic Growth*.

Finally, Hudson and I consider Zero Energy Growth from 1975 levels with greater energy conservation induced by an *ad valorem* tax on energy. We show that these reductions in energy utilization would require relatively modest sacrifices in future U.S. economic growth. Wilcoxen and I have considered taxes for stabilizing emissions of carbon dioxide by means of a carbon tax, levied on alternative fuels in proportion to their carbon content. One of the objectives we consider is stabilization of emissions at 1990 levels. We summarize the results in our 1993 survey paper.

In chapter 8, Ben Bernanke and I integrate the Hudson-Jorgenson model of energy and U.S. economic growth with a detailed econometric model of the U.S. natural gas industry constructed by Paul W. MacAvoy and Robert S. Pindyck (1973). Each of the models had been employed in isolation to study the impact of specific energy policies. For example, the MacAvoy–Pindyck Natural Gas Model had been used to study the effects of deregulation of natural gas markets within a partial equilibrium framework. The purpose of combining these two energy policy models is to analyze the impacts of energy policies on a particular sector, the natural gas industry, as well as the energy sector as a whole and the growth of the U.S. economy in a general equilibrium setting.

The Natural Gas Model incorporates the production, distribution, and consumption of natural gas, broken down by twenty-nine producing regions and forty consuming regions. This model determines the level of exploration and development of new reserves as well as production of natural gas and depletion of existing resources. Prices of natural gas are exogenous to the model, reflecting the regulation of well-head prices by the Federal Power Commission. Bernanke and I simulate the impact of deregulation of natural gas prices and imposition of a quota on petroleum imports. We show that the cost of imposing an oil import quota in terms of economic growth would be substantial. We also show that the deregulation of natural would stimulate the supply of natural gas while alleviating costly gas shortages.

In chapter 9, Kenneth C. Hoffman and I combine the Hudson-Jorgenson econometric general equilibrium model with a linear activity analysis model of the U.S. energy sector. The activity analysis model includes information from detailed engineering studies of technologies that are not currently available, but could be developed through government sponsorship of research and development programs. By contrast, econometric representations of producer and consumer behavior are limited to technologies already in existence. Technology assessment requires an economic evaluation of the costs and benefits of future adoption of new technologies. This must include the impact of these technologies on the energy sector and the growth of the U.S. economy.

Our integrated general equilibrium model is based on an expanded system of inter-industry accounts with explicit detail for energy resource sectors, energy conversion processes, and energy product sectors. Data for the energy sectors is provided by an engineering description taken from the Brookhaven Energy Systems Optimization Model (BESOM), while data for the non-energy sectors is obtained from the econometric general equilibrium model. BESOM can be formulated as a linear programming model and was employed as a leading illustration of linear activity analysis by Tjalling C. Koopmans (1975). The dual to this linear programming model generates prices for energy resources, conversion processes, and final products. These are combined with prices for the non-energy products in the integrated model.

Hoffman and I present an integrated economic and engineering analysis of The National Plan for Energy Research, Development, and

Demonstration prepared by the U.S. Energy Research and Development Administration (1975). We show that this plan would result in a
rapid rise in imports of petroleum over the following decade. We consider an alternative policy with a tariff on imported petroleum and
taxes on domestic energy producers. New technologies such as oil
from shale, direct use of solar energy, generation of electricity from
geothermal sources, and coal gasification and liquefaction are introduced in greater quantities under the alternative policy. In addition,
electric automobiles are introduced on a modest scale to conserve
gasoline.

In chapter 10, Hudson and I present a second version of the combined econometric general equilibrium model and linear activity analysis model. In addition to the features of the model Hoffman and I
discuss in chapter 9, this model integrates investment in new capacities for producing energy resources, conversion processes, and utilization of energy products with investment in the non-energy sectors.
Investments in the energy and non-energy sectors are balanced with
saving for the U.S. economy as a whole. We consider alternative policies to reduce dependence on imported energy and reduce the growth
of energy consumption in the U.S. economy. Unlike the policies we
consider for the Energy Policy Project, the required increases in energy
prices and energy conservation measures have a widespread and
significant impact on the structure and growth of the U.S. economy.

In chapter 13, Hudson and I analyze alternative policies for the
reduction of petroleum imports in greater detail. We first consider
taxes on U.S. petroleum production that would bring domestic
petroleum prices to world levels. We allow natural gas price controls
to continue, but raise natural gas prices. Energy conservation is stimulated by taxes on the use of oil and gas in industry, restrictions on the
use of oil and gas by utilities, subsidies for the insulation of structures,
and mandatory performance standards for energy-using prices.
Second, we add a tariff on imported petroleum. Finally, we consider
excise taxes on delivered energy sufficient to reduce delivered energy
to levels required to reduce or eliminate petroleum imports.

Hudson and I simulate the impact of the four alternative policies
for the reduction of petroleum imports on input patterns in the four
non-energy sectors—agriculture, manufacturing, transportation, and
services. We describe these changes in terms of Allen elasticities of
substitution, defined as proportional changes in ratios of inputs with
respect to proportional changes in the corresponding ratios of input

prices. This reveals patterns of substitution and complementarity among inputs. Energy and capital are complements in agriculture, manufacturing, and transportation, while these inputs are substitutes in services. Energy and materials are complements in manufacturing and services, but substitutes in agriculture and transportation. Finally, energy and labor are complements in transportation, but substitutes in the other three sectors. All combinations of capital, labor, and materials are substitutes in all four sectors.

Hudson and I simulate the impact of the four policies on the composition of final demand—personal consumption expenditures, gross private domestic investment, government purchases, and net exports. The overall level of final demand is reduced considerably. Energy shrinks in relation to other components of final demand, while the energy intensive sectors—agriculture, manufacturing, and transportation—decline relative to services. Combining changes in final demands and the composition of inputs, we find that the energy intensity of national product declines dramatically. We conclude that the objectives of slower energy growth and reduction of import dependence can be achieved, but at unacceptable costs in terms of slower economic growth and foregone output.

In chapter 11, I present an overview of U.S. energy policy in the aftermath of the Oil Crisis of 1973. At the time of the crisis the U.S. had a system of wage and price controls in effect. Energy policy evolved into a complex system of price controls on domestically produced crude petroleum and refined products that had the effect of maintaining petroleum prices below world levels. The system of price controls averaged the price of imported crude with domestic crude in pricing refined products. In effect, foreign producers received a subsidy financed by means of a tax on domestic producers. Not surprisingly, domestic output fell while imports of petroleum rose.

In 1977, the U.S. government announced a National Energy Policy with gradual decontrol of petroleum and natural gas prices. A system of taxes on the use of oil and gas by industrial and utility users of these fuels was proposed, together with an elaborate system of tax credits for conversion to other forms of energy. Finally, regulations on fuel efficiency of automobiles and mandatory energy efficiency standards for appliances were introduced. I show that these policies would have the effect of raising U.S. energy prices above world levels and would stimulate energy conservation and a reduction in imports.

However, I argue that world energy prices could eventually fall and that U.S. policy should take this possibility into account.

I present the outlook for U.S. economic growth with higher energy prices. I draw attention to the combination of lower investment, more rapid employment growth, and slower growth of labor productivity. I attribute this to patterns of substitution and complementarity among energy and other inputs. The substitution of labor for energy stimulates growth of employment, but depresses productivity growth. Lower investment reflects the decline in growth of economic activity. I project slower economic growth as a consequence of reduced productivity growth and lower investment.

In chapter 12, Hudson and I provide a more detailed analysis of the impact of higher energy prices on the U.S. economy during the period 1972–1976. We simulate the growth of the U.S. economy with and without the energy price increases that resulted from the first Oil Crisis. We compare the input-output coefficients with and without these price increases. Energy-output ratios fall in all sectors with the most substantial declines in manufacturing and services. Capital-output ratios also decline in agriculture, manufacturing, and transportation, while labor-output ratios rise in all four non-energy sectors. Materials-output ratios fall slightly in agriculture and manufacturing, rise in transportation, and decline substantially in services.

We decompose the change in energy utilization in the U.S. economy among three sources: slower aggregate growth, change in the composition of final demand, and reduced energy intensity of production. We attribute about a quarter of the decline in energy use to a lower level of economic activity. Reduced energy intensity of final demand accounts for a little more than a third of the decline in energy use, while reduced energy intensity of production explains the remaining forty percent. A similar decomposition of the reduction in capital input shows that the decline is proportional to the reduction in overall activity. This decline generates large losses in employment, but these are offset by increases in the labor intensity of production and final demand.

In chapter 14, Hudson, David O'Connor, and I integrate the Hudson–Jorgenson model with the Regionalized Electricity Model constructed by Martin L. Baughman and Paul L. Joskow (1974). The purpose of the combined model is to analyze the impact of policies for electricity regulation on the electricity industry, the energy sector, and U.S. economic growth. Conceptually, the electricity sector of the combined model replaces the corresponding sector of the Hudson–

Jorgenson model. Electricity prices and fuel input requirements are generated within the Regionalized Electricity Model, while the demand for electricity and fuel prices are determined within the Hudson–Jorgenson model. The price system of the combined model balances demands and supplies for electricity and other forms of energy, as well as non-energy products and the factors of production.

The focus of chapter 14 is on the impact of restrictions on generating capacity. These include a nuclear moratorium, that is, a prohibition on the initiation of construction for new nuclear plants, restrictions on the expansion of coal-burning capacity, and higher fuel prices and capital costs for electric utilities. Each of these restrictions, considered individually, has a negative impact on the electricity utility sector by raising the electricity price and reducing the growth of demand for electricity. Slower electrification spills over into the market for other forms of energy, especially petroleum, resulting in increases in petroleum imports.

However, the most important finding of the study of electricity regulation is that there are powerful interactions among the various restrictions on the growth of generating capacity. For example, a nuclear moratorium produces a shift toward the expansion of coal-burning capacity. Similarly, restrictions on the expansion of coal-burning capacity produce a shift toward nuclear generation of electricity. Either of these restrictions, by itself, has a relatively modest economic impact. However, the combination of restrictions on both coal and nuclear results in a severe curtailment of increases in electricity production and substantially dampens economic growth.

The overall conclusion of chapter 14 is similar to that of the study of import restrictions in chapter 13. Even a relatively drastic change in energy policy, such as a nuclear moratorium, has a modest economic impact because of the flexibility of the energy sector and the possibility of adapting to changes in the availability of energy resources through the price system. The simultaneous imposition of several restrictions of this type causes severe and long-lasting economic damages. In fact, the U.S. regulatory system did impose what amounts to a nuclear moratorium with the predictable effect of stimulating the expansion of coal-burning capacity. The environmental consequences are analyzed in the companion volume, *Energy, the Environment, and Economic Growth*.

The studies of energy policy and U.S. economic growth summarized in this volume were evaluated in terms of the impact on the growth and structure of the U.S. economy without appealing to formal welfare economics. The transcendental logarithmic model of aggregate consumer behavior presented in my 1982 paper with Lau and Thomas M. Stoker, included in the volume, *Aggregate Consumer Behavior*, made it possible to fill this gap. Following John R. Hicks (1942), Lau, Stoker, and I developed methods for computing compensating and equivalent variations in the welfare of individual consumers. This made it possible to analyze economic policies in terms of Pareto optimality, the welfare concept employed in the theory of general equilibrium.

In 1985, Daniel T. Slesnick and I presented a new approach to economic policy evaluation based on the concept of a social welfare function introduced by Abram Bergson (1938). For this purpose, we introduced cardinal and interpersonally comparable measures of individual welfare, derived from the transcendental logarithmic model of aggregate consumer behavior. We decomposed changes in social welfare into components that can be identified with efficiency and equity. In two papers included in the volume, *Measuring Social Welfare*, we applied this approach to policy evaluation to issues in energy policy, alternative policies for petroleum taxation and petroleum and natural gas price regulation. We estimated the impact of the alternative policies by means of simulations based on the Hudson–Jorgenson econometric general equilibrium model.

I would like to thank June Wynn of the Department of Economics at Harvard University for her excellent work in assembling the manuscripts for this volume in machine-readable form. Renate d'Arcangelo of the Editorial Office of the Divison of Engineering and Applied Sciences at Harvard edited the manuscripts, proofread the machine-readable versions, and prepared them for typesetting. Warren Hrung, then a senior at Harvard College, checked the references and proofread successive versions of the typescript. William Richardson and his associates provided the index. Gary Bisbee of Chiron Incorporated typeset the manuscript and provided camera-ready copy for publication. The staff of The MIT Press, especially Terry Vaughn, Victoria Richardson, Andrea Werblin, and Michael Sims, has been very helpful at every stage of the project. Financial support was provided by the Program on Technology and Economic Policy of the Kennedy School of Government at Harvard. As always, the author retains sole responsibility for any remaining deficiencies in the volume.

List of Sources

1. Dale W. Jorgenson, "A Dual Stability Theorem," *Econometrica*, Vol. 28, No. 4, October 1960, pp. 892–899. Reprinted by permission.

2. Dale W. Jorgenson, "The Development of a Dual Economy," *Economic Journal*, Vol. 71, No. 282, June 1961, pp. 309–334. Reprinted by permission.

3. A. Dale W. Jorgenson, "The Structure of Multi-Sector Dynamic Models," *International Economic Review*, Vol. 2, No. 3, September 1961, p. 276–291. B. Dale W. Jorgenson, "The Structure of Multi-Sector Dynamic Models: Some Further Examples," *International Economic Review*, Vol. 4. No. 1, January 1963, pp. 101–104. Reprinted by permission.

4. Dale W. Jorgenson, "Testing Alternative Theories of the Development of a Dual Economy," in I. Adelman and E. Thorbecke (eds.), *The Theory and Design of Development*, Baltimore, Johns Hopkins Press, 1966, pp. 45–60. Reprinted by permission.

5. Dale W. Jorgenson, "Surplus Agricultural Labor and the Development of a Dual Economy," *Oxford Economic Papers*, Vol. 19, No. 3, November 1967, pp. 288–312. Reprinted by permission of Oxford University Press.

6. Edward A. Hudson and Dale W. Jorgenson, "U.S. Tax Policy and Energy Conservation," in D. W. Jorgenson (ed.), *Econometric Studies of U.S. Energy Policy*, Amsterdam, North-Holland, 1976, pp. 7–94. Reprinted by permission from Elsevier Science Publishers B.V.

7. Edward A. Hudson and Dale W. Jorgenson, "Economic Analysis of Alternative Energy Growth Patterns," in David Freeman et al., *A Time to Choose*, Cambridge, Ballinger, 1974, pp. 493–511. Reprinted by permission from Harper Collins Publishers.

8. Ben Bernanke and Dale W. Jorgenson, "The Integration of Energy Policy Models," *Computers and Operations Research*, Vol. 2, No. 3, pp. 225–249. Reprinted by permission from Pergamon Press Ltd, Headington Hill Hall, Oxford OX3 OBW, UK.

9. Kenneth C. Hoffman and Dale W. Jorgenson, " Economic and Technological Models for Evaluation of Energy Policy," *Bell Journal of Economics*, Vol. 8, No. 2, Autumn 1977, pp. 444–466. Reprinted by permission.

10. Edward A. Hudson and Dale W. Jorgenson, "Energy Policy and U.S. Economic Growth," *American Economic Review*, Vol. 68, No. 2, May 1978, pp. 118–123. Reprinted by permission.

11. Dale W. Jorgenson, "The Role of Energy in the U.S. Economy," *National Tax Journal*, Vol. 31, No. 3, September 1978, pp. 209–220. Reprinted by permission.

12. Edward A. Hudson and Dale W. Jorgenson, "Energy Prices and the U.S. Economy, 1971–1976," *Natural Resources Journal*, Vol. 18, No. 4, October 1978, pp. 877–897. Reprinted by permission.

13. Edward A. Hudson and Dale W. Jorgenson, "The Economic Impact of Policies to Reduce U.S. Energy Growth," *Resources and Energy*, Vol. 1, No. 3, November 1978, pp. 205–230. Reprinted by permission.

14. Edward A. Hudson, Dale W. Jorgenson, and David C. O'Connor, "The Impact of Restrictions on Electric Generating Capacity," in J. Moroney (ed.), *Advances in the Economics of Energy and Resources*, Vol. 3, Greenwich, JAI Press, 1980, pp. 111–157. Reprinted by permission.

Growth
Volume 1: Econometric General
Equilibrium Modeling

1   A Dual Stability Theorem

Dale W. Jorgenson

A dual interpretation of the Leontief dynamic input-output system suggests the problem: What is the relationship between the stability of the output system and the stability of the dual? If the output system is stable, the dual must be unstable and *vice versa*, at least for the closed system. For the open system the statement is true except under rather implausible circumstances.

1.1   Introduction

The dynamic input-output system introduced into the economic literature by Hawkins (1948) and Leontief (1953), has been the subject of much recent discussion.[1] In Hawkin's original presentation of the system, the problem of macroeconomic stability for the system is discussed in detail (Hawkins, 1948). The problem is also discussed at length by Georgescu-Roegen (1951). Macroeconomic instability arises when for certain capital structures the unique, positive vector of sector output levels is dominated by some other solution of the system, violating, for arbitrary but nonnegative initial output levels, the requirement that outputs be nonnegative for all time. Dorfman, Samuelson, and Solow (1958) have reexamined this problem which they call that of "causal indeterminacy." Where the positive solution is not stable, they propose to open the dynamic input-output system to admit "excess capacity," and to impose explicit nonnegativity conditions on the output levels. Two alternative interpretations of the system under a regime of excess capacity have been given: Leontief (1953) and McManus (1957) propose a lower limit on the rate of decumulation of capital stocks; Dorfman, Samuelson, and Solow (1958) propose to interpret the system as a model of optimum capital accumulation. An optimal capital accumulation program is obtained by linear programming.

More recently, a dual interpretation of the dynamic input-output system has been given by Morishima (1958) and Solow (1959).[2] This raises an interesting question: What is the relationship between the macroeconomic stability or causal determinacy of the output system and that of the dual? Solow (1959) finds: If the balanced growth path of outputs is definitely unstable and the rate of interest is less than the equilibrium rate of growth, the price system is stable (it converges to a stationary state with positive prices). Solow offers the conjecture: If the balanced growth path is stable, "then it seems likely that the price model will be unstable (1959)." For the open system the conjecture cannot be verified. For the closed system the conjecture is true and leads to the following Dual Stability Theorem: If the output system is globally relatively stable, then the price system is unstable in this sense, and *vice versa*. If excess capacity is not admitted and the dual interpretation of the dynamic input-output system is retained, then Hawkins's macroeconomic stability of the dynamic input-output system implies instability of the dual; causal determinacy of the prices requires causal indeterminacy of the outputs. The conclusion is that excess capacity (or positive profit levels or both) is necessary and not merely sufficient[3] for the interpretation of the dynamic input-output system and its dual as a model of an actual economy.

1.2   Relative Stability

Verification of the Dual Stability Theorem necessitates an explicit theory of relative stability.[4] It is well-known that the dominant root of a system of linear differential equations governs the course of the system eventually (Leontief, 1953). This fact has application in the familiar power methods of extracting characteristic roots of a matrix (Iversen, 1954). The problem of relative stability for the dynamic input-output system is this: There is a given solution of interest, a balanced growth (or constant relative price) solution with all elements positive; furthermore, this solution is unique under mild restrictions on the input-output or stock-flow matrices. Under what conditions will this solution dominate the behavior of the system? The fact of significance is not the relationship of the other roots to zero (or to modulus one in the case of difference equations) but rather the relationship of these roots to the equilibrium rate of growth or rate of interest of the economy. For example, suppose that the equilibrium rate of growth of the economy is 10 percent and there is a transient with a rate of growth of 5 percent. Eventually, the proportion of the transient in the solution will be negligible; and in growth only the proportion matters. Although the transient grows, it dies out *relative* to the part of the solution associated with the equilibrium rate of growth. These ideas may now be formalized.

Let $x = A_x + B\dot{x}$ represent a closed, dynamic, input-output system, where x is a vector of output levels, A is an input-output matrix, B a stock-flow matrix and $\dot{x}$ the first time derivate of x. Let $C = B^{-1} (I - A)$. The solution to this system is given by:

$$x(t) = e^{Ct} x(0) \tag{1.1}$$

where B is assumed to be nonsingular. If it is not, the standard procedure for reduction of the order of the system to the rank of C may be applied (Iversen, 1954). We assume that this reduction has already taken place. Let us assume that A is indecomposable. The C^{-1} is an indecomposable Frobenius matrix. Hence there is a real, positive, simple characteristic root γ of C such that to γ can be associated a unique, positive, characteristic vector ξ (Debreu and Herstein, 1953). The particular solution $e^{\gamma t}\xi$ is referred to as the balanced growth solution.

The theory of relative stability may be summarized as follows:

Definition: The unique, positive solution to the system of linear differential equations $\dot{x} = Cx$ is globally relatively stable if and only if for every $\varepsilon > 0$, there exists a time T such that for every $t > T$:

$$\left| \frac{x_i(t)}{x_1(t)} - \frac{\xi_i}{\xi_1} \right| < \varepsilon \qquad \text{(for all } i) \tag{1.2}$$

where $x_i(t)$ is the ith component of the general solution $x(t) = e^{Ct} x(0)$, $x(0) \geq 0$, and $e^{\gamma t}\xi_i$ is the ith component of the characteristic solution $e^{\gamma t}\xi$. The first component of $x(t)$ may be chosen to be any nonzero component of $x(t)$. There is always at least one such component for any time t.

We may also define relative stability in the small:

Definition: The unique positive solution $e^{\gamma t}\xi$ to the system of linear differential equations $\dot{x} = Cx$ is *locally relatively stable* if and only if for every $\varepsilon > 0$, there exists a vector $\delta > 0$, such that for any perturbation $|\phi| < \delta$ there exists a time T such that for every t greater than T

$$\left| \frac{x_i(t)}{x_1(t)} - \frac{\xi_i}{\xi_1} \right| < \varepsilon \qquad \text{(for all } i) \tag{1.3}$$

where $x_i(t)$ is the ith component of the general solution $x(t)$

$$x(t) = e^{Ct} (\xi + \phi) \tag{1.4}$$

and

$$\xi + \phi \geq 0. \tag{1.5}$$

In the event that there is no other characteristic root of C which has a real part equal to γ, the theory of relative stability may be summarized in the:

Equivalence Theorem: *The following three statements are equivalent*:
(1) $e^{\gamma t}\xi$ *is locally relatively stable.*
(2) $e^{\gamma t}\xi$ *is globally relatively stable.*
(3) *All the characteristic roots of C have real parts which are less than γ.*

In the event that roots with real part equal to γ occur, global relative stability is no longer equivalent to local relative stability. The system will never be globally stable for initial conditions in which the characteristic vector associated with the characteristic value equal to γ in real part enters with nonzero constant coefficient. These facts are summarized in the:

Theorem: *If there are some roots of C with real part equal to γ and no roots with real part greater than γ, then $e^{\gamma t}\xi$ is locally relatively stable if and only if all such roots have index one,[5] further, $e^{\gamma t}\xi$ is not globally relatively stable.*

1.3   Dual Stability Theorem

With notions of global and local relative stability fixed, we are ready to consider the Dual Stability Theorem: If the output system is relatively stable, the price system cannot be, and *vice versa*. The dual interpretation of the dynamic input-output system is the "long-run equilibrium" of the following dual

$$p = (1 + \pi)(pA + rpB - pB + wa_0) \tag{1.6}$$

where p is a vector of prices, π is the rate of profit, A is the input-output matrix of the primal system, B is the stock-flow matrix, r is the rate of interest, p is a vector of first time derivatives of the price levels p, w is the wage rate, and a_0 is the vector of labor requirements: In words, the price level in each sector is equal to the costs of one unit of output of that sector—current costs, pA, interest charges, rpB, capital losses, pB, wage costs, wa_0—multiplied by one plus the rate of profit.

This dual incorporates the features of the dual interpretations presented by Morishima (1958) and Solow (1959). In long-run equilibrium it is true by definition that $\pi = 0$, i.e., profits disappear in all sectors. For convenience in presentation we set the rate of interest $r = 0$. In a closed model the rate of interest has no effect on the relative stability of prices.[6]

We begin by discussing a closed system, that is, a model in which the household sector is treated in the manner of any other "sector." Its outputs are labor services, its inputs are items for consumption. The model we consider is then:

$$p = pA - pB. \tag{1.7}$$

Solving for p, we obtain:

$$p = - p(I - A)B^{-1} = pD. \tag{1.8}$$

But $-D^{-1}$ is a Frobenius matrix; therefore, there is an equilibrium set of relative prices and an associated negative characteristic value $-\rho$ of D such that all prices are positive. We have then the:

Dual Stability Theorem: *For systems of order greater than one, if the output system is globally relatively stable, the price system is globally relatively unstable, and vice versa.*

For systems of order greater than the number of characteristic roots of C of index one with real part equal to γ, if the output system is locally relatively stable, the price system is locally relatively unstable and vice versa.

Proof: Let s be the number of roots of C less than γ in real part, u_1 be the number of such roots greater than γ in real part, u_2 be the number of roots equal to γ in real part with index greater than one, and n the number of roots of C equal to γ in real part with index one. Let the corresponding roots for D and $-\rho$ be s', u_1', u_2', and n', respectively.

The necessary and sufficient condition for global relative stability for the output system is that $u_1 + u_2 + n - 1 = 0$. The similar condition for the price system is that $u_1 + u_2' = n' - 1 = 0$. These statements are immediate implications of the Equivalence Theorem and the Theorem of page 4. Note that the characteristic roots of C and $-D$ are the same (MacDuffee, 1933), and $\gamma = \rho$. Hence it is easily seen that $s = u_1'$, $u_1 = s'$, $u_2 = u_2'$ and $n = n'$. Global relative stability of the multisector theory of growth implies that $s' + u_2' + n' - 1 = 0$. If the order of the system is greater than one, $u_1' \neq 0$ and the price system is unstable.

Secondly, the necessary and sufficient condition for local relative stability of the dynamic input-output system is that $u_1 + u_2 = 0$. The necessary and sufficient condition for local relative stability in the dynamic theory of prices is that $u'_1 + u'_2 = 0$. But if $u_1 + u_2 = 0$, $s' = 0$. If the order of the system is greater than n', $u'_1 + u'_1 \neq 0$ and the price system is unstable. If the order of the system is n', then the price system is locally relatively stable.[7]

We have shown that global relative stability and local relative stability of the output system imply instability in the same senses for the price system; that this holds *vice versa* follows easily.[8]

1.4   Dual Instability in the Open System

An open system admits of the possibility of output and price systems which are stable simultaneously. For this to occur the solution corresponding to the equilibrium rate of growth must dominate all other solutions and all solutions of the homogeneous part of the dual must die out, leaving a positive set of prices determined by the nonhomogeneous term. We have the

Theorem: *For global relative stability of the dynamic input-output system and its dual it is necessary and sufficient that any root $\alpha + \beta i$ of C except γ satisfies*:

$$0 \leq r < \alpha < \gamma.$$

This condition implies the existence of positive prices for a nonnegative vector of unit labor costs.

Proof: To verify these facts consider the open system and its dual:

$$x = Ax + B\dot{x} + y,$$
$$p = pA + rpB - p\dot{B} + wa_0, \tag{1.9}$$

where y is a vector of final demands and other terms are defined as above in section 1.3. It is assumed that y, wa_0 are nonnegative vectors with at least one positive element each. If $0 \leq r < \alpha < \gamma$ for all characteristic roots $\alpha + \beta i$ of C except γ, the system and its dual are easily seen to be relatively stable and stable, respectively, since γ is the dominant characteristic root of the output system and since all the roots of $-(I - A - rB)B^{-1}$ in the solution of the dual,

$$p = -p(I - A - rB)B^{-1} + wa_0 B^{-1}, \tag{1.10}$$

are negative so that the solution approaches:

$$p = wa_0(I - A - rB)^{-1}.$$ (1.11)

Moreover, prices are positive for any wa_0 which is nonnegative with at least one positive element, if and only if $(I - A - rB)^{-1}$ is composed of positive elements. For this it is necessary and sufficient that $r < \gamma$,[9] which is implied by $r < \alpha < \gamma$. This completes the proof of sufficiency; necessity is obtained by noting that if $\alpha \geq \gamma$, the output system is globally relatively unstable; if $\alpha \leq r$, the steady state solution to the dual is globally unstable in the usual sense. The condition $r \geq 0$ is required for an economic interpretation of the results. $\alpha < 0$ implies global instability of the price system for any nonnegative rate of interest.[10]

At this point we state a peculiar result. Since γ is the root of C smallest in modulus, α must be the real part of a complex root $\alpha + \beta i$ with modulus $\sqrt{\alpha^2 + \beta^2}$ greater than γ. But if there are any real roots of the system, other than γ, the system is characterized by dual instability. Since complex roots always occur in pairs this implies that any even-ordered open system must be unstable, either in its prices or its outputs or both. Among open systems with an odd number of sectors, only those are stable in both prices and outputs for which all the roots except γ are complex, and the real part of each complex root satisfies $\alpha < \gamma$. The notion that the number of commodities should affect the stability properties of an actual economic system seems unreasonable. But the possibility of obtaining a system of odd order *and* complex roots with real parts satisfying the conditions we have given seems remote. Except for this unlikely occurrence, Solow's conjecture is true.

Notes

1. A bibliography is given by Solow (1959).
2. Reference is made to papers by Leontief (1953) and Morishima (1958) for proposed economic interpretations of the dynamic input-output system and its dual, respectively.
3. As shown by Dorfman, Samuelson, and Solow (1958).
4. "Relative stability" is used in the same sense by Samuelson and Solow (1953).
5. For the definition of "index," see Friedman (1956, p. 69).
6. For an arbitrary rate of interest, if $D = - (I - A)B^{-1}$, $p = p (D + rI)$ is the closed version of the price model. From this it is obvious that the effect of a nonzero rate of interest is simply to add a constant—namely r, the rate of interest—to the real part of each root of D. But this does not affect the relative stability of the unique, positive set of prices. Roots larger than, equal to, or less than $- \gamma$ for a zero rate of interest remain in

the same relationship to $r - \gamma$ for an arbitrary rate of interest, r. The relationship of the real parts of each root to the quantity $r - \gamma$ is all that matters for relative stability.

7. Let $s\ (= u_1')$ and $u_1\ (= s')$ be positive. Then the actual paths $x(t)$ and $p(t)$ may be stable for some initial conditions, since $x(0)$ and $p(0)$ are assumed to be independent.

8. The results may be extended to systems of difference equations. For example, consider Solow's model (1959) in closed form with $r = 0$:

$$x_t = Ax_t + B(x_{t+1} - x_t) = B^{-1}(I - A + B)x_{t-1} = (C + I)x_{t-1},$$

and its dual

$$p_t = p_t^A - (p_t - p_{t-1})B = p_{t-1}B(I - A + B)^{-1} = p_{t-1}(I - D)^{-1}.$$

The essential fact is that $1 + \gamma$ is the equilibrium rate of growth of the output system and $1/1 + \rho$ is the root of the price system corresponding to the uniquely positive relative prices. Any root larger than $1 + \gamma$ in modulus implies the existence of a root which is less than $1/1 + \rho$ in modulus for the dual. That this holds *vice versa* is easily verified. But this is the Dual Stability Theorem.

9. Necessity is given by Solow (1959). Proof of sufficiency, for which the author is indebted to the referee, is as follows: From Debreu-Herstein (1953, Theorem III), $[1/rI - (I - A)^{-1}B]^{-1} > 0$, since $1/\gamma$ is the dominant characteristic root of $(I - A)^{-1}B$, a positive matrix. But $(I - A)^{-1} > 0$, hence $[1/rI - (I - A)^{-1}B]^{-1}[I - A]^{-1} = [1/r(I - A) - B]^{-1} > 0$ implies $[I - A - rB]^{-1} > 0$.

10. We also have the **Theorem**: *The analogous necessary and sufficient condition required for local relative stability of the output system and local stability of its dual is simply $0 \leq r \leq \alpha \leq \gamma$; if equality holds in either of the last two inequalities, the index of the corresponding root must be one.*

2

The Development of a
Dual Economy

Dale W. Jorgenson

2.1 Introduction

Two decades of rapid progress in the theory of economic growth and development[1] have left some curious gaps in the received doctrine. On the one hand there is a large and steadily increasing battery of theories of "models" alleged to apply to advanced economies. Of these the most familiar and time-tested is the Harrod–Domar theory of growth.[2] Three recent entries to the field which must be noted are the Duesenberry–Smithies model[3] of cycles and growth, the Tobin–Solow "neoclassical" growth model[4] and the Kaldor model of growth.[5] Of course, this is only part of the array of theoretical devices now available to students of growth in advanced economies.[6] Whatever the differences among these growth theories, they share one distinctive feature: The analysis throughout is on the highest level of aggregation. There is assumed to be a single commodity and a single producing sector. On the other hand, there is a smaller number of theories of development for backward economies. Most important among these contributions, from a theoretical point of view, is the recent work of Leibenstein (1957), carrying forward the program of creating an economic-demographic theory of development (Leibenstein, 1954). As in the theory of growth for an advanced economy, the analysis is carried through on a level of aggregation which permits only one output and a single production relation. The differences between the theory of growth (for advanced economies) and the theory of development (for backward economies) are so great that one might be tempted to conclude that there is little in common between them. In the theory of development emphasis is laid on the balance between capital accumulation and the growth of population, each adjusting to the other. In the theory of growth the balance between investment and saving is all-important and the growth of population is treated as constant or

shunted aside as a qualification to the main argument.[7] However
great the differences between theories of growth and development
appear to be, it is hard to escape the conclusion that each of the theories is true, sometimes. No simple model seems to be true all of the
time or even very often. In particular, limitation of the analysis to situations in which there is effectively one producing sector rules out
much of what is interesting about growth and development, at least if
the empirical and institutional literature is any guide.[8] A few examples of "special situations" or "unsolved problems" created by concen-
tration on a single output or a single production relation are: balance
between industries in economic growth, imbalance between advanced
and backward countries in international trade and the development of
a dual economy, that is, of an economy with an advanced or modern
sector and a backward sector as well.[9] These problems remain virtually untouched in the theoretical literature.[10] The purpose of this
chapter is to begin a frontal attack on the gap between theories of
growth and theories of development by presenting a theory of development of a dual economy. The theory to be presented here is not
intended to be yet another candidate for *the* universal theory of
economic growth and development,[11] but only a theory which is
applicable to a few well-defined and empirically significant historical
situations. Whatever loss of generality is suffered in striving for
something less than a single theory of growth must be balanced
against the gain in specific implications for those situations to which
the theory of development of a dual economy does apply.[12]

Very briefly, the situation envisaged in the theory of a dual economy
is this: The economic system may be divided into two sectors—the
advanced or modern sector, which we will call, somewhat inaccurately,
the manufacturing sector, and the backward or traditional sector,
which may be suggestively denoted agriculture.[13] Productive activity
in each sector may be characterized by a function relating output to
each of the factors of production—land, labor and capital. The special
character of the theory of development of a dual economy is a certain
asymmetry in the productive relations. If the two production functions
were essentially symmetric, that is, if each function included all three
productive factors, the resulting model would be suited to the problems of industrial balance in an advanced economy or to dynamic
problems in the theory of international trade (Johnson, 1954). In the
theory of a dual economy the output of the traditional or agricultural
sector is a function of land and labor alone; there is no capital accumu-

lation, except where investment takes the form of land reclamation. For the purposes of the present analysis it seems best to assume that all potentially arable land is under cultivation, so that land is fixed in supply. Land does not appear as a factor of production in the manufacturing sector; the level of manufacturing output is a function of capital and labor alone. Agricultural activity is characterized by diminishing returns to scale. Although there are many ways to account for diminishing returns—e.g., declining quality of the land as more and more is put under cultivation as in Ricardo's (1911) extensive margin—the initial assumption that land is fixed in supply (and of one uniform quality, arable) implies that the diminishing returns encountered in agricultural production arise at the intensive margin of the Ricardian scheme. The interpretation of diminishing returns and increasing returns as the effect of a fixed factor has been stressed by Kaldor (1934). In manufacturing, expansion of productive activity proceeds with constant returns to scale. This appears to be a reasonable assumption, at least on the basis of evidence from the manufacturing industries of advanced economies.[14] A second feature of the production functions for agriculture and industry is that each function will shift over time so that a given bundle of factors will generate a higher level at one date than at an earlier date. The autonomous shifts in the production function correspond to technological changes. Although it is possible to devise purely economic explanations for some observed changes in technology,[15] we will assume that the changes take place at some more or less constant rate and that all changes are neutral.[16]

The assumption that technical changes are neutral is by now customary in the analysis of growth; whatever the theoretical importance of biased technical progress, it is hard to see how one may distinguish empirically between shifts of a production function, movements along it and shifts in the relative factor productivities, simultaneously.[17]

The characteristic feature of the theory of development of a dual economy is the asymmetry between production relations in the industrial and agricultural sectors. The remaining elements of the theory may be enumerated briefly: Population growth depends on the supply of food *per capita* and the force of mortality; the force of mortality is assumed given—it may be altered only by an alteration in medical technique. The birth rate depends on the supply of food *per capita*; however, it may attain a physiological maximum, or a maximum given by a particular social situation and by the state of medical knowledge, provided that the supply of food is sufficient. If the food supply is more than sufficient there exists an agricultural surplus, and labor may be freed from the land for employment in manufacturing. Labor is divided between the two sectors in a straightforward manner: if there is no agricultural surplus, all labor remains on the land; if an agricultural surplus can be generated, a labor force available for employment in manufacturing grows at a rate which is equal to the rate of growth of the agricultural surplus. Of course, no manufacturing production is possible without some initial capital stock, however small the initial bundle may be. Once the initial injection of capital is made, capital formation proceeds at a pace determined by the growth of the manufacturing labor force and by the terms of trade between the two sectors. It would not be correct to assume, as one might more readily assume in an advanced economy, that the real wage-rate is the same in the two sectors. In the first place only laborers in the advanced urbanized sector can be assumed to respond to wage differentials between employment opportunities in agriculture and industry. Since the course of development will result, with few lapses, in a steady migration of labor from the backward agricultural sector to the modern sector, some differential between wages in agriculture and wages in manufacturing may be expected to persist. We will assume that this differential is proportional to the manufacturing wage-rate and is stable in the long run. This differential determines the terms of trade between manufacturing and agricultural sectors, and thereby the rate of investment in the modern or advanced sector. Under this interpretation of the model it must be assumed either that the economy is closed to trade or that trade is in balance, not only overall but also in the goods of each sector. Such a balance could occur, for example, whenever there are no imports or exports of food and trade is in balance. Then manufactured goods would be traded for manufactured goods and the production function of the advanced sector would consist of a relationship between factors employed in manufacturing and domestic utilization of manufactured goods, including imports and excluding exports. The assumption that the economy is essentially closed to trade follows the practice of most recent contributions to the theory of growth and development.[18] An alternative interpretation of the model is that the terms of trade between agriculture and industry in domestic commerce are determined by the rate of substitution of manufactured goods for agricultural goods in international trade. Then the wage differential between agriculture and industry would be determined by the terms of trade. In what follows we confine the analysis to a closed economy or an economy in which trade is in balance for goods of both sectors.

2.2   The Traditional Sector

To begin the analysis we consider an economic system in which no development of manufacturing activity has taken place; all productive activity is concentrated in the traditional or backward sector. Then, if P is the total population and Y is agricultural output with L the fixed quantity of land available to the society, a simple version of the production function in agriculture, characterized by constant returns with all factors variable is given by the Cobb–Douglas production function[19]

$$Y = e^{\alpha t} L^{\beta} P^{1-\beta}$$

where $e^{\alpha t}$ represents the shift factor corresponding to technological progress. Changes in techniques are assumed to take place at a constant rate, α. The constant β represents the elasticity of output with respect to an increase in the supply of land; as is well known, it also corresponds to the share of landlords in the product of the traditional sector; if the supply of land is fixed, as in the model described here, this share takes the form of rent, defined as the unimputed residual remaining after the share of labor in the product, $1 - \beta$, has been paid to the agricultural labor force. Since the supply of land is assumed fixed, it is possible to choose the origin for measuring the passage of time so that the production function may be rewritten in the simpler form

$$Y = e^{\alpha t} P^{1-\beta} \, .$$

Dividing both sides by the agricultural population, we have

$$y = \frac{Y}{P} = e^{\alpha t} P^{-\beta}$$

where y is agricultural output per man. Differentiating with respect to time and dividing through by output per man, this production function takes the form

$$\frac{\dot{y}}{y} - \alpha - \beta \frac{\dot{P}}{P}$$

where α is the rate of technical progress and β is defined as before. This equation characterizes the agricultural production function completely for the analysis to follow.

The second characteristic feature of the agricultural system is described by the function which governs the growth of population. It is assumed that if there is literally no agricultural production the reproduction rate falls to zero and the force of mortality is constant at the level δ. Secondly, it is assumed that the rate of gross reproduction is an increasing function of agricultural output per head up to some physiological maximum, say $\varepsilon + \delta$. It is simplest to assume that the rate of increase in the gross reproduction rate is constant as *per capita* income increases, so that the population theory may be written in the form

$$\frac{\dot{P}}{P} = \min \begin{cases} \gamma y - \delta \\ \varepsilon \end{cases}$$

where γ is the rate of increase in the gross reproduction rate with respect to an increase in the output of food per man. The net reproduction rate $\dot{P}/P$ is the gross reproduction rate less the force of mortality, where the gross reproduction rate is the minimum of the two rates determined by the physiologically maximum rate of reproduction and the rate determined by the output of food per head.

For the first phase of development, in which reproduction is below its physical maximum, the population function and the production function may be combined to give a single differential equation in output per head alone

$$\frac{\dot{y}}{y} = \alpha - \beta(\gamma y - \delta) = \alpha + \beta\delta - \beta\gamma y .$$

Now, multiplying by y, we obtain the fundamental differential equation for the theory of development of the agricultural sector

$$\dot{y} = (\alpha + \beta\delta)y - \beta\gamma y^2 .$$

To characterize the possible modes of development for an economic system which satisfies the conditions defining the production function and the theory of population growth, we will analyze the solutions of this equation. It should be noted first that there are two stationary solutions of the equations, that is, values of *per capita* income, which once established will maintain themselves. All such stationary solutions may be found by setting the rate of change in *per capita* income to zero as follows

$$(\alpha + \beta\delta)y - \beta\gamma y^2 = 0.$$

This equation has two roots, $y_1 = 0$, and $y_2 = (\alpha + \beta\delta)/\beta\gamma$, which is necessarily positive. If the level of agricultural output reaches zero the rate of population growth falls to the negative rate given by the force of mortality, $-\delta$, and population dies off exponentially. No further attention need to be devoted to this case; we confine further analysis to the stationary solution y_2. We have already characterized y_2 as a situation in which *per capita* output of food remains constant. The rate of population growth must, however, be positive. This may be seen by inserting the given value for y_2 into the equation for determining the rate of growth of population

$$\frac{\dot{P}}{P} = \gamma[(\alpha + \beta\delta)/\beta\gamma] - \delta = \frac{\alpha}{\beta} > 0$$

so that population and the food supply grow at the same positive rate with no progress, that is, no increase in the output of food *per capita*. The situation in which output per head remains stagnant and population growth is positive is precisely that envisioned in Leibenstein's low-level equilibrium trap.[20] Although there are important differences between the model described here and that of Leibenstein, the existence of a kind of "trap" level of income suggests the problem: Under what conditions is the low-level equilibrium trap stable? In formal terms: Under what conditions is y_2 a stable solution of the fundamental differential equation? The answer is simple: If a low-level equilibrium trap would be stable, if it existed, then it must exist. In this case existence of stationary equilibrium and its stability are equivalent.

To complete the analysis of a pure traditional or agricultural system, let us denote by y^+ the minimum level of income at which $\dot{P}/P$ attains its physiological maximum. Then, using the model for population growth, we may solve for y^+ as follows

$$\frac{\dot{P}}{P} = \gamma y^+ - \delta = \varepsilon.$$

Hence

$$y^+ = (\varepsilon + \delta)/\gamma$$

is the value of production of food per head at which population growth attains its maximum rate. The two cases into which solutions to the fundamental differential equation may be divided are distinguished as follows: If the critical level of income, y^+, is below y_2, the stationary level assuming that population growth has not attained its maximum, y_2 will not be attained, since it would require a rate of growth in population higher than the physiological maximum. In the event that y_2 exceeds y^+ the growth path will be given instead by the expression

$$\frac{\dot{y}}{y} = \alpha - \beta\varepsilon.$$

Multiplying both sides by y we have

$$\dot{y} = (\alpha - \beta\varepsilon)y$$

which has the general solution

$$y(t) = e^{(\alpha - \beta\varepsilon)t}y(0)$$

where the rate of growth in *per capita* income, $\alpha - \beta\varepsilon > 0$, will be attained from any positive initial level of output. Note that if this rate of growth is positive, $y_2 > y^+$ and no stationary level of equilibrium (except $y_1 = 0$) exists. The second case is that in which $y_2 < y^+$. In this case the stationary level y_2 exists and is stable in the large, that is y_2 will be approached for any positive initial level of agricultural output. If the initial level of output is sufficiently high that population growth attains its maximum the rate of growth in output per head, $\alpha - \beta\varepsilon$, is negative and output declines at this rate to the level y^+. From this point the original fundamental differential equation describes the further decline of *per capita* production of food to its equilibrium level, y_2. The obverse situation is that in which y_2 does not exist, but *per capita* income is initially below the rate at which population growth attains its maximum. In this case the original fundamental differential equation describes the movement of *per capita* output to the level y^+, at which point population growth attains its maximum rate. After y^+ is attained, the growth of *per capita* output is described as taking place at the constant positive rate, $\alpha - \beta\varepsilon$. The intermediate case in which $y^+ = y_2$ and $\alpha - \beta\varepsilon = 0$ seems unlikely. But the resulting movements of the economy would be characterized by movements toward y_2 for any initial output level below $y_2 = y$. At any higher level the output of agricultural goods is in equilibrium; thus y_2 is stable from below and neutrally stable from above. All solutions $y > y_2$ are neutrally stable equilibrium values for the system, both from above and from below.

So far as the implication of the foregoing analysis for policy is concerned: Any change in social policy corresponds to an alteration in the parameters of the system. If a society finds itself in a low-level equilibrium trap and the parameter β, representing diminishing returns to additions in the agricultural labor force, remains constant, only two parameters remain to be altered by social policy, namely, α, the rate of technical progress, and ε, the maximum net rate of reproduction. If the rate of technical progress can be increased (without the creation of a manufacturing sector) the sign of the expression $\alpha - \beta\varepsilon$ may be changed from negative, the trap situation, to positive, in which case there is a steady increase in the output of food *per capita*. An alternative avenue for social policy would be a change in the rate of reproduction. Any improvement in medical technique would be reflected in a reduced force of mortality, so that δ, the previous mortality rate, would be reduced. For the same level of the gross reproduction rate, $\delta + \varepsilon$, population would increase at a rate which was more rapid than before; that is, the net rate of reproduction, ε, would rise. Thus an improvement in medical technique with no other alterations in the parameters of the model would lead to a decrease in the test criterion, $\alpha - \beta\varepsilon$, leading to retardation of the rate of growth. If this criterion is already negative, inspection of the expression for the stationary solution, y_2, reveals that the new stationary level of food output *per capita* is lower than before, so that improvements in medical technique with no other changes lead to immiseration of the surviving members of the population. On the other hand, institutional changes, leading to a restriction of the gross reproduction rate below its physiological maximum, will result in no rise in the stationary level of income; however, they may reduce the critical level of income, y^+, to a level at which it falls below the stationary level, y_2. In this event the test criterion changes from negative to positive and the system enters a phase of steady progress in the level of food output *per capita*. It may be helpful to contrast this model of economic development of a backward economy with the familiar low-level equilibrium trap model of Leibenstein. The only resemblance between the two models is that it is possible to have constant *per capita* output with a growing population. However, in the theory just presented there is at most one equilibrium level of output per head corresponding to each set of parameter values, while in Leibenstein's (1957) analysis there are two equilibrium solutions at which *per capita* income is constant, one stable in the small and the other unstable. The implications for social policy are correspondingly different. To escape the low-level equilibrium trap of the present model, changes in the rate of introduction of new techniques or measures of birth control are prescribed; in Leibenstein's analysis the parameters of the model are regarded as essentially fixed and progress is possible only by a massive infusion of capital into the system. The role played by capital accumulation in the development of the agricultural sector will be discussed in more detail below, after the development of the advanced sector has been described.

2.3   Modes of Development

In this section a rigorous analysis of the fundamental differential equation for a backward economy is presented. Readers who are willing to take the mathematics for granted should go on to the next section. The preceding analysis of the fundamental differential equation revealed that there are essentially two modes of development for an economy which is purely traditional or wholly agricultural—either steady growth in output per man or equilibrium at some level of output per man which remains constant. Any given situation will be described by one of these two cases, depending on the net rate of reproduction, the elasticity of output with respect to increases in the labor supply and the rate of technological progress. In this section we present a detailed proof of the stability of the stationary solution $y_2 = (\alpha + \beta\delta)/\beta\gamma$ where such a solution exists, and the equivalence of the existence of such an equilibrium to the condition $\alpha - \beta\varepsilon < 0$. We will also show that if $\alpha - \beta\varepsilon > 0$ the long-run steady growth solution will be attained from any positive initial output levels. We begin by solving the fundamental differential equation

$$\dot{y} = (\alpha + \beta\delta)y - \beta\gamma y^2 .$$

First, changing variables, let $y = y_2 - 1/u$ define the new variable, u; then the fundamental equation is written

$$\frac{\dot{u}}{u^2} = (\alpha + \beta\delta)(y_2 - 1/u) - \beta\gamma(y_2 - 1/u)^2 .$$

Eliminating y_2 and multiplying by u^2 we have

$$\dot{u} = (\alpha + \beta\delta)u - \beta\gamma$$

which has the solution

$$u(t) = e^{(\alpha + \beta\delta)t} \left[\frac{1}{y_2 - y(0)} - \frac{\beta\gamma}{\alpha + \beta\delta} \right] + \frac{\beta\gamma}{\alpha + \beta\delta} .$$

Substituting this expression into the fundamental differential equation, we obtain

$$y(t) = y_2 + \cfrac{1}{e^{\alpha + \beta\delta)t}\left[\dfrac{\beta\gamma}{\alpha + \beta\delta} + \dfrac{1}{y(0) - y_2} \right] - \dfrac{\beta\gamma}{\alpha + \beta\delta}}$$

which is the general solution for $y(t) < y^+$ and for $y(0) \neq y_2$.[21]

Case I. Suppose $y_2 < y^+$. Then $0 < (\alpha + \beta\delta)/\beta\gamma < (\varepsilon + \delta)/\gamma$, since y_2 is always positive. But since γ is positive this reduces to

$$\frac{\alpha}{\beta} + \delta < \varepsilon + \delta .$$

Hence

$$(\alpha - \beta\varepsilon) < 0$$

which is necessary and sufficient for the steady growth path of output corresponding to $y > y^+$ to be characterized by a negative rate of growth. If $y(0) > y^+$ income declines to y^+. If $y_2 < y(0) \leq y^+$ the general solution reveals that $y(t) - y_2$ diminishes to zero. If $0 < y(0) < y_2$, $y(t) - y_2$ increases to zero. Hence, for any positive initial level of output whatever, y_2 is a stable equilibrium solution. If $y(0) = y_2$, $y(t) = y_2$, since y_2 is an equilibrium of the fundamental differential equation.

Case II. Suppose $y_2 > y^+$. Then $\alpha - \beta\varepsilon > 0$ by analogous reasoning and if $y(0) > y^+$ the system grows at the long-run equilibrium rate. If $0 < y(0) < y^+ < y_2$ the general solution has the form

$$y(t) = y_2 + \cfrac{1}{e^{(\alpha + \beta\delta)t}\left[\cfrac{1}{y_2} + \cfrac{1}{y(0) - y_2}\right] - \cfrac{1}{y_2}}$$

where $y(0) - y_2$, the initial value of the fraction on the right-hand side, is negative. Since $1/y_2 < 1/(y_2 - y(0)) < 0$, the fraction remains negative and approaches zero from below. But $y(t) = y^+ < y_2$ for t sufficiently large, since $y(t)$ approaches y_2 from below. Hence the equilibrium growth path is stable.

Case III. $y_2 = y^+$. If $0 < y(0) < y^+$, $y(0)$ approaches $y_2 = y^+$ from below. If $y(0) \geq y_2$, $y(t) = y(0)$ for all t, since $\alpha - \beta\varepsilon = 0$ by reasoning analogous to the previous two cases.

Note that the fundamental condition $y^+ \gtrless y_2$, which determines whether or not a stationary equilibrium exists, is equivalent to the condition $\alpha - \beta\varepsilon \gtrless 0$, which determines whether or not such an equilibrium is stable, if it exists. The theoretical analysis which applies to a given case is determined by the three parameters α, β and ε, the rate of technical progress, the elasticity of output with respect to land (unity less the elasticity of output with respect to labor) and the net rate of reproduction.

2.4 A Dual Economy

In previous sections we presented an analysis of the development of a backward or purely traditional economic system. Depending on the conditions of production and the net reproduction rate, the system is characterized either by a low-level equilibrium, in which output per head is constant and population is growing at less than its physiologically maximum rate, or by a steady growth equilibrium, in which output per head is rising and population is growing at its physiologically maximum rate. Where output per head is constantly rising, an agricultural surplus is generated. Using the notation of the previous discussion, the agricultural surplus, per member of the agricultural labor force, is defined by

$$y - y^+ = s$$

where s is the agricultural surplus. From the point of view of economic-demographic development, y^+ is the level of output of food necessary to bring about the maximum rate of increase in population. If agricultural output exceeds this rate, part of the labor force may be freed from the land to produce industrial goods with no diminution in the rate of growth of the total labor force. Let us denote the agricultural population by A and the manufacturing population by M; then the total population is the sum of these two quantities

$$P = A + M.$$

The theory of population growth for a dual economy is essentially the same as that for a backward economy: The net rate of reproduction is the minimum of the physiologically maximum rate and the gross reproduction rate which corresponds to the output of food *per capita* for the total population, less the force of mortality. The function describing the growth of population may be written

$$\frac{\dot{P}}{P} = \min \begin{cases} \varepsilon \\ \gamma y \, \dfrac{A}{P} - \delta \end{cases}$$

where $A = P$, the whole labor force is engaged in agricultural production, and the model of population growth reduces to that discussed previously.

In a dual economy labor may be freed from the land at a rate which is just sufficient to absorb the agricultural surplus. Of course, if the growth of manufacturing is not sufficiently rapid some of the excess labor force will remain on the land and part or all of the surplus may be consumed in the form of increased leisure for agricultural workers; this condition will eventuate in the virtual destruction of manufacturing activity or in some arrangement whereby manufactured goods are exported and food is imported. The latter situation is ruled out by our assumption of balance in trade in both classes of commodities. The balance between the expansion of the manufacturing labor force and the production of food is simply described: Total agricultural output is simply output per man employed in agriculture multiplied by the agricultural population. Total food consumption is y^+, multiplied by total population, so that the proportion of the total labor force employed in agriculture is the ratio of the subsistence level of agricultural production to the actual agricultural output per man in the agricultural population

$$\frac{y^+}{y} = \frac{A}{P}.$$

This relationship holds only when an agricultural surplus exists; that is, when there is a positive agricultural surplus rather than a shortage of food, and $y > y^+$. Hence, the relationship governing the distribution of labor between agriculture and industry may be represented by

$$\frac{A}{P} = \min \begin{cases} 1 \\ y^+/y \end{cases}.$$

To complete the model the conditions of production in manufacturing and of capital accumulation in the manufacturing sector must be described. If M is the manufacturing labor force and K is capital stock, then the level of manufacturing output is a function of the quantities of each of these factors employed; but since technical progress in manufacturing may be expected to be quite rapid, the output of manufactured goods for a given bundle of the two factors may be expected to depend not only on the amounts of each of the two factors employed but also on the time at which production takes place. The production function for manufacturing may be written in the form

$$X = F(K, M, t)$$

where X is manufacturing output. For any given time, it will be assumed that the production function exhibits constant returns to scale; this assumption is equivalent to the assumption that manufacturing output is exhausted by factor payments to labor and to the owners of capital. If, further, the relative share of labor in manufacturing output is constant and all technical change is neutral, the production function may be represented in the Cobb–Douglas form

$$X = A(t)M^{1-\sigma}K^{\sigma}$$

where $1 - \sigma$ is the relative share of labor and $A(t)$ is some function of time. If the rate of growth is A is constant, say

$$\frac{\dot{A}}{A} = \lambda$$

then we have

$$\dot{A} = \lambda A$$

and solving this relation as a differential equation we have

$$A(t) = e^{\lambda t} A(0)$$

so that the production function takes the form

$$X = e^{\lambda t} A(0) M^{1-\sigma} K^{\sigma}.$$

Dividing X and K by M, and representing output per man and capital per man by x and k, respectively; further, changing the units of X so that $A(0) = 1$, we have the final version of the production function

$$x = e^{\lambda t} k^{\sigma}.$$

Differentiating this function with respect to time and dividing through by output per man, this expression reduces to

$$\frac{\dot{x}}{x} = \lambda + \sigma \frac{\dot{k}}{k}$$

which may be compared with Kaldor's (1961) technical progress function for a single-sector model. The production function described here implies the existence of a technical progress function which is linear.[22] Whatever the difficulties which exist in expressing output per man as a function of capital per man,[23] it is clear that no distinction can be made between such a production function and a *linear* technical progress function from the point of view of empirical observation. The interpretation of the underlying mechanism is, of course, vastly different in the two cases; but the effects of the two distinct mechanisms cannot be separately identified empirically.

The remaining problem for the theory is this: What determines the rate of capital accumulation? The first approach to this problem is through the fundamental *ex post* identity between the sum of investment and the consumption of manufactured goods, on the one hand, and manufacturing output, on the other. We assume with Kaldor (1955–1956) that industrial workers do not save and that property owners do not consume, at least out of their property income. Then, the consumption of manufactured goods, in both the manufacturing and the agricultural sector, is equal to the share of labor in the product of the manufacturing sector. The industrial wage-rate is determined by the usual marginal productivity condition

$$\frac{\partial M}{\partial X} = (1 - \sigma)x = w$$

where x is output per man, $1 - \sigma$ is the relative share of labor in the total product and w is the industrial wage-rate. The condition that the industrial wage-rate is equal to the marginal product of labor is a necessary condition for the maximization of profit. While it is not unreasonable to assume that profits are maximized in the advanced sector, there seems to be much less reason for making such an assumption for the agricultural sector. In fact, agricultural workers can be expected to respond to wage differentials between industry and agriculture only if industrial wages are greater than agriculture income, where agricultural income includes both wages and rent. Following the Weber–Fechner law of proportional effect, we can assume that the differential which is necessary to cause movement of agricultural labor into the industrialized sector is roughly proportional to the industrial wage-rate. Let $\mu < 1$ denote the ratio between agricultural income per man and the industrial *wage-rate* per man. Then the total wage bill for the economy is given by the expression

$$wM + \mu wA = (1 - \sigma)X + qY$$

where wM is the industrial wage bill, μwA is total agricultural income (expressed in manufactured goods), $(1 - \sigma)X$ is total consumption of manufactured goods by workers in both sectors and qY is the value of agricultural output measured in manufactured goods. The variable q is the term of trade between agriculture and industry. It is assumed that all of agricultural income, whether this income accrues in the form of rent or wages, is consumed. If part of agricultural income, say income from property, were available for investment inside or outside the agricultural sector, the balance relation given above could not hold. It is assumed that all agricultural incomes are consumed, so that investment in the manufacturing sector is financed entirely out of the incomes of property-holders in that sector. The assumption that landholders do not accumulate capital accords with the classical theories of land-rent, especially the theory of Smith and the physiocrats.[24] If agricultural activity is fully rationalized it would be necessary to replace the theory just described by one which is more neoclassical: Agricultural incomes could be divided into property incomes; the agricultural wage-rates (and hence the terms of trade) would be determined by the condition that real wages be equal in the two sectors in the long run. It is assumed through the analysis that follows that agriculture is traditional in its organization and that the classical model applies.

Once the share of labor in manufacturing output is distributed to workers in the form of food and consumption goods, and agricultural workers have received the proportion of manufacturing output which must be traded for food, the remainder of manufacturing output is available for capital accumulation, or more properly, for investment. Capital accumulation is defined as investment less depreciation, where depreciation (calculated by the declining-balance method) is a constant fraction of capital stock

$$\dot{K} = I - \eta K$$

where η is the rate of depreciation, I is investment and $\dot{K}$ is net capital accumulation. Then, by definition, total industrial output is equal to consumption plus investment

$$X = (1 - \sigma)X + I$$

which implies the following relation between output and capital stock

$$X = (1 - \sigma)X + \dot{K} + \eta K .$$

This relation closes the system and completes the formulation of a theory of development for a dual economy.

2.5   Agricultural Surplus

To study the development of a dual economy for the case which is of greatest interest—that in which an agricultural surplus eventually emerges so that development of an advanced sector is possible—we must assume at the outset that $\alpha - \beta\varepsilon > 0$, which is necessary and sufficient for the emergence of an agricultural surplus. If no such surplus comes into existence the economy remains in an undeveloped state, producing only food and other products of the traditional sector. The level of production stagnates, that is, remains constant with a rising population, while population increases at less than its maximum rate. The theory of a dual economy under these conditions reduces to the theory of a backward economic system, and nothing need be added to the analysis of the earlier sections. To characterize the development of an advanced sector we will begin by analyzing the growth of the manufacturing labor force. This will be followed by a detailed consideration of capital accumulation and growth in the level of output. The analysis will be concluded by a discussion of wages, interest and the terms of trade between industry and agriculture. An industrial labor force comes into being when $y = y^+$, that is, when agricultural output attains the minimum level necessary for population to grow at its maximum rate. From this point forward, population grows at the rate ε, the maximum rate of net reproduction. This implies that

$$P(t) = e^{\varepsilon t} P(0)$$

where $t = 0$ is taken as that point of time at which $y = y^+$. From the fact that population is growing at a constant rate and that *per capita* consumption of food is stationary, it is easily seen that food output and population grow at the same rate

$$\frac{Y}{P} = y^+$$
$$Y = Py^+ = P(0)e^{\varepsilon t} y^+ .$$

Given the agricultrual production function, the required rate of growth in the agricultural labor force necessary to maintain the growth of the agricultural surplus may be calculated as follows

$$Y = e^{\alpha t} A^{1-\beta} = P(0)e^{\varepsilon t} y^+$$

which implies

$$A^{1-\beta} = P(0)y^+ e^{[\varepsilon - \alpha]t}$$

which may be further simplified

$$A = [P(0)y^+]^{\frac{1}{1-\beta}} e^{\left[\frac{\varepsilon-\alpha}{1-\beta}\right]t} .$$

But, recalling the fact that the origin of time is taken as the point at which the maximum rate of population growth begins, we have the following relation between $P(0)$, total population (entirely employed in agriculture) and y^+, the critical level of agricultural output

$$y^+ = P(0)^{-\beta}$$

substituting this expression for y^+ into the formulas given above, we obtain the following equivalent expressions for the agricultural labor force

$$A = P(0)e^{\left[\frac{\varepsilon-\alpha}{1-\beta}\right]t} = A(0)e^{\left[\frac{\varepsilon-\alpha}{1-\beta}\right]t}$$

where $P(0) = A(0)$. It is easily seen that agricultural population may grow, decline or remain constant, depending solely on the relative magnitude of the two parameters ε, the maximum rate of population growth, and α, the rate of technological progress in the agricultural sector.

The manufacturing labor force (or population; no distinction between the two concepts is needed here) is total population less the agricultural population. Hence the growth of the manufacturing labor force is governed by the following expression

$$M = P(0)\left[e^{\varepsilon t} - e^{\left(\frac{\varepsilon-\alpha}{1-\beta}\right)t}\right]$$

which is zero at time $t = 0$ and grows at a rate which is always more rapid than the rate of population growth. This is an immediate consequence of the condition equivalent to the existence of a positive agricultural surplus, namely

$$\alpha - \beta\varepsilon > 0$$

which implies

$$\varepsilon - \alpha < \varepsilon(1 - \beta)$$

so that

$$\varepsilon > \frac{\varepsilon - \alpha}{1 - \beta}$$

so that population is growing more rapidly than the agricultural labor force, hence the manufacturing labor force is growing more rapidly than population, since the rate of growth of population is simply the weighted average of the rates of growth of each of its two components. A second consequence which may be derived from the expression for the size of the manufacturing labor force is that the rate of growth is always declining and approaches, as a limit, the rate of growth of population, ε. This result may be deduced from the relative stability of the component $P(0)e^{\varepsilon t}$ in the solution for M, the manufacturing labor force.

To study capital accumulation, it is necessary to analyze the relationship between growth of the industrial labor force, investment and output. In addition to the expression for the size of the manufacturing labor force

$$M = P(0)\left[e^{\varepsilon t} - e^{\left(\frac{\varepsilon-\alpha}{1-\beta}\right)t} \right]$$

the fundamental relations include the production function

$$X = e^{\lambda t} K^{\sigma} M^{1-\sigma}$$

and the identity in industrial output

$$X = (1 - \sigma)X + \dot{K} + \eta K$$

which may be simplified as follows

$$\sigma X = \dot{K} + \eta K$$

which is, in familiar terms, saving equals investment. Investment is made up of two components—net capital accumulation, $\dot{K}$, and replacement investment, ηK. Using the production function to eliminate X, the level of output in the manufacturing sector, we have

$$\dot{K} + \eta K = \sigma e^{\lambda t} K^{\sigma} M^{1-\sigma}.$$

Using the expression for the size of the manufacturing labor force, we have

$$\dot{K} = -\eta K + \sigma K^{\sigma} P(0)^{1-\sigma} e^{\lambda t}\left[e^{\varepsilon t} - e^{\left(\frac{\varepsilon-\alpha}{1-\beta}\right)t} \right]$$

which is the fundamental differential equation for the development of a dual economy. To study capital accumulation it is necessary to solve the fundamental differential equation and to characterize its solutions. In the case of a purely traditional economy it was possible to obtain a solution of the fundamental equation in closed form so that a complete characterization of the modes of development of the system could be obtained. It is apparently impossible to solve the equation for a dual economy in the same way, so that only long-run tendencies of the system can be characterized.

The first thing to be noted is that there is no stationary situation for any economy in which capital accumulation is possible, that is, for which there is a positive and growing agricultural surplus. Once the economy has begun to grow it must continue to do so. The actual pattern of growth is determined by two fixed initial conditions: First, the size of the total population at the time at which sustained growth begins; secondly the size of initial capital stock. Of these parameters, only the influence of the initial size of population has any effect on the long-run growth of the economy. The influence of initial capital stock dies out quickly; the greater the rate of depreciation η and the greater the relative share of labor $(1 - \sigma)$, the more rapidly the effects of the initial capital endowment disappear. Secondly, there is no critical level of initial capital endowment below which no sustained growth is possible. Even the smallest initial stock gives rise to sustained growth; that is, the combination of a positive and growing agricultural surplus and a small positive initial capital endowment must give rise to the well-known and much-discussed take-off into sustained capital accumulation and increase in output. If sustained growth can be achieved, the long-run characteristics of capital accumulation, increases in the level of output and growth of population eventually assume easily recognizable form. For long-run equilibrium growth, capital and output grow at the same rate, even in the presence of neutral technological change. If there is no technical progress in manufacturing, capital, output and population all grow at the maximum rate of growth of population, ε. If technical progress takes place, population grows at its maximum rate, ε; capital and output grow at a more rapid rate, namely $\lambda/(1 - \sigma) + \varepsilon$, where λ is the rate of technical progress and $(1 - \sigma)$ is the share of labor. Growth in the level of manufacturing output is more rapid the greater the rate of growth of the labor force and the more rapid the pace of technological change; growth is less rapid the greater the share of labor in current output or more rapid the greater the saving ratio. The rate $\lambda/(1 - \sigma) + \varepsilon$ is a kind of natural rate of growth, Harrod's G_n. The fact that in the long run the accumulation of capital and the growth of output adjust themselves to the natural rate when substitution in production is permitted is due to Solow (1956),[25] whose analysis of the growth of an advanced economy provides an approximation the model of development for a dual economy which improves as a larger and larger proportion of the total activity of the system shifts from the traditional to the advanced sector. Since capital and output grow at the same rate in long-run equilibrium, the capital-output ratio approaches a fixed value. Whether or not the accelerator is fixed in the short-run, long-run equilibrium growth will be characterized by a constant ratio of capital to output, even in the presence of technological change, factor substitution and an underdeveloped sector of the economy. For an advanced economy characterized by a pattern of development like that of the dual economy we have analyzed, the familiar Harrod–Domar growth model is a perfectly valid theory of growth in long-run equilibrium.[26] It must be noted that this result is strictly correct *only* in long-run equilibrium; the validity of the short-run aspect of Harrod's model, with its knife-edge instability under the impact of short-run disequilibrium movements, cannot be assessed here.

We have been able to discuss only the features of the theory of development of a dual economy which characterize long-run equilibrium. One further aspect of the theory which should be noted is the absence of a critical "minimum effort" necessary for take-off into sustained growth. Whatever the initial capital endowment of the advanced sector, sustained growth must eventuate. Secondly, no matter how small the initial endowment, the beginning of growth of manufacturing output is invariably accompanied by a "big push" of activity associated with an extraordinarily high rate of growth of output. But for a dual economy this high initial rate of growth may be viewed as essentially a statistical artifact. Using the production function for the advanced sector, it is possible to derive the relation

$$\frac{\dot{X}}{X} = \lambda + (1 - \sigma) \frac{\dot{M}}{M} + \sigma \frac{\dot{K}}{K}$$

so that the rate of growth of output in the industrial sector is the rate of technological progress plus a weighted average of the rates of growth of the manufacturing labor force and the rate of growth of capital stock. Since capital stock always grows at some positive rate and the growth of the manufacturing labor force begins at an extremely high rate and declines gradually to the rate of growth of population, the initial rate of growth of manufacturing output must be extremely high, declining gradually and approaching its equilibrium value. The existence of a statistically observable "big push" in manufacturing output is no evidence for the necessity of a massive infusion of capital from outside the system. There may be other reasons for which such an infusion might be desirable;[27] it is clearly unnecessary for development leading to sustained growth.

To complete the discussion we must consider the development of wages, interest and the terms of trade between the advanced and the underdeveloped agricultural sector. First, wages per man must be equal to the share of labor multiplied by output per man. Real wages in manufacturing must therefore rise at the rate $\lambda/(1 - \sigma)$ in long-run steady growth; this may be seen as follows

$$\frac{\dot{w}}{w} = \frac{\dot{x}}{x} = \left[\frac{\dot{X}}{X} - \frac{\dot{M}}{M}\right] = \left[\frac{\lambda}{1 - \sigma} + \varepsilon\right] - \varepsilon = \frac{\lambda}{1 - \sigma}$$

since output per man grows at a rate given by the rate of growth of output less the rate of growth of the manufacturing labor force. If there is no technological progress in the advanced sector real wages eventually reach some constant level. If technical progress is possible, real wages rise more rapidly, the more rapid the rate of technological change and the higher the saving ratio. Another way to state the relationship of the growth of real wages and the savings ratio is this: The higher the share of labor in the product of any given period, the more slowly must real wages rise. Unlike wages, the real rate of interest attains a constant level whether or not there is technical progress. Provided that activity in the advanced sector is highly rationalized, that is, predominantly "capitalistic" in its mode of organization, the rate of interest is determined by the usual marginal productivity condition

$$\frac{\partial X}{\partial K} = \sigma \frac{X}{K} = r$$

which is necessary for maximization of profit in the advanced sector. But the ratio of capital to output is constant in long-run sustained growth; where C is the capital-output ratio of Harrod, this yields the familiar

$$r = \frac{\sigma}{C}$$

where σ is the saving ratio. The rate of interest is equal to Harrod's warranted rate, which is essentially the gross rate of capital accumulation or I/K, in the notation of the last section. The rate of growth of output (and the rate of net capital accumulation) is less than the warranted rate by the amount of depreciation on capital stock. This implies that

$$r = \frac{\sigma}{C} \left[\frac{\lambda}{1 - \sigma} + \varepsilon \right] + \eta = G_n + \eta$$

where G_n is Harrod's notation for the natural rate of growth. The rate of interest rises with an increase in the rate of technical progress, with an increase in the rate of population growth or in the rate of depreciation on capital, and with a rise in the saving ratio. Another way to stage the relation between the rate of interest (the rate of gross capital accumulation) and the rate of depreciation on capital is this: Interest increases with a decline in the durability of capital equipment. Another way to derive the basic relationship between interest and the rate of growth on capital stock is to note that all property income is "interest" in the sense in which interest is used here, so that the total volume of interest payments is equal to gross investment

$$rK = \dot{K} + \eta K$$

which implies

$$r = \frac{\dot{K}}{K} + \eta = G_n + \eta$$

as before. From these relationships it is possible to compute the long-run sustained growth capital-output ratio, Harrod's C. The capital-output ratio is given by

$$C = \frac{\sigma(1 - \sigma)}{\lambda + (1 - \sigma)(\varepsilon + \eta)}$$

which increases with the saving ratio and diminishes with the rate of growth of population, the rate of technical progress and the rate of depreciation on capital goods. Turning finally to the terms of trade between agriculture and industry, we have

$$wM + \mu wA = (1 - \sigma)X + qY$$

as the balance relation between industry and agriculture. This reduces to the simpler expression

$\mu wA = qY$.

This may be used to derive the expression

$$\mu wP(0)e^{\left(\frac{\varepsilon-\alpha}{1-\beta}\right)t} = qe^{\varepsilon t}\, y^+$$

hence

$$q = w\,\frac{\mu}{y^+}\,e^{\left[\left(\frac{\varepsilon-\alpha}{1-\beta}\right)-\varepsilon\right]t}$$

from which the following expression

$$\frac{\dot{q}}{q} = \left[\frac{\varepsilon-\alpha}{1-\beta} - \varepsilon\right] + \frac{\dot{w}}{w}$$

is derived by differentiating both sides with respect to time and then by dividing through by q, where q is the term of trade, that is, the price of agricultural goods in terms of manufactured goods. The first two terms of this expression are negative by the condition that $\alpha - \beta\varepsilon > 0$, which is necessary and sufficient for the emergence of an agricultural surplus. This third term, the rate of growth of real wages, is positive and equal to $\lambda/(1 - \sigma)$. If technical progress in the manufacturing sector declines to zero the terms of trade for the agricultural sector must deteriorate. The more rapid the rate of technical progress in manufacturing, the less rapidly the terms of trade for agriculture deteriorate; if technical progress is sufficiently rapid the terms of trade may even improve for agriculture. Not unexpectedly, precisely the opposite holds for changes in the terms of trade with respect to changes in the rate of technical progress in agriculture. The more rapid the rate of technical progress, the more rapidly the terms of trade deteriorate. A second consequence of the fundamental balance relation is that the more rapidly population increases, the less rapidly the terms of trade of agriculture deteriorate. Finally, the effects of diminishing returns in agriculture depend on the relative magnitude of technical progress in agriculture and the rate of growth of population. If $\varepsilon > \alpha$ the terms of trade improve if returns diminish more rapidly than before; if $\varepsilon = \alpha$ the terms of trade remain unaltered by a change in the rate at which returns to additions in the agricultural labor force diminish; finally if $\varepsilon < \alpha$ the terms of trade deteriorate if returns to scale in agriculture diminish more rapidly.

2.6   Fundamental Differential Equation

In this section a rigorous analysis of the fundamental differential equation of the theory of development of a dual economy is given. This analysis is necessary to provide a detailed derivation of the conclusions of the previous section; as in section 2.3 above, readers who trust the mathematics should go on to the following section. The fundamental differential equation is given by

$$\dot{K} = -\eta K + \sigma K^{\sigma} P(0)^{1-\sigma} e^{\lambda t} \left[e^{\varepsilon t} - e^{\left(\frac{\varepsilon - \alpha}{1-\beta}\right)t} \right]^{1-\sigma}$$

where K is the size of capital stock, P is the size of the total population, and the various parameters are derived from the expression for growth of the manufacturing labor force, the production function for the advanced sector and the identity in manufacturing output and its allocation to consumption and investment. To solve this equation, we begin by transforming variables so that

$$K = U^{\frac{1}{1-\sigma}}$$

hence,

$$\dot{K} = \frac{1}{1-\sigma} U^{\frac{\sigma}{1-\sigma}} \dot{U} .$$

The fundamental equation may be rewritten in the form

$$\dot{U} = -(1-\sigma)\eta U + \sigma(1-\sigma)P(0)^{1-\sigma} e^{\lambda t} \left[e^{\varepsilon t} - e^{\left(\frac{\varepsilon - \alpha}{1-\beta}\right)t} \right]^{1-\sigma}$$

$$= -(1-\sigma)\eta U + q(t)$$

which is linear in U and may be integrated as follows

$$U(t) = e^{-(1-\sigma)\eta t} U(0) + e^{-(1-\sigma)\eta t} \int_0^t e^{(1-\sigma)\eta t_1} q(t_1)\, dt_1$$

Now, consider the integral

$$\int_0^{} e^{(1-\sigma)\eta t_1} \, q(t_1) \, dt_1$$

$$= \sigma(1-\sigma)P(0)^{1-\sigma} \int_0^t e^{[(1-\sigma)(\epsilon+\eta) + \lambda]t_1} \left[1 - e^{\frac{-(\alpha-\beta\epsilon)}{1-\beta}t_1} \right]^{1-\sigma} dt_1$$

$$= \sigma(1-\sigma)P(0)^{1-\sigma} \int_0^t e^{p t_1} [1 - e^{-q t_1}]^r \, dt_1$$

where p, q and r are defined as in the second line above and are used to simplify notation for the computations that follow. It is apparently impossible to evaluate this integral in closed form except for special cases (such as $r = 1$, which is ruled out for the problem at hand). It is necessary to expand $[1 - e^{-q t_1}]^r$ in MacLaurin series as follows

$$[1 - e^{q t_1}]^r = 1 - r e^{-q t_1} + \frac{r(r-1)}{2!} e^{-2q t_1} - \cdots$$
$$+ (-1)^n \frac{r(r-1)\cdots(r-n+1)}{n!} e^{-nq t_1} + \cdots.$$

Hence, the integral is written

$$\int_0^t \left[e^{pt} - r e^{(p-q)t_1} + \frac{r(r-1)}{2!} e^{(p-2q)t_1} - \cdots \right.$$
$$\left. + (-1)^n \frac{r(r-1)\cdots(r-n+1)}{n!} e^{(p-nq)t_1} + \cdots \right].$$

Integrating term by term we obtain

$$\int_0^t e^{p t_1} [1 - e^{-q t_1}]^r \, dt_1$$

$$= \frac{1}{p} [e^{pt} - 1] - \frac{r}{p-q} [e^{(p-q)t} - 1] + \frac{r(r-1)}{2!(p-2q)} [e^{(p-2q)t_1} - 1] - \cdots$$
$$+ (-1)^n \frac{r(r-1)\cdots(r-n+1)}{n!(p-nq)} [e^{(p-nq)t} - 1] + \cdots.$$

Hence

$$U(t) = e^{-(1-\sigma)\eta t} U(0) + \frac{\sigma(1-\sigma)P(0)^{1-\sigma}}{(1-\sigma)(\epsilon+\eta) + \lambda} e^{[\lambda+\epsilon(1-\sigma)]t} + R(t)$$

where $R(t)$ is a remainder, defined as the sum of the appropriate infinite series. Each term of $R(t)$ grows at a rate which is strictly less than the rate $\lambda + \varepsilon(1 - \sigma)$, which is the "dominant" term in the expression for $U(t)$. If $p > q$, $R(t) \to 0$ as t increases without limit; otherwise $R(t)$ grows over time, diminishing relative to the dominant term. Noting that the dominant term, which grows at a positive rate, and the remainder depend only on the initial value of population, and further than $U(0) = K(0)^{1-\sigma}$, it is clear that the effects of the initial endowment of capital die out, absolutely, and relative to the dominant term. To compute the long-run equilibrium value of the rate of growth for capital stock we note first that

$$\frac{\dot{U}}{U} \to [\lambda + \varepsilon(1 - \sigma)] \text{ as } t \to \infty.$$

But also, using the expressions for U and $\dot{U}$ derived previously we have

$$\frac{\dot{K}}{K} = \frac{1}{(1 - \sigma)} \frac{U^{\frac{\sigma}{1-\sigma}}\dot{U}}{U^{\frac{1}{1-\sigma}}} = \frac{1}{(1 - \sigma)} \frac{\dot{U}}{U}$$

so that

$$\frac{\dot{K}}{K} \to \frac{\lambda}{(1 - \sigma)} + \varepsilon \text{ as } t \to \infty.$$

Secondly, using the expression

$$\frac{\dot{X}}{X} = \lambda + (1 - \sigma) \frac{\dot{M}}{M} + \sigma \frac{\dot{K}}{K}$$

we have the result that

$$\frac{\dot{X}}{X} \to \lambda + (1 - \sigma)\varepsilon + \sigma \left[\frac{\lambda}{(1 - \sigma)} + \varepsilon \right] = \frac{\lambda}{(1 - \sigma)} + \varepsilon \text{ as } t \to \infty \text{ }[28]$$

so that capital and output grow at the same rate in long-run equilibrium. To compute the long-run equilibrium capital-output ratio, we can compute the ratio of the dominant components in the expressions for each of the terms, capital and output.

First, we may utilize the production function to derive

$$X(t) = e^{\lambda t}\, P(0)^{1-\sigma} \left[e^{\varepsilon t} - e^{\left(\frac{\varepsilon-\alpha}{1-\beta}\right)t} \right]^{1-\sigma} K(t)^{\sigma}$$

$$= e^{\lambda t}\, P(0)^{1-\sigma} \left[e^{\varepsilon t} - e^{\left(\frac{\varepsilon-\alpha}{1-\beta}\right)t} \right]^{1-\sigma} U(t)^{\frac{\sigma}{1-\sigma}}$$

and we also have

$$K(t) = U(t)^{\frac{1}{1-\sigma}}$$

so that

$$C(t) = \frac{K(t)}{X(t)} = -\frac{U(t)}{e^{\lambda t} P(0)^{1-\sigma}\left[e^{\varepsilon t} - e^{\left(\frac{\varepsilon-\alpha}{1-\beta}\right)t} \right]^{1-\sigma}}$$

$$\rightarrow \frac{\dfrac{\sigma(1-\sigma)P(0)^{1-\sigma}}{(1-\sigma)(\varepsilon+\eta)+\lambda} e^{[\lambda \times \varepsilon(1-\sigma)]t}}{P(0)^{1-\sigma}e^{[\lambda-\varepsilon(1-\sigma)]t}}$$

$$= \frac{\sigma(1-\sigma)}{(1-\sigma)(\varepsilon+\eta)+\lambda} \quad \text{as } t \rightarrow \infty .$$

This completes the analysis of the fundamental differential equation.

2.7 Low-level Equilibrium Trap

The development of a dual economy has been discussed under the assumption that if an agricultural surplus comes into existence it will persist. If such a surplus is already in existence, and a change in the parameters of the system, particularly in the net rate of reproduction, results in a diminution of the agricultural surplus, implying its eventual disappearance, the course of development of the economy is considerably different. Eventually manufacturing activity is brought to a halt, capital is allowed to depreciate without replacement and the situation previously described as a low-level equilibrium trap is approached as a limit. If a low-level equilibrium trap exists, it is stable for any initial level of agricultural and industrial output, and for any initial stock of capital. To trace the decline of the economy to its trap level of output, note first that from the point at which the agricultural surplus begins to diminish, the agricultural labor force grows at a rate which is more rapid than the rate of growth of population and the manufacturing force declines absolutely, eventually becoming zero at some finite time, which is easily computed. At the point at which all labor has returned to the land, manufacturing output drops to zero and capital is decumulated at the rate given by the rate of depreciation; in the limit it disappears entirely. From the point at which industrial output drops to zero, the theory of a traditional economic system governs the further decline of the system to its trap level. Population growth is reduced from its maximum rate. Food output *per capita* declines to a stationary level.

The critical condition, which marks the dividing line between economies caught in the low-level equilibrium trap and economies capable of sustained growth, is simply that for sustained growth an agricultural surplus must come into existence and must persist.[29] Formally, the condition which is necessary and sufficient for sustained growth of output in both the manufacturing and agricultural sectors is $\alpha - \beta\varepsilon > 0$, where α is the rate of technical progress, ε is the maximum rate of population growth and $1 - \beta$ is the elasticity of output in the agricultural sector with respect to an increase in the agricultural labor force. The characteristics of an economy which moves toward a low-level equilibrium trap are completely described by the theory of a traditional or backward economy. The characteristics of an economy which experiences steady growth depend not only on the existence of an agricultural surplus but also on technical conditions in the advanced sector. The more rapid the rate of technical change, the higher the saving ratio, and the more rapid the rate of growth of population, the more rapid is the pace of growth in the advanced sector. Eventually, the economy is dominated by the development of the advanced sector and becomes more and more like the advanced economic systems described by the familiar Harrod–Domar theory of economic growth.

Of course, the theory of a dual economy is far from the whole story concerning the growth of an advanced economic system. From the outset the possibility of capital accumulation in agriculture was ruled out. While this assumption holds remarkably well for Asian agriculture, including the highly productive agricultural sector of the Japanese economy, in the "newly settled" lands of the United States, Canada, Argentina, Australia and New Zealand agriculture has experienced rapid increases in labor productivity due to infusions of capital. We have already noted that there is no "minimum critical effort" of investment in dual economies in which substitution between capital and labor in manufacturing is possible, and there is no capital accumulation in agriculture; however, one of the critical parameters of the expression dividing economies into developing and stationary systems is the rate of technological progress in agriculture. If technical progress can be accelerated by the accumulation of capital in agriculture the balance between food shortage and agricultural surplus may be tipped in favor of surplus. It must be remarked that this possibility presumes not only the availability of resources for investment in agriculture but also drastic changes in the social organization of the 'traditional' or backward sector. The infusion of capital must be accompanied by the infusion of the spirit of capitalism;[30] the traditional way of life must be replaced by a way of life in which production in both agriculture and industry is fully rationalized.

Notes

1. Dating the beginning of serious work in this field with R.F. Harrod (1939, pp. 14–33).
2. R.F. Harrod (1939, 1948); E.D. Domar (1946, pp. 137–147).
3. J.S. Duesenberry (1958); A. Smithies (1957, pp. 1–52).
4. R.M. Solow (1956, pp. 65–94); J. Tobin (1955, pp. 103–115).
5. N. Kaldor (1957, pp. 591–624); reprinted in *Essays in Economic Stability and Growth* (Duckworth, 1960); reference should also be made to "Capital Accumulation and Economic Growth" in Proceedings of the International Economic Association's Corfu conference on *Capital Theory*, September 1958.
6. A helpful review and exposition of dynamic theory is W. Baumol (1959).
7. For an exception to this rule see the interesting but brief theoretical treatment of population growth in Solow (1956, pp. 90–91).
8. See especially: W.A. Lewis (1955); and Part II of G.M. Meier and R.E. Baldwin (1957); for a survey of the historical and institutional literature on development. For references to a dual economy see footnote 9, below.
9. The source of the notion of a dual economy is: J.H. Boeke (1953) (earlier edition in two vols., 1942, 1946), which deal with the case of Indonesia; following Boeke's orientation is the important study by R. Firth (1946) which discusses the traditional sector of the Malayan economy. For a critical view of Boeke's thesis and his policy recommendations, see B. Higgins (1956, pp. 99–115). The notion of a "dual economy" has been employed by Chenery, Clark, Mandelbaum, Rosenstein–Rodan and Singer, among others.
10. But see G.O. Gutman (1957, pp. 323–329) with mathematical appendix by J. Black. Black uses the well-known two-country trade model of H. Johnson (1954, pp. 462–485) reprinted in *International Trade and Economic Growth* (London: Allen and Unwin, 1958), pp. 94–119.
11. For recent assaults on the summit see Joan Robinson (1958); D.G. Champernowne (1958, pp. 218–244); and the references of footnotes 3–5.

12. The situation envisaged is that of Japan, as well as areas of Southeast Asia studied by Boeke and Firth. The idea of a dual economy evidently has considerably broader empirical relevance.

13. In the primary-producing countries of Southeast Asia the advanced sector is plantation agriculture, mining and extraction of petroleum. The traditional sector is peasant agriculture and fishing. In Japan the traditional sector includes agriculture, small manufacturing and most construction; the advanced sector should be identified with Japanese heavy industry.

14. Reference may be made to the theory of the L-shaped cost curve; P. Wiles (1956, Chapter 12 and appendix, pp. 202–251); and J.S. Bain (1956, Chapter 3, pp. 53–113).

15. See, for example, the interesting work of Zvi Griliches (1957).

16. A technological change is "neutral" provided that for a given bundle of factors the marginal rate of substitution between factors with output held constant is the same before and after the change.

17. There is considerable literature on this problem, mainly unpublished. The key reference is R.M. Solow (1957, pp. 313–320), where shifts of a production function and movements along it are separately identified. It is an open question whether it is possible to test the assumption of neutrality of technical change which underlies Solow's work.

18. See the references in footnotes 3–5.

19. The basic reference to the work is Douglas (1948, pp. 1–42); many further references are listed there. The so-called Cobb–Douglas form was apparently introduced into the literature by Wicksell in his notable article "A Mathematical Analysis of Dr. Åkerman's Problem" (1923), translated into English by E. Classen, and reprinted as part of an appendix to Wicksell's *Lectures on Political Economy* (1934). For a recent discussion of "Åkerman's problem" reference must be made to the contribution of R.M. Solow to the Corfu conference on capital theory.

20. Leibenstein (1957, Chapter 3), and the references listed there, p. 15.

21. This solution has the form of a "logistic" curve, familiar from many biological and economic applications.

22. This was pointed out to me by F.H. Hahn.

23. For a discussion of the difficulties of constructing a production function see Joan Robinson (1953–1954, pp. 81–106); R.M. Solow (1955, pp. 101–108); Joan Robinson (1955–1956, pp. 247); and recently Joan Robinson (1959, pp. 157–166).

24. See, for example, F. Quesnay (1894, first edition, 1758).

25. R.M. Solow (1956). The result that capital and output grow at the same rate with neutral technological change does not accord with the analysis of Solow, *op cit.*, p. 86. In correspondence he points out that a minor arithmetical slip in his argument is responsible for the discrepancy.

26. For the basic references see footnote 9, above.

27. A persuasive case for capital-intensive investments is made by H. Leibenstein and W. Galenson (1955); see also: H. Leibenstein (1954, Chapter 15).

28. This expression may be compared with an essentially equivalent expression derived by N. Kaldor (1957, p. 615). Neo-classical, Kaldor and dual economy models of growth all tend, in the limit, to the equilibrium growth path described by the Harrod–Domar model.

29. This condition is given its due weight by Kaldor in his paper "Characteristics of Economic Development" read to the International Conference on Underdeveloped Areas in October 1954, now printed in *Essays on Economic Stability and Growth* (London: Duckworth, 1960), pp. 233–242. See especially the discussion of this problem on p. 240.

30. The rationalization of production in the traditional sector is, obviously, one of the great "costs" of economic advancement in underdeveloped areas. The view that the cost is too great to pay is not without its adherents; see especially the work of Boeke, cited in footnote 9.

3   The Structure of Multi-Sector Dynamic Models

Dale W. Jorgenson

3A   Introduction

In this chapter we consider multi-sector generalizations of various Keynesian type macroeconomic models and investigate the existence, uniqueness, and nonnegativity of solutions to these models. On the basis of the seemingly elementary consideration that national income and capital stock or sectoral income and stock levels must be nonnegative, doubt is cast on the general validity of the well-known models of the trade cycle proposed by Samuelson (1939a,b), Hicks (1950), and Smithies (1957), and the augmented dynamic input-output system of Leontief (1953). Using the same elementary consideration, we can deduce stringent conditions which must be satisfied by the ordinary dynamic input-output system, Hicks' "basic equation," and Duesenberry's (1958) multi-sector model of growth and fluctuations.

On the constructive side, techniques are provided for the analysis of solutions to the linear and piece-wise linear systems which dominate the literature on Keynesian macroeconomics. If the solution to the macroeconomic model can be shown to be nonnegative for any nonnegative initial conditions, methods associated with the spectral theory of nonnegative matrices may be employed to characterize the solutions in detail. In particular, the existence and relative stability of a nonnegative characteristic solution are assured. Using more specific information, we may find it possible to obtain bounds to the equilibrium rate of growth.

Application of these techniques requires information only on the signs of elements in the matrices associated with the reduced form of a macroeconomic model. In many of the cases examined in this chapter, this information can be obtained directly from the economic interpretation of the corresponding coefficients of investment and consumption functions or other relationships.

3A.1   Two Theorems on Nonnegativity

The investigation will be based on the following theorems:

Theorem 3.1. *For a system of linear differential equations*

$$\dot{x} = Ax + f(t), \tag{3A.1.1}$$

where A is a constant matrix, $f(t) \geq 0$ for $t \geq 0$ is a vector-valued function of t, $x(0) \geq 0$ is a vector of initial conditions, a necessary and sufficient condition that $x(t) \geq 0$ for $t \geq 0$ is that there is a nonnegative scalar c so that $cI + A \geq 0$.[1]

The corresponding result for difference equations is as follows:

Theorem 3.2. *For a system of linear difference equations*

$$x(t) = Ax(t - 1) + f(t), \tag{3A.1.2}$$

where A is a constant matrix, $f(t) \geq 0$ for $t \geq 0$ is a vector-valued function of t, $x(0) \geq 0$ is a vector of initial conditions, a necessary and sufficient condition that $x(t) \geq 0$ for $t \geq 0$ is that $A \geq 0$ and A has at least one element strictly positive in each column.[2]

These theorems provide simple criteria for the nonnegativity of solutions to macroeconomic models formulated as linear difference of differential equations or for piece-wise linear systems.[3] Proof of the theorems is based on a series of lemmas which provide alternative and equivalent conditions for the nonnegativity of solutions to systems of difference and differential equations in terms of certain functions of a matrix.

Lemma 3.1. *$Ax \geq 0$ for $x \geq 0$ if and only if $A \geq 0$ and A has at least one element strictly positive in each column.*

Lemma 3.2. *A necessary and sufficient condition that $A^t \geq 0$ and A^t has at least one element strictly positive in each column for any integer t, nonnegative, is that $A \geq 0$ and A has at least one element strictly positive in each column.*

Proof: Sufficiency is obtained by observing that the lemma is trivial for $t = 1$; suppose the lemma is true for $t = n - 1$, then we may write

$$A^n = A \cdot A^{n-1},$$

where A, $A^{n-1} \geq 0$, and each matrix has at least one element strictly positive in each column. Applying lemma 3.1 to each column of A^n

considered as a vector, we observe that each such column is nonnegative and not zero. Necessity is obtained from consideration of $t = 1$.

Theorem 3.2 is an immediate consequence of lemmas 3.1 and 3.2.

Lemma 3.3.[4] *A necessary and sufficient condition that $e^{At} \geq 0$ for $t \geq 0$ is that there is a positive scalar c so that $cI + A \geq 0$.*

Proof: Expanding the matrix exponential function e^{At} in power series

$$E^{At} = I + At + \frac{A^2 t^2}{2!} + \cdots,$$

we observe that for small t, e^{At} has at least one negative element if there is no positive scalar c so that $cI + A \geq 0$. For sufficiency we observe that the existence of such a positive scalar implies the nonnegativity of e^{At} for small t, but for any t and any n we have

$$(e^{At/n})^n = e^{At}.$$

Choose n sufficiently large so that $e^{At/n}$ is nonnegative; then, since e^{At} is nonsingular for any t (Bellman, 1960, p. 166), $e^{At/n}$ has at least one element strictly positive in each column. Hence, $e^{At} \geq 0$ by lemma 3.2.

Proof of Theorem 3.1: The general solution to the system (3A.1.1) is

$$x(t) = e^{At} x(0) + \int_0^t e^{A(t-2)} f(s) \, ds.$$

If there is nonnegative scalar c so that $cI + A \geq 0$, $e^{At} \geq 0$ by lemma 3.3. Since e^{At} is nonsingular, $x(0) \geq 0$ implies $e^{At} x(0) \geq 0$ by lemma 3.1. Secondly, for $s \leq t$, $e^{A(t-s)} f(s) \geq 0$, for $f(s) \geq 0$, by lemma 3.1. Hence $\int_0^t e^{A(t-s)} f(s) \, ds \geq 0$ for $t \geq 0$. But $x(t)$ is the sum of two nonnegative vectors, one of which is not zero. Hence $x(t) \geq 0$ for $t \geq 0$, which completes proof of sufficiency.

For necessity, let $f(t) = 0$ for all t; then $e^{At} \geq 0$ only if there is a nonnegative scalar c so that $cI + A \geq 0$ by lemma 3.3. By lemma 3.1, $e^{At} x(0) \geq 0$ for $x(0) \geq 0$ only if $e^{At} \geq 0$ for all $t \geq 0$, $x(t) = e^{At} x(0)$, which completes the proof.

Theorems 3.1 and 3.2 may be applied to piece-wise linear systems by making use of the observation that the initial conditions for each linear "phase" are the end conditions for the previous phase, so that the homogeneous part of such solutions can be written as the product of a sequence of matrix exponential or matrix power functions, each such function corresponding to one phase of the system.

In the following section, theorems 3.1 and 3.2 will be applied to a series of disaggregated macroeconomic models of the Keynesian type. All the models examined are based on a separation of total output into two parts—consumption and investment. Consumption is determined by some version of the consumption function; investment may be taken as autonomous, as in the Kahn (1931) dynamic multiplier, or as determined by the acceleration principle; i.e., investment is proportional to changes in income. The three versions of the acceleration principle to be examined are (i) unlagged or instantaneous adjustment of capital stock to changes in income, (ii) lagged adjustment with a fixed lag, and (iii) adjustment distributed over time (distributed lags). When combined with the consumption function, these alternative versions of the acceleration principle generate (i) the Harrod–Domar growth model (Harrod, 1939, 1948; Domar, 1946, 1957), (ii) the Samuelson–Hicks model of the trade cycle (Samuelson, 1939a,b; Hicks, 1950), and (iii) the Smithies–Duesenberry model of fluctuations and growth (Smithies, 1957; Duesenberry, 1958). The corresponding multi-sector model are (i) the dynamic input-output system of Hawkins (1948) and Leontief (1953), (ii) a multi-sector model of the trade cycle described by Allen (1956, p. 364), (iii) Duesenberry's multi-sector model (1958, pp. 222–225).

3A.2   Multiplier Theory

The simplest Keynesian macrodynamic theory is based on a determination of investment outside the model, i.e., investment is autonomous. In the discussion that follows it will be assumed that autonomous expenditures are nonnegative.

It is well known that disaggregation of the static multiplier of Keynes for determination of national income leads to a model which is formally identical with the Leontief static system of the open type (Chipman, 1951; Goodwin, 1949, 1950; Solow, 1952)

$$(I - A)x = y, \tag{3A.2.1}$$

where x is a vector of sector income levels, $y \geq 0$ is a vector of final or autonomous demands, and $A \geq 0$ is an input-output matrix.[5] The conditions under which there is a unique, nonnegative solution to this system of equations have been carefully investigated by Solow (1952) and by Hawkins and Simon (1949). Solow's results are as follows:

There exists a unique solution $x \geq 0$ of the system (3A.2.1) for any $y \geq 0$ if (i) A is an irreducible input-output matrix with at least one row sum $\sum_j a_{ij}$ strictly less than one,[6] or (ii) A is a reducible input-output matrix, but arranged in normal form so that each irreducible submatrix along the main diagonal has at least one row sum strictly less than one (Solow, 1952, pp. 36–38).[7] In the disaggregated form of Kahn's (1931) dynamic multiplier, $x(t)$ and $y(t)$ are vectors with elements representing the income and autonomous demand for the output of the corresponding sector. If A is a matrix with nonnegative elements $[a_{ij}]$, where a_{ij} is the marginal (and average) propensity of the jth sector to consume the output of the ith sector, the dynamic multiplier may be represented in the form given by Goodwin (1949, 1950) and Solow (1952)

$$x(t) = Ax(t - 1) + y(t).$$ (3A.2.2)

Applying theorem 3.2, we find that the solution

$$x(t) = A^t x(0) + y(t) + Ay(t - 1) + \cdots + A^{t-1} y(1)$$ (3A.2.3)

is nonnegative and not zero for any initial levels of income $x(0)$, non-negative and not zero, if and only if the matrix $A \geq 0$ has at least one element strictly positive in each column. This latter condition means that each sector consumes the output of at least one other sector (possibly its own). If the coefficients a_{ij} are interpreted as technologically given constants, this assumption corresponds to Koopmans' "impossibility of the Land of Cockaigne" (Koopmans, 1951a, pp. 49–52; 1957, pp. 77–79). There is no *necessary* connection between the existence and uniqueness of a nonnegative solution to the multi-sector dynamic multiplier (3A.2.2) and the convergence of the multiplier process to a stationary nonnegative solution

$$x = (I - A)^{-1} y,$$ (3A.2.4)

where $y \geq 0$ is a constant vector. The *sufficient* condition that this solution of the model be stable and nonnegative given by Solow (1952) also implies that the solution to the dynamic multiplier (3A.2.2) is nonnegative for all values of time. The irreducibility of A implies that the complete solution (3A.2.3) is nonnegative and *not zero* for all values of time.

3A.3   The Dynamic Input-Output System

In the Harrod–Domar growth model, investment is taken as determined within the system by an unlagged accelerator. In the discussion that follows the closed, continuous time formulation of the
Harrod–Domar theory will be used. Consumption is determined by a
static multiplier; investment is proportional to the rate of change of
income.

In the dynamic input-output system A is an input-output matrix,
and $B \geq 0$ is a stock-flow matrix with elements $[b_{ij}]$, showing the stock
of the ith commodity required for production of one unit of the jth.
The vectors $x(t)$ and $\dot{x}(t)$ have elements representing the output and
rate of change of output of the corresponding sector. The complete
dynamic input-output system may be written in the form

$$x(t) = Ax(t) + B\dot{x}(t).$$ (3A.3.1)

To simplify the following discussion, it will be assumed at the outset
that B^{-1} exists and that $B^{-1}(I - A)$ is nonsingular and irreducible. The
solution to the dynamic input-output system may be written

$$x(t) = e^{B^{-1}(I-A)t}x(0), \qquad x(0) \geq 0.$$ (3A.3.2)

Various attempts have been made to obtain conditions that the
solution of $x(t)$ be nonnegative and not zero (Chipman, 1954;
Georgescu-Roegen, 1951; Hawkins, 1948; Jorgenson, 1960; Solow,
1959). Previous results may be summarized as follows: Since A is an
input-output matrix, $(I - A)^{-1}$ exists and is nonnegative; hence
$(I - A)^{-1}B$ is the product of two nonnegative matrices and is itself
nonnegative. Since $B^{-1}(I - A)$ is irreducible, $(I - A)^{-1}B$ is an irreducible nonnegative matrix. By Frobenius' theorem (Gantmacher,
1959, p. 65), $(I - A)^{-1}B$ has a unique positive characteristic vector, say
ζ, and no other characteristic vector which is nonnegative. Secondly,
associated with this vector is a characteristic value of $(I - A)^{-1}B$, say
$1/\gamma$, which is simple, positive, and largest in modulus of all the characteristic values of $(I - A)^{-1}B$. The corresponding uniquely nonnegative
characteristic solution of (3A.3.2), $e^{\gamma t}\zeta$, is relatively stable if and only if
all characteristic values of $B^{-1}(I - A)$ are less than γ in real part (Jorgenson, 1960). Various other conditions on $B^{-1}(I - A)$ for relative stability have been given for two and three sector models (Hawkins,
1948; Georgescu-Roegen, 1951) using determinants; however, these

conditions are equivalent to the condition on characteristic values just given. It will be shown that relative stability is necessary for nonnegativity of solutions to (3A.3.1). However, no sufficient conditions for nonnegativity have been given in the literature.

To obtain a necessary and sufficient condition for nonnegativity of solutions to the dynamic input-output system, we apply theorem 3.1. For nonnegativity of solutions to (3A.3.1), it is necessary and sufficient that for the matrix $B^{-1}(I - A)$ there is a scalar c such that

$$cI + B^{-1}(I - A) \geqq 0,$$

that is $B^{-1}(I - A)$ has only nonnegative off-diagonal elements. If $B^{-1}(I - A)$ is acyclic and irreducible, all diagonal elements of $B^{-11}(I - A)$ must be negative; otherwise, $B^{-1}(I - A)$ could not be the inverse of a positive matrix.[8] It can be shown that the condition for nonnegativity of solutions for the dynamic input-output system is sufficient for relative stability of the characteristic solution $e^{\gamma t}\zeta > 0$. Since the matrix $cI + B^{-1}(I - A)$ is nonnegative and irreducible, it has a uniquely nonnegative characteristic vector $\zeta > 0$ associated with a characteristic value $c + r > 0$, which is the characteristic value of $B^{-1}(I - A)$ largest in modulus and hence largest in real part. The γ is the characteristic value of $B^{-1}(I - A)$ largest in real part, and $e^{\gamma t}\zeta$ is relatively stable. It should be observed that this sufficient condition for relative stability of the uniquely nonnegative solution makes no use of determinant conditions or conditions on the characteristic values of the matrix $B^{-1}(I - A)$.[9]

3A.4 The Lagged Accelerator

In the complete theory of the trade cycle proposed by Hicks, Samuelson's linear multiplier-accelerator is combined with two nonlinear relations—a "floor" to capital decumulation and a "ceiling" to the rise of output imposed by capacity. In this section the linear part of the Samuelson–Hicks model, Hicks' elementary case, will be analyzed. In section 3A.6 a nonlinear model in which capital accumulation is irreversible will be discussed. For the elementary case, consumption is determined by the income of the previous period as in Kahn's dynamic multiplier; investment is determined by a lagged accelerator and is proportional to the change in income in the previous period.

It is possible to derive a multi-sector analogue to the Samuelson–Hicks model of the trade cycle along the lines suggested by Allen (1956, p. 364). The marginal propensity to consume is replaced by an input-output matrix and the stock-flow coefficient by a stock-flow matrix. Let $x(t)$ be a vector with components equal to the level of output in each sector. The system may be written in the form

$$
\begin{bmatrix} x(t) \\ x(t-1) \end{bmatrix} = \begin{bmatrix} A+B & -B \\ I & 0 \end{bmatrix} \begin{bmatrix} x(t-1) \\ x(t-2) \end{bmatrix} + \begin{bmatrix} y(t) \\ 0 \end{bmatrix}. \tag{3A.4.1}
$$

Applying theorem 3.2 it is easily seen that the condition $B \geq 0$ is sufficient to imply that solutions to (3A.4.1) cannot be nonnegative for all nonnegative initial conditions.

A number of alternative versions of the consumption function have been combined with the lagged accelerator to form a model of the trade cycle. Two examples will be discussed. Consumption is a fraction of the current period's income, $Ax(t)$, and consumption is some weighted average of the previous two periods' incomes, $A_1 x(t-1) + A_2 x(t-2)$. The resulting models are

$$x(t) = (I - A)^{-1} Bx(t-1) - (I - A)^{-1} Bx(t-2) + (I - A)^{-1} y(t),$$
$$x(t) = (A_1 + B)x(t-1) + (A_2 - B)x(t-2) + y(t). \tag{3A.4.2}$$

In the first case, if autonomous expenditure is nonnegative, the nonhomogeneous term is nonnegative, since for A an input-output matrix $(I - A)^{-1}$, if it exists, will be nonnegative. But $-(I - A)^{-1}B$ is nonpositive and not zero, so that the first model cannot satisfy the conditions for nonnegativity given by theorem 3.2. In the second case, the conditions of theorem 3.2 are satisfied if and only if $A_2 \geq B$, that is, if and only if the marginal propensity of each sector to consume from each other sector with respect to its own output, two periods previous, is greater than the corresponding stock-flow coefficient for the output of that sector. This condition appears to be economically implausible.

Essentially the same analysis can be applied to the various distributed lag consumption and investment models discussed by Hicks (1950, p. 182 *et seq.*) and by Allen (1956, pp. 228–39). It will suffice to consider Hicks' "basic equation," which may be written

$$x_t = \sum_1^p a_i x_{t-i} + \sum_1^{p-1} b_i (x_{t-i} - x_{t-i-1}) + y_t, \tag{3A.4.3}$$

where the coefficients a_i, b_i are consumption and stock-flow coefficients, x_t is the level of output in the current period and y_t is the level of autonomous expenditure. This system can be rewritten in matrix form as

$$
\begin{bmatrix} x_t \\ x_{t-1} \\ \vdots \\ x_{t-p+1} \end{bmatrix} = \begin{bmatrix} a_1+b_1 & a_2+b_2-b_1 & \cdots & a_p-b_{p-1} \\ 1 & 0 & \cdots & 0 \\ \vdots & \vdots & & \vdots \\ 0 & 0 & \cdots & 0 \end{bmatrix} \begin{bmatrix} x_{t-1} \\ x_{t-2} \\ \vdots \\ x_{t-p} \end{bmatrix} + \begin{bmatrix} y_t \\ 0 \\ \vdots \\ 0 \end{bmatrix}. \quad (3A.4.4)
$$

Theorem 3.2 may be applied to demonstrate that the system has only nonnegative solutions if and only if

$$ a_i + b_i \geqq b_{i-1}, \qquad (i = 2, \ldots, p-1) $$

$$ a_p > b_{p-1}. \qquad (3A.4.5) $$

The economic interpretation of the first set of conditions is that the marginal propensity to consume with respect to the income of the ith period must be greater than or equal to the difference between the accelerator coefficient associated with changes in output of the succeeding period and the coefficient associated with current changes in output. The second condition is simply that the final term in the series of consumption coefficients must be larger than the final term in the series of accelerator coefficients. If the effects of past income levels on consumption die out before the effects of such income levels on investment, these conditions would be violated.

If the conditions required for nonnegativity are satisfied, it may be observed that the matrix (3A.4.4) is a nonnegative irreducible matrix; there is a unique, simple, positive characteristic root associated with a positive characteristic vector; furthermore, if $\sum_1^p a_1 < 1$, the modulus of this characteristic value is less than one. There are no roots of the system with modulus greater than or equal to one, and the possibility of progressive equilibrium described by Hicks (1950, p. 183) is ruled out. The system (3A.4.4) approaches a stationary state in essentially the same way as an ordinary dynamic multiplier like that of Solow (1952) or the distributed lag multiplier described by Hicks (1950, pp. 180–182). A multi-sector analogue of the general distributed lag model is easy to formulate; the conditions required for nonnegativity of solutions are analogous to those of the second system (3A.4.2).

3A.5 The Capital Stock Adjustment Model

The most significant difference between the older multiplier-accelerator models and the models proposed by Smithies and Duesenberry is that in the latter investment is determined by income and capital stock. There are important analogies between the complete models considered by Smithies (1957) and Duesenberry (1958, pp. 46–50); however, a difference in the formulation of the consumption function turns out to be critical for the existence of nonnegative solutions. To begin the analysis, we consider Duesenberry's model, given by investment and consumption function

$$I_t = \alpha Y_{t-1} - \beta K_{t-1} \; ; \qquad \alpha, \beta > 0 \; ;$$
$$C_t = a Y_{t-1} + b K_{t-1} \; ; \qquad a, b > 0 \; ; \qquad (3A.5.1)$$

together with identities in income and capital stock

$$Y_t = I_t + C_t \; ;$$
$$K_t = I_t + K_{t-1} - R_t \; ; \qquad (3A.5.2)$$

where I_t, C_t are investment and consumption, Y_t, K_t are income and capital stock, and R_t is physical depreciation, assumed to be a constant proportion of capital stock

$$R_t = k K_{t-1} \; ; \qquad 0 < k < 1 \; . \qquad (3A.5.3)$$

Since investment and income are measured gross of depreciation, each must be nonnegative. It is easily seen that capital stock must also be nonnegative.

The model proposed by Smithies consists of two phases, each of which is linear; the complete model is piece-wise linear. The linear model for the first phase associated with expansion is analogous to that of Duesenberry.[10] To show this, we consider Smithies' investment and consumption functions with time trends omitted

$$I_t = (\beta_1 + \beta_2 + \beta_3)Y_{t-1} - \beta_3 \sigma K_{t-1} \; ; \qquad \beta_1, \beta_2, \beta_3, \sigma > 0 \; ;$$
$$C_t = (1 - \alpha_1 + \alpha_2)Y_t \; ; \qquad \alpha_1, \alpha_2 > 0 \; . \qquad (3A.5.4)$$

This system may be compared with equations (3A.5.1); the principal difference is that capital stock does not enter the consumption function. The system is completed by two identities in income and capital

$$Y_t = I_t + C_t \, ,$$

$$K_t = I_{t-1} + K_{t-1} - \frac{1}{\sigma}(D_1 + D_2) \, , \tag{3A.5.5}$$

where $D_1 + D_2$ corresponds to depreciation. The second identity may be written

$$K_t = I_{t-1} + K_{t-1} - (\delta_1 + \delta_2)K_{t-1} + \frac{\delta_2}{\sigma} Y_{t-1} \, . \tag{3A.5.6}$$

The complete system reduces to

$$\begin{bmatrix} Y_t \\ K_t \end{bmatrix} = \begin{bmatrix} \dfrac{\beta_1 + \beta_2 + \beta_3}{\alpha_1 - \alpha_2} & \dfrac{-\beta_3\sigma}{\alpha_1 - \alpha_2} \\ \dfrac{\delta_2}{\sigma} + \alpha_1 - \alpha_2 & 1 - \delta_1 - \delta_2 \end{bmatrix} \begin{bmatrix} Y_{t-2} \\ K_{t-1} \end{bmatrix} . \tag{3A.5.7}$$

Applying theorem 3.2, it is evident that since either the first or second coefficient in the first row of the matrix in (3A.5.7) must be negative, Smithies' first phase model cannot satisfy the requirement that solutions be nonnegative for all nonnegative initial conditions.

Since the model is piece-wise linear there are implicit restrictions on the initial conditions. There remains the possibility that a given set of initial conditions would dictate a change of phase. Hence the second phase of the model must also be examined. The complete system becomes

$$\begin{bmatrix} Y_t \\ K_t \end{bmatrix} = \begin{bmatrix} \dfrac{\beta_1}{\alpha_2} & \dfrac{-\beta_3\sigma}{\alpha_1} \\ \alpha_1 + \dfrac{\delta_2}{\sigma} & 1 - \delta_1 - \delta_2 \end{bmatrix} \begin{bmatrix} Y_{t-1} \\ K_{t-1} \end{bmatrix} + \begin{bmatrix} \dfrac{\alpha_2 + \beta_2 + \beta_3}{\alpha_1} \bar{Y} \\ - \alpha_2 \bar{Y} \end{bmatrix} . \tag{3A.5.8}$$

Applying theorem 3.2 as before, it is clear that the second phase does not satisfy the conditions required for nonnegativity; in particular, it is always possible to choose a level of excess capacity sufficiently high so that the actual level of income is negative in the succeeding period, applying either the model of phase one or that of phase two. The model which should be applied depends not on the initial conditions alone but on whether the initial value of income is the highest ever.

A multi-sector version of the capital stock adjustment model has been given by Duesenberry (1958, pp. 222–225). A single consumption function of essentially the same form as (3A.5.1) is given by

$$C_t = aY_{t-1} + \sum_1^n b_i K_{i,t-1},$$ (3A.5.9)

where $K_{i,t-1}$ is the capital stock in the ith sector. Individual investment functions are provided for all sectors:

$$I_{i,t} = \alpha l_i Y_{t-1} - \beta_i K_{i,t-1}, \quad (i = 1, \ldots, n), \quad \sum_{i=1}^n l_i = 1,$$ (3A.5.10)

where $I_{i,t}$ is gross investment in the ith industry and $l_i > 0$ is a constant of proportionality. Finally, there are two sets of identities.

$$Y_t = C_t + \sum_1^n I_{i,t},$$

$$K_{i,t} = I_{i,t} + K_{i,t-1} - R_{i,t}, \quad (i = 1, \ldots, n),$$ (3A.5.11)

where $R_{i,t}$ is the physical depreciation in the ith industry, assumed proportional to the capital in that industry

$$R_{i,t} = k_i K_{i,t-1}, \quad (i = 1, \ldots, n).$$ (3A.5.12)

The complete system may be written in the form

$$\begin{bmatrix} Y_t \\ K_{1t} \\ K_{2t} \\ \vdots \\ K_{nt} \end{bmatrix} = \begin{bmatrix} \alpha + a & b_1 - \beta_1 & b_2 - \beta_2 & \cdots & b_n - \beta_n \\ \alpha l_1 & 1 - \beta_1 - k_1 & 0 & \cdots & 0 \\ \alpha l_2 & 0 & 1 - \beta_2 - k_2 & \cdots & 0 \\ \vdots & \vdots & \vdots & & \vdots \\ \alpha l_n & 0 & 0 & \cdots & 1 - \beta_n - k_n \end{bmatrix} \begin{bmatrix} Y_{t-1} \\ K_{1,t-1} \\ K_{2,t-1} \\ \vdots \\ K_{n,t-1} \end{bmatrix}.$$

(3A.5.13)

Necessary and sufficient conditions for nonnegativity of solutions to (3A.5.13) are

$$\begin{bmatrix} b_i \\ 1 \end{bmatrix} \ge \begin{bmatrix} \beta_i \\ \beta_i + k_i \end{bmatrix}, \quad (i = 1, \ldots, n).$$ (3A.5.14)

If the conditions for nonnegativity (3A.5.14) are satisfied, the matrix in (3A.5.13) is nonnegative. If, in addition, the elements of the top row are positive, the matrix is irreducible. A nonnegative irreducible matrix has a uniquely positive characteristic vector associated with a positive, real, simple characteristic root largest in modulus of all the characteristic values of the matrix. The vector may be interpreted as the equilibrium proportions between the capital stocks held by each sector and the output of the economic system; the characteristic value is the long-run equilibrium growth factor. Clearly, the corresponding uniquely positive solution of the system is relatively stable so that, asymptotically, the movement of the economic system is characterized by balanced growth (or decline) at a constant rate of growth. The rate of growth may be calculated by subtracting unity from the equilibrium growth factor.

3A.6   Irreversibility of Capital Accumulation

Nonlinear relationships play an important role in extensions of the multiplier-accelerator models discussed in the previous sections. Specifically, irreversibility of capital accumulation has been discussed by Leontief (1953), Hicks (1950), Duesenberry (1950), and Smithies (1957). In this section the existence of nonnegative solutions for the piece-wise linear model of Leontief will be investigated.

The possibility that the ordinary dynamic input-output system may generate negative output levels has led to many attempts to augment the ordinary system with certain additional relationships. In particular, Dorfman, Samuelson, and Solow (1958, pp. 335–345) have interpreted the system as a model of optimal capital accumulation. An alternative proposal, made by Leontief (1953, pp. 68–76), is to imbed the ordinary system in an augmented system in which capital accumulation is irreversible. As Leontief points out, the augmented system may be inconsistent. The problem of consistency has been discussed by Uzawa (1956) and McManus (1957). It will be shown that for the augmented system there always exist economically meaningful initial conditions for which inconsistency will occur and that Leontief's proposal cannot surmount the difficulties associated with solutions have negative components for nonnegative initial conditions.

To begin the discussion, we follow Uzawa's lucid interpretation of the augmented dynamic input-output model. If all stocks are irreversible the model is given by the following system of differential equations

$$(I - A)x = B^0 \max(\dot{x}, 0),$$ (3A.6.1)

where $B^0 \geq 0$ is a matrix with elements $b_{i,j}^0$ such that

$$b_{ij}^0 = \begin{cases} b_{ij} & \text{if } s_{ij} = b_{ij} \, x_j \\ 0 & \text{otherwise}. \end{cases} \tag{3A.6.2}$$

b_{ij} is an element of B, a stock-flow matrix; x_j is an element of the vector x of output levels; s_{ij} is the stock of the ith commodity held by the jth industry; and max $(\dot{x}, 0)$ is a vector with elements, max $(\dot{x}_j, 0)$. If the initial output and stock levels are denoted $x(0)$, $S(0)$, output must be less than capacity:

$$B[\text{diag } x(0)] \leqq S(0), \tag{3A.6.3}$$

where diag $x(0)$ is a diagonal matrix with elements $x_j(0)$; furthermore, the usual nonnegativity conditions must be satisfied,

$$x(0) \geq 0, \qquad S(0) \geq 0. \tag{3A.6.4}$$

$S(0) \geq 0$ is implied by (3A.6.3) and the condition that $x(0) \geq 0$ if at least one of the commodities corresponding to strictly positive elements of $x(0)$ cannot be produced without stocks. Any set of initial conditions $x(0), S(0)$ satisfying (3A.6.3) and (3A.6.4) will be said to be *economically meaningful*.

A second set of relations, not given by Uzawa, completes the augmented dynamic input-output system

$$\dot{S} = B^0(\text{diag}[\max(\dot{x}, 0)]). \tag{3A.6.5}$$

If all stocks are irreversible, stock levels are constant unless $s_{ij} = b_{ij} x_j$, and $\dot{x}_j > 0$.

For this model, we have the following result: For any augmented dynamic input-output system, if at least one off-diagonal element of A is not zero, there exist economically meaningful initial conditions $x(0)$, $S(0)$, for any B^0 such that there is no solution to the augmented dynamic input-output system.[11]

Proof: Suppose $a_{ij} > 0$, $i \neq j$; then by lemma 3.1, there is a vector $x * (0) \geq 0$ so that $(I - A)x * (0)$ has at least one negative element. For fixed B^0, choose $S * (0)$ so that $s *_{ij} (0) = b_{ij}^0 x *_j (0)$ if $b_{ij}^0 = b_{ij}$, and $s *_{ij} (0) > b_{ij}^0 x *_j (0)$ otherwise. Clearly, $x * (0)$ and $S * (0)$ comprise an economically meaningful set of initial conditions.

Since $B^0 \geq 0$ and $\max(\dot{x}, 0) \geqq 0$, $B^0 \max(\dot{x}, 0) \geqq 0$. Hence, for initial conditions $x * (0)$, $S * (0)$ the equality in (3A.6.1) cannot hold.

The interpretation of this theorem is that for any of the possible "phases" of Leontief's dynamic input-output system there are economically meaningful initial conditions, nonnegative, for which no solution to the system exists. In Uzawa's formulation of the dynamic input-output system, it is assumed that all stocks are irreversible. For the general augmented dynamic input-output system, the relation (3A.6.2) holds only for irreversible stocks. However, the usual causes to which the irreversibility of capital accumulation is attributed— technical irreducibility as in the case of land or buildings or nontransferability as in the case of equipment and inventories—would imply that if a stock is irreversible in one sector, it must be irreversible in all others. It is easily observed that the proof just given goes through provided that there is just one commodity which is irreversible as a stock in every industry if the commodity is used as an input on current account in any industry except the industry which produces it. In such a case, there are economically meaningful initial conditions for which no solution to the system exists.

3B   Some Further Examples

3B.1. In my recent paper, three classes of macroeconomic models are distinguished models which *never* satisfy the criterion that all variables are nonnegative for all nonnegative initial conditions, models which *may* satisfy this criterion for some numerical values of the structural parameters, and models which *always* satisfy this criterion.[12] This is apparently a subtle point, for it is easily missed.[13]

I demonstrated that the only model ready at hand which falls in the latter class is the ordinary matrix multiplier, analyzed by several writers.[14] But many models fall in the second of the three classes; so it is easy to provide other examples of models which satisfy the criterion.[15] A numerical example illustrating this point is given in section 3B.3 below.

3B.2. There are many ways to supplement the matrix multiplier by adding to it a theory of investment. In fact practically all theories of growth and the business cycle of the Keynesian variety, to which my paper was devoted, are generated in this way. Some of these models *may* satisfy the criterion given above and others definitely do not.[16] An example of the latter type is presented by M.C. Lovell in his accompanying note.

Lovell's model may be written

$$
\begin{bmatrix} I & 0 \\ A & I \end{bmatrix} \begin{bmatrix} x(t) \\ s(t) \end{bmatrix} = \begin{bmatrix} A & 0 \\ A & I \end{bmatrix} \begin{bmatrix} x(t-1) \\ s(t-1) \end{bmatrix} + \begin{bmatrix} y(t) \\ 0 \end{bmatrix}, \tag{3B.1}
$$

or

$$
\begin{bmatrix} x(t) \\ s(t) \end{bmatrix} = \begin{bmatrix} A & 0 \\ A(I-A) & I \end{bmatrix} \begin{bmatrix} x(t-1) \\ s(t-1) \end{bmatrix} + \begin{bmatrix} y(t) \\ -Ay(t) \end{bmatrix}. \tag{3B.2}
$$

To provide a correct analysis of this model, we appeal to theorem 3.2 of my paper, namely:

For a system of linear difference equations

$$
x(t) = Bx(t-1) + f(t), \tag{3B.3}
$$

where B is a constant matrix, $f(t) \geq 0$ for $t \geq 0$ is a vector-valued function of t, $x(0) \geq 0$ is a vector of initial conditions, a necessary and sufficient condition that $x(t) \geq 0$ for $t \geq 0$ is that $B \geq 0$ and B has at least one element strictly positive in each column.[17]

Lovell argues that ". . . the feasibility of initial conditions combined with the restriction that the final demand vector be nonnegative does not suffice to guarantee that the anomaly of negative stocks will not occur" (p. 2). But, of course, this argument is not a correct application of theorem 3.2. In fact, from the statement of theorem 3.2 given above it is obvious that the hypothesis of the theorem, $f(t) \geq 0$, is not satisfied by Lovell's model; the error in the statement quoted apparently arises from his regarding the vector of final demands, $y(t)$ given above, as playing the role of $f(t)$; but regarding the model in the form (3B.2), it is obvious that the vector $f(t)$ is given by

$$
f(t) = \begin{bmatrix} y(t) \\ -Ay(t) \end{bmatrix}, \tag{3B.4}
$$

which, in view of the condition that $A \geq 0$, does not satisfy the hypothesis of theorem 3.2. It should come as no surprise that the conclusion does not follow. Lovell's argument is irrelevant for application of the criterion of nonnegativity; this criterion is easily applied by correctly checking the hypothesis of theorem 3.2.

3B.3. In this section, a model which satisfies the correctly inter-preted nonnegativity condition of my paper is given. The example is a two-sector version of the ordinary dynamic input-output system

$$\dot{x} = B^{-1}(I - A)x + y, \tag{3B.5}$$

the solution of which is written

$$x(t) = e^{B^{-1}(I-A)t}x(0) + \int_0^t e^{B^{-1}(I-A)(t-s)}y(s)\, ds. \tag{3B.6}$$

To satisfy the hypothesis of theorem 3.1 of my paper any $y(s) \geqq 0$ will do. For (A, B), I chose

$$A = \begin{bmatrix} \dfrac{3}{5} & \dfrac{1}{10} \\ \dfrac{1}{10} & \dfrac{3}{5} \end{bmatrix}, \qquad B = \begin{bmatrix} \dfrac{1}{3} & \dfrac{2}{3} \\ \dfrac{2}{3} & \dfrac{1}{3} \end{bmatrix},$$

so that

$$B^{-1}(I - A) = \begin{bmatrix} -\dfrac{3}{5} & \dfrac{9}{10} \\ \dfrac{9}{10} & -\dfrac{3}{5} \end{bmatrix},$$

which satisfies the remaining hypothesis of theorem 3.1.

3B.4. Since not all the models considered in my paper fail to satisfy the nonnegativity criterion, there are no grounds for following Lovell into Webster's unabridged dictionary or elsewhere in search of a weaker condition.[18] Of course, the literature on multi-sector dynamic models continues to proliferate with further models which *never* sat-isfy the elementary consideration that national income and capital stock and sectoral income and stock levels must be nonnegative. In a further paper, I will continue the pruning operation begun in this note and my previous article by a consideration of some additional exam-ples, chosen mainly from recent publications.

For those who would prefer to await the harvest which will sup-posedly follow the spread of serious empirical work in economics, I can offer only an adage of physics: The hard thing in science is not to

invent new ideas; there are always plenty of those. The difficult thing
is to get rid of bad ideas quickly and expeditiously. In my paper I
attempted to improve the conceptual framework of multi-sector models by adding to the criterion of completeness introduced by Frisch[19]
the criterion of nonnegativity. Hopefully, these two principles will
prove to be as fruitful in economic dynamics as the corresponding
principles have proved to be in the static theory of general
equilibrium.[20]

Notes

1. That is, A is a Metzler matrix; off-diagonal elements are nonnegative. A recent
review of mathematical properties of Metzler and related matrices together with a summary of economic applications of such matrices is contained by McKenzie (1960).
Although the following discussion is confined to models of the Keynesian type, some
results are already available for models of the Walrasian type (Morishima, 1960;
Nikaido and Uzawa, 1960). In certain elementary cases, like the Leontief static system
discussed below in section 3A.2, the difference between Walrasian and Keynesian models is simply a matter of the economic interpretation.
For vectors (and matrices) the following notation will be useful. If x is a vector with ele-
ments x_i, $x > 0$ if $x_i > 0$ for all i; $x \geq 0$ if $x_i \geq 0$ for all i; $x = 0$ if $x_i = 0$ for all i; $x \geq 0$ if
$x \geq 0$ and $x \neq 0$.
2. This condition is equivalent to assumption (**) (i) of Kemeny, Morgenstern, and
Thompson (1956, p. 118). The system is also seen to satisfy assumption (**) (ii) since B,
the output matrix, is the identity matrix, I. I am indebted to Professor Morishima for
these observations.
3. A system is piece-wise linear if its solutions may be represented as a continuous
sequence of solutions to linear systems. Since the existence and uniqueness of solutions
to each "phase" are usually assured, problems of existence center on the transition from
one phase to another, that is, on the consistency of "switching" conditions (Leontief,
1953, pp. 72–76). For other examples of piece-wise linear systems, see Goodwin (1951,
1952, 1955). So far as existence and uniqueness of solutions to piece-wise linear system
is concerned, it may be possible to approximate such equations by nonlinear equations
which have continuously differentiable solutions and to apply standard techniques for
analysis of such nonlinear equations (Ichimura, 1954; Morishima, 1958). Here, however,
few results are available for equations of order greater than two. The fact that the theory of positive matrices play an important role in nonnegativity of solutions to linear
equations suggests that it may be possible to make some progress in the nonlinear case
through application of the theory of positive operators (Krein and Rutman, 1950; Karlin,
1959).
4. Lemma 3.3, with a proof suggested by Karlin, and application of the results to differential equations are given in a slightly different form by Bellman (1960, p. 172). Arrow
(1960, pp. 6 and 14) gives a different proof for the sufficiency part of theorem 3.1. The
matrix exponential function is discussed in detail by Bellman.
5. An input-output matrix is a matrix $A \geq 0$ with elements (a_{ij}) such that $\sum_j a_{ij} \leq 1$.
6. A matrix is irreducible if it is not reducible. For a reducible matrix there is a simultaneous permutation of rows and columns such that

$$A = \begin{bmatrix} A_{11} & A_{12} \\ 0 & A_{22} \end{bmatrix},$$

where A_{11}, A_{22} are square submatrices. A matrix is decomposable if there is a simultaneous permutation of rows and columns such that

$$A = \begin{bmatrix} A_{11} & 0 \\ 0 & A_{22} \end{bmatrix},$$

where A_{11}, A_{22} are square submatrices. Many different systems of terminology are used to describe reducible and decomposable matrices. For example, Solow (1952) and Debreu and Herstein (1953) use the terms decomposable and completely decomposable. The terminology employed here appears to be standard in the mathematical literature (Gantmacher, 1959).
7. The normal form of a reducible matrix A is

$$A = \begin{bmatrix} A_{11} & A_{12} & \cdots & A_{1m} \\ 0 & A_{22} & \cdots & A_{2m} \\ \cdots & \cdots & \cdots & \cdots \\ 0 & 0 & & A_{mm} \end{bmatrix},$$

where A_{11}, A_{22}, ..., A_{mm} are irreducible square submatrices along the main diagonal. Such a normal form is unique except for the order of submatrices along the main diagonal (Gantmacher, 1959, pp. 89–92).
8. A matrix is acyclic if it not cyclic. For a cyclic matrix, there is simultaneous permutation of rows and columns such that

$$A = \begin{bmatrix} 0 & A_1 & 0 & \ldots & 0 \\ 0 & 0 & A_2 & \ldots & 0 \\ \cdots & \cdots & \cdots & \cdots & \cdots \\ A_p & 0 & 0 & \ldots & 0 \end{bmatrix}.$$

The necessity of a condition involving acyclicity for the fact that a nonnegative irreducible matrix cannot have a nonnegative inverse was pointed out to me by Professor Morishima.
9. A final observation on the dynamic input-output system is that if the system for the determination of output levels (3A.4.3) has nonnegative solutions for all nonnegative initial conditions, the dual discussed by Morishima (1958) and Solow (1959) cannot have such solutions. The proof is as follows: If the output system has nonnegative solutions for any nonnegative initial conditions not zero, it is relatively stable. Then by the dual stability theorem (Jorgenson, 1960), the dual is relatively unstable and therefore has solutions which have negative components for nonnegative initial conditions, not zero. Of course, this dual stability theorem does not hold for the open system.
10. To facilitate comparison with the Duesenberry model, Smithies' variable Y_F, full employment income, is transformed to K, capital stock, using the reaction $Y_F = \sigma K$, where σ is Domar's coefficient (Allen, 1960, p. 47). In what follows, D_1 represents depreciation and D_2 extraordinary obsolescence (Smithies, 1957, p. 21). The parameters δ_1 and δ_2 are the corresponding rates of depreciation, where depreciation is calculated by the declining balance method.
11. The form of the result and method of proof are due to Professor Morishima.
12. Jorgenson (1961a, pp. 276–291).

13. See the accompanying note of M.C. Lovell (1963).

14. See Chipman (1951), Goodwin (1949, 1950) and Solow (1952).

15. A list containing only those mentioned explicitly in my paper is: The ordinary dynamic input-output system, Hicks' "basic equation," and Duesenberry's multi-sector model of growth and fluctuations, discussed in Chipman (1954), Dorfman, Samuelson and Solow (1958), Duesenberry (1958), Georgescu-Roegen (1951), Hawkins (1948), Hawkins and Simon (1949), Hicks (1950), Jorgenson (1960), Leontief (1953), Morishima (1958) and Uzawa (1956). (The remainder of the sentence quoted by Lovell at the beginning of his comment contains this list of models.)

16. Examples of some that do are given in footnote 15; examples of some that do not are: The Samuelson-Hicks and Smithies models of the trade cycle and the augmented dynamic input-output system.

17. This theorem is quoted from p. 277 of my paper, with changes of notation only.

18. This statement, sufficient proof of which is given by the example of section 3B.3, is at variance with the principal conclusion reached by Lovell. Lovell's conclusion is in error. For further examples, see the discussion in my paper of the models listed in footnote 15 above.

19. Frisch (1933, pp. 171–205).

20. A discussion of the development of the static theory of general equilibrium with emphasis on the role played by the criteria of existence, uniqueness, and nonnegativity is contained in T.C. Koopmans (1951a), esp. 1–4.

4

Testing Alternative Theories of the Development of a Dual Economy

Dale W. Jorgenson

4.1 Introduction

As a branch of general economic theory, that of development of a dual economy is of relatively recent origin. It is widely recognized that under contemporary conditions most backward economic systems have important relations with advanced economies, either through international trade or through the establishment of a modern "enclave" in an otherwise backward social and economic setting.[1] Either relationship gives rise to economic and social "dualism" in which a given economic or social system consists of two component parts—an advanced or modern sector and a backward or traditional sector. Neither theories of economic growth for an advanced economy nor theories of development for a backward economy are directly applicable to the development of a dual economy.

In a previous paper we have described two alternative approaches to the theory of development of a dual economy.[2] In order to facilitate comparison of the two approaches, we attempted to develop both within the same framework. The basic differences between the two are in assumptions made about the technology of the agricultural sector and about conditions governing the supply of labor. In the "classical" approach it is assumed that there is some level of the agricultural labor force beyond which further increments to this force are redundant. In the "neoclassical" approach the marginal productivity of labor in agriculture is assumed to be always positive so that labor is never redundant. In the "classical" approach the real wage rate, measured in agricultural goods, is assumed to be fixed "institutionally" so long as there is disguised unemployment in the agricultural sector. In the "neoclassical" the real wage rate is assumed to be variable rather than fixed; it is further assumed that at very low levels of income the rate of population growth depends on the level of income. These are the basic differences between the "neoclassical" and "classical" approaches to the theory of development of a dual economy.

The neoclassical and classical theories differ in characterization of the backward or traditional sector of the economy. These differences have implications for the behavior of the backward sector. Among the implications we may note that according to the classical approach, the agricultural labor force must decline absolutely before the end of the phase of disguised unemployment; in the neoclassical approach the agricultural labor force may rise, fall, or remain constant. The differences between the two approaches also have implications for the behavior of the advanced sector; unfortunately, these implications depend on the actual behavior of the terms of trade between the backward and advanced sectors. In the neoclassical approach the terms of trade may rise or fall; in the classical approach, they cannot be determined endogenously. Alternative assumptions about the course of the terms of trade may be made. Corresponding to each assumption, there is an alternative theory for the behavior of the advanced sector. Since any assumption about the course of the terms of trade is consistent with the classical approach, the behavior of these terms cannot provide a test of this approach. The classical approach may be tested only by deriving the implications of this approach for the advanced sector, given the observed behavior of the terms of trade, and confronting these implications with empirical evidence.

We have developed the classical theory in detail only on the assumption that the terms of trade between the backward and advanced sectors remain constant. Proceeding on this assumption, we have derived the following implications of the classical approach: (1) output and employment in the advanced sector grow at the same rate so long as there is disguised unemployment in the backward sector, that is, labor productivity in the advanced sector remains constant; (2) capital grows at a slower rate than output and labor so that capital-output ratio falls; (3) the rates of growth of manufacturing output, employment, and capital increase during the phase of disguised unemployment. For the neoclassical approach, the corresponding results are: (1) output and capital in the advanced sector grow at the same rate, asymptotically, so that the capital-output ratio remains constant; (2) manufacturing unemployment grows more slowly than either output or capital so that labor productivity in the advanced sector rises; (3) the rates of growth of manufacturing output and employment decrease throughout the development process. Since the classical approach reduces to the neoclassical approach after the phase of disguised unemployment is completed, the two approaches have different implications only for situations where it is alleged that disguised unemployment exists.

In view of the similarities between classical and neoclassical approaches to the development of a dual economy, it is not surprising that many implications of one model are also implications of the other. For example, both models imply that if the proportion of manufacturing output to agricultural output increases, the share of saving in total income also increases. Thus, either model suffices to explain an increase in the fraction of income saved in the course of economic development. The fact that the implications of the two approaches for the share of saving are identical is of considerable significance. According to Lewis: "The central problem in the theory of economic development is to understand the process by which a community which was previously saving and investing [four or five percent] of its national income or less, converts itself into an economy where voluntary savings is running at about [twelve to fifteen percent] of national income or more. This is the central problem because the central fact of economic development is rapid capital accumulation (including knowledge and skills with capital)."[3] Both classical and neoclassical theories of the development of a dual economy provide an explanation of an increase in the share of saving. In each case the explanation is based on the relationship between saving and industrial profits. Disguised unemployment is neither necessary nor sufficient to generate a sustained rise in the share of saving. Ultimately, a sustained increase in the saving share depends on a positive and growing agricultural surplus and not on the presence or absence of disguised unemployment.

We conclude that tests of the classical versus the neoclassical approach to the development of a dual economy can be carried out only for situations in which it is alleged that disguised unemployment exists. For all other situations the implications of the two approaches are identical. Even where disguised unemployment is alleged to exist, some implications of the two approaches are identical. The implications that are different may be classified into two groups: (1) direct implications of the basic assumptions about agricultural technology and the conditions governing the supply of labor; (2) indirect implications about the behavior of both backward and advanced sectors of the economy. In reviewing the evidence pertaining to the development of a dual economy, we will first discuss the evidence for and against the existence of disguised unemployment and historical evidence for and against the constancy of the real wage rate in certain historical circumstances where disguised unemployment allegedly exists. Secondly, we will discuss the evidence for and against the indirect implications of the two alternative approaches. Since the indirect implications refer mainly to historical trends in economic development, we will concentrate on the historical development of the Japanese economy, which is cited in support of the classical approach by Fei and Ranis (1962) and by Johnston (1964).[4]

4.2   Evidence: Direct Implications

In Lewis's original presentation of the classical approach the scope of validity of the assumption of disguised unemployment is delimited as follows: "It is obviously not true of the United Kingdom, or of North West Europe. It is not true either of some of the countries usually now lumped together as underdeveloped; for example, there is an acute shortage of male labor in some parts of Africa and of Latin America. On the other hand it is obviously the relevant assumption for the economies of Egypt, of India, or of Jamaica."[5] In *The Theory of Economic Growth*, Lewis (1955) characterizes the phenomenon of disguised unemployment as follows: "This phenomenon is rare in Africa and in Latin America, but it repeats itself in China, in Indonesia, in Egypt and in many countries of Eastern Europe."[6] In a later presentation he states: "More than half of the world's population (mainly in Asia and in Eastern Europe) lives in conditions which correspond to the classical and not to the neoclassical assumptions."[7] Fei and Ranis are not so specific in delimiting the scope of application of their version of the Lewis model. However, they state: "The empirical support of both our theory and policy conclusions draw heavily on the experience of nineteenth century Japan and contemporary India."[8]

Lewis's allegations that disguised unemployment exists in Asia and Eastern Europe are based on a substantial literature on the problem dating from the 1930s and early 1940s. This literature has been surveyed by Kao, Anschel, and Eicher.[9] Estimates of disguised unemployment in the early literature are based on what Kao, Anschel, and Eicher call the "indirect method" of measurement. Labor requirements for production of the current level of agricultural output and labor available from the agrarian population are estimated; the difference between labor available and labor required is called "disguised unemployment." One fallacy underlying this method is that agricultural work in all countries is highly seasonal. Substantial parts of the agricultural labor force may be unemployed in agriculture during a part of the year without being redundant. The critical test is whether the agricultural labor force is fully employed during peak periods of demand for labor such as planting and harvesting. Only if labor is redundant during periods of peak demand could the agricultural labor force be reduced without reducing agricultural output. A second fallacy underlying the indirect method is that all members of the agricultural population older than some minimum age, usually fifteen, are treated as members of the labor force, and that younger members of the population are not treated as members of the labor force. All of the studies of the 1930s and early 1940s are based on the indirect method of measurement. Examples are provided by the work of Buck (1930) on China and of Warriner (1939), Rosenstein-Rodan (1943), and Mandelbaum (1945) on southeastern Europe.[10] More recent examples may be found in the work of Warriner (1948) on Egypt, Mellor and Stevens (1956) on Thailand, and Rosenstein-Rodan (1957) on southern Italy.[11]

Warriner (1955) has subsequently withdrawn from her position on disguised unemployment in Egypt,[12] noting that her earlier estimate was based on a fallacious set of assumptions. Kenadjian (1961) has corrected Rosenstein-Rodan's estimate of disguised unemployment for southern Italy to take into account seasonal demands for labor. By this single adjustment the estimate of disguised unemployment is reduced from 10 to 12 percent of the agricultural labor force to less than 5 percent.[13] Pepelasis and Yotopoulos have attempted to measure disguised unemployment in Greece from 1953 to 1960, taking into account the seasonal pattern of demand for labor. Their conclusion is the following: "From the eight years of our series, [disguised unemployment] existed only in 1953 and 1954 to a degree of 3.4 and 2.3 [percent] respectively. The other years of the period are marked by a seasonal shortage of labor."[14] A corrected version of Buck's estimate of disguised unemployment has been presented by Hsieh: "The conclusion that in the majority of the localities . . . there was at the seasonal peak a shortage of male labor, which had to be reinforced by a large number of female workers, probably applies not only to many other areas of China but also to other Asian countries. Field investigations of several other localities in China and the rural districts of Bengal in

India reveal a similar situation. Considering the extremely intensive input of labor in their farm operations, this is not unexpected.[15] We conclude that estimates of disguised unemployment based on the so-called indirect method of measurement always overestimate the amount of disguised unemployment. When these estimates are corrected to take into account the seasonality of demands for agricultural labor, the situation in southeastern Europe, Egypt, China, and Southeast Asia appears to be one of labor shortage rather than labor surplus.

Almost all of the evidence for the existence of disguised unemployment is based on the indirect method of measurement. However, attempts have been made to test for the existence of disguised unemployment by examining historical instances in which substantial parts of the agricultural labor force have been withdrawn in a short period of time. This type of test is always subject to the criticism that one cannot generalize from isolated historical examples. Nonetheless, the evidence is worth reviewing. One class of examples consists of studies of agricultural production after labor is withdrawn for a public works project. Two such examples are summarized by Schultz (1956): "In Peru a modest road was recently built down the east slopes of the Andes to Tingo Maria, using some labor from farms along the way mostly within walking distances; agricultural production in the area dropped promptly because of the withdrawal of this labor from agriculture. In Belo Horizonte, Brazil, an upsurge in construction in the city drew workers to it from the nearby countryside, and this curtailed agricultural production.[16]

Another class of examples consists of studies of the effects of famines and epidemics. Schultz has studied in detail the effects of the influenza epidemic of 1918–1919 in India on agricultural production. He summarizes the results:

The agricultural labor force in India may have been reduced by about 8 percent as a consequence of the 1918–19 epidemic. The area sown to crops was reduced sharply the year of the influenza, falling from 265 million in 1916–17 to 228 million in 1918–19. This drop, however, is confounded by some adverse weather and by the many millions of people who became ill and who were therefore incapacitated for a part of the crop year. For reasons already presented, 1919–20 is the appropriate year to use in this analysis. The area sown in 1919–20 was, however, 10 million acres below, or 3.8 percent less than that of the base year 1916–17. In general, the provinces of India with the highest death rates attributed to the epidemic also had the largest percentage decline in acreage sown to crops. It would be hard to find any support in these data for the doctrine that a part of the labor force in agriculture in India at the time of the epidemic has a marginal productivity of zero.[17]

A third type of evidence used to test for the existence of disguised unemployment consists of anthropological studies of peasant agriculture. Eighteen studies by anthropologists and economists are cited by Oshima in support of the following position:

Despite the limitations of the empirical material, there is no denying the general picture that emerges for Asia. The labor requirement during busy seasons exceeds the male, adult population so that female and juvenile labor must be recruited into the labor force. And, from the description found in the books cited, no part of this larger labor requirement seems redundant, given the existing technology and organization. A withdrawal of portions of the labor force may be expected to reduce total output (in the sense that insufficient plowing, inadequate planting, and untimely harvesting will diminish the size of the final crop).[18]

The studies reviewed by Oshima refer to India, China, and Southeast Asia. Schultz gives a detailed summary of two exceptionally complete anthropological studies, that of Panajachel, Guatemala, by Sol Tax and that of Senapur, India, by W. David Hopper. Schultz concludes "that no part of the labor force working in agriculture in these communities has a marginal productivity of zero."[19]

Evidence from anthropological studies is subject to the same criticism as the examination of historical instances of rapid withdrawal of agricultural labor, namely, that one cannot generalize from particular examples. However, the consistency of the evidence from indirect estimates of disguised unemployment for the entire agricultural labor force of countries such as Greece, southern Italy, Egypt, and China, with the evidence from both historical and anthropological studies, leads to the conclusion that disguised unemployment simply does not exist for a wide range of historical and geographical situations where it has been alleged to exist. Lewis admits that disguised unemployment is not typical of Africa and Latin America. This is consistent with the historical and anthropological evidence for Brazil, Mexico, and Peru cited by Schultz. Lewis claims that disguised unemployment exists in southeastern Europe, Egypt, and Asia. But this is inconsistent with the evidence from indirect measurement in the case of southeastern Europe, Egypt, and China and with both historical and anthropological evidence in the case of India, China, and Southeast Asia. We may conclude, with Kao, Anschel, and Eicher that it is an understatement to say that the development literature in [the early 1950s] was optimistic about development through the transfer of redundant agricultural labor to other occupations. We have shown that the empirical studies supporting this optimism were often poorly conceived. In addition, we have noted that by considering temporary rather than permanent labor transfers and by allowing some reorganization of production, various writers have arrived at a high percentage of disguised unemployment. To date, there is little reliable empirical evidence to support the existence of more than token—5 percent—disguised unemployment in underdeveloped countries....[20]

4.3   Evidence: Indirect Implications

We have reviewed the evidence for and against the existence of disguised unemployment. The indirect evidence suggests that the conditions governing the supply of labor in southeastern Europe and Asia are no different from those in Latin America and Africa to which Lewis refers. This evidence does not demonstrate that disguised unemployment never exists in any historical or geographical circumstances, but only that the scope of applicability of the classical approach to the development of a dual economy is severely limited. More specifically, the classical assumptions do not apply to Latin America, Africa, southeastern Europe, India, China, or the remainder of Southeast Asia. Thus far we have reviewed direct evidence for most of Asia except for Japan, for which it is possible to check out the indirect implications of the classical and neoclassical approaches for historical trends in economic development. Japan is the only Asian country for which long-term data exists for trends in agricultural and nonagricultural labor force, agricultural and nonagricultural output, and capital formation. Furthermore, Japanese historical development has been cited in support of the classical approach by Fei and Ranis and by Johnston.[21] Fei and Ranis state that: "Continuous capital shallowing in Japanese industry between 1888 and the end of World War I is evidence that Japan made maximum use of her abundant factor, surplus agricultural labor."[22] They continue: "The empirical evidence on Japan ... indicates clearly that ... a change of regime from capital shallowing to capital deepening occurred at about the end of World War I. Moreover, we have convincing evidence that Japan's unlimited supply of labor condition came to an end at just about that time.... The virtual constancy before and rapid rise of the real wage after approximately 1918 is rather startling. We thus have rather conclusive evidence in corroboration of our theoretical framework."[23] Since the

Japanese data are the only empirical support Fei and Ranis offer for their assumption of an unlimited labor supply at a constant real wage, Japanese economic development up to 1918 provides an important test case for the classical approach to the theory of development of a dual economy.

We first consider the indirect implications of the classical approach for the agricultural sector. For this sector Fei and Ranis assume that there is an institutionally fixed real wage, equal to the initial average productivity of labor.[24] Ohkawa and Rosovsky provide data from which real labor income per capita in agriculture for the period 1878–1917 may be estimated. The share of rents in agricultural income fluctuates during this period, beginning at an average level of 59 percent in 1878–1887 and ending at an average level of 58 percent in 1908–1917.[25] Labor income may be estimated by deducting the share of rents from real income per capita. This results in the series for labor income presented in table 4.1. Total real income per capita is 100.0 in 1913–1917.[26] We conclude that for the period 1878–1917, the assumption of a constant real wage rate in the agricultural sector is inconsistent with the evidence. The hypothesis of a constant real wage rate in the agricultural sector where disguised unemployment exists is the most important assumption underlying the classical approach to the theory of development of a dual economy. The classical approach stands or falls on this hypothesis.

A second implication of the classical approach for the behavior of the agricultural sector is that the agricultural labor force must decline absolutely as redundant labor leaves the land and later as disguised

Table 4.1
Real labor income per capita in Japanese
agriculture, five-year averages, 1878–1917

1878–1882	18.0
1883–1887	18.1
1888–1892	18.2
1893–1897	21.1
1898–1902	27.0
1903–1907	31.3
1908–1912	39.4
1913–1917	42.0

Source: Computed from K. Ohkawa and
H. Rosovsky (1964), pp. 129–143.

unemployment is eliminated. This decline must include all of the redundant labor force together with that part of the labor force with marginal productivity less than the real wage rate. The typical pattern of economic development in Europe is a constant or moderately rising agricultural labor force until just before or after the relative importance of nonagricultural population surpasses that of agricultural population. Subsequently, the agricultural labor force begins to fall.[27] In short, absolute reductions in the size of the agricultural labor force occur after industrialization is well under way rather than during its early stages. This pattern also characterizes Japan. The agricultural labor force is essentially constant from 1878–1882 to 1903–1907, falling slightly from an average level of 15,573,000 to 15,184,000 over this period of twenty-five years. From 1903–1907 to 1913–1917 the agricultural labor force falls from an average level of 15,184 thousand to an average of 14,613 thousand. The total decline over the thirty-five-year period is 7 percent.[28] Since Fei and Ranis date the end of the surplus labor period at 1918, we may conclude that 7 percent can serve as an upper bound for the percentage of the labor force that could be classified as redundant at any time during the period 1878–1917. A second useful comparison may be made between the number of farm households in 1884, a total of 5,437 thousand, and the number in 1920, 5,573 thousand, a slight increase.[29] The movement of labor from the rural areas to the advanced sector did not involve the transfer of a reserve army of the disguised unemployed. The process is described by Ohkawa and Rosovsky: "During the early period of industrialization necessary increases in the labor force did indeed come from the rural areas. But laborers were usually young and left single. There was only very little movement in terms of family units, and no formation of an agricultural proletariat. Thus, a fairly typical Asian type of agriculture remained in existence and was utilized to promote impressive increases in productivity, while Western technology was making rapid progress in manufacturing."[30] The Japanese pattern may be regarded as similar to that of many European countries, including countries of northwestern Europe, where the period preceding the predominance of the nonagricultural labor force in the total labor force is characterized by a stable agricultural labor force, rising or declining at very moderate rates throughout the period of initial industrialization. This pattern is inconsistent with the hypothesis of redundant labor or of disguised unemployment. However, the pattern is entirely consistent with the neoclassical theory of the development of a dual economy.

We may conclude with Ohkawa and Minami that "in the light of Japanese experience with the initial phase of economic development, traditional agriculture based on household production grew at a considerable rate in terms of both output and productivity; technological progress had taken place and the level of living and wage rates increased to a certain extent. These responses occurred together with the increase in population. In view of this, it seems that the features of models of the Lewis type are too rigorous to be applied to such historical realities."[31]

We have discussed the empirical validity of the implications of the classical approach to the theory of development of a dual economy for the agricultural sector. These implications—the constancy of the real wage rate, measured in agricultural goods, and the absolute decline of the agricultural labor force during the phase of disguised unemployment—are directly contradicted by the evidence we have reviewed. In particular, the interpretation of Japanese economic development prior to 1917 by Fei and Ranis is inconsistent with the evidence on real labor income in agriculture. The pattern of development of the agricultural labor force up to 1917 is inconsistent with the existence of substantial surplus labor in the agricultural sector during the initial period of industrialization. The development of the agricultural labor force follows the pattern of most European countries and is fully consistent with the neoclassical approach to the development of a dual economy. At this point we turn to the development of the advanced or nonagricultural sector of the Japanese economy during the period preceding 1917. As we have already pointed out, the implications of the classical approach for the advanced sector depend on the historical development of the terms of trade between agriculture and industry. Data on the terms of trade are presented by Ohkawa and Rosovsky.[32] These data are consistent with the assumption that the terms of trade are essentially constant throughout the period before 1917. Accordingly, the implications of the classical approach on this assumption may be confronted with data on the development of the nonagricultural sector of the Japanese economy for this period.

The first implication of the classical approach for the advanced sector is that labor productivity remains constant during the phase of disguised unemployment. The corresponding implication of the neoclassical approach is that labor productivity is always rising. Real income per member of the labor force in secondary and tertiary industry for the period 1878–1971 are given by Ohkawa[33] (see table 4.2).

Table 4.2
Real income per capita in Japanese industry,
five-year averages, 1878–1917

	Secondary industry	Tertiary industry
1878–1882	137	156
1883–1887	173	199
1888–1892	189	197
1893–1897	217	227
1898–1902	268	261
1903–1907	237	261
1908–1912	266	313
1913–1917	327	333

Source: K. Ohkawa (1957), p. 34.

The data show an increase in labor productivity from 1878–1882 to 1913–1917 of 239 percent in secondary industry and 213 percent in tertiary industry. These increases in productivity are inconsistent with the implication of the classical theory that labor productivity remains constant throughout the phase of disguised unemployment. Increases in labor productivity are a direct implication on the neoclassical approach. We conclude that the data on labor productivity provide very powerful support for the neoclassical theory.

A second implication of the classical approach for the advanced sector is that the rates of growth of output and employment increase over time. The corresponding implication of the neoclassical approach is that rates of growth of both variables decline over time. Rates of growth of real income and occupied population in secondary and tertiary industry for the period 1878–1917 are presented in table 4.3. The rate of growth of real income has a substantial downward trend for this period, which is inconsistent with the implications of the classical approach. The rate of growth of the nonagricultural labor force shows a high initial value but declines monotonically as development proceeds. This trend is also inconsistent with the implications of the classical approach. We conclude that data on the rates of growth of output and employment provide additional support for the neoclassical theory. It should be pointed out that for the period subsequent to 1918, the date at which disguised unemployment disappears, according to Fei and Ranis, there is an increase in the rates of growth in the secondary and tertiary sectors. This is evidence neither for nor against the classical as opposed to the neoclassical approach, since the

Table 4.3
Rates of growth of output, employment and capital in Japanese industry, five-year averages, 1878–1917

	Output	Employment	Capital
1878–1882 to 1883–1887	10.1	5.4	—
to 1888–1892	4.4	4.4	4.7
to 1893–1897	6.3	3.8	5.2
to 1898–1902	6.7	3.4	5.7
to 1903–1907	1.9	3.0	4.6
to 1908–1912	5.8	2.6	6.5
to 1913–1917	5.2	2.4	5.8

Source: Rates of growth of output and employment computed from Ohkawa (1957), pp. 20, 34; rate of growth of capital computed from S. Ishiwata (1957), p. 12.

implications of these approaches are identical for periods in which there is no disguised unemployment.

A third implication of the classical approach for the advanced sector is that the capital-output ratio falls throughout the phase of disguised unemployment and that the rate of growth of capital increases over time. The corresponding implications of the neoclassical approach are based on asymptotic results; the capital-output ratio eventually becomes constant since the rate of growth of output and the rate of growth of capital tend to the same limit. Data on net capital stock for the period 1883–1917 are given by Ishiwata.[34] Rates of growth computed from these data are presented in table 4.3. There is essentially no trend in the rate of growth of capital during this period. We conclude that data on the rate of growth of capital stock are inconsistent with the implications of the classical approach. The capital-output ratio for the advanced sector may be computed from the data on capital given by Ishiwata and the data on real income given by Ohkawa. The resulting capital-output rates are presented in table 4.4, along with the capital-output ratio for the advanced sector computed

Table 4.4
Capital-output ratio in Japanese industry,
five-year averages, 1883–1917

	Ohkawa real income	Ishiwata real income
1883–1887	1.96	1.56
1888–1892	1.99	1.51
1893–1897	1.88	1.53
1898–1902	1.80	1.52
1903–1907	2.03	1.72
1908–1912	2.10	1.82
1913–1917	2.24	1.79

Source: Computed from K. Ohkawa
(1957), p. 34, and S. Ishiwata (1957), p. 15.

by Ishiwata from an alternative set of data on real income.[35] For the period as a whole, both series of capital-output ratios show a substantial increasing trend. For Ishiwata's series of capital-output ratios the trend is especially strong. We conclude that the implication of the classical approach of "capital-shallowing" throughout the period prior to 1917 is inconsistent with the evidence. The data on capital-output ratios provide additional support for the neoclassical theory.

4.4   Summary and Conclusion

We have considered implications of the classical and neoclassical approaches to the development of a dual economy for both agricultural and nonagricultural sectors. The assumption of a constant real wage rate in the agricultural sector made in the classical approach is inconsistent with the evidence presented by Ohkawa and Rosovsky. Real labor income per capita in agriculture more than doubles during the period 1878–1917. The implication of the classical approach that the agricultural labor force must decline absolutely as redundant labor leaves the land is also inconsistent with the evidence. Data on the occupied population in agriculture show a decline from 1878–1917 of only 7 percent; data on the number of farm households show a 2.5 percent increase. The Japanese pattern is similar to that of many European countries where the agricultural labor force is essentially stable throughout the period of initial industrialization.

Implications of the classical approach for the nonagricultural sector are also inconsistent with the evidence. First, the implication that labor productivity remains constant is inconsistent with the data presented by Ohkawa; these data show an increase in labor productivity over the period 1878–1917 of 239 percent in secondary industry and 213 percent in tertiary industry. Secondly, the implication that rates of growth of output and employment increase over time is inconsistent with evidence on the growth of real income and employment in the nonagricultural sector presented by Ohkawa. Finally, the implications that the rate of growth of capital increases over time and that the capital-output ratio falls is inconsistent with the data of Ishiwata on capital stock for the period 1883–1917. The rate of growth of capital stock shows no trend over this period; the capital-output ratio actually rises substantially over the period 1883–1917.

The evidence on Japanese economic development from 1878–1917 supports the neoclassical rather than the classical approach to the theory of development of a dual economy. The basic assumptions of the classical approach are inconsistent with the evidence. The implications of the classical approach are also inconsistent with the evidence while the implications of the neoclassical approach are also strongly supported. Our knowledge of Japanese economic development corroborates the evidence we have reviewed for and against the existence of disguised unemployment in Latin America, Africa, southeastern Europe, India, China, and Southeast Asia. We conclude that the neoclassical theory of the development of a dual economy is strongly supported by the empirical evidence and that the classical approach must be rejected.

Notes

1. This point of view is elaborated in Jorgenson (1961b), especially, pp. 309–311. The same point of view is expressed by Luigi Spaventa (1959), especially, pp. 386–390. An excellent review of the literature on economic dualism through 1960 is given by Howard S. Ellis (1961), pp. 3–17.
2. Dale Jorgenson (1965).
3. W.A. Lewis (1954), p. 155.
4. J.C.H. Fei and G. Ranis (1964), pp. 263–264; B.F. Johnston (1962), pp. 223–275.
5. Lewis (1954), p. 140.
6. W.A. Lewis (1955), p. 327.
7. W.A. Lewis (1958), p. 1.
8. Fei and Ranis (1964), p. 6.
9. C.H.C. Kao, K.R. Anschel, and C.K. Eicher (1964), pp. 129–143.

10. J.L. Buck (1930); P.N. Rosenstein-Rodan (1943), pp. 202–211; K. Mandelbaum (1945); D. Warriner (1939).

11. D. Arriner (1948); J.W. Mellor and R.D. Stevens (1956), pp. 780–791; P.N. Rosenstein-Rodan (1957), pp. 1– 7. P. 12. D. Warriner (1955), p. 26 P. 13. B. Kenadjian (1961), pp. 216--223.

14. Quoted in Kao, Anschel, and Eicher (1964), p. 140.

15. H. Oshima (1958), p. 259–263; Oshima cites C. Hsieh (1952), "The Nature and Extent of Underemployment in Asia," *International Labor Review*, LV (1952), 703–725; the passage quoted is from pp. 716–717.

16. Theodore Schultz (1956), p. 375; see also Schultz (1964), p. 62.

17. Schultz (1964), p. 66–67. Amartya K. Sen has pointed out to me that the estimates of changes in working-age population used by Schultz are too high, since only deaths between 1917–1918 and 1918–1919 are recorded as changes in the labor force. The natural increase of the population from 1916–1917 and 1919–1920, the base dates for the measurement of acreage sown, are ignored. Taking 8.35 percent per decade as the rate of natural increase, Schultz's estimates of changes in the agriculture labor force should be reduced by 2.4 percent. Making these changes, Sen obtains an estimate of the labor coefficient of 0. 412 ± 0. 252. Sen's estimate is closer to the *a priori* value of 0.4 given by Schultz than Schultz's own estimate of 0. 349 ± 0. 152. Both results support the conclusion cited in the text.

18. Oshima (1958), p. 261.

19. Schultz (1964), p. 52.

20. Kao, Anschel, and Eicher (1964), p. 141.

21. Fei and Ranis (1961), pp. 134, 263–64; B.F. Johnston (1962), pp. 223–275.

22. *Ibid.*, p. 132.

23. *Ibid.*, pp. 263–264.

24. *Ibid.*, p. 22.

25. K. Ohkawa and H. Rosovsky (1964), p. 52.

26. *Ibid.*, p. 55.

27. F. Dovring (1959), p. 1–11. For a study of the development of agricultural population during the English industrial revolution revealing a similar pattern, see J.D. Chambers (1953), pp. 319–343. I am indebted to Henry Rosovsky for this reference.

28. Ohkawa and Rosovsky (1964), p. 46.

29. *Ibid.*, p. 49.

30. *Ibid.*, p. 48.

31. K. Ohkawa and R. Minami (1964), pp. 1–15; the quotation given here may be found on p. 8.

32. Ohkawa and Rosovsky (1964), p. 48, table 4.

33. K. Ohkawa (1957), p. 34.

34. S. Ishiwata, "Estimation of Capital Stocks in Prewar Japan (1868–1940)" (Unpublished Paper D27, Institute of Economic Research, Hitotsubashi University, Tokyo, in Japanese), p. 12.

35. *Ibid.*, p. 15.

5   Surplus Agricultural Labor and the Development of a Dual Economy

Dale W. Jorgenson

5.1   Introduction

The point of departure for this chapter is the well-established empirical association between the degree of industrialization and the level of economic development. This association characterizes both time series data for individual countries and international cross sections at a given point of time. High income per head is associated with a relatively large proportion of the total population engaged in industry. Low income per head is associated with a predominance of employment in the agricultural sector. The process of economic development may be studied as an increase in income per head or as an increase in the role of industrial activity relative to that in agriculture. Quantitatively speaking, gross domestic product *per capita* for the world excluding centrally planned economies increased from $334 to $534 in U.S. dollars of 1958 between 1938 and 1961. In the same period value added in industrial activity increased from $117 to $223. Similarly, in 1961 gross domestic product *per capita* for industrialized countries was $1,486 U.S. dollars of 1958; the corresponding figure for less industrialized countries was $132 *per capita*. Value added in industry *per capita* was $666 for industrialized countries and $36 for less industrialized countries.[1] For both time series and cross sections high levels of output are associated with a high degree of industrialization.

The great disparity in degree of industrialization in developed and less developed countries is mirrored by a bifurcation in theories of economic growth. In models of a developed economy the analysis is concentrated on the allocation of national product between consumption and investment. Technology may be characterized by fixed factor proportions, as in Harrod's model of economic growth, or by variable factor proportions, as in Tinbergen's model.[2] Technological change may be embodied or disembodied, neutral or biased. Similarly, the model may be closed by assuming that investment is a constant fraction of national output or that investment depends on the distribution of income as in Kaldor's theory of economic growth.[3] For present purposes the similarities of theories of growth for an advanced economic system are more important than the differences. The industrial composition of output, that is, the proportion of output generated by industry, by agriculture, and by the remaining sectors of the economy, is entirely ignored. The central feature of the process of increasing income *per capita*, namely, an increase in the role of industry relative to that of agriculture, is left entirely out of account.

By contrast, in models of a less developed economy the analysis is concentrated on the relationship between the growth of income and the growth of population. One branch of the modern literature on theories of development originated with the paper "Economic Development with Unlimited Supplies of Labor," by W.A. Lewis.[4] Lewis postulates that the fundamental characteristic of certain less developed economies is the existence of disguised unemployment. Lewis's analysis of the role of the unemployed in the determination of wages during economic development is strictly analogous to that of Marx. Wages are tied to a subsistence level so that agricultural output *per capita* remains constant so long as disguised unemployment persists. A second branch of the modern theory of development originates with Harvey Leibenstein's book of 1954.[5] The central result of Leibenstein's theory is the existence of a low-level equilibrium trap, a kind of Malthusian equilibrium of population and sustenance. The Malthusian equilibrium level of income is stable for small changes in income; to achieve sustained economic growth something like a massive infusion of capital is required. As in theories of economic growth, the industrial composition of output is entirely ignored in theories of economic development.

It is widely recognized that under contemporary conditions many less developed countries have important relations with developed countries either through international trade or through the establishment of a modern "enclave" in an otherwise purely traditional social and economic setting.[6] Either relationship gives rise to economic and social "dualism" in which a given economic or social system consists of two component parts—an advanced or modern sector and a less advanced or traditional sector. To capture the essence of dualistic development it is necessary to focus on the association between the degree of industrialization and the level of economic development. A theory of development of a dual economy requires a theory of the industrial composition of output and its relationship to the level of economic development. The process of economic development must be studied as an increase in the role of industrial activity relative to that in agriculture. In the development of a dual economy these two developments are intimately related.

The purpose of this chapter is to present a theory of development of a dual economy, focusing on the relationship between the degree of industrialization and the level of economic development. The theory of development of a dual economy has been approached within both classical and neoclassical frameworks. The chief difference between these two approaches to the development of a dual economy is in conditions governing the supply of labor to the industrial sector. In the classical approach to the theory, the real-wage rate is assumed to be fixed in terms of agricultural goods; from the point of view of industry labor is available in unlimited amounts at a fixed real wage. In the neoclassical approach labor is never available to the industrial sector without sacrificing agricultural output. From the point of view of the industrial sector the real-wage rate rises steadily over time, depending on the rates of technological progress in both sectors and the rate of capital accumulation. Disguised unemployment is assumed to be nonexistent. As Lewis points out, a phase of development characterized by disguised unemployment may be followed by a phase without unemployment: "When the labor surplus disappears our model of the closed economy no longer holds. Wages are no longer tied to a subsistence level."[7] Within both frameworks it is possible to examine aspects of industrialization of strategic importance for developing countries such as changes in the structure of output and employment and changes in the rate of investment, capital intensity, and factor substitution.

5.2   Development of a Dual Economy: A Classical Approach

In presenting the classical approach to the theory of development of a dual economy the essential assumption proposed by Lewis, unlimited supplies of labor at a fixed real-wage rate, will be retained. In the theory of development of a dual economy, the economic system may be divided into two sectors—the advanced or modern sector, which we will call, somewhat inaccurately, the industrial sector or manufactur-

ing, and the backward or traditional sector, which may be suggestively denoted agriculture. This terminology has been used by Lewis
and by Fei and Ranis as well as by the present author.[8] It is clear that
industry includes a good many traditional activities and that these
activities have many of the characteristics of the backward sector; similarly, the agricultural sector may include a relatively advanced sub-
sector. Examples of the former would include small-scale industry in
Japan; examples of the latter would include plantation agriculture in
Asia and agriculture in areas of European settlement in parts of
Africa. Nevertheless, it is useful to regard the backward sector as
mainly agricultural and the advanced sector as primarily industrial.

Productive activity in each sector may be characterized by a function relating output to each of the factors of production—land, labor,
and capital. The special character of the theory of development of a
dual economy is an asymmetry in the productive relations. The output of the traditional sector is a function of land and labor alone; there
is no accumulation of capital except in the form of land reclamation.
This assumption is made by the present author and also by Lewis and
by Fei and Ranis.[9] Of course, other assumptions are possible. Even in
relatively primitive societies, there are important uses of capital in
agricultural production.[10] Capital is accumulated in the form of land
reclamation and in the form of equipment for agriculture, fishing, and
hunting. In the study of primitive societies, saving and investment,
ownership of property, and even credit cannot be ignored. For present
purposes, the assumption of no capital in agriculture is useful. The
essential distinction is between agriculture which uses capital produced in the advanced or modern sector and agriculture which uses
only traditional forms of capital. We will refer to any agricultural sector utilizing modern forms of capital as commercialized agriculture.
For present purposes the special role of commercialized agriculture
will be ignored. The resulting theory of development of a dual economy is of special relevance to the less developed countries.

It will be assumed that land is fixed in supply. Further, it is
assumed that agricultural activity is characterized by constant returns
to scale with all factors variable. These assumptions are made by the
present author and by Fei and Ranis.[11] Although there are many ways
to account for diminishing returns, e.g., declining quality of land as
more and more is put under cultivation as in Ricardo's extensive margin—the initial assumption that land is fixed in supply implies that
the diminishing returns arise at the intensive margin of the Ricardian

scheme. In the neoclassical theory of development of a dual economy it is assumed that the marginal productivity of labor in agriculture is always positive. In the classical theory it is assumed that there is some point at which the marginal productivity of labor becomes zero. If population exceeds the quantity at which the marginal productivity of labor becomes zero, labor is available to the manufacturing sector without loss of agricultural output. This assumption, made by Lewis and by Fei and Ranis,[12] will be retained in the present version of the classical theory of development of a dual economy.

Land does not appear as a factor of production in the manufacturing sector; the level of manufacturing output is a function of capital and labor alone. In manufacturing, expansion of productive activity proceeds with constant returns to scale. This appears to be a reasonable assumption, at least on the basis of evidence from the manufacturing industries of advanced economies.[13] A second feature of the production functions for agriculture and manufacturing is that each function will shift over time so that a given bundle of factors will generate a higher level of output at one date than at an earlier date. In short, technological change will be assumed to take place in the manner indicated by Tinbergen and other contributors to the neoclassical theory of economic growth. A special problem arises in applying this assumption to the classical theory of development of a dual economy. For simplicity, it will be assumed that the size of labor force for which the marginal productivity of labor becomes zero remains the same for all technological changes. Of course, the output of the agricultural sector at this point increases over time as the agricultural production function shifts upward.

In the classical approach to the theory of development of a dual economy population growth is ignored or shunted aside as a qualification to the main argument. Lewis discusses a demographic theory quite similar to that of Leibenstein, as outlined above. However, this demographic theory is not integrated into the theory of economic development in a satisfactory way. For Lewis's main line of argument it suffices to assume that unlimited quantities of labor are available to the industrial sector at a fixed real wage; an unlimited supply of labor may have its origin in population growth, but population growth is not affected by activity in either the agricultural or industrial sectors until the phase of disguised unemployment is completed. A similar assumption is made by Fei and Ranis: "Population growth will be treated as a known phenomenon exogenous to our model."[14] This assumption must be qualified in that so long as the real wage remains fixed, the consumption of workers consists entirely of products of the agricultural sector. In the words of Fei and Ranis: ". . . as a consequence of the natural austerity condition arising from the same unlimited supply of labor situation, much industrial output must take the form of capital goods due to the absence of a domestic market for consumer goods."[15] For simplicity, it will be assumed that so long as there is disguised unemployment, population expands at the same rate as the growth of agricultural output. This is the only assumption which is consistent with the view of Lewis and of Fei and Ranis that the real-wage rate remains fixed and equal to the initial level of real income in the agricultural sector. At this level of income all of the income of workers in either sector is used for consumption of agricultural products.

The chief difference between the classical approach to the development of a dual economy and the neoclassical approach is in the conditions governing the supply of labor. In the classical theory, labor is available to the industrial sector in unlimited quantities at a fixed real-wage rate, measured in agricultural goods. Lewis suggests that it is immaterial to his argument whether the marginal productivity of labor in agriculture is zero or simply less than the real-wage rate.[16] Fei and Ranis distinguish between phases of development in which the marginal productivity of labor is zero and in which the marginal productivity of labor is positive but less than the real wage.[17] In the first of these phases labor may be supplied to the industrial sector at no loss in agricultural output; in the second of these phases, labor may be supplied to the industrial sector only at some sacrifice in agricultural output. In both phases labor is available to the industrial sector at a fixed real-wage rate only if the terms of trade between agriculture and industry remain fixed and if population growth is precisely equal to the growth of agricultural output. If the terms of trade should turn against industry, a constant real wage (measured in agricultural goods) will imply a rising price of labor relative to the price of industrial goods.

Finally, in the present version of the classical approach to the development of a dual economy, it will be assumed that saving is equal to total profits in the industrial sector. This assumption is consistent with Lewis's observation that: "We have seen that if unlimited labor is available at a constant real wage, the capitalist surplus will rise continuously, and annual investment will be a rising proportion of the national income."[18] As Lewis emphasizes; "Practically all saving is done by people who receive profits or rents. Workers' savings are very small."[19] The present assumption implies that agricultural rents, in so far as they exist at all, are exchanged for goods produced by the industrial sector. The agricultural products represented by these rents are then provided to the industrial workers. The institutional mechanism by which this transaction takes place may vary from one economy to another. For example, agricultural rents may be taxed away and the proceeds spent on governmentally financed investment; alternatively, landlords may themselves invest in the industrial sector, becoming industrial capitalists; finally, landlords may consume goods produced by the industrial sector so that all investment is done by the owners of industrial capital. For present purposes it suffices to assume that saving is equal to total profits in the industrial sector without specifying whether the resulting accumulation of capital is owned by the government, the landlords, or the industrial capitalists.

We are now in a position to lay out a more concrete version of the classical approach to the development of a dual economy. To begin the analysis we consider an economic system in which no development of manufacturing activity has taken place; all productive activity is concentrated in the traditional or backward sector. We will assume that there is some maximum quantity of labor which may be employed in the agricultural sector with positive marginal productivity; the agricultural labor force, say A, is always less than this maximum quantity of labor. If we let Y be the level of agricultural output and L the fixed quantity of land available to the economy, then a simple version of the production function for agriculture, characterized by constant returns to scale with all factors variable, is given by the Cobb-Douglas function

$$Y = e^{\alpha t} L^{\beta} A^{1-\beta},$$

where $e^{\alpha t}$ represents the shift factor corresponding to technological progress. Changes in techniques are assumed to take place at a constant percentage rate, α. The constant β represents the elasticity of output with respect to an increase in the supply of land; if the supply of land is fixed it is possible to choose the origin for measuring the passage of time so that the production function can be rewritten in the simpler form

$$Y = e^{\alpha t} A^{1-\beta} .$$

For a total population in excess of the maximum quantity which may be employed at positive marginal productivity, we may distinguish between the labor force employed at positive marginal productivity, say A, the agricultural labor force, and the labor force which is redundant, say R. Then total population is the sum of the agricultural labor force and redundant labor

$$P = A + R .$$

If we represent the maximum labor force which may be employed at positive marginal productivity by A^+, then the agricultural labor force is the minimum of total population and this maximum labor force

$$A = \min \begin{cases} P \\ A^+ . \end{cases}$$

Of course, if the agricultural labor force is equal to total population, disguised unemployment is zero: if the agricultural labor force is equal to the maximum level, A^+, redundant labor is equal to the difference between total population and this maximum level.

Under the assumptions that the rate of technological progress in agriculture is positive and that the maximum quantity of labor which may be employed with positive marginal productivity is fixed over time, the development of an economy in which all productive activity is concentrated in the traditional or backward sector is simple to describe. At a constant real-wage rate, measured in agricultural goods, population increases at the same rate as agricultural output. In the presence of redundant labor, the rate of growth of agricultural output and population is constant and equal to the rate of technological progress in agriculture, α. In the absence of redundant labor, population growth can exceed the rate of technological progress since the rate of growth of output is equal to the rate of technological progress, α, plus the elasticity of output with respect to labor, $1 - \beta$, multiplied by the rate of growth of population. With a constant real-wage rate the rate of growth of population is simply α/β, a positive quantity. Hence, in an economy in which there is no redundant labor initially, population will grow at a positive rate until the maximum quantity of labor which can be employed with positive marginal productivity is reached. After this point the rate of population growth will slow to the rate of technological progress, α, and all increments in population will become part of the redundant labor force.

We next consider an economic system in which development of manufacturing activity has taken place. Conditions of production in the manufacturing sector must be described. We have assumed that the production function in manufacturing exhibits constant returns to scale. We have also assumed that the output of manufactured goods for a given bundle of capital and labor increases over time. If we denote the quantity of manufacturing output by X, the manufacturing labor force by M, and the quantity of capital by K, then a simple version of the production function for manufacturing is given by the Cobb–Douglas function

$$X = e^{\lambda t} K^{\sigma} M^{1-\sigma},$$

where $e^{\lambda t}$ represents technological change, as before, and the constant σ represents the elasticity of manufacturing output with respect to an increase in the supply of land.

With respect to the supply of labor to the manufacturing sector, we have assumed that redundant labor is available to the industrial sector at a fixed real wage, measured in agricultural goods. We may also assume that the terms of trade between agriculture and manufacturing are fixed. If we assume further that competitive conditions prevail in manufacturing, the marginal product of labor is equal to the fixed real wage, measured in either agricultural or manufacturing goods. This assumption is made by Lewis and by Fei and Ranis.[20] If we denote the fixed real wage measured in manufactured goods by w, the marginal product of labor in the manufacturing sector is then

$$\frac{\partial X}{\partial M} = (1 - \sigma) \frac{X}{M} = w.$$

If there is no redundant labor, the marginal productivity of labor in the agricultural sector may still be below the real-wage rate, measured in agricultural goods. However, labor may be transferred from the agricultural sector to the industrial sector only by sacrificing agricultural output. Under these conditions it may still be assumed that the terms of trade between agriculture and manufacturing are fixed. This assumption is made by Lewis.[21] Alternatively, it may be assumed that the terms of trade turn against manufacturing, so that the wage rate measured in manufactured goods increases. This assumption is made

by Fei and Ranis.[22] In the present version of the classical approach to
the theory of development of a dual economy, the terms of trade
between agriculture and manufacturing cannot be determined
endogenously. For simplicity, we will begin with Lewis's assumption
that the terms of trade are fixed; under this assumption the marginal
product of labor in manufacturing is fixed. Using the marginal productivity relationship given above to eliminate the manufacturing
labor force from the production function for manufacturing, we may
write

$$X = \left(\frac{1-\sigma}{w}\right)^{(1-\sigma)/\sigma} e^{(\lambda/\sigma)t} K .$$

If we assume that saving is equal to the share of profits in the
industrial sector, ignoring depreciation we may set the rate of change
of capital equal to the share of profits in manufacturing output

$$\dot{K} = \sigma X ,$$

so that the rate of growth of capital may be written

$$\frac{\dot{K}}{K} = \sigma \left(\frac{1-\sigma}{w}\right)^{(1-\sigma)/\sigma} e^{(\lambda/\sigma)t} .$$

Using the production function and the fact that the output per man
remains constant, the rate of growth of manufacturing output may be
written

$$\frac{\dot{X}}{X} = \frac{\lambda}{\sigma} + \sigma \left(\frac{1-\sigma}{w}\right)^{(1-\sigma)/\sigma} e^{(\lambda/\sigma)t} .$$

The rate of growth of manufacturing employment is, of course, equal
to the rate of growth of manufacturing output.

For an economy with total population in excess of the maximum
quantity which may be employed at a positive marginal productivity
in agriculture plus the manufacturing labor force, there is redundant
labor. Total population is the sum of the agricultural labor force, the
industrial labor force, and redundant labor

$$P = A + M + R .$$

The agricultural labor force is the minimum of total population less the manufacturing labor force and the maximum labor force which may be employed at positive marginal productivity

$$A = \min \begin{cases} P - M \\ A^+ \end{cases}.$$

So long as there is redundant labor in the agricultural sector, manufacturing output and manufacturing employment grow at a rate which is positive and increasing. Capital in manufacturing also grows at a rate which is positive and increasing, but always less than the rate of growth of output. This implies that the capital-output ratio is always falling; a similar result is obtained by Fei and Ranis.[23] Since agricultural output is increasing at a constant rate, equal to the rate of technological progress in agriculture, population is increasing at this same rate. Whatever the initial value of the rate of growth of manufacturing output, this rate of growth eventually exceeds any fixed rate of growth. The sum of redundant labor and manufacturing employment grows at a rate which exceeds the rate of growth of population; but this rate must fall to the rate of growth of population. Hence, the rate of growth of manufacturing employment eventually becomes so large as to force the rate of growth of redundant labor to become negative and decreasing. Under these conditions redundant labor eventually disappears altogether. This concludes the description of the first phase of development with unlimited supplies of labor. The point at which redundant labor disappears is called the "Lewis turning-point" by Fei and Ranis.[24]

After the Lewis turning-point is reached the marginal productivity of labor in the agricultural sector is positive but less than the real-wage rate, measured in agricultural goods. Under the assumption that the real-wage rate remains fixed when measured in agricultural goods, the rate of growth of population is equal to the rate of technological change in the agricultural sector less the elasticity of agricultural output with respect to labor multiplied by the rate of decline of the agricultural labor force. Where w_A is the proportion of the agricultural labor force in total population and w_M the proportion of the manufacturing labor force, this condition on the rate of population growth implies

$$\alpha + (1 - \beta) \frac{\dot{A}}{A} = w_A \frac{\dot{A}}{A} + w_M \frac{\dot{M}}{M},$$

or simply,

$$\alpha + (w_M - \beta) \frac{\dot{A}}{A} = w_M \frac{\dot{M}}{M} \, .$$

For this condition to be satisfied, the manufacturing proportion, w_M, must be such that the rate of growth of the agricultural labor force is negative at the Lewis turning-point. Furthermore, the rate of growth of the agricultural labor force must remain negative until the labor force itself reaches the level at which the marginal product of labor in agriculture, measured in agricultural goods, is equal to the real wage. For this it suffices to assume that the share of manufacturing in the total labor force exceeds the elasticity of agricultural output with respect to land. Under this condition the agricultural labor force declines at an increasing rate until the marginal product of labor is equal to the real wage. At this point a third phase of the development of dual economy is reached. In this phase the wage rate of labor is the same in agriculture and in manufacturing.

The third phase of development of a dual economy under the classical approach is described by Lewis as follows: "When capital catches up with labor supply, an economy enters upon the [third] phase of development. Classical economics ceases to apply; we are in the world of neoclassical economics, where all the factors of production are scarce, in the sense that their supply is inelastic. Wages are no longer constant as accumulation proceeds; the benefits of improved technology do not all accrue to profits; and the profit margin does not necessarily increase all the time. . . ."[25] Fei and Ranis describe the third phase as follows: "The transition into phase [three] constitutes a major landmark in the developmental process. With the completion of the transfer of the disguisedly unemployed, there will occur a switch, forced by circumstance in employer behavior, i.e., the advent of a fully commercialized agricultural sector. This landmark may be defined as the end of the take-off process. We know of no other way to establish a nonarbitrary criterion for an economy reaching the threshold of so-called self-sustaining growth."[26] The basic point made by Lewis and by Fei and Ranis is that a neoclassical theory of growth for an advanced economy applies after the third phase of development has been reached. Hence, further discussion of this phase will be postponed until the neoclassical theory of development for a dual economy has been discussed.

Parenthetically, it should be remarked that Fei and Ranis attempt to combine Lewis's notion of disguised unemployment with the critical

minimum effort hypothesis of Leibenstein. Their criterion for a critical minimum effort is that the rate of growth of population must be
less than the rate of growth of the industrial labor force. In the presence of disguised unemployment, this condition is always satisfied,
provided only that the rate of technological change in the industrial
sector is positive. With a positive rate of technological change the rate
of growth of the industrial labor force eventually exceeds any fixed
rate of growth; with a fixed real wage, measured in agricultural goods,
the growth of population is limited by the rate of technological change
in the agricultural sector. In the absence of disguised unemployment,
the critical minimum effort criterion is satisfied only under a somewhat different set of conditions. We will return to the discussion of
this problem after our review of the neoclassical theory.

5.3   Development of a Dual Economy: A Neoclassical Approach[27]

The distinguishing characteristics of the neoclassical theory of the
development of a dual economy are the technology of the agricultural
sector and the conditions governing the supply of labor. First, in the
neoclassical approach it is assumed that the productivity of labor in
agriculture is always positive so that labor is never redundant. Secondly it is assumed that the real-wage rate is variable rather than
fixed; wage rates in the backward sector are assumed to be proportional to those in the advanced sector. The interpretation of this relationship will be discussed below. Except for the possibility that labor
may be redundant, the description of technology for the agricultural
sector is the same for both classical and neoclassical theories. In the
neoclassical approach there is no level of the agricultural labor force at
which the marginal productivity of labor is zero. It is assumed that
the agricultural production function for any level of the agricultural
labor force may be characterized by the Cobb–Douglas production
function

$$Y = e^{\alpha t} L^\beta A^{1-\beta},$$

where variables and parameters have the same interpretation as in the
classical approach. Assuming that the supply of land is fixed, this
production function may be rewritten in the form

$$y = e^{\alpha t} A^{-\beta},$$

where $y = Y/A$ is agricultural output per head.

Conditions of production in the manufacturing sector are the same as those of the classical theory. We have assumed that the manufacturing production function may be characterized by constant returns to scale and that the output of manufactured goods for a given quantity of capital and labor increases over time; a simple version of the manufacturing production function is the Cobb-Douglas function

$$X = e^{\lambda t} K^\sigma M^{1-\sigma},$$

where variables and parameters have the same interpretation as in the classical theory. Second, we assume that saving is equal to the share of profits in the manufacturing sector; as before, we ignore depreciation so that the rate of change of capital may be set equal to the share of profits in manufacturing output

$$\dot{K} = \sigma X.$$

This assumption is identical to that made in the classical approach.

To close the model for the neoclassical theory of the development of a dual economy it is necessary to describe the allocation of labor between the backward and advanced sectors of the economy. To simplify the discussion we will assume that as agricultural output per head increases, all output is consumed up to a level of agricultural output per head equal to the critical value, y^+. We assume that once the critical value is attained all further increases in consumption per head take the form of manufactured goods. Under these assumptions agricultural output per head in excess of the critical value, y^+, constitutes a surplus; we may define the agricultural surplus per head, say s, as the difference between agricultural output per head and the critical value, y^+

$$s = y - y^+.$$

If agricultural output per head exceeds the critical level, part of the labor force may be released from the land to produce manufactured goods with no reduction in the rate of growth of total population.[28]

As before, we denote agricultural population by A and manufacturing population by M; total population, say P, is the sum of these two components

$$P = A + M.$$

The demographic theory for the development of a dual economy is as follows: The net rate of reproduction is the minimum of the rate corresponding to the minimum force of mortality ε and a rate which corresponds to output of food per head; the basic demographic relationship may be written

$$\frac{\dot{P}}{P} = \min \left\{ \begin{array}{l} \gamma y \, \dfrac{A}{P} - \delta \\ \varepsilon \end{array} \right.$$

where yA/P is output of food per head for the whole economy and δ is the minimum net reproduction rate equal to the maximum possible force of mortality (mass starvation) and ε is a fixed birth-rate that depends on medical technique and social institutions. For an economy with an agricultural surplus, total food consumption is the critical level, y^+, multiplied by total population; the proportion of the total labor force employed in agriculture is the ratio of this critical level of agricultural production per head to the actual level of output per head

$$\frac{y^+}{y} = \frac{A}{P} .$$

Of course this relationship holds only when an agricultural surplus exists, that is, if $y > y^+$. Under these assumptions, the relationship governing the distribution of labor between the backward sector and the advanced sector may be represented by

$$\frac{A}{P} = \min \left\{ \begin{array}{l} 1 \\ y^+/y \end{array} \right. .$$

To study the development of a dual economy for the case in which the advanced sector is economically viable, we must assume at the outset that an agricultural surplus eventually emerges, that is, that $\alpha - \beta\varepsilon > 0$, which is both necessary and sufficient for the emergence of an agricultural surplus. The case in which the advanced sector is not economically viable will be treated subsequently. We assume first that the initial level of agricultural output per head is below the critical level, y^+. An industrial labor force comes into being when agricultural output per head attains the critical value, y^+, that is, when agricultural output attains the minimum level necessary for population to grow at its maximum rate. From this point forward, population grows at the maximum rate of net reproduction, ε.

From the fact that population is growing at a constant rate and that consumption of food per head is stationary, we obtain the following expression for the growth of the agricultural labor force

$$A = P(0)e^{[\varepsilon-\alpha/1-\beta]t} = A(0)e^{[\varepsilon-\alpha/1-\beta]t} \,.$$

Agricultural population may grow, decline, or remain constant, depending on the magnitude of the parameters ε, the rate of growth of total population, and α, the rate of technological progress in agriculture.

The manufacturing population is equal to total population less agricultural population; hence the growth of the manufacturing labor force is governed by the following expression

$$M = P(0)[e^{\varepsilon t} - e^{[\varepsilon-\alpha/1-\beta]t}]\,,$$

which is zero at time $t = 0$ and grows at a rate which is always more rapid than the rate of growth of total population. To show this we begin with the assumption that an agricultural surplus eventually emerges, namely

$$\alpha - \beta\varepsilon > 0,$$

which implies

$$\varepsilon - \alpha < \varepsilon(1 - \beta)\,,$$

so that

$$\varepsilon > \frac{\varepsilon - \alpha}{1 - \beta} \,.$$

The rate of growth of population is greater than that of the agricultural population alone; hence the manufacturing labor force is growing at a rate which exceeds that of total population. The rate of growth of the manufacturing labor force is always declining and approaches, as a limit, the rate of growth of population, ε.

To study the growth of manufacturing output, it is necessary to characterize the process of capital accumulation in the advanced sector of the economy. The fundamental relationships include the expression given above the the growth of the manufacturing labor force, the production function for the manufacturing sector, and the savings function. Combining these relationships we may eliminate the output of the manufacturing sector and the manufacturing labor force to obtain a differential equation in capital alone

$$\dot{K} = \sigma K^{\sigma} P(0)^{1-\sigma} e^{\lambda t} [e^{\varepsilon t} - e^{[\varepsilon-\alpha/1-\beta)t}]^{1-\sigma},$$

which is the fundamental differential equation for the neoclassical theory of development of a dual economy. From this fundamental equation it may be deduced immediately that there is no stationary situation for any economy in which the advanced sector is economically viable; that is; provided that there is a positive and growing agricultural surplus, the advanced sector must continue to grow. The pattern of growth of the advanced sector is determined by two initial conditions, the size of total population at the time that the growth of the advanced sector begins and the size of the initial capital stock. Only the initial size of the population has any effect on the long-run pattern of growth of the economy; the influence of the initial size of capital stock eventually dies out.[29] Secondly, it may be shown that there is no critical minimum level of the initial capital stock required for sustained economic growth. Given any positive initial capital stock, no matter how small, the existence of a positive and growing agricultural surplus generates sustained economic growth.

For the neoclassical theory of the development of a dual economy capital and output grow at the same rate in the long run, namely, $\lambda/(1 - \sigma) + \varepsilon$, where λ is the rate of technological progress in industry, $1 - \sigma$ is the share of labor in manufacturing output, and ε is the rate of growth of population. Population grows at the rate ε; since the share of labor in manufacturing output is constant, the wage rate of the manufacturing labor force eventually grows at the rate $\lambda/1 - \sigma$. In the short run the beginning of the growth of the advanced sector is always characterized by a "big push," that is, an extraordinarily high rate of growth of manufacturing output. From the viewpoint of the neoclassical theory of the development of a dual economy, such a high initial rate of growth may be interpreted as a statistical artifact. Using the production function for the advanced sector, we may derive the relation

$$\frac{\dot{X}}{X} = \lambda + \sigma \frac{\dot{K}}{K} + (1 - \sigma) \frac{\dot{M}}{M}$$

so that the rate of growth of manufacturing output is equal to the rate of technological progress plus a weighted average of the rates of growth of capital stock and of the manufacturing labor force. But the initial rate of growth of the manufacturing labor force is essentially unbounded; this rate of growth declines gradually, approaching a long-run equilibrium value equal to the rate of growth of total population. The existence of a statistically observable "big push" is no evidence for the necessity of a massive infusion of capital from outside the system for a "take-off" into sustained growth; sustained growth depends on the economic viability of the advanced sector and not on the initial level of capital stock. The advanced sector is economically viable if and only if there is a positive and growing agricultural surplus.

We have assumed that wage rates in the backward sector of a dual economy are proportional to those in the advanced sector. Using this relationship and the saving function it is possible to determine the terms of trade between agriculture and industry. The balance of trade between agriculture and industry requires that the value of labor income in both sectors is equal to the value of manufacturing output not used for additions to capital together with the value of total agricultural output. This balance relation may be written

$$wM + \mu wA = (1 - \sigma)X + qY,$$

where q is the terms of trade between agriculture and industry and μ is the constant of proportionality between wage rates in the agricultural sector and wage rates in the industrial sector.

The constant of proportionality may be interpreted in a number of different ways. First, in a "strict" neoclassical theory wage rates in the two sectors must be equal. In this case the constant of proportionality, μ, is unity. Alternatively, if the process of development of a dual economy is characterized by a steady flow of labor from agriculture to industry, a differential between agricultural and industrial wages may be required to sustain this flow.[30] As a third alternative, if land is owned by the cultivators but the full value of the land cannot be realized by outright sale, the industrial wage rate must be sufficiently high to cover both labor and property income for a member of the agricultural labor force.[31] If nothing can be realized by the sale of land, the industrial wage rate would have to be equal to unity divided by the share of labor in total agricultural output. Other interpretations of the constant of proportionality could doubtless be given. Provided that μ is a fixed constant the balance relation may be rewritten in the form

$$\mu wA = qY,$$

so that

$$\frac{\dot{w}}{w} + \frac{\dot{A}}{A} = \frac{\dot{q}}{q} + \frac{\dot{Y}}{Y}$$

and

$$\frac{\dot{q}}{q} = \left[\frac{\varepsilon - \alpha}{1 - \beta} - \varepsilon \right] + \frac{\dot{w}}{w}.$$

In the long run the rate of growth of the wage rate in manufacturing is equal to $\lambda/1 - \sigma$, so that the rate of growth of the terms of trade is the sum of a negative and a positive quantity; hence the terms of trade may turn in favor of agriculture or industry, depending on the relative magnitude of the two quantities.

5.4   Beyond Disguised Unemployment

Where the advanced sector is already in existence, wage rates in the advanced and backward sectors may be taken to be equal, as in the "strict" neoclassical approach. Then the neoclassical theory of the development of a dual economy may be reinterpreted as a theory of the neoclassical phase of Lewis's theory of economic development. The growth of the manufacturing labor force and manufacturing output and the accumulation of capital are described by the relations given above for the neoclassical theory. However, the initial phases of the development of the advanced sector are not the same as in the neoclassical theory. In the classical theory the phase of redundant labor initiates the development of manufacturing. This sector develops further in the phase of disguised unemployment, where there is no redundant labor but the marginal product of labor in the agricultural sector is below the real-wage rate, measured in agricultural goods. Finally, the marginal products of labor in both sectors are brought into equality with the fixed real-wage rate. By this time a certain amount of capital has been accumulated in the manufacturing sector. Given the manufacturing labor force, the second initial condition for the fundamental relations of the neoclassical theory of development of a dual economy, namely, the size of total population when agricultural output per head reaches its critical value, y^+, can be computed by inserting the manufacturing labor force into the equation

$$M(t) = P(0)[e^{\varepsilon t} - e^{[\varepsilon - \alpha/1 - \beta]t}],$$

by inserting total population into the equation

$$P(t) = P(0)e^{\varepsilon t},$$

and by computing $P(0)$ and the origin for the measurement of time. These constants may then be used to determine the course of economic growth in the neoclassical phase of the classical theory of the development of a dual economy. Of course, the fundamental relations of the neoclassical theory are valid for the classical theory only *after* the beginning of the neoclassical phase.

Up to this point we have considered only the case in which the advanced sector is economically viable. A necessary and sufficient condition for the economic viability of the advanced sector is the eventual emergence of a positive and growing agricultural surplus. Provided that an agricultural surplus eventually emerges, the development of a dual economy may be characterized in two ways. If there is disguised unemployment as in the classical approach, the manufacturing sector develops in three separate phases. First, manufacturing output and employment grow at a rate which is positive and increasing. Capital in manufacturing also grows at a rate which is positive and increasing, but always less than the rate of growth of manufacturing output. Redundant labor eventually disappears. Secondly, provided that the share of manufacturing in the total labor force exceeds the elasticity of agricultural output with respect to land, the agricultural labor force declines at an increasing rate until the marginal product of labor is equal to the real wage in both sectors. The realization of this condition marks the end of disguised unemployment. Finally, the manufacturing sector enters onto the neoclassical phase. This phase is the same as the phase of "dualistic" development in the neoclassical theory, provided that the initial conditions of the fundamental relations of the neoclassical theory are properly reinterpreted. If there is no disguised unemployment as in the neoclassical approach, the backward sector develops according to the fundamental relations describing an increase in agricultural output per head until the critical level, y^+, is reached. At this level the force of mortality reaches its minimum and the net reproduction rate for total population reaches its maximum. From this point forward the development of the manufacturing sector is described by the fundamental relations for capital accumulation and for the growth of manufacturing output and employment. These relations are the same as those describing the neoclassical phase of development of a dual economy in the classical approach.

We may now consider the case in which the advanced sector is not economically viable. First, we will describe the neoclassical theory of development for this case. If capital for the advanced sector is already in existence, the condition for economic viability of this sector, $\alpha - \beta\varepsilon > 0$, is not satisfied. There are two possibilities. First, suppose that $\alpha = \beta\varepsilon$; then the manufacturing labor force is equal to zero and there is no manufacturing production. Secondly, suppose that $\alpha < \beta\varepsilon$ and the initial value of the manufacturing labor force is positive. Then this labor force declines to zero after which there is no further manufacturing production. Total population becomes entirely concentrated in the agricultural sector and agricultural output per head eventually declines to that associated with the low-level equilibrium trap.

The classical theory of development where the advanced sector is not economically viable at the maximum net reproduction rate is somewhat more complex. We consider development only in the third or neoclassical phase. In this phase the development of a dual economy is characterized by the same fundamental relations as in the neoclassical approach. If the advanced sector is not economically viable, two possibilities exist. First, if $\alpha = \beta\varepsilon$, the existence of a positive manufacturing labor force contradicts the fundamental differential equation for the neoclassical theory of development of a dual economy. Hence, for the classical approach this condition must be ruled out by assumption. Secondly, if $\alpha < \beta\varepsilon$, the manufacturing labor force begins to decline as soon as disguised unemployment is eliminated. This decline continues until the agricultural labor force reaches its maximum level, so that further increases in the agricultural labor force are redundant. Throughout the decline of the manufacturing labor force the real wage in both sectors remains constant with no disguised unemployment.

With a fixed real wage, measured in agricultural goods, the rate of population growth must decline to the rate of technological progress in agriculture when the agricultural labor force reaches its maximum, so that $\varepsilon = \alpha$ from this point forward. At this lower rate of population growth the advanced sector is always economically viable. The labor force in manufacturing begins to grow at a rate exceeding that of population growth, but eventually declines to this rate of growth. The renewed growth of the manufacturing labor force is characterized by a "big push," that is, an extraordinarily high rate of growth of the manufacturing labor force. As in the neoclassical theory of the development of a dual economy, this high initial rate of growth may be interpreted as a statistical artifact. The existence of such a statistically observable "big push" is no evidence for the necessity of a massive infusion of capital from outside the system for a "take-off." Sustained growth depends on the economic viability of the advanced sector at the new rate of population growth and not on the initial level of capital stock.

In the second phase of growth in the manufacturing labor force the labor force in agriculture remains constant at its maximum level, while agricultural output grows at the same rate as population. Manufacturing output and capital stock eventually increase at the rate $\lambda/(1 - \sigma) + \alpha$ and the real wage, measured in manufacturing goods, grows at the rate $\lambda/1 - \sigma$. Throughout the second phase of growth in the manufacturing labor force, the real wage, measured in agricultural goods, is increasing at the rate of technological progress in agriculture, α. The terms of trade between agriculture and industry eventually grows at the rate $\lambda/(1 - \sigma) - \alpha$. This rate may be positive or negative, depending on the relative rates of technological progress in the two sectors.

In the classical theory of the development of a dual economy the phase of development beginning with no manufacturing production but with redundant agricultural labor or disguised unemployment is characterized by a rate of growth of the manufacturing labor force that exceeds the rate of growth of population. This characterization is a necessary consequence of the classical theory whether or not the advanced sector is economically viable at the maximum rate of net reproduction. If the advanced sector is not economically viable at this rate of population growth, the initial phase of disguised unemployment is followed by a phase of absolute decline in the manufacturing labor force that terminates with the agricultural labor force at its maximum level and with a reduced rate of population growth. This phase is followed by a second phase of growth in the manufacturing labor force. Again, the rate of growth of the manufacturing labor force exceeds the rate of growth of population.

We conclude that the criterion for a critical minimum effort proposed by Fei and Ranis, that the rate of growth of population must be less than the rate of growth of the industrial labor force, provides no indication whatever concerning the economic viability of the advanced sector. The advanced sector is economically viable if and only if there is a positive and growing agricultural surplus, that is $\alpha > \beta\varepsilon$. During the phase of disguised unemployment, the critical minimum effort criterion of Fei and Ranis is satisfied whether or not the advanced sector is economically viable. Where their criterion is satisfied, the elimination of disguised unemployment may be followed by sustained economic growth or by a period of absolute decline in the manufacturing labor force. Only the existence of a positive and growing agricultural surplus assures that growth will be sustained.

5.5   Summary and Conclusion

In the preceding sections we have described two alternative approaches to the theory of development of a dual economy. In order to facilitate comparison of the two approaches, we have attempted to develop both within the same framework. Within this framework the basic differences between the two approaches are in assumptions made about the technology of the agricultural sector and about conditions governing the supply of labor. In the classical approach it is assumed that there is some level of the agricultural labor force beyond which further increments in this labor force are redundant. In the neoclassical approach the marginal productivity of labor in agriculture is assumed to be always positive so that labor is never redundant. In the classical approach the real-wage rate, measured in agricultural goods, is assumed to be fixed "institutionally" so long as there is disguised unemployment in the agricultural sector. In the neoclassical approach the real-wage rate is assumed to be variable rather than fixed; it is further assumed that at very low levels of income the rate of growth of population depends on the level of income. These are the basic differences between the neoclassical and classical approaches to the theory of development of a dual economy.

The neoclassical and classical theories differ in the characterization of the backward or traditional sector of the economy. These differences have implications for the behavior of the backward sector. Among the implications we may note that according to the classical approach, the agricultural labor force must decline absolutely before the end of the phase of disguised unemployment; in the neoclassical approach the agricultural labor force may rise, fall, or remain constant. The differences between the two approaches also have implications for the behavior of the advanced sector; unfortunately, these implications depend on the actual behavior of the terms of trade between the backward and advanced sectors. In the neoclassical approach the terms of trade may rise or fall. In the classical approach the terms of trade cannot be determined endogenously. Alternative assumptions about the course of the terms of trade may be made. Corresponding to each assumption about the terms of trade, there is an alternative theory for the behavior of the advanced sector. Since any assumption about the course of the terms of trade is consistent with the classical approach, the behavior of the terms of trade cannot provide a test of this approach. The classical approach may be tested only be deriving the implications of this approach for the advanced sector, given the observed behavior of the terms of trade, and confronting these implications with empirical evidence.

We have developed the classical theory in detail only on the assumption that the terms of trade between the backward and advanced sectors remain constant. Proceeding on this assumption, we have derived the following implications of the classical approach: (1) output and employment in the advanced sector grow at the same rate so long as there is disguised unemployment in the backward sector; that is, labor productivity in the advanced sector remains constant; (2) capital grows at a slower rate than output and labor so that capital-output ratio falls; this result corresponds to that of Fei and Ranis;[32] (3) the rates of growth of manufacturing output, employment, and capital increase during the phase of disguised unemployment. For the neoclassical approach, the corresponding results are: (1) output and capital in the advanced sector grow at the same rate, asymptotically, so that the capital-output ratio remains constant; (2) manufacturing employment grows more slowly than either output or capital so that labor productivity in the advanced sector rises; (3) the rates of growth of manufacturing output and employment decrease throughout the development process. Since the classical approach reduces to the neoclassical approach after the phase of disguised unemployment is completed, the two approaches have different implications only for situations where it is alleged that disguised unemployment exists.

In view of the similarities between classical and neoclassical approaches to the development of a dual economy it is not surprising that many implications of one model are also implications of the other. For example, both models imply that if the proportion of manufacturing output to agricultural output increases, the share of saving in total income also increases. Thus, either model suffices to explain an increase in the fraction of income saved in the course of economic development. The fact that the implications of the two approaches for the share of saving are identical is of considerable significance. According to Lewis: "The central problem in the theory of economic development is to understand the process by which a community which was previously saving and investing (four or five percent) of its national income or less, converts itself into an economy where voluntary saving is running at about twelve to fifteen percent of national income or more. This is the central problem because the central fact of economic development is rapid capital accumulation (including knowledge and skills with capital)."[33] Both classical and neoclassical theories of the development of a dual economy provide an explanation of an increase in the share of saving. In each case the explanation is based on the relationship between saving and industrial profits. Disguised unemployment is neither necessary nor sufficient to generate a sustained rise in the share of saving. Ultimately, a sustained increase in the saving share depends on a positive and growing agricultural surplus and not on the presence or absence of disguised unemployment.

The role of the industrial sector in economic development is critical for the elimination of disguised unemployment. In the absence of industrialization an economy with redundant labor is characterized by population growth at a rate equal to the rate of growth of agricultural output. Agricultural output grows at the rate of technological progress in agriculture. All increments in population become part of the redundant labor force. In the presence of industrialization the rate of growth of manufacturing employment eventually becomes so large as to force the rate of growth of redundant labor to become negative; redundant labor eventually disappears altogether. The disappearance of disguised unemployment is, however, no indication that the industrial sector is economically viable. If the condition for persistence of an agricultural surplus is not satisfied, the initial phase of disguised unemployment is followed by a phase of absolute decline in the manufacturing labor force that terminates with the agricultural labor force at its maximum level and with a reduced rate of population growth. The condition that population grows more slowly than the manufacturing labor force provides no indication of the economic viability of the advanced sector at a given rate of population growth.

In the theory of development of a dual economy, there is no critical minimum level of initial capital stock required for sustained economic growth. Given any positive initial capital stock, no matter how small, the existence of a positive and growing agricultural surplus generates sustained growth of the industrial sector. In the long run the development of a dual economy is characterized by a growth in industrial output at a rate equal to the sum of the rate of growth of population and the ratio of the rate of technological progress in industry to the share of labor in that sector. Agricultural output grows at a rate equal to the rate of growth of population; hence the ratio of industrial output to agricultural output is always increasing. Similarly, the rate of growth of the industrial labor force is equal to the rate of growth of population in the long run. The rate of growth of the agricultural labor force is equal to the difference between the rate of growth of total population and the rate of technological progress in agriculture divided by the share of labor in agriculture. The existence of a positive and growing agricultural surplus assures that this rate of growth is less than that of population; accordingly, the ratio of industrial labor force to agricultural labor force is always increasing. Finally, capital and output in the industrial sector eventually grow at the same rate so that capital per man increases at a rate equal to the rate of growth of output per man, namely the rate of technological progress in industry divided by labor's share in industry. The share of capital formation in national product is always increasing, ultimately approaching the share of property in the product of the industrial sector.

We conclude that the industrial sector plays a strategic role in the development of a dual economy with or without disguised unemployment. Industrial output and industrial labor force ultimately come to dominate a developed economy as a consequence of the shift in a consumer demand from agricultural to industrial products and as a result of the rising proportion of investment demand in total output as income *per capita* increases. However, supply conditions for the agricultural sector must not be neglected in any analysis of prospects for industrialization. Unless technological progress in agriculture is sufficiently rapid to outpace the growth of population and the force of diminishing returns, the industrial sector may not be economically viable.

In the absence of a growing agricultural surplus, forced industrialization at fixed real wages may result in a phase of growth in the relative importance of industry with no improvement in levels of living, followed by an absolute reduction in the size of the industrial sector as population growth is forced down to the Malthusian level consistent with the increase of sustenance. Since the criterion for the persistence of an agricultural surplus depends on the rate of growth of population, the rate of advance of agricultural technology required for improvement in levels of living is larger the larger the rate of population growth. The recent increase of rates of population growth in low-income countries has increased the threshold for rates of improvement in agricultural technology required to sustain industrial development. Where the condition for viability of the industrial sector is not met, any policy for industrialization must be accompanied by policies for population control and for the introduction of nontraditional factors into the agricultural sector.[34]

Notes

1. Statistical Office of the United Nations, Department of Economic and Social Affairs (1965, pp. 194–195). For more detailed support of the association between degree of industrialization and the level of economic development for time series, the following may be consulted: F. Dovring (1959, pp. 1–11), reprinted in Carl K. Eicher and Lawrence W. Witt (1964, pp. 78–98); S. Kuznets (1957). Similar support for the association on international cross sections may be obtained from: C. Clark (1957); H.B. Chenery (1960, pp. 624–654); Centre for Industrial Development, Department of Social and Economic Affairs (1965).
2. R.F. Harrod (1939, pp. 14–33); J. Tinbergen (1942, pp. 511–549), translated and reprinted in L.H. Klaasen, L.M. Koyck, and H.J. Witteveen (1959, pp. 182–221).
3. N. Kaldor (1957, pp. 591–624), reprinted in N. Kaldor (1960, pp. 259–300). N. Kaldor (1961, pp. 177–222). N. Kaldor and J. Mirrlees (1962, pp. 172–192).
4. W.A. Lewis (1954, pp. 139–191); W.A. Lewis (1958, pp. 1–32).
5. H. Leibenstein (1954); see also H. Leibenstein (1957).
6. This point of view is elaborated in my paper, Jorgenson (1961b, especially pp. 309–311). The same point of view is expressed by Luigi Spaventa (1959, especially pp. 386–390). An excellent review of the literature on economic dualism through 1960 is given by Howard S. Ellis (1961, pp. 3–17).
7. Lewis (1954, p. 176).
8. Lewis (1954, pp. 146–148); Jorgenson (1961b, p. 311); Fei and Ranis (1961a, pp. 533–534).
9. Lewis (1954, p. 146); Jorgenson (1961b, p. 311); Fei and Ranis (1964, p. 16).
10. See, for example, the essays in Firth and Yames (1964).
11. Jorgenson (1961b, p. 311); Fei and Ranis (1964, pp. 15–16).
12. Lewis (1954, p. 141); Fei and Ranis (1961, p. 30).
13. See Jorgenson (1961b, p. 311), and the references given there.
14. Fei and Ranis (1961, p. 550).

15. Fei and Ranis (1964, p. 118).
16. Lewis (1954, p. 142).
17. Fei and Ranis (1961, p. 537).
18. Lewis (1954, p. 171).
19. Lewis (1954, p. 157).
20. Lewis (1954, pp. 146–149); Fei and Ranis (1964, pp. 16–19).
21. Lewis (1954, p. 142).
22. Fei and Ranis (1964, p. 209).
23. Fei and Ranis (1963, p. 288).
24. Fei and Ranis (1961, p. 540).
25. Lewis (1954, pp. 26–27).
26. Fei and Ranis (1961, p. 537).
27. This section is based on Jorgenson (1961b).
28. The relationship between the existence of an agricultural surplus and development of the advanced sector has been discussed by Lewis and by Fei and Ranis. This relationship is also discussed by N. Kaldor (1960, pp. 233–242). The necessity of an agricultural surplus has been emphasized by William H. Nicholls (1964, pp. 11–44; 1963, pp. 1–29).
29. A proof of this proposition is given in Jorgenson (1961b, pp. 330–333).
30. See, for example, Jorgenson (1961b, pp. 322–333).
31. Lewis (1954, pp. 148–149).
32. Fei and Ranis (1963, p. 288).
33. Lewis (1954, p. 155).
34. Schultz (1964). The importance of policies of this type for low-income countries has been emphasized by Schultz in this book.

6

U.S. Tax Policy and Energy Conservation

Edward A. Hudson and Dale W. Jorgenson

6.1 Introduction

The dramatic increase in world petroleum prices associated with the Arab oil embargo of October 1973 has highlighted the need for a new approach to the quantitative analysis of economic policy. Econometric models in the Tinbergen-Klein mold have proved to be very useful in studying the impact of economic policy on aggregate demand.[1] At the same time these models do not provide an adequate basis for assessing the impact of economic policy on supply. Input-output analysis in the form originated by Leontief is useful for a very detailed analysis of supply, predicated on a fixed technology at any point of time.[2] Input-output analysis does not provide a means of assessing the impact of changes in technology induced by price variations associated with changes in economic policy.

The purpose of this chapter is to present a new approach to the quantitative analysis of U.S. energy policy.[3] This approach is based on an integration of econometric modeling and input-output analysis and incorporates an entirely new methodology for assessing the impact of economic policy on supply. We combine the determinants of energy demand and supply within the same framework and relate patterns of U.S. economic growth to both demand and supply. Our approach can be used to project U.S. economic growth and energy utilization for any proposed U.S. energy policy. It can be employed to study the impact of specific policy changes on energy demand and supply, energy price and cost, energy imports and exports, and on U.S. economic growth.

The first component of our framework for energy policy analysis is an econometric model of inter-industry transactions for nine domestic industries. We have subdivided the business sector of the U.S. economy into nine industrial groups in order to provide for the detailed analysis of the impact of U.S. energy policy on the sectors most directly affected by policy changes. The nine sectors included in the model are:

1. Agriculture, nonfuel mining, and construction;
2. Manufacturing, excluding petroleum refining;
3. Transportation;
4. Communications, trade, and services;
5. Coal mining;
6. Crude petroleum and natural gas;
7. Petroleum refining;
8. Electric utilities;
9. Gas utilities.

Our inter-industry model includes a model of demand for inputs and supply of output for each of the nine industrial sectors. The model is closed by balance equations between demand and supply for the products of each of the nine sectors.

The principal innovation of our inter-industry model is that the input-output coefficients are treated as endogenous variables rather than exogenously given parameters. Our model for producer behavior determines the input-output coefficients for each of the nine sectors listed above as functions of the prices of products of all sectors, the prices of labor and capital services, and the prices of competing imports. We determine the prices of all nine products and the matrix of input-output coefficients simultaneously. In conventional input-output analysis the technology of each sector is taken as fixed at any point in time. Prices are determined as functions of the input-output coefficients, but the input-output coefficients themselves are treated as exogenously given parameters. Our approach integrates conventional input-output analysis with a determination of the structure of technology through models of supply for each industrial sector.

The second component of our framework for energy policy analysis is a macroeconometric growth model. The complete model consists of endogenous business and household sectors and exogenous foreign and government sectors. The chief novelty of our growth model is the integration of demand and supply conditions for consumption, investment, capital and labor. The model is made dynamic by links between investment and changes in capital stock and between capital service prices and changes in investment goods prices. The model determines both components of gross national product in real terms, generated by conventional macroeconometric models, and relative prices of labor and capital services required by our econometric model of inter-industry transactions.

Our approach to the analysis of macroeconomic activity can be contrasted with the analysis that underlies macroeconometric models used for short-term forecasting. Short-term forecasting is based on the projection of demand by foreign and government sectors and the determination of the responses of households and businesses in the form of demands for consumption and investment goods. The underlying economic theory is essentially the Keynesian multiplier, made dynamic by introducing lags in the responses of households and businesses to changes in income. In short-term macroeconometric models the supply side is frequently absent or present in only rudimentary form.[4] Our approach integrates the determinants of demand employed in conventional macroeconometric models with the determinants of supply; this integration is essential to the successful implementation of our inter-industry model.

Given a framework that incorporates the determinants of demand and supply for energy in the U.S. economy, our first objective is to provide a reference point for the analysis of energy policy by establishing detailed projections of demand and supply, price and cost, and imports and exports for each of the nine industrial sectors included in our model. For this purpose we project the level of activity in each industrial sector and relative prices for the products of all sectors for the years 1975–2000. Our projections include the level of macroeconomic activity in the U.S. economy and the matrix of input-output coefficients for each year. Projections for the five industrial sectors that form the energy sector of the U.S. economy provide the basis for translating our detailed projections into the energy balance framework that has become conventional in the analysis of patterns of energy utilization.[5]

Our inter-industry approach imposes the same consistency requirements as the energy balance approach, namely, that demand is equal to supply in physical terms for each type of energy. In addition, our approach requires that demand and supply are consistent with the same structure of energy prices. This additional consistency requirement is absent from energy balance projections and requires the integration of energy balance projections with projections of energy prices. Our inter-industry model provides a means of combining these projections within a framework that also includes prices and inter-industry transactions for the sectors that consume but do not produce energy.

To illustrate the application of our model to the analysis of U.S. energy policy we have analyzed the effects of tax policies to stimulate energy conservation on the future pattern of energy utilization. Our methodology for policy analysis begins with a set of projections that assume no major new departures in energy policy. We then prepare an alternative set of projections incorporating the proposed change in policy. In analyzing the impact of tax policy we have incorporated the effect of energy taxes on demand and supply for energy. We find that price increases provide the economic incentive for the adoption of energy conservation measures that will result in considerable savings of energy. Tax policies or other measures to increase the price of energy could result in U.S. independence from energy imports by 1985.

We present our model for inter-industry transactions in section 6.2 of the chapter. In section 6.3 we present econometric models of producer behavior for each of the nine sectors included in our inter-industry model. We then outline our macroeconometric growth model in section 6.4. In section 6.5 we present projections of economic activity and energy utilization for the period 1975–2000. In section 6.6 we discuss the methodology for analyzing energy policy. In section 6.7 we analyze the impact of alternative oil prices on the level and composition of energy policies for stimulating energy conservation and eliminating reliance of the U.S. economy on energy imports.

6.2   Inter-Industry Model

6.2.1   Introduction

The first component of our framework for energy policy analysis is a model of inter-industry transactions for the United States. Rather than analyzing energy utilization in isolation, we begin with an analysis of the entire U.S. economy and then proceed to a detailed examination of the energy sector as one among many interdependent components of the economy. This perspective is necessarily more complex and more detailed than traditional perspectives on the analysis of the energy sector, but is indipensable to the study of the interaction of energy resources and the growth of the U.S. economy.

Our inter-industry model permits the analysis of the entire chain of production from the purchase of primary inputs through the various intermediate stages of production to the emergence of final products to be absorbed in consumption, investment, government, or export final demand. The structure of production includes all of U.S. domestic supply of goods and services, but our specification provides for detailed analysis of the impact of U.S. energy policy on the sectors most directly affected by policy changes. We have classified production into nine industrial sectors, each of which purchases primary inputs, makes purchases from and sales to the other producing sectors, and sells finished output to final users. The flow of inter-industry transactions is represented in diagrammatic form in figure 6.1.

Our inter-industry model consists of balance equations between supply and demand for the products of each of the nine sectors included in the model. The model also includes accounting identities between the value of domestic availability of these products and the sum of values of intermediate input into each industry, value added in the industry, and imports of competing products. Demands for the products include demands for use as inputs by each of the nine sectors included in the model. The rest of domestic availability is allocated among four categories of final demand: personal consumption expenditures, gross private domestic investment, government expenditures, and exports.

In the model for projecting energy demand and supply we take the levels of final demand for all industries from the macroeconometric model presented in section 6.4 below. Second, for the five energy sectors of the model we take the price and quantity of imports to be exogenous. For the four nonenergy sectors we take the prices of imports as exogenous and determine import quantities along with the quantities of capital and labor services in each industry.[6] The prices of capital and labor services are determined within the macroeconometric model. We take the quantities of exports and government purchases of the output of each industry as exogenous. We also take the allocation of investment among the industries of origin to be exogenous.

Our inter-industry model consists of models of producer behavior for each of the nine industries included in the model. Producer behavior in each industry can be characterized by input-output coefficients for the input of products of each of the nine sectors, inputs of

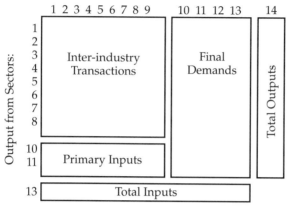

Input to Sectors:

INTERMEDIATE SECTORS:
1. Agriculture, nonfuel mining and construction
2. Manufacturing, excluding petroleum refining
3. Transportation
4. Communications, trade, services
5. Coal mining
6. Crude petroleum and natural gas
7. Petroleum refining
8. Electric utilities
9. Gas utilities

PRIMARY INPUTS, ROWS:
10. Imports
11. Capital services
11. Labor services

FINAL DEMAND, COLUMNS:
10. Personal consumption expenditures
11. Gross domestic private investment
12. Government purchases of goods and services
13. Exports

Figure 6.1
Inter-industry transactions: diagrammatic representation.

capital and labor services, and, for the four nonenergy sectors, the level of competitive imports. An inter-industry approach to the study of energy resources is essential since most energy is consumed as an intermediate rather than a final product of the economy. Examples of intermediate products would be fossil fuels consumed by the electric generating sector. Examples of final products would be gasoline and heating oil consumed by the household and government sectors.

Given the prices of domestic availability of the output of each sector included in our model, we determine the allocation of personal consumption expenditures among commodity groups distinguished in the model, using our model of consumer behavior. Personal consumption expenditures include deliveries to the household sector by eight of the nine sectors included in our inter-industry model of the producing sector. There are no direct deliveries of crude petroleum and natural gas to personal consumption expenditures. These products are delivered first to the petroleum refining and gas utility sectors and then to personal consumption expenditures and to other categories of intermediate and final demand.

Personal consumption expenditures also include noncompetitive imports and the services of dwellings and consumers' durables. The levels of personal consumption expenditures on each of the eleven commodity groups included in our model of the household sector are determined from the projected level of personal consumption expenditures from the macroeconometric model, from the prices of domestic availability of the output of each sector included in the inter-industry model, and from the prices of noncompetitive imports, consumers' durables services, and housing services. The price of noncompetitive imports is taken to be exogenous. The capital service prices for consumers' durables services and housing services are determined from the price of capital services determined in the macroeconometric model.

The equations representing the balance of demand and supply for each of the nine sectors of the inter-industry model set domestic availability equal to the sum of intermediate demands and final demand. Intermediate demands are determined simultaneously with the levels of output of each industry, given input-output coefficients determined in the model of producer behavior. The input-output coefficients are determined simultaneously with the prices of domestic availability of the output of each industry. Finally, levels of capital and labor services for all sectors and competitive imports for the four nonenergy sectors are determined from the levels of domestic availability and the corresponding input-output coefficients. These levels can be compared with the levels projected in the macroeconometric model.

6.2.2   Inter-Industry Transactions

We first describe our model of inter-industry transactions and then outline the application of this model to the projection of energy demand and supply. Our notation is as follows:

XIJ = intermediate demand for the output of industry I by industry J;
YI = final demand for the output of industry I;
XI = domestic availability of the output of industry I;
PI = price of the output of industry I.

To simplify the notation we take the price of the output of each industry to be the same in all uses. The deflators for each category of intermediate and final demand can differ. In projecting energy demand and supply we take the ratios of the deflator for the individual categories of demand to the deflator for domestic availability of output of the industry to be exogenous.

The inter-industry model consists of equality between demand and supply for each of the nine sectors included in the model. The balance equations for the nine sectors are

$$I = \sum_{J=1}^{9} XIJ + YI, \qquad I = 1, 2, \ldots, 9.$$

In addition, the model includes accounting identities between the value of domestic availability and the sum of values of intermediate input into the industry, value added in the industry, and, for the four nonenergy sectors, the imports of competing products,

$$PI * XI = \sum_{J=1}^{9} PJ * XJI + PK * KI + PL * LI + PRI * RI,$$

$$I = 1, 2, \ldots, 9,$$

where

KI = quantity of capital services in industry I;

LI = quantity of labor services in industry I;

RI = competitive imports of the output of industry I;

PK = price of capital services;

PL = price of labor services;

PRI = price of competitive imports of the output of industry I.

Again, prices of capital and labor services can differ among industries. To simplify notation we take the prices of these productive factors to be the same in all industries. In projecting energy demand and supply we take the ratios of service prices for each industry to the corresponding prices from the macroeconometric model to be exogenous.

Our inter-industry model includes models of producer behavior for each of the nine industrial sectors included in the model. These models of producer behavior can be derived from price possibility frontiers for the nine sectors,

$$AI * PI = GI(P1, P2, \ldots, P9; PK, PL, PRI), \quad I = 1, 2, \ldots, 9,$$

where AI ($I = 1, 2, \ldots 9$) is an index of Hicks-neutral technical efficiency in industry I. The price possibility frontier for each sector can be derived from price possibility frontiers for each of the three submodels employed in our analysis of production structure.[7] These submodels are:

(1) a model giving the price of output as a function of prices of four aggregate inputs in each sector-capital (K), labor (L), energy (E), and materials (M);

(2) a model giving the price of aggregate energy input in each sector as a function of the prices of the five types of energy included in the model-coal, crude petroleum and natural gas, refined petroleum products, electricity, and gas as a product of gas utilities;

(3) a model giving the price of aggregate nonenergy input in each sector as a function of the prices of the five types of nonenergy input into each sector—agriculture, manufacturing, transportation, communications, and, for the four nonenergy sectors, competitive imports.

Given the prices of capital services, labor services, and competitive imports in each of the four nonenergy sectors, we can determine the prices of domestic availability of output PI ($I = 1, 2, \ldots 9$) for all nine sectors. To determine these prices we solve twenty-seven equations for prices of domestic availability, prices of aggregate energy input, and prices of aggregate nonenergy input into all nine sectors. This system of twenty-seven equations consists of three equations for each sector. These three equations correspond to production possibility frontiers for each of the three submodels for each sector. In these computations we are making use of a nonsubstitution theorem of the type first discussed by Samuelson.[8] This theorem states that for given prices of the factors of production and competitive imports, the prices of domestic availability of the output of each sector are independent of the composition of final demand.

The second step in our analysis of inter-industry transactions is to derive input-output coefficients for each of the nine industrial sectors included in our inter-industry model. The input-output coefficients can be expressed as functions of the prices. First, the relative share of the Jth intermediate input can be determined from the identity:

$$\frac{\partial \ln PI}{\partial \ln PJ} = \frac{Pj * XJI}{PI * XI} = \frac{PJ}{PI} * AJI, \quad I, J = 1, 2, \ldots, 9,$$

where AJI is the input-output coefficient corresponding to XJI; it represents the input of the output of industry J per unit of output of industry I. Similar identities determine the relative shares of capital and labor services and competitive imports.[9]

Second, we can divide the relative shares by the ratio of the price of domestic availability of the output of the Jth industry, PJ, to the price for the Jth industry, PJ, to obtain the input-output coefficients,

$$XJI/XI = AJI(P1, P2, \ldots, P9; PK, PL, PRI), \quad I, J = 1, 2, \ldots, 9,$$

and

$$KI/XI = AKI(P1, P2, \ldots, P9; PK, PL, PRI),$$

$$LI/XI = ALI(P1, P2, \ldots, P9; PK, PL, PRI),$$

$$RI/XI = ARI(P1, P2, \ldots, P9; PK, PL, PRI), \quad I = 1, 2, \ldots, 9.$$

For each industry we derive the input-output coefficients in two steps: First, we determine the input-output coefficients for the aggregate inputs—capital (K), labor (L), energy (E), and materials (M). Second, we determine the input-output coefficients for the input of each type of energy input per unit of total energy input and the input of each type of nonenergy input per unit of total nonenergy input. To obtain the input-output coefficients required for our inter-industry model we multiply the input-output coefficients for each type of energy by the input-output coefficient for total energy. Similarly, we multiply the input-output coefficients for each type of nonenergy input by the input-output coefficient for total nonenergy input. We obtain input-output coefficients for capital services, labor services, five types of energy inputs into each sector and five types of nonenergy inputs into each sector.

The input-output coefficients for each of the nine industrial sectors included in our model of inter-industry transactions are functions of the prices of capital services, labor services, and competitive imports for the four nonenergy sectors and the prices of domestic availability of the output of each of the nine sectors. The prices of domestic availability are functions of the prices of capital services, labor services, and competitive imports for the four nonenergy sectors. By the nonsubstitution theorem both prices of domestic availability and input-output coefficients are independent of the composition of final demand.[10]

6.2.3   Final Demand

Final demand for domestic availability of the output of each of the nine sectors included in our inter-industry model is allocated among personal consumption expenditures, gross private domestic investment, government expenditures, and exports. In projecting energy demand and supply we take aggregate levels of each category of final demand from our macroeconomic projections. We allocate personal consumption expenditures among the nine sectors included in our model, employing aggregate personal consumption expenditures as total expenditures, on the basis of the prices of domestic availability of the output of all nine sectors. Government expenditures and exports of the output of each sector are exogenous. Imports of the output of the five energy sectors are also exogenous so that we include only exports net of imports in final demand for these sectors. We take aggregate private domestic investment from our macroeconomic projections. We take the relative proportion of investment in the output of each industrial sector included in our inter-industry model to be exogenous.

The final step in determining the level and composition of inter-industry transactions is to determine the levels of output, employment, and utilization of capital for each of the nine industrial sectors included in our model and competitive imports for the four nonenergy sectors included in the model. This part of our model coincides with conventional input-output analysis. Given the input-output coefficients for all nine sectors, we can determine the level of output for each sector for any given levels of final demand for the output of all nine sectors. We present projected matrices of inter-industry transactions in energy for the years 1975, 1985, and 2000 in summary form in section 6.5 below. We also present projections of energy prices for each year.

Final demand for domestic availability of the output of each of the nine sectors included in the model is allocated among personal consumption, investment, government expenditures, and exports.

$$YI = CI + II + GI + ZI, \quad I = 1, 2, \ldots, 9,$$

where

$CI =$ personal consumption expenditures on the output of industry I;

$II =$ gross private domestic investment in the output of industry I (the sum of gross private fixed investment and net inventory change);

$GI =$ government expenditure on the output of industry I;

$ZI =$ exports of the output of industry I (exports less imports for the five energy sectors).

In our model for projecting energy demand and supply we take the levels of final demand for all industries from the macroeconomic projections. We link our inter-industry model to our macroeconometric model through the identities,

$$PC * C = \sum_{I=1}^{9} PI * CI,$$

$$PI * I = \sum_{I=1}^{9} PI * II,$$

$$PG * G = \sum_{I=1}^{9} PI * GI,$$

$$PZ * Z = \sum_{I=1}^{9} PI * ZI.$$

The values of personal consumption expenditures $PC * C$, gross private domestic investment $PI * I$, government expenditures $PG * G$, and exports $PZ * Z$ from the macroeconometric model are set equal to the sums of each of these categories of expenditures over all nine industries included in the inter-industry model.

In the macroeconometric model government expenditures on goods and services are divided into two parts,

$$PG * G = PIG * IG + PCG * CG,$$

where

IG = quantity of government expenditures on investment goods;

CG = quantity of government expenditures on consumption goods;

PIG = price of government expenditures on investment goods;

PCG = price of government expenditures on consumption goods.

In making projections of energy demand and supply we project total government expenditures in current and constant prices. Government expenditures on goods and services are exogenous to the macroeconometric model. We then allocate total government expenditures among the nine industry groups included in the inter-industry model.

In our macroeconometric model net exports of goods and services are taken to be exogenous. For the purposes of projecting energy demand and supply we divide net exports between imports and exports, allocate exports among the nine industry groups included in the model, and project the prices of competitive imports for each of the nine sectors of the model. Since net exports in current and constant prices are exogenous to the macroeconometric model, this change in the treatment of net exports does not alter the structure of the complete model. In projecting energy demand and supply we take the prices of imports for each industrial sector together with prices of capital services for each sector as given.

We project gross private domestic investment in current and constant prices in our macroeconometric model. To project energy demand and supply we allocate gross private domestic investment among the nine industry groups included in the model. The relative proportions of investment originating in each sector are taken to be exogenous. In a completely dynamic model the allocation of investment by sector of origin and sector of destination would be endogenous. Our macroeconometric model incorporates the dynamics of saving and investment only in the projection of total investment. The allocation of capital by sector of destination is endogenously determined, but the allocation of investment by sector of origin is exogenous.

The final step in determining final demand for the domestic availability of the output of each sector included in our inter-industry model is to allocate personal consumption expenditures among the products of the nine sectors included in the model and expenditures on noncompetitive imports and the services of consumers' durables, which are not included among the products of the nine sectors. For this purpose we employ an econometric model of consumer behavior.

This model is based on an indirect utility function that can be represented in the form[11]

$$\ln V = \ln V\left(\frac{P1}{PC * C}, \frac{P2}{PC * C}, \ldots, \frac{P11}{PC * C}\right),$$

where V is the level of utility, PI is the price of the Ith commodity, and $PC * C$ is total personal consumption expenditures. There are eleven commodity groups included in our model of consumer behavior: one for each of the nine industrial sectors, excluding crude petroleum and natural gas, housing, services of consumers' durables and noncompetitive imports.

For each commodity group we take the budget share to be fixed. This assumption corresponds to a linear logarithmic indirect utility function. The quantity demanded for each of the eleven commodity groups included in our model of consumer behavior is a function of the prices of the corresponding commodity group and the level of total personal consumption expenditures. We determine the level of total personal consumption expenditures in our macroeconometric model. We determine the prices of domestic availability of the output of each sector in the inter-industry model from our models of producer behavior. Given total expenditures and the prices, we can determine the quantities demanded of the output of each sector of the model for personal consumption expenditures.

Final demand for all nine industrial sectors included in our inter-industry model is the sum of final demands for personal consumption expenditures, gross private domestic investment, government expenditures, and exports. We add personal consumption expenditures for the output of communications, trade and services, less housing, to personal consumption expenditures for housing to obtain personal consumption expenditures on communications, trade and services. Otherwise, there is a direct correspondence between commodity groups in our model of consumer behavior and the sectors included in our inter-industry model. Given all final demands, the prices of domestic availability of the output of each sector and the matrix of input-output coefficients, we can determine the matrix of inter-industry transactions in both current and constant prices.

The equations representing the balance of demand and supply for each of the nine industrial sectors included in our inter-industry model can be represented in the form

$$XJ = \sum_{J=1}^{9} XIJ + YI \,,$$

$$= \sum_{J=1}^{9} AIJ * XJ + CI + II + GI + ZI \,, \quad I = 1, 2, \ldots, 9 \,.$$

The input-output coefficients $\{AIJ\}$ are determined together with the prices of domestic availability of the output of each industry $\{PI\}$. Given prices and the level of aggregate personal consumption expenditures, the levels of personal consumption expenditures $\{CI\}$ are determined. The remaining components of final demand $\{II, GI, ZI\}$ are projected by industry of origin. These projections are consistent with levels of gross private domestic investment, government expenditures and exports from our macroeconometric model.

In matrix form the demand and supply balance equation for the model can be represented as

$$x = Ax + y$$

where x and y are vectors of outputs and final demands,

$$x = \begin{bmatrix} X1 \\ X2 \\ \vdots \\ X9 \end{bmatrix} \text{ and } y = \begin{bmatrix} Y1 \\ Y2 \\ \vdots \\ Y9 \end{bmatrix}.$$

and A is the matrix of input-output coefficients,

$$A = \begin{bmatrix} A11 & A12 & \ldots & A19 \\ A21 & A22 & \ldots & A29 \\ \vdots & \vdots & & \vdots \\ A91 & A92 & & A99 \end{bmatrix}.$$

Levels of domestic availability of the output of each sector are obtained by solving this system of equations,

$$x = (I - A)^{-1} y \,.$$

Levels of capital and labor services and competitive imports are determined from the levels of domestic availability and the corresponding input-output coefficients,

$KI = AKI * XI$,

$LI = ALI * XI$,

$RI = ARI * XI$, $I = 1, 2, \ldots, 9$.

The input-output coefficients for capital and labor services and competitive imports are functions of the prices of the outputs of the nine sectors included in our inter-industry model, the prices of capital and labor services and the prices of competitive imports for the four nonenergy sectors of the model. Our complete econometric model for inter-industry transactions is presented in diagrammatic form in figure 6.2.

The model solution, at this point, consists of the simultaneous determination of the pattern of economic interactions that results from a given specification of the economic environment. The behavior of the energy sectors is one component of this determination. The simulated performance of the energy sectors reflects not only the characteristics of these sectors *per se*, but also their interrelationships with the rest of the economic system. In short, the model solution already contains a simulated picture of the energy characteristics of the U.S. economy. It only remains to express these characteristics in terms of physical units rather than dollar flows. This transformation is performed in the final segment of the inter-industry energy model.

Fuel prices are part of the solution of the inter-industry model, although these prices are expressed in terms of price indices. The conversion from price indices to dollar prices is simply a matter of scaling. Thus, as the price of each fuel is known relative to its price in 1971, the multiplication of these price indices by the actual 1971 dollar price gives the simulated price in terms of dollars per physical unit. Analogously, fuel outputs are simulated in terms of 1971 dollars so, by multiplying these by the number of physical units of fuel that could be purchased for one dollar in 1971, the output of each fuel can be reexpressed in physical units-tons of coal, barrels of petroleum, kilowatt hours of electricity, and cubic feet of gas.

The inter-industry model also simulates the flow of fuels into each intermediate production and final use sector. This information is in 1971 dollars, so it remains to reexpress it in terms of flows of British Thermal Units of energy. These Btu flows can be found by multiplying each transaction by the Btu per $1971 ratio found from 1971 data. In this way a five by thirteen matrix of energy flows can be found, i.e., energy flows from the five supplying sectors—coal, petroleum,

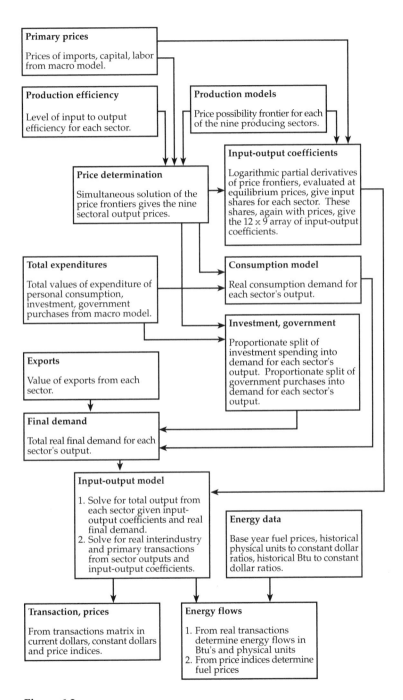

Figure 6.2
Inter-industry econometric model: diagrammatic representation.

electricity, gas and fuel imports—into the thirteen energy-using sectors. In addition, as a final step, the output format can be brought into line with the Department of Interior energy balance system: our thirteen-way classification can be aggregated into a four-way classification in which the energy-consuming sectors are classified into industrial, household and commercial, transportation, and electricity generation sectors.

6.3   Producer Behavior

6.3.1   Introduction

Our inter-industry model includes econometric models of producer behavior for each of the nine industrial sectors included in the model.[12] In implementing an econometric model of producer behavior for each sector our primary objective is to explore the interrelationships between relative demand for energy and relative demand for capital services, labor services, and nonenergy inputs. Similarly, we wish to explore the interrelationships among relative demands for the five types of energy included in our model—coal, crude petroleum and natural gas, refined petroleum products, electricity and gas as a product of gas utilities. We have imposed a structure on the price possibility frontier that permits us to deal with relative demand for energy as a whole and relative demands for the five types of energy included in our model as two separate problems.

To construct a model of the interrelationship of relative demands for energy, capital services, labor services, and nonenergy inputs, we first define groups of inputs that are aggregates of the twelve inputs included in our model of inter-industry production structure. These commodity groups are:

(1) Capital (K)

(2) Labor (L)

(3) Energy (E). This group consists of inputs of coal, crude petroleum and natural gas, refined petroleum products, electricity, and gas as a product of gas utilities.

(4) Materials (M). This group consists of inputs of agriculture, manufacturing, transportation, communications, trade and services, and competitive imports for the nonenergy sectors.

We first construct a model for producer behavior in terms of the four aggregates—capital, labor, energy, and materials. We represent the price of domestic availability of the output of each sector as a function of the prices of each of the aggregates. A sufficient condition for the price possibility frontier to be defined on the prices of the four aggregates is that the overall price possibility frontier is separable and homogenous in the inputs within each aggregate.[13] The price possibility frontier is separable in the commodities within an aggregate if and only if the ratio of the relative shares of any two commodities within an aggregate is independent of the prices of commodities outside the aggregate.[14] For example, the five types of energy make up an appropriate aggregate if the relative value shares of any two types of energy depend only on the prices of energy and not on the prices of nonenergy intermediate inputs or the prices of capital and labor services.

The second step in constructing a model of producer behavior is to represent the price possibility frontier for the energy and materials aggregates as functions of the prices of inputs that make up each of the aggregates. For the energy aggregate the price of energy is represented as a function of the prices of the five types of energy that make up the aggregate—coal, crude petroleum and natural gas, refined petroleum products, electricity, and gas as a product of gas utilities. For the materials aggregate the price of materials is represented as a function of the five types of inputs that make up the aggregate—agriculture, manufacturing, transportation, communications, trade, and services, and competitive imports for the nonenergy sectors.

6.3.2 Econometric Specification

The system of relative demand functions employed in our econometric model of producer behavior for each of the nine industrial sectors of our model is generated from the price possibility frontier for the corresponding sector. For each of the three submodels that make up our model of producer behavior we represent the price possibility frontier by a function that is quadratic in the logarithms of the prices of the inputs into the sector. The resulting price possibility frontier provides a local second-order approximation to any price possibility frontier. We refer to our representation as the transcendental logarithmic price possibility frontier or, more simply, the *translog price possibility frontier*. The price possibility frontier is a transcendental function of the logarithms of the prices of inputs. The translog price possibility frontier was introduced by Christensen, Jorgenson, and Lau (1971).

As an example, the price possibility frontier for the aggregate (KLEM) submodel takes the form

$$\ln AI + \ln PI = \alpha_0^I + \alpha_K^I \ln PK + \alpha_L^I \ln PL + \alpha_E^I \ln PE + \alpha_M^I \ln PM$$
$$+ \frac{1}{2} [\beta_{KK}^I (\ln PK)^2 + \beta_{KL}^I \ln PK \ln PL + \cdots],$$

where PK is the price of capital services, PL the price of labor services, PE the price of energy, and PM the price of materials. For this form of the price possibility frontier, the equations for the relative shares of the four input aggregates take the form

$$(PK * KI)/(PI * XI)$$
$$= \alpha_K^I + \beta_{KK}^I \ln PK + \beta_{KL}^I \ln PL + \beta_{KE}^I \ln PE + \beta_{KM}^I \ln PM,$$
$$(PL * LI)/(PI * XI)$$
$$= \alpha_L^I + \beta_{LK}^I \ln PK + \beta_{LL}^I \ln PL + \beta_{LE}^I \ln PE + \beta_{LM}^I \ln PM,$$
$$(PE * EI)/(PI * XI)$$
$$= \alpha_E^I + \beta_{EK}^I \ln PK + \beta_{EL}^I \ln PL + \beta_{EE}^I \ln PE + \beta_{EM}^I \ln PM,$$
$$(PM * MI)/(PI * XI)$$
$$= \alpha_M^I + \beta_{MK}^I \ln PK + \beta_{ML}^I \ln PL + \beta_{ME}^I \ln PE + \beta_{MM}^I \ln PM,$$
$$I = 1, 2, \ldots, 9,$$

where KI is the quantity of capital services in the Ith sector, LI the quantity of labor services, EI the quantity of energy input, and MI the quantity of materials input.[15]

The dependent variable in each of the four functions generated from the translog price possibility frontier is the relative share of the corresponding input. To derive the input-output coefficient for that input, we divide the relative share by the ratio of the price of the input to the price of the output of the sector. For example, the input-output coefficients for capital services are

$$AKI = KI/XI,$$
$$= (\alpha_K^I + \beta_{KK}^I \ln PK + \beta_{KL}^I \ln PL + \beta_{KE}^I \ln PE$$
$$+ \beta_{KM}^I \ln PM)/(PK/PI), \quad I = 1, 2, \ldots, 9.$$

Similar expressions can be obtained for the input-output coefficients for labor services, energy, and materials.

The value of domestic availability of the output of each sector is equal to the sum of the values of capital and labor services in that sector and the value of energy and nonenergy inputs into the sector,

$$PI * XI = PK * KI + PL * LI + PE * EI + PM * MI , \quad I = 1, 2, \ldots, 9.$$

Given this accounting identity, the relative shares of the four aggregate inputs into each sector add to unity. The parameters of the four relative demand functions for capital and labor services and energy and nonenergy inputs must satisfy the restrictions,

$$\alpha_K^I + \alpha_L^I + \alpha_E^I + \alpha_M^I = 1 ,$$

$$\beta_{KK}^I + \beta_{LK}^I + \beta_{EK}^I + \beta_{MK}^I = 0 ,$$

$$\beta_{KL}^I + \beta_{LL}^I + \beta_{EL}^I + \beta_{ML}^I = 0 ,$$

$$\beta_{KE}^i + \beta_{LE}^I + \beta_{EE}^I + \beta_{ME}^I = 0 ,$$

$$\beta_{KM}^I + \beta_{LM}^I + \beta_{EM}^I + \beta_{MM}^I = 0 , \quad I = 1, 2, \ldots, 9.$$

Given estimates of the parameters of any three equations for the relative shares, estimates of the parameters of the fourth equation can be determined from these restrictions.

The logarithm of the price possibility frontier for each sector is twice differentiable in the logarithms of the prices of inputs, so that the Hessian of this function is symmetric. This gives rise to a set of restrictions relating the parameters of cross-partial derivatives. For the aggregate (KLEM) submodel three of these restrictions are explicit in the three equations we estimate directly, namely,

$$\beta_{KL}^I = \beta_{LK}^I ,$$

$$\beta_{KE}^I = \beta_{EK}^I ,$$

$$\beta_{LE}^I = \beta_{EL}^I , \quad I = 1, 2, \ldots, 9.$$

In addition, we estimate the parameters β_{MK}^I, β_{ML}^I, and β_{ME}^I $(I = 1, 2, \ldots, 9)$ from

$$\beta_{MK}^I = -\beta_{KK}^I - \beta_{LK}^I - \beta_{EK}^I,$$

$$\beta_{ML}^I = -\beta_{KL}^I - \beta_{LL}^I - \beta_{EL}^I,$$

$$\beta_{ME}^I = -\beta_{KE}^I - \beta_{LE}^I - \beta_{EE}^I, \qquad I = 1, 2, \ldots, 9,$$

so that three additional symmetry restrictions are implicit in the equations we estimate, namely,

$$\beta_{KM}^I = \beta_{MK}^I,$$

$$\beta_{LM}^I = \beta_{ML}^I,$$

$$\beta_{EM}^I = \beta_{ME}^I, \qquad I = 1, 2, \ldots, 9.$$

For each of the nine industrial sectors, the aggregate (KLEM) submodel involves six symmetry restrictions.

The price possibility frontier for each sector is homogeneous of degree one; proportional changes in the prices of all inputs result in a proportional change in the price of output. Homogeneity of the price possibility frontier is implied by the symmetry restrictions outlined above and the restrictions implied by the accounting identity between the value of output and the value of input. In the absence of the symmetry restrictions and the restrictions implied by the accounting identity between the value of output and the value of input, the aggregate (KLEM) submodel involves twenty unknown parameters. Taking these restrictions into account, we reduce the number of unknown parameters to nine.

We have presented (KLEM) submodel of our model of producer behavior in detail. The forms of the energy (E) and materials (M) submodels are analogous to the form of the aggregate submodel. For the energy submodel we can write the translog price possibility frontier in the form

$$\ln PE = \alpha_0^{EI} + \alpha_1^{EI} \ln PE1 + \alpha_2^{EI} \ln PE2 + \alpha_3^{EI} \ln PE3 + \alpha_4^{EI} \ln PE4$$

$$+ \alpha_5^{EI} \ln PE5$$

$$+ \frac{1}{2} [\beta_{11}^{EI}(\ln PE1)^2 + \beta_{12}^{EI} \ln PE1 \ln PE2 + \cdots], \qquad I = 1, 2, \ldots, 9,$$

where $PE1$ is the price of coal, $PE2$ the price of crude petroleum and natural gas, $PE3$ the price of refined petroleum products, $PE4$ the price of electricity, and $PE5$ the price of gas as a product of gas utilities. Similarly, we can write the translog price possibility frontier for the materials submodel in the form

$$\ln PM = \alpha_0^{MI} + \alpha_1^{MI} \ln PM1 + \alpha_2^{MI} \ln PM2 + \alpha_3^{MI} \ln PM3 + \alpha_4^{MI} \ln PM4$$
$$+ \alpha_5^{MI} \ln PM5$$
$$+ \frac{1}{2} [\beta_{11}^{EI}(\ln PM1)^2 + \beta_{12}^{EI} \ln PM1 \ln PM2 + \cdots], \quad I = 1, 2, \ldots, 9,$$

where $PM1$ is the price of agriculture, nonfuel mining, and construction, $PM2$ the price of manufacturing, excluding petroleum refining, $PM3$ the price of transportation, $PM4$ the price of communications, trade and services, and $PM5$ the price of competitive imports.

For both energy (E) and materials (M) submodels we can derive a system of five equations for determining the relative shares of the five commodity groups making up each submodel. Each equation gives the relative share of one of the commodity groups as a function of the prices of all five groups included in the submodel. We can derive the relative demand functions for each commodity group by dividing the relative value share of the group by the ratio of the price of that group to the price of the corresponding aggregate. For example, to derive the demand for coal relative to total energy we divide the relative value share of coal by the ratio of the price of coal to the price of total energy. We can derive the input-output coefficient for coal by multiplying the demand for coal relative to total energy by the demand for energy relative to the output of the corresponding industrial sector.

The value of each aggregate is equal to the sum of the values of the commodity groups that make up that aggregate. For example, the value of energy is equal to the sum of the values of each of the five types of energy,

$$PE * EI = PE1 * E1I + PE2 * E2I + PE3 * E3I + PE4 * E4I + PE5 * E5I,$$
$$I = 1, 2, \ldots, 9,$$

where $E1I$ is the quantity of coal, $E2I$ the quantity of crude petroleum and natural gas, $E3I$ the quantity of refined petroleum products, $E4I$ the quantity of electricity, and $E5I$ the quantity of gas as a product of gas utilities. As before, the relative shares of the five energy inputs add to unity, so that the parameters of the five relative demand functions for these inputs must satisfy restrictions analogous to the restrictions given above for the parameters of the aggregate (KLEM) submodel. Similar restrictions hold for the five relative demand functions for nonenergy inputs.

6.3.3   Parameter Estimation

For each of the nine industrial sectors included in our inter-industry
model of production structure the aggregate (KLEM) submodel consists of four equations. We fit the three equations for relative shares of
capital (K), labor (L), and energy (E). The relative shares of materials
(M) can be determined from these three equations and the accounting
identity between the value of output and the value of input. Taking
into account the symmetry restrictions on the parameters of the three
equations of the aggregate (KLEM) submodel, the number of
unknown parameters to be estimated is reduced to nine. Taking convexity restrictions into account where appropriate, we further reduce
the number of unknown parameters.[16]

For four of the industrial sectors included in our inter-industry
model the energy (E) submodel consists of five equations for the relative shares of coal, crude petroleum and natural gas, refined
petroleum products, electricity, and gas as a product of gas utilities.
These four sectors are:

(1) Agriculture, nonfuel mining, and construction.

(2) Manufacturing, excluding petroleum refining.

(4) Communications, trade, and services.

(7) Petroleum refining.

For these industrial sectors we fit the four equations for relative shares
of coal, crude petroleum and natural gas, refined petroleum products,
and electricity. The relative share of gas as a product of gas utilities
can be determined from these four equations and the accounting identity between the total value of energy and the sum of the values of the
five types of energy.

For the four industrial sectors listed above the energy (E) submodel
involves six symmetry restrictions in the four equations we estimate
directly and four additional restrictions that are implicit in these equations and the accounting identity for the total value of energy. In the
absence of these restrictions and the restrictions implied by the
accounting identity, the energy (E) submodel for the four industrial
sectors involves thirty unknown parameters. Taking these restrictions
into account, we reduce the number of unknown parameters to fourteen.

For four of the industrial sectors included in our inter-industry
model the energy (E) submodel consists of four equations for relative

shares of four types of energy. For transportation, coal mining, and electric utilities the relative share of crude petroleum and natural gas is zero. For gas utilities the relative share of electricity is zero. For these four sectors the form of energy (E) submodel is analogous to the form of the aggregate (KLEM) submodel. We fit three equations for the relative shares of three types of energy, excluding the equation for the relative share of gas as a product of gas utilities. The relative share of gas can be determined from the accounting identity for the total value of energy. We fit these three equations subject to symmetry restrictions so that the number of unknown parameters is reduced to nine.

For crude petroleum and natural gas sector of our inter-industry model the energy (E) submodel consists of three equations for relative shares of three types of energy. For this sector the relative shares of coal and gas as an output of gas utilities are equal to zero. We fit two equations for the relative shares of crude petroleum and natural gas and refined petroleum products. The relative share of electricity can be determined from the accounting identity for the total value of energy. Fitting these equations subject to symmetry restrictions, we reduce the number of unknown parameters to five.

For the four nonenergy sectors included in our inter-industry model the materials (M) submodel consists of five equations for the relative shares of agriculture, manufacturing, transportation, communications, and competitive imports. The five energy sectors the materials submodel consists of four equations for the relative shares of agriculture, manufacturing, transportation, and communications. The form of the materials (M) submodel for the four nonenergy sectors, is analogous to the form of the energy (E) submodel with five equations for the relative shares of five types of energy. For these sectors we fit four equations for the relative shares of nonenergy inputs, excluding competitive imports. The relative shares of competitive imports can be determined from these four equations and the accounting identity between the total value of materials and the sum of the values of the five types of nonenergy inputs. Each of these submodels involves fourteen unknown parameters.

For the five nonenergy sectors we fit three equations for the relative shares of nonenergy inputs, excluding inputs of communications, trade and services. The materials (M) submodels for these sectors are analogous to the aggregate (KLEM) submodel and involve nine unknown parameters.

For each of the nine industrial sectors included in our inter-industry model of production all three submodels-aggregate (KLEM), energy (E), and materials (M)—have been fitted to annual data on inter-industry transactions, capital and labor services, and competitive imports for the period 1947–1971.[17] Our method of estimation is the minimum distance estimator for nonlinear simultaneous equations, treating the prices of competitive imports as exogenous variables.[18] For each of these submodels the system of equations is nonlinear in the variables but linear in the parameters.

In tables 6.1–6.3 we present estimates of the parameters of the translog price possibility frontier for each of the three submodels of our econometric model of producer behavior for all nine industrial sectors. For the convenience of the reader we list again the nine sectors:

(1) Agriculture, nonfuel mining, and construction.

(2) Manufacturing, excluding petroleum refining.

(3) Transportation.

(4) Communications, trade, and services.

(5) Coal mining.

(6) Crude petroleum and natural gas.

(7) Petroleum refining.

(8) Electric utilities.

(9) Gas utilities.

Table 6.1 contains estimates of the parameters of the translog price possibility frontier for the aggregate submodel. The aggregate price possibility frontier is defined on the prices of capital (K), labor (L), energy (E), and materials (M). For each of the nine industrial sectors the parameters of the aggregate submodel are estimated from a system of three equations. The dependent variables in these equations are the relative shares of capital, labor, and energy in the value of total output. Parameters in the equation for the relative share of materials are estimated from the restrictions implied by the accounting identity between the value of output and the value of input. We employ constraints across the equations arising from symmetry restrictions on the price possibility frontier for each sector, reducing the number of parameters to be estimated to nine. We also employ convexity restrictions, where appropriate, further reducing the number of parameters to be estimated.

Table 6.1
Estimates of the parameters of the translog price possibility frontier for the aggregate (KLEM) submodel for nine industrial sectors of the U.S. economy; 1947–1971

Parameter	Sectors								
	1	2	3	4	5	6	7	8	9
α_K^I	0.1785	0.1149	0.1799	0.2994	0.1277	0.5616	0.0753	0.3458	0.3206
α_L^I	0.2354	0.2940	0.4096	0.4171	0.4139	0.0838	0.1162	0.1925	0.1008
α_E^I	0.0244	0.0202	0.0380	0.0182	0.1857	0.0947	0.5490	0.2120	0.4895
α_M^I	0.5616	0.5708	0.3726	0.2653	0.2727	0.2599	0.2595	0.2496	0.0891
α_{KK}^I	0.0851	0.5790	0.1018	0.0595	0.0280	0.2462	0.0402	0.1330	0.1224
α_{KL}^I	-0.0366	0.0030	-0.0601	0.0114	-0.0357	-0.0470	0.0620	0.0288	0.0179
α_{KE}^I	-0.0052	-0.0055	-0.0137	0.0011	0.0099	-0.0532	-0.0706	-0.1682	-0.0975
α_{KM}^I	-0.0434	-0.0565	-0.0280	-0.0719	-0.0022	-0.1460	-0.0316	0.0064	-0.0429
α_{LL}^I	0.0287	0.0737	0.0582	0.0848	-0.0751	0.0655	-0.0674	-0.0968	0.0642
α_{LE}^I	0.0023	0.0054	-0.0180	0.0098	0.1145	0.0284	0.0066	0.0239	-0.0806
α_{LM}^I	0.0056	-0.0821	0.0199	-0.1059	-0.0037	-0.0469	-0.0012	0.0441	-0.0015
α_{EE}^I	0.0072	0.0188	0.0198	0.0020	0.0087	-0.0319	0.1846	0.0638	0.2128
α_{EM}^I	-0.0044	-0.0187	0.0119	-0.0129	-0.1332	0.0566	-0.1205	0.0805	-0.0347
α_{MM}^I	0.0422	0.1573	-0.0038	0.1907	0.1392	0.1362	0.1533	-0.1311	0.0790

Table 6.2
Estimates of the parameters of the translog price possibility frontier for the energy (E) submodel for nine industrial sectors of the U.S. economy; 1947–1971

Parameter	Sectors								
	1	2	3	4	5	6	7	8	9
α_1^{EI}	0.0053	0.2040	0.0799	0.1142	0.8510	0.0000	0.0021	0.3165	0.0068
α_2^{EI}	0.0021	0.0002	0.0000	0.0111	0.0000	0.8885	0.8475	0.0000	0.3958
α_3^{EI}	0.8389	0.3384	0.8107	0.3520	0.0400	0.0365	0.1180	0.1173	0.0190
α_4^{EI}	0.1212	0.2858	0.0406	0.4136	0.1062	0.0750	0.0057	0.3829	0.0000
α_5^{EI}	0.0325	0.1716	0.0688	0.1091	0.0029	0.0000	0.0267	0.1829	0.5785
β_{11}^{EI}	0.0052	0.1624	0.0735	0.1011	−0.0118	0.0000	0.0017	0.0762	0.0068
β_{12}^{EI}	0.0000	0.0000	0.0000	−0.0013	0.0000	0.0000	−0.0095	0.0000	−0.0027
β_{13}^{EI}	−0.0068	−0.0690	−0.0648	−0.0402	0.0220	0.0000	0.0067	0.0833	−0.0001
β_{14}^{EI}	0.0011	−0.0583	−0.0032	−0.0472	−0.0100	0.0000	0.0009	−0.0578	0.0000
β_{15}^{EI}	0.0005	−0.0350	−0.0055	−0.0125	−0.0002	0.0000	0.0003	−0.1017	−0.0040
β_{22}^{EI}	0.0010	−0.0029	0.0000	0.0110	0.0000	0.0239	−0.0254	0.0000	0.0557
β_{23}^{EI}	0.0007	−0.0001	0.0000	−0.0039	0.0000	−0.0249	0.0389	0.0000	−0.0075
β_{24}^{EI}	−0.0007	0.0073	0.0000	−0.0046	0.0000	0.0010	0.0126	0.0000	0.0000
β_{25}^{EI}	−0.0010	−0.0043	0.0000	−0.0012	0.0000	0.0000	−0.0165	0.0000	−0.0455
β_{33}^{EI}	−0.0252	0.2239	0.1534	0.2281	−0.0287	−0.0232	−0.0206	0.0001	0.0186
β_{34}^{EI}	0.0128	−0.0967	−0.0329	−0.1456	0.0064	0.0481	−0.0164	−0.0966	0.0000
β_{35}^{EI}	0.1854	−0.0581	−0.0557	−0.0384	0.0003	0.0000	−0.0086	0.0162	−0.0110
β_{44}^{EI}	−0.0410	0.1868	0.0389	0.2425	0.0055	−0.0490	0.0038	0.2077	0.0000
β_{45}^{EI}	0.0278	−0.0390	−0.0028	−0.0451	−0.0019	0.0000	−0.0008	−0.0502	0.0000
β_{55}^{EI}	−0.0458	0.1364	0.0640	0.0972	0.0018	0.0000	0.0257	0.1357	0.0604

Table 6.3
Estimates of the parameters of the translog price possibility frontier for the materials (M) submodel for nine industrial sectors of the U.S. economy; 1947–1971

Parameter	Sectors								
	1	2	3	4	5	6	7	8	9
α_1^{MI}	0.2578	0.1348	0.1221	0.0819	0.0193	0.0738	0.0448	0.1134	0.0909
α_2^{MI}	0.3777	0.5933	0.1373	0.2548	0.4270	0.1464	0.2131	0.1046	0.1408
α_3^{MI}	0.0653	0.0472	0.1932	0.0532	0.0675	0.0894	0.2289	0.1200	0.0940
α_4^{MI}	0.2674	0.1643	0.4382	0.5774	0.4839	0.6904	0.5132	0.6620	0.6743
α_5^{MI}	0.0318	0.0603	0.1091	0.0327	0.0023	0.0000	0.0000	0.0000	0.0000
β_{11}^{MI}	0.0799	0.0376	0.1072	-0.0454	0.0190	-0.0557	-0.0165	0.0170	-0.0752
β_{12}^{MI}	-0.1012	-0.0200	-0.0168	0.0848	-0.0083	0.1098	0.0483	0.0755	0.1850
β_{13}^{MI}	0.0629	0.0043	-0.2360	-0.0094	-0.0013	-0.0255	0.0005	-0.0292	-0.0192
β_{14}^{MI}	-0.0672	-0.0571	-0.0535	-0.0806	-0.0094	-0.0286	-0.0323	-0.0633	-0.0906
β_{15}^{MI}	0.0256	0.0352	-0.0133	0.0506	-0.0000	0.0000	0.0000	0.0000	0.0000
β_{22}^{MI}	0.2349	0.1958	0.1185	0.0973	0.2447	0.0077	0.1113	0.0023	-0.1416
β_{23}^{MI}	-0.0219	-0.0361	-0.0265	-0.0091	-0.0288	0.0053	-0.0592	0.0037	0.0455
β_{24}^{MI}	-0.1009	-0.0710	-0.0602	-0.1179	-0.2066	-0.1228	-0.1003	-0.0815	-0.0889
β_{25}^{MI}	-0.0109	-0.0687	-0.0150	-0.0550	-0.0010	0.0000	0.0000	0.0000	0.0000
β_{33}^{MI}	0.0039	0.0435	0.1559	0.0502	0.0629	-0.0418	0.0680	0.1027	-0.0553
β_{34}^{MI}	-0.0187	-0.0030	-0.0847	-0.0321	-0.0327	0.0620	-0.0092	-0.0773	0.0289
β_{35}^{MI}	-0.0263	-0.0087	-0.0211	0.0005	-0.0002	0.0000	0.0000	0.0000	0.0000
β_{44}^{MI}	0.1959	0.1218	0.2462	0.2348	0.2497	0.0894	0.1418	0.2221	0.1505
β_{45}^{MI}	-0.0090	0.0093	-0.0478	-0.0042	-0.0011	0.0000	0.0000	0.0000	0.0000
β_{55}^{MI}	0.0206	0.0329	0.0972	0.0081	0.0023	0.0000	0.0000	0.0000	0.0000

Table 6.2 contains estimates of the parameters of the translog price possibility frontier for the energy (E) submodel. The energy price possibility frontier gives the price of energy for each sector as a function of the prices of five types of energy inputs. The five types of energy are:

1. Coal.
2. Crude petroleum and natural gas.
3. Refined petroleum products.
4. Electricity.
5. Gas as a product of gas utilities.

For each of the nine industrial sectors the parameters of the energy submodel are estimated from a system containing as many as four equations. The dependent variables in these equations are the relative shares of each type of energy in the total value of energy. We employ the restrictions implied by the accounting identity between the total value of energy and the sum of the values of all types of energy, the symmetry restrictions, and, where appropriate, convexity restrictions in reducing the number of parameters to be estimated.

Finally, table 6.3 contains estimates of the parameters of the translog price possibility frontier for the materials (M) submodel. For the four nonenergy sectors the materials price possibility frontier is defined on the prices of the five types of nonenergy inputs:

1. Agriculture, nonfuel mining, and construction.
2. Manufacturing, excluding petroleum refining.
3. Transportation.
4. Communications, trade, and services.
5. Competitive imports.

For the five energy sectors the materials price possibility frontier is defined on the prices of four types of nonenergy inputs, excluding competitive imports. The dependent variables are relative shares of each type of nonenergy input. We employ restrictions on the parameters that are analogous to the restrictions used for the energy submodel.

6.4   Growth Model

6.4.1   Introduction

The second component of our framework for energy policy analysis is a model of long-term U.S. economic growth. A model of U.S. economic growth is required to provide totals for consumption, investment, government and export final demand in our econometric model of inter-industry transactions. For this purpose conventional econometric models could be used as an alternative to our macroeconometric growth model. However, a growth model is also required to provide the relative prices of capital and labor services which enter as primary inputs into the nine sectors of our inter-industry model. Prices of primary inputs must be generated within a framework that also incorporates primary input quantities and the prices and quantities of final products. For this purpose a new approach to macroeconometric model building is required.

Our approach to the explanation of economic growth is closely related to the neoclassical theory of economic growth.[19] The building blocks of our model are submodels of household and production sectors and submodels of foreign and government sectors. Economic growth results from the link between current capital formation and future productive capacity. In our model this link is provided by a macroeconometric production function, relating the output of consumption and investment goods to the input of capital and labor services. Preferences between present and future consumption, which determine the allocation of income between saving and consumption, complete our model of economic growth.

Our macroeconometric growth model of the U.S. economy provides for the simultaneous determination of the values of products and factors of production in both current and constant prices. The model links demand for capital formation by savers to the supply of investment goods by producers. Similarly, the model links demand for consumption goods and supply of labor services by households to supply of consumption goods and demand for labor by producers. Finally, given the supply of capital stock, the demand for capital services determines the overall rate of return to capital.

The theory of U.S. economic growth that underlies our macroeconometric growth model is a theory of the behavior of the private sector of the U.S. economy. The behavior of the foreign and government sectors is taken to be exogenous. Demographic trends—the growth of population, labor force, and unemployment—are also exogenous to the model. The main determinant of growth in productivity is capital formation. Growth in productivity over and above growth due to capital formation is exogenous to the model. We have projected demographic trends and trends in productivity growth on the basis of postwar experience in the United States.[20]

6.4.2   Variables

Our econometric growth model is summarized in the following series of tables. In table 6.4, we present our notation for the variables that appear in the model. The first group of variables convert aggregates from one basis of classification to another. For example, the index of total factor productivity A converts input to output. The index of AW converts investment weights for capital formation to the weights appropriate for the measurement of wealth. All of the aggregation variables are taken to be exogenous.

The second group of variables appearing in table 6.4 comprises the quantities of products and factors of production, broken down by sector of origin and destination. Variables beginning with C are quantities of consumption goods. Similarly, variables beginning with I are quantities of investment goods. Variables beginning with L are quantities of labor services, while variables beginning with K are quantities of capital services. The third group of variables includes prices corresponding to the quantities of products and factors of production. Each price begins with P and continues with the corresponding quantity. For example, the variable C is personal consumption expenditures and the variable PC is the price of personal consumption expenditures.

The fourth group of variables are financial variables: rates of depreciation and replacement, the nominal rate of return, gross private national saving, and private national wealth. Finally, the fifth group of variables are tax and transfer variables. The variable EL represents government transfer payments to persons other than from social insurance funds, an expenditure category. The variables beginning with T are tax rates. Each of the products and factors included in the model—consumption goods, investment goods, capital services, and labor services—is associated with an effective tax rate. The variable TP is the effective tax rate for capital stock.

Table 6.4
Macroeconometric growth model: notation

---

1. Aggregation variables

A   Total factor productivity (input to output)
ACI   Investment to change in business inventories, consumption goods
AI   Investment to capital stock
AL   Investment to capital stock, lagged
AK   Capital stock, lagged to capital service
APC   Implicit deflator of consumption to implicit deflator of change in business inventories, consumption goods
AW   Investment to wealth

2. Quantities

C   Personal consumption expenditures, including services of consumers' durables
CE   Supply of consumption goods by government enterprises
CG   Government purchases of consumption goods
CI   Change in business inventories of consumption goods
CR   Net exports of consumption goods less income originating, rest of the world
CS   Supply of consumption goods by private enterprises
G   Net claims on government
R   Net claims on rest of the world
I   Gross private domestic investment, including purchases of consumers' durables
IG   Government purchases of investment goods
IR   Net exports of investment goods
IS   Supply of investment goods by private enterprises
L   Supply of labor services
LD   Private purchases of labor services
LGE   Government enterprises purchases of labor services
LGG   General government purchases of labor services
LH   Time available
LJ   Leisure time
LR   Net exports of labor services
LU   Unemployment
K   Capital stock
KD   Capital services

3. Prices

PC   Implicit deflator, personal consumption expenditures, including services of consumers' durables
PCE   Implicit deflator, supply of consumption goods by government enterprises
PCG   Implicit deflator, government purchases of consumption goods

---

Table 6.4 (continued)

3. Prices (continued)

PCI   Implicit deflator, change in business inventories of consumption goods
PCR   Implciti deflator, net exports of consumption goods, less income originating, rest of the world
PCS   Implicit deflator, supply of consumption goods by private enterprises
PG   Implicit deflator, net claims on government
PR   Implicit deflator, net claims on rest of world
PI   Implicit deflator, gross private domestic investment, including purchases of consumers' durables
PIG   Implicit deflator, government purchases of investment goods
PIR   Implicit deflator, net exports of investment goods
PIS   Implicit deflator, supply of investment goods by private enterprises
PL   Implicit deflator, supply of labor services
PLD   Implicit deflator, private purchases of labor services
PLGE   Implicit deflator, government enterprises purchases of labor services
PLGG   Implicit deflator, general government purchases of labor services
PLR   Implicit deflator, net exports of labor services
PHD   Implicit deflator, capital services

4. Financial variables

D   Rate of depreciation, private domestic tangible assets
M   Rate of replacement, private domestic tangible assets
N   Nominal rate of return, private domestic tangible assets
S   Gross private national saving
W   Private national wealth

5. Tax and transfer variables

EL   Government transfer payments, other than social insurance funds, to persons
TC   Effective tax rate, consumption goods
TI   Effective tax rate, investment goods
TK   Effective tax rate, capital services
TL   Effective tax rate, labor services
TP   Effective tax rate, capital stock

6.4.3   Equations

In table 6.5 we present the equations for our macroeconometric growth model. The model includes five behavioral equations, describing the behavior of household and business sectors.[21] The demand for labor is determined by the total level of production, the amount of capital services available, and the relative prices of capital and labor services. Output of investment goods is determined by the price of investment goods, the prices of capital services and the available supply of capital services, and the amount of productive capacity being

Table 6.5
Macroeconometric growth model: equations

1. Behavioral equations

Investment supply:
$$(PIS * IS) / (PKD * KD) = 1.717 - 0.5006 * (\log CS - \log IS)$$

Labor demand:
$$(PLD * LD) / (PKD * KD) = 1.5655$$

Production possibility frontier:
$$(0 = -\log KD - 1.5655 * \log LD + 1.3938 * \log CS - 2.5655 * \log A$$
$$+ 1.717 * \log IS + 0.2503 * (\log CS - \log IS) ** 2$$

Consumption demand:
$$PC * C = 0.0034 * W(-1) + 0.1469 * (PL * LH + EL)$$

Leisure demand:
$$PL * LJ = 0.0196 * W(-1) + 0.8403 * (PL * LH + EL)$$

2. Accounting identities

Capital stock and investment:
$$K = AI * I + (1 - M) * K(-1)$$

Capital service and capital stock:
$$KD = AK * K(-1)$$

Value of output and input:
$$PIS * IS + PCS * CS = PKD * KD + PLD * LD$$

Value of consumption goods:
$$(1 + TC) * PCS * CS + PCE * CE$$
$$= PC * C + PCG * CG + PCI * CI + PCR * CR$$

Value of investment goods:
$$(1 + TI) * PIS * IS + PCI * CI = PI * I + PIG * IG + PIR * IR$$

Value of capital services:
$$(1 - TK) * (PKD * KD - TP * PI(-1) * AW(-1) * K(-1))$$
$$= N * PI(-1) * AW(-1) * K(-1) + D * PI * AL * K(-1)$$
$$+ PI(-1) * AW(-1) * K(-1) - PI * AL * K(-1)$$

Value of labor services:
$$(1 - TL) * (PLD * LD + PLGE * LGE + PLGG * LGG + PLR * LR)$$
$$= PL * L$$

Saving:
$$S = PI * I + PG * (G - G(-1)) + PR * (R - R(-1))$$

Wealth:
$$W = PI * AW * K + PG * G + PR * R$$

Table 6.5 (continued)

---

3. Balance equations
  Consumption:
    CS + CE = C + CG + CI + CR
  Investment:
    IS + CI = I + IG + IR
  Time:
    LH = L + LJ
  Labor:
    L = LD + LGE + LGG + LR + LU

4. Aggregation equations
  Implicit deflator, change in business inventories, consumption goods:
    PCI = PC * APC
  Change in business inventories, consumption goods:
    PCI * CI = PI * I * ACI

---

devoted to the output of consumer goods and services. The production that takes place in the U.S. private sector, whether of consumption or of investment goods, is limited by the total productive capacity which in turn depends on available supplies of capital and labor services as well as on the level of technology.

The level of household expenditure on consumer goods and services is determined by the wealth and resources held by the household sector, including the time of endowment of the sector. The desired amount of work input provided by the household sector is determined by the total amount of time available, the wage rate, and the extent of other resources available to the household sector in the form of wealth and transfer payments.

The behavioral equations of our macroeconometric growth model have been estimated from historical data for the United States for the period 1929–1971.[22] In addition to the five behavioral equations, the model includes accounting identities for capital stock, investment and capital services, for the value of input and output, for saving and wealth, and for the value of consumption goods, investment goods, capital services and labor services. These accounting identities incorporate the budget constraints for household and business sectors and the flow of each product and factor of production in current prices.

The model is completed by balance between demand and supply of products and factors of production in constant prices and by aggregation equations that determine inventory accumulation of consumption goods. Although gross private domestic investment is determined in the model, the allocation of investment between fixed investment and inventory accumulation is not determined in the model. An allocation between inventory accumulation in the form of consumption goods and other components of gross private domestic investment is required for the balance between demand and supply of consumption and investment goods. In figure 6.3 we outline the working of our macroeconometric growth by means of a diagram.

6.5   Energy Projections

6.5.1   Introduction

Our next objective is to provide a reference point for the analysis of energy policy by establishing detailed projections of energy demand and supply, energy price and cost, and energy imports and exports. Our projections cover the years 1975–2000 and are based on the assumption that there are no major changes in energy policy, either by U.S. or foreign governments, over the forecast period. The principal energy assumption underlying these projections is that the average real crude oil price remains at $7 over the forecast period. The projections include the entire matrix of inter-industry transactions in current dollar and in constant dollar flow. We translate this information into physical terms by converting the constant dollar energy transactions into British Thermal Units (Btu) for each fuel.[23] We also convert the price indexes into dollars per physical unit. This transformation permits the expression of our detailed inter-industry projections in the energy balance framework that is conventional in energy analysis.[24]

A summary of the composition and growth of the inter-industry transactions for the U.S. economy is given in table 6.6. This table presents information on the gross output of each producing sector, together with information on the product side of GNP. The rate of growth of real GNP is expected to slow somewhat from recent levels, in large part because of the expected decline in the rate of increase of the labor force, but only to around 3.85 percent a year. Inflation also is expected to slow from rates experienced in the recent past but, at 3.95 percent a year, to remain above typical historical rates.

The composition of GNP is expected to change gradually. Net exports absorb an increasing fraction of GNP as the terms of trade,

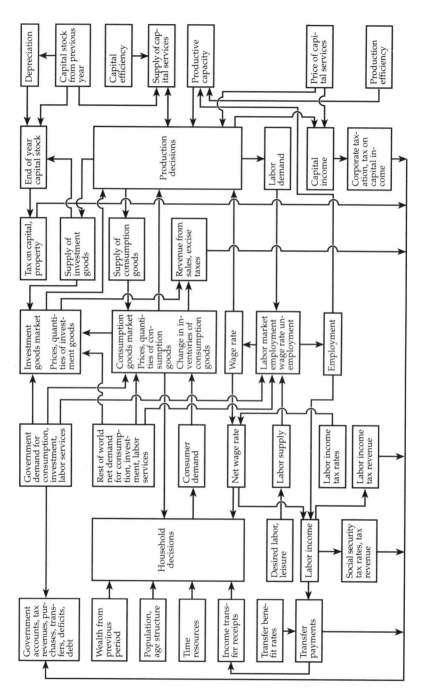

Figure 6.3
Macroeconomic growth model: diagrammatic representation.

Table 6.6
U.S. industry output and prices; 1975–2000 (average annual growth rates, percent)

Output of sector	Real dollars	Prices	Current dollars
(1) Agriculture, etc.	2.83	4.96	7.93
(2) Manufacturing	3.93	3.48	7.55
(3) Transport	4.31	2.31	6.72
(4) Services	3.51	4.14	7.80
(5) Coal	2.64	5.57	8.36
(6) Crude petroleum, gas	2.41	3.95	6.46
(7) Refined petroleum	2.42	5.02	7.56
(8) Electricity	5.18	3.79	9.17
(9) Gas	1.04	6.97	8.08
Consumption	3.82	3.99	7.96
Investment	3.81	3.94	7.90
Government	3.75	4.12	8.02
Net exports	6.15	—	—
GNP	3.85	3.95	7.95

particularly relating to raw materials, continue to move against the U.S. Real government purchases fall in relation to total output although the rapid rate of increase in the price of government purchases, primarily of its purchases of labor and services, offsets this and results in a small increase in the current dollar share of government purchases of GNP. Personal consumption in real terms increases in line with GNP and the current dollar share of consumption in GNP also remains stable. Private investment in both real and current dollar terms increases slightly less rapidly than GNP.

The composition of production changes more noticeably. Agriculture, nonfuel mining and construction output increases relatively slowly, as its output is income inelastic, while the expected productivity advance in manufacturing and transport permits a comparatively rapid increase in output from these sectors with less than average increase in prices. Communications, trade and services output continues to increase but less rapidly than real GNP and, due to the slow productivity advance in this sector and its relative intensity in an increasing cost input, labor, its prices increase comparatively rapidly.

6.5.2   Energy Balance

The base case projection of total U.S. energy utilization for the period 1975–2000 is summarized in table 6.7. Total energy input is forecast to increase from 77.230 quadrillion Btu in 1975 to 163.383 quadrillion Btu in 2000, an average annual growth rate of 3.0 percent. The rate of increase of this total varies over time. In the past the rate of increase of total input has varied from 3.7 percent a year over the 1960–1965 period, to 4.8 percent over 1965–1970, to 3.9 percent for 1970–1973. Our forecast 1975 total corresponds to a 2.7 percent increase for the 1970–1975 period.

The historical rates of increase in energy use are not expected to continue, in fact, these base case projections show a gradual decline in the rate of increase. This decline is due to several factors. Some of the

Table 6.7
U.S. energy input; 1970–2000

	1970	1975	1980	1985	1990	2000
1. U.S. total energy input (quadrillion Btu)						
Coal	12.922	13.219	14.304	16.741	19.887	26.160
Petroleum	29.614	33.783	39.195	45.031	50.783	61.432
Natural gas (exc. synthetic gas)	22.029	24.753	26.800	28.022	28.612	28.639
Hydro, nuclear, other	2.879	5.474	10.115	16.010	23.616	47.152
Total	67.444	77.230	90.414	105.804	122.897	163.383
2. Total energy input, growth rates (average percent per annum)						
Coal		0.46	1.59	3.20	3.50	2.78
Petroleum		2.67	3.02	2.81	2.43	1.92
Natural gas		2.36	1.60	0.90	0.42	0.01
Hydro, nuclear, other		13.72	13.06	9.62	8.08	7.16
Total		2.75	3.20	3.19	3.04	2.89
3. Total energy input, composition (percent of total)						
Coal	19.16	17.12	15.82	15.82	16.18	16.01
Petroleum	43.91	43.74	43.35	42.56	41.32	37.60
Natural gas	32.66	32.06	29.64	26.48	23.28	17.53
Hydro, nuclear, other	4.27	7.09	11.19	15.13	19.22	28.86
Total	100.00	100.00	100.00	100.00	100.00	100.00

deceleration is largely independent of the recent increases in energy prices since it is due to the continuing trend in production and spending towards nonenergy intensive goods and, in particular, to services. Also, the gradual approach to saturation of such energy expensive capital as air-conditioning, single family suburban homes, and large automobiles would have produced a decline in the growth rate of energy use. The recent, and projected future, increases in fuel prices provide additional stimulus to this trend as wasteful energy use is reduced, as existing capital is gradually replaced by more energy efficient capital, and as the implementation of more energy efficient production and consumption patterns is promoted. All these forces act to limit the rate of increase in energy consumption. The result is a gradual decline in this rate, with U.S. gross energy input rising at 3.2 percent a year over the 1975–1980 period, at 3.2 percent between 1980 and 1985, at 3.0 percent between 1985 and 1990, and at only 2.9 percent a year over the 1990–2000 period.

The composition of total energy input is also expected to change markedly. Coal is projected to decline slightly in relative importance during the 1970s but then to retain, and even to increase, its importance after the mid-1980s as new demand for coal for synthetic gas projection is superimposed on the continuing demand for coal for electricity generation. The net result is that the share of coal in total input in 2000 is only fractionally below its 1975 level.

Petroleum shows a continuing decline in relative importance. Use of petroleum continues to increase at around 2.9 percent a year until 1985, but this increase gradually slows as the introduction of more energy efficient capital and change in economic patterns have significant effects in reducing demand for petroleum. For example use of more efficient automobiles, more use of public transport, better building insulation, use of heat pumps in heating and cooling all have a major effect in slowing the increase in petroleum use. Thus, by 2000, petroleum is projected to form 38 percent of total energy input, compared to 44 percent in the 1970s.

Natural gas is predicted to decline dramatically in relative importance. This is due primarily to expected supply limitations which prevent its use from keeping pace with other fuels. The share of natural gas in total energy input falls from 32 percent in 1975 to 18 percent in 2000 (although, in terms of consumption, synthetic gas supplements the availability of gaseous fuels). Finally, the hydro, nuclear and other share in total input is expected to increase dramatically. This is due to

Table 6.8
U.S. energy consumption; 1970–2000[a]

	1970	1975	1980	1985	1990	2000
1. U.S. energy consumption (quadrillion Btu)						
Coal	12.922	13.219	14.304	16.741	19.887	26.160
Petroleum	29.614	33.783	39.195	45.031	50.783	61.432
Electricity	5.218	6.713	8.853	11.478	14.984	23.720
Gas	22.029	24.753	26.800	28.712	30.408	32.279
2. Energy consumption, growth rates (average percent per annum)						
Coal		0.46	1.59	3.20	3.50	2.78
Petroleum		2.67	3.02	2.81	2.43	1.92
Electricity		5.17	5.69	5.33	5.48	4.70
Gas		2.36	1.60	1.39	1.15	0.60
3. Energy consumption (physical units)						
Coal (million short tons)	525	572	618	724	860	1131
Petroleum (million barrels a day)	14.70	16.77	19.45	22.35	25.20	30.49
Electricity (billion kilowatt hours)	1530	1958	2582	3347	4370	6917
Gas (trillion cubic feet)	21.37	23.99	25.90	27.71	29.33	31.10

[a] Coal consumption includes coal used in electricity generation and in the production of synthetic gas. Petroleum consumption includes petroleum inputs into electricity generation and synthetic gas. Gas consumption includes both natural and synthetic gas.

the rapidly increasing use of electricity and to the steadily increasing importance of nuclear generation within the electricity sector. The 9 percent average annual increase of hydro and nuclear input over the 1975–2000 period results in its share in total input increasing from 7 percent to 29 percent.

Consumption of each type of energy is shown in table 6.8. Coal consumption increases at an average rate of 2.8 percent over the 1975–2000 period, petroleum consumption at a rate of 2.4 percent, electricity at 5.2 percent and gas (natural plus synthetic) at 1.1 percent. These growth rates vary within the forecast interval. Typically, the growth rates increase over the 1975–1980 period, compared to rates for 1970–1975 which are reduced as a result of the 1973–1974 energy crisis. After 1980 the growth rates steadily decline over the remainder of the century.

The dominant trend in these aggregate consumption figures is the continued rapid increase in electricity consumption. The growth in electricity use has several implications. First, since electricity is a secondary form of energy suffering large energy losses in the conversion from primary fuels, it is very expensive in terms of energy input and its rapid growth produces a rapid growth in the use of primary fuels. In other words, the cost of the electricity growth in energy terms is the absorption of ever increasing proportions of total energy input in electricity conversion loss. For example, in 1975 electricity conversion losses are projected to amount to 14.1 quadrillion Btu, or 18.2 percent of total energy input, but in 2000 these losses are projected to be about 49.7 quadrillion Btu which is 30.4 percent of total energy input.

The second implication of electricity use is derived from the fact that any fuel can be used as the primary input to electricity generation. Uranium and hydro resources, at present, have no alternative use, although uranium enrichment for present generation nuclear reactors is a heavy user of electricity. Also, the ability to use any fossil fuel gives electricity generation some degree of comparative advantage over final use of these fuels. Electricity generation can exploit coal, which is in relative abundance in the U.S., and residual oil, which, for technical reasons, has only limited value as a fuel in other uses. In short, electricity has a property that partially offsets its large energy requirements for the cheapest and most abundant fuels can be used in its generation, leaving scarce oil and gas supplies available for direct use.

Projected fuel prices are shown in table 6.9. All prices are expected to increase in current dollars, coal by an average of 5.6 percent a year over the 1975–2000 period, crude petroleum by 4.0 percent, electricity by 3.8 percent and gas by 7.0 percent. These rates of increase reflect both supply and demand factors. The increase in coal prices is due largely to the slow productivity advance and increasingly stringent production controls for both safety and environmental reasons, expected in the coal mining industry. These base case forecasts correspond to crude oil being available at $7, in 1975 prices, so that the crude oil price increases with the rate of inflation. Electricity prices increase but, due to continued productivity advance in the electric utilities sector, at a less rapid rate than other fuel prices. Gas prices are projected to rise rapidly as an increasing demand faces a relatively inelastic supply (this presupposes a relaxation of price controls on natural gas and the assumption is made that this relaxation occurs in the latter part of the 1970s).

Table 6.9
U.S. energy prices; 1970–2000

	1970	1975	1980	1985	1990	2000
1. Fuel prices (current dollars)						
Coal ($/short ton)	7.59	11.49	16.89	22.49	28.65	44.54
Crude petroleum ($/barrel)	3.39	7.00	8.82	10.73	12.86	18.43
Electricity (¢/kilowatt hours)	1.61	2.10	2.63	3.17	3.77	5.32
Gas ($/thousand cubic feet)	0.83	0.99	1.54	2.07	2.79	5.34
2. Fuel prices, growth rates (average percent per annum)						
Coal		8.65	8.01	5.89	4.96	4.51
Crude petroleum		15.61	4.75	3.98	3.69	3.66
Electricity		5.46	4.60	3.81	3.53	3.50
Gas		3.59	9.24	6.09	6.15	6.71
GNP price deflator		5.63	4.75	3.98	3.69	3.66
3. Total energy input, composition (percent of total)						
Coal ($1975/short ton)	9.98	11.49	13.40	14.67	15.59	16.92
Crude petroleum ($1975/barrel)	4.46	7.00	7.00	7.00	7.00	7.00
Electricity (¢ 1975/kilowatt hours)	2.12	2.10	2.09	2.07	2.05	2.02
Gas ($1975/thousand cubic feet)	1.09	0.99	1.22	1.35	1.52	2.03

When the rates of increase of fuel prices are compared to general inflation, which averages 4.0 percent over the 1975–2000 period, a somewhat different picture emerges. First, coal and gas prices show a significant increase in real terms, which is in marked contrast to historical experience, e.g., between 1951 and 1971 real coal prices fell at 1.5 percent a year and the real average price for gas sold by gas utilities rose by only 0.52 percent a year. The projected upward price trend provides a strong incentive for economy in the use of these fuels. The second price feature is that electricity prices, in real terms, fall slightly although the 0.2 percent annual rate of decline between 1975 and 2000 is again much less than the 2.5 percent annual decrease that occurred between 1951 and 1971. Compared to past experience, the virtual constancy of real electricity prices exerts some pressure to slow the rate of increase in electricity use, but the main effect is to continue to promote the substitution of electricity for other fuels as electricity becomes slightly less expensive compared to other fuels.

The fuel supply sections of the energy forecasts are shown in table 6.10. Although the inter-industry model takes account of production and supply possibilities after the primary extractive stage it does not include any detailed information on the supply characteristics of the

Table 6.10
U.S. energy supply; 1970–2000

	1970	1975	1980	1985	1990	2000
1. Coal (million short tons)						
Production	598	656	707	828	972	1260
Exports	72	84	89	104	112	129
U.S. consumption	525	572	618	724	860	1131
2. Petroleum (million barrels a day)						
U.S. crude output						
(including gas liquids)	11.54	10.60	13.90	17.60	19.00	20.60
U.S. output of shale oil	0	0	0	0	0.81	4.29
Imports	3.42	6.42	5.78	4.97	5.58	5.73
U.S. consumption	14.70	16.77	19.45	22.35	25.20	30.49
Exports	0.26	0.25	0.23	0.22	0.19	0.13
3. Gas (billion cubic feet)						
U.S. output of natural gas	20616	21862	22512	23541	23941	23662
U.S. output of synthetic gas	0	0	0	690	1796	3640
Imports	821	2210	3444	3526	3621	3814
U.S. consumption	21367	23991	25898	27714	29325	31098
Exports	70	81	58	44	33	18
4. Total (quadrillion Btu)						
U.S. energy input	67.444	77.230	90.414	105.804	122.897	163.383
Exports	2.610	2.667	2.672	2.961	3.043	3.297
Total demand	70.054	79.897	93.086	108.765	126.940	166.680
Imports	8.235	15.917	15.890	14.235	15.688	16.100
Supplemental (synthetic gas, shale oil)	0	0	0	0.690	3.428	12.284
Imports as percentage of total demand)	11.76	19.92	17.07	13.09	12.46	9.66
Supplemental as percentage of total demand	0	0	0	0.01	2.72	7.37

U.S. fuel extracting industries. Indeed, given current knowledge, any supply predictions, particularly to 2000, are dubious. The supply figures shown in table 6.10 represent, essentially, estimates appended to the model. Coal has no supply problems concerning its existence, the only problems concern the prices at which mining and land reclamation become economic. Our coal supply information represents an extrapolation of past data and is embodied in the coal sector production structure of the model. The U.S. oil output figures are based on an *ad hoc* combination of past price elasticities and currently available information concerning future oil fields, such as the North Slope and other Alaskan fields. Imports make up the difference between U.S. demand and supply at each oil price. Our estimates for U.S. output of natural gas are based upon estimates made by various government and private agencies, as are our estimates for the output of synthetic gas and of shale oil.

The energy forecasts for the 1975–2000 period are shown by sector of origin and destination in table 6.11. This table shows, for each of the forecast years, the energy supplied by each type of fuel-coal, petroleum, natural gas, hydro and nuclear, electricity and synthetic gas—into each consuming sector. There are four fuel-consuming sectors, following the Department of the Interior classification—household and commercial (excluding use of vehicles), industrial (excluding use of vehicles), electricity generation, and transportation (which includes all travel in all vehicles).

Coal is used almost entirely as an intermediate input, in manufacturing, coal mining and electricity generation, and in exports. This pattern is not projected to alter but the composition of its use in production is. Manufacturing and coal mining uses are relatively unchanged; the projected growth in coal consumption comes in its use in electricity generation, its use for export and, in the latter part of the forecast period, as an input to the production of synthetic gas.

Petroleum products are, at present, used heavily in all sectors and this feature is projected to continue. However, the rates of growth of petroleum use in the different sectors are expected to show substantial differences. Petroleum consumption by households (in personal consumption expenditure) shows the most striking changes—it increases comparatively slowly, at an average 2.6 percent a year, until 1985 but then levels off and increases at only 0.2 percent a year for the rest of the century. This corresponds to an average 1.1 percent a year increase in household use between 1975 and 2000. This has the result of reducing the growth of transportation demand for petroleum to an average 2.1 percent a year over the 1975–2000 period. Commercial demand rises more rapidly than household demand so that the average household and commercial growth rate between 1975 and 2000 is 2.5 percent a year. Industrial consumption of petroleum increases more rapidly, at 3.2 percent a year, while use of petroleum in electricity generation grows at 2.2 percent a year over the forecast period.

The slow growth of petroleum use, in particular in the household sector, can be attributed to various forces. Higher prices and the conservation ethic stimulate economy in the use of petroleum through the

Table 6.11
Composition of U.S. energy use; 1970–2000 (energy flows in trillion Btu)

		Consuming sector					
		Household, commercial	Industrial	Transportation	Electricity generation	Synthetic gas	Total input
1970	Coal	427	5004	8	7483	0	12922
	Petroleum	6453	5267	15592	2087	0	29614
	Natural gas	7108	10162	745	4015	0	22029
	Hydro, nuclear	0	0	0	2879	0	2879
	Total input	13988	20433	16345	16464	0	67444
	Electricity	3000	2210	16	0	0	5218
	Synthetic gas	0	0	0	0	0	0
	Total	16988	22643	16361	16464	0	67444
1975	Coal	200	4393	0	8625	0	13219
	Petroleum	6819	6627	17937	2400	0	33783
	Natural gas	8415	11102	945	4290	0	24753
	Hydro, nuclear	0	0	0	5475	0	5475
	Total input	15435	22122	18882	20790	0	77230
	Electricity	3982	2709	22	0	0	6713
	Synthetic gas	0	0	0	0	0	0
	Total	19418	24831	18904	20790	0	77230
1980	Coal	180	3897	0	10227	0	14304
	Petroleum	7996	7665	20967	2567	0	39195
	Natural gas	8515	12778	1003	4505	0	26800
	Hydro, nuclear	0	0	0	10115	0	10115
	Total input	16691	24340	21970	27413	0	90414
	Electricity	5427	3396	30	0	0	8853
	Synthetic gas	0	0	0	0	0	0
	Total	22118	27736	22000	27413	0	90414

Table 6.11 (continued)

			Consuming sector			
	Household, commercial	Industrial	Transportation	Electricity generation	Synthetic gas	Total input
1985						
Coal	175	3677	0	11779	1111	16741
Petroleum	9149	8938	23948	2907	89	45031
Natural gas	7499	14690	993	4840	0	28022
Hydro, nuclear	0	0	0	16010	0	16010
Total input	16822	27304	24942	35536	1199	105804
Electricity	7490	3951	37	0	0	11478
Synthetic gas	310	379	0	0	0	690
Total	24623	31635	24978	35536	1199	105804
1990						
Coal	135	3612	0	13545	2594	19887
Petroleum	9964	10655	25902	4053	208	50783
Natural gas	6462	15978	1000	5173	0	28612
Hydro, nuclear	0	0	0	23616	0	23616
Total input	16561	30245	26902	46387	2802	122897
Electricity	10064	4876	43	0	0	14984
Synthetic gas	808	988	0	0	0	1798
Total	27434	36109	26945	46387	2802	122897
2000						
Coal	174	5048	0	15878	5061	26160
Petroleum	12727	14405	29810	4085	405	61432
Natural gas	4742	16632	954	6310	0	28639
Hydro, nuclear	0	0	0	47152	0	47152
Total input	17643	36085	30764	73425	5466	163383
Electricity	16737	6927	56	0	0	23720
Synthetic gas	1638	2002	0	0	0	3640
Total	36017	45014	30820	73425	5466	163383

operation of existing energy using capital less intensively and through the introduction of more energy efficient capital. Also other forces operate to accentuate the trend to slower growth in petroleum use. For example, the decline in population growth, more expensive housing and more stringent insulation regulations in building codes produce a trend to slower increases in housing construction, to smaller houses, and towards multi-family housing units all of which operate to greatly reduce energy requirements for space heating, and cooling, from past growth rates. Also more expensive cars, together with concern over air pollution and with the disincentive to driving caused by traffic congestion, operate to slow the growth of transportation demand for petroleum by stimulating reductions in the size and use of cars. The time involved in these changes is rather long for first attitudes must be changed, by economic, regulatory and other pressures, and then these attitudes must be translated into new capital stock which typically, must wait upon the depreciation and replacement of existing stock. (Although some significant changes in use can be achieved very quickly by altering the rate of utilization of existing capital stock.) Thus, a substantial time lag can be expected before the full effects of prices on petroleum consumption are felt, but in time the scope for conservation is large enough to permit increasing levels of effective services to be sustained from only a very small rate of growth in the input of petroleum energy.

Electricity consumption increases at a rapid rate—at 5.2 percent a year between 1975 and 20000. The rate of increase is highest in the late 1970s, as the 1975 consumption figure is depressed as a result of the 1974 energy problems. But, thereafter, the rate of increase steadily falls and is consistently below the growth rates experienced in the past. As with petroleum use, consumption in different sectors shows widely different rates of increase, but here it is final demand that increases the most rapidly. Household electricity consumption increases at an average annual rate of 6.9 percent between 1975 and 2000, with household and commercial demand increasing at an average of 5.9 percent and industrial demand at 3.8 percent. The increase in household use of electricity is the most rapid of any use of any fuel and, in this, it continues the trend that has been observed in the past. However, the projected rate of increase is slower than those observed in the past due to the more rapid increase in electricity prices, the approach to saturation of heavy electricity using appliances such as home air-conditioning, laundries, dishwashers and so on, and to the decline in the rate of new dwelling construction.

Gas consumption is forecast to increase comparatively slowly and at a declining rate. This slow growth is due to supply rather than to demand limitations. The actual allocation of scarce gas supplies may be controlled by regulation rather than by market processes. If so, then the sectoral split contained in these projections may not be accurate. The allocation shown here is based on a simulated market process, in line with the assumption of virtually complete deregulation of gas by 1980. Under this assumption the growth in gas consumption occurs in industrial uses. Industrial consumption of gas is projected to increase at an average 1.6 percent a year between 1975 and 2000. This increase is significantly more rapid than total gas supply so it must be offset by slow growth elsewhere. The slow growth occurs in the household and commercial sector where gas use declines by 2.3 percent a year. The reason for the decline in gas use in nonindustrial areas lies in the price behavior of the fuels—the rapid gas price increase, together with the ease of substitution of other fuels for gas in household and commercial uses leads to the shift away from gas in these areas. In addition, this pressure is supplemented by nonprice factors such as the expected slowing in new construction rates and the downward trend in new house sizes which operate to reduce space heating demands for gas.

The composition of inputs into the electricity generation sector is shown in table 6.12. The dominant feature here is the projected increase in hydro and nuclear generation, with virtually all the increase being in nuclear. In 1970 hydro and nuclear provided 17.5 percent of total input but this proportion increases to 64 percent by 2000. Coal input, although growing rapidly in absolute terms, declines in relative importance as an input from supplying almost half of total inputs in 1970 to one-fifth in 2000. Similarly, although petroleum and gas inputs increase in absolute terms, this increase is relatively slow and they show a steady decline in proportion to total input.

The changing composition of inputs into electricity generation reflects relative prices and is undertaken by the electricity generation sector in response to market forces. But, these forces also reflect, in part at least, a basic characteristic of U.S. fuel supply possibilities. Coal, uranium and hydro power are not only relatively abundant but also have a low economic opportunity cost for, apart from electricity

Table 6.12
Energy inputs into U.S. electricity generation; 1970–2000

	1970	1975	1980	1985	1990	2000
1. Energy inputs (quadrillion Btu)						
Coal	7.483	8.625	10.227	11.779	13.545	15.878
Petroleum	2.087	2.400	2.567	2.907	4.053	4.085
Gas	4.015	4.290	4.505	4.840	5.173	6.310
Hydro, nuclear, other	2.879	5.475	10.115	16.010	23.616	47.152
Total	16.464	20.790	27.413	35.536	46.387	73.425
2. Energy inputs (percent of total)						
Coal	45.4	41.5	37.3	33.2	29.2	21.6
Petroleum	12.7	11.5	9.4	8.2	8.7	5.6
Gas	24.4	20.6	16.4	13.6	11.2	8.6
Hydro, nuclear, other	17.5	26.3	36.9	45.1	50.9	64.2
Total	100.0	100.0	100.0	100.0	100.0	100.0

absorbed in uranium enrichment, they have comparatively few alternative uses, whereas petroleum and gas fuels are not only in relatively short supply but also have many alternative uses that render their opportunity cost, for use in electricity generation, very high. In these respects, and omitting nuclear safety from consideration, the forecast outcome of market forces, as they affect inputs to electricity generation, appears to be entirely consistent with the objectives of currently proposed national energy policies.

6.5.3   Alternative Projections

This section presents summary comparisons between our energy projections and alternative projections. This comparison is conducted for two purposes, first, to obtain an independent check that our forecasts are of reasonable orders of magnitude and, second, to pinpoint the differences between economically based forecasts and technologically based forecasts. The alternative forecasts considered are those prepared by the Committee on the U.S. Energy Outlook of the National Petroleum Council[25], the U.S. Department of the Interior forecasts prepared by Dupree and West, and, for electricity, various forecasts reported in Chapman, Mount and Tyrrell.[26] (These alternative fore-

Table 6.13
Alternative forecasts of U.S. energy utilization (energy use is in quadrillion Btu; growth rates are average annual rates of increase)

	Dupree-West		Hudson-Jorgenson		National Petroleum Council	
	Energy use	Growth rate	Energy use	Growth rate	Energy use	Growth rate
Coal						
1970	12.922		12.922		12.922	
1975	13.825	1.4	13.219	0.5	16.1	4.5
1985	21.470	4.5	16.741	2.4	22.7	3.5
2000	31.360	2.6	26.160	3.0		
Petroleum						
1970	29.614		29.614		29.614	
1975	35.090	3.5	33.783	2.7	39.8	6.1
1985	50.700	3.7	45.031	2.9	56.2	3.5
2000	71.380	2.3	61.432	2.1		
Gas						
1970	22.029		22.029		22.029	
1975	25.220	2.7	24.753	2.4	21.3	−0.7
1985	28.390	1.2	28.022	1.2	21.1	−0.1
2000	33.980	1.2	28.639	0.1		
Total input						
1970	67.444		67.444			
1975	80.265	3.5	77.230	2.7		
1985	116.630	3.8	105.804	3.2		
2000	191.900	3.4	163.383	2.9		

casts were prepared before the 1973–1974 oil price increases; the NPC forecast was published in 1971, the Dupree and West forecast in 1972 and the Chapman, Mount and Tyrrell forecast in 1973.)

The fossil fuel projection of our inter-industry model, of the NPC and of Dupree and West are shown in table 6.13. For 1975 our forecasts and those of Dupree and West are similar, although for each fuel and for total input, ours are lower. The higher fuel prices incorporated into our projections reduce fuel use below the extrapolations of past trends used by Dupree and West. This same relationship continues for 1985 and 2000, i.e., our forecasts and those of Dupree and West are reasonably close, but the divergence increases over time, with our energy use always being below that in Dupree and West. This indicates first, that the orders of magnitude of our forecast are consistent with past energy trends, used by Dupree and West, and second, that simple extrapolations of these trends are insufficient. Expected fuel

Table 6.14
Alternative forecasts of U.S. electricity consumption (trillion kilowatt hours)[a]

	1970	1975	1980	1985	1995	2000
Chapman-Mount-Tyrrell						
High	1.53	2.14	3.05	—	5.66	9.89
Medium	1.53	1.98	2.38	—	3.01	3.45
Low	1.53	1.88	2.07	—	2.11	2.01
Cornell-National Science						
Foundation	1.57	2.15	2.92	3.96	5.38	10.25
Dupree-West	1.53	2.13	3.00	4.14	—	9.01
Federal Power Commmission	1.53	—	3.07	—	5.83	—
Hudson-Jorgenson	1.53	1.96	2.58	3.35	4.37	6.92
National Petroleum						
Council	1.59	2.29	3.29	4.54	—	—

[a] Sources: Cornell-NSF, FPC, NPC forecasts are given in Chapman, Mount and Tyrrell (1972) table 1, p. 3. The Chapman-Mount-Tyrrell "low" forecast assumes that the real electricity price doubles by 2000, the "medium" forecast corresponds to the FPC estimates of a 19 percent real price increase over 1970–1990, "high" corresponds to a 24 percent real price decline over 1970–1980, and a 12 percent decline over each of the 1980–1990 and 1990–2000 intervals.

price increases and changes in the nonenergy sections of the economy do exert a significant influence working to depress energy use below historical trends. The NPC forecasts for 1975 do not, at the present time, appear very realistic and the 1985 NPC forecasts are also open to question. The fact that our projections are well below those of NPC gives further weight to the need to take account of price and other factors that affect demand.

The alternative projections of electricity consumption are given in table 6.14. The striking impression gained from these forecasts is one of great variations—the projected 2000 consumption ranges from 2.0 to 10.3 trillion kilowatt hours. Our forecasts are never the extreme entry but are always towards the lower end of the range of forecasts. To the extent that such a diversity of forecasts permits any conclusion, we can say that the above conclusions are reinforced: our projections are in line with other forecasts but, by taking price and other economic factors into account, our projections are comparatively low.

All the alternative energy forecasts considered here, apart from Chapman, Mount and Tyrrell's electricity forecasts, have been prepared without explicit assumptions about the growth of real or relative fuel prices, without explicit consideration of interfuel substitutions and without explicit account of the interactions between energy and the rest of the economy or of future developments in the rest of economy. This lack of analysis of the underlying forces at work in determining energy demand is a serious conceptual drawback. The omission is particularly significant in view of the present need to use energy models to aid the formation of future U.S. energy policy. Our inter-industry model, however, avoids these problems and can provide a more realistic basis for policy analysis.

6.6   Energy Policy

6.6.1. Introduction

This section describes the application of the inter-industry energy model to the analysis of one specific energy policy—a Btu tax designed to reduce dependence on imported fuels. This application serves to illustrate the methodology of the model and provides an evaluation of a specific tax proposal currently under consideration. The actual tax considered is a uniform rate of tax levied on the energy content of all fuels used outside the energy generation and processing sectors.[27]

The starting point for the analysis of the impact of a tax on energy is the base case energy projections which were presented above. These projections are based on the assumption of a continuation of current policies and conditions and so can be used as a reference point against which the changes induced by the introduction of a new tax policy can be measured.

A tax on energy use has the effect of creating a wedge between the price paid by the energy consumer and that received by the producer. Since the forecast supply prices already equal average costs, it can be taken that the tax is added onto the sales price so that it causes an increase in the selling price while leaving the supply price unchanged (apart from indirect impact on the supply price due to any production cost increases that are caused by the tax). Therefore, the tax leads to a change in energy use solely by acting on the demand side of the energy equation.

The tax is inserted into the inter-industry model by means of price markups that increase the sales prices of fuels above the output price received by the seller. The Btu tax is simply a tax on energy sales with the tax base being the Btu content of each dollar of sales, rather than the sales dollar itself. This means that the rate of tax on sales is equal to the Btu tax rate multiplied by the Btu content of each dollar of fuel. Thus, the markups vary between fuels being, in general, greatest for coal, then progressively smaller for gas, petroleum and electricity. The tax is assumed to be levied only on energy as it emerges from the fuel sector into domestic production, i.e., energy inputs into fuel production, including the generation of electricity, and fuel exports are considered exempt from the tax. After the price markups have been inserted, the model is solved to obtain a new set of economic and energy projections. This involves solving for new output prices and input-output coefficients, new final demand components and the associated industry output levels and inter-industry transactions. In this way, the new simulations incorporate both the direct and indirect effects of the energy conservation induced by the price increases—the direct saving by the redirection of final demands towards nonenergy intensive goods and services and the indirect energy saving obtained by the substitution of other inputs for energy in production.

6.6.2   Tax Policy and Conservation

The impact of three different rates of Btu tax on energy demand in 1980 is shown in table 6.15. These figures show that the tax can induce significant reductions in energy use. The highest rate shown, $0.5 per million Btu, leads to a decline of 6.5 quadrillion Btu, or 7.2 percent, in energy use relative to the no tax projection. This reduction is made up of substantial cuts in both final and intermediate uses of energy. The greater part of the reduction comes from the decline in energy input to intermediate production but the relative cutback in use is greater in final demand where energy input is reduced by 10.6 percent, compared to the 5.6 percent fall in intermediate use. These results indicate that although final users of energy may be more responsive to price increases than business users, the sheer volume of energy absorbed in production requires that, for maximum effect, energy conservation policies give at least as much weight to reducing intermediate demand as to reducing final demand. The response of both intermediate and final users to the tax varies with the tax level with, in both cases, the tax having a diminishing marginal impact on energy use. The decline in effectiveness is, however, gradual so that a reasonable first approximation is that each dollar of tax per million Btu's reduces total energy input by about 14 quadrillion Btu. This

Table 6.15
Impact of Btu taxes on total energy input; 1980

Tax rate ($/million Btu)	0	0.1	0.3	0.5
1. Total energy input (quadrillion Btu)	90.414	89.020	86.361	83.949
Change from base		−1.394	−4.053	−6.465
Change/tax rate		−13.94	−13.51	−12.93
Percent change from base		−1.54	−4.48	−7.15
2. Intermediate use (quadrillion Btu)	62.474	61.757	60.332	58.982
Change from base		−0.717	−2.142	−3.492
Change/tax rate		−7.17	−7.14	−6.98
Percent change from base		−1.15	−3.43	−5.59
3. Final use (quadrillion Btu)	27.940	27.263	26.029	24.967
Change from base		−0.677	−1.911	−2.973
Change/tax rate		−6.77	−6.37	−5.95
Percent change from base		−2.42	−6.84	−10.64
4. Energy imports (quadrillion Btu)	15.890	14.628	12.145	9.948
Imports in total input (1%)	17.6	16.4	14.1	11.9
Tax revenue ($ billion)	0	6.655	19.238	30.988

corresponds to an elasticity of Btu use to Btu price of approximately −0. 22.

The detailed adjustments by energy users to the imposition of the tax are shown in table 6.16. These figures show, first, the different degrees of energy conservation in the four major energy-consuming sectors—manufacturing, services, electricity generation and personal consumption. Substantial economies are made in the energy input to each sector but there is a wide difference in the proportionate response: energy used in personal consumption is reduced by 9.5 percent in response to the $0.5 tax rate, with services use being cut by 7.6 percent, manufacturing use by 6.3 percent, and input into electricity generation by 1.8 percent. (Energy input into electricity generation is not taxed, it is reduced only in response to the decline in demand for electricity caused by the tax on electricity purchases.)

Energy use can be split into two broad categories—discretionary use and process use. Discretionary use includes inputs for comfort functions such as heating and cooling as well as personal services such as automobile travel. Process use covers fuel inputs for driving machinery, heating materials, turning generators and so on. Discretionary uses are, typically, characterized by greater flexibility than process uses firstly because the associated capital stock is generally less

Table 6.16
Impact of Btu taxes on input patterns; 1980

Tax rate ($/million Btu)	0	0.1	0.3	0.5
1. Energy input, including use of electricity (quadrillion Btu)				
Manufacturing	21.607	21.314	20.754	20.241
Services	9.237	9.095	8.806	8.539
Electricity generation	27.413	27.334	27.119	26.908
Personal consumption	25.092	24.556	23.566	22.705
2. Percentage change in total inputs				
Energy input		−1.54	−4.48	−7.15
Capital input		0.10	0.28	0.49
Labor input		0.13	0.41	0.67
3. Input-output coefficients for total energy inputs				
Agriculture	0.0244	0.0238	0.0225	0.0215
Manufacturing	0.0234	0.0232	0.0231	0.0230
Transport	0.0447	0.0440	0.0425	0.0413
Services	0.0189	0.0188	0.0185	0.0182
4. Input-output coefficients for manufacturing				
Coal	0.0025	0.0025	0.0024	0.0024
Petroleum	0.0069	0.0068	0.0068	0.0067
Electricity	0.0085	0.0086	0.0087	0.0088
Gas	0.0055	0.0054	0.0052	0.0051
Total energy	0.0234	0.0232	0.0231	0.0230
Capital services	0.1201	0.1200	0.1199	0.1198
Labor services	0.2887	0.2889	0.2893	0.2897
Materials input	0.5165	0.5163	0.5162	0.5160

durable and easier to replace with more energy efficient capital, and secondly because discretionary uses are input to the generation of psychologically rather than technically specified performance, e.g., desired miles driven rather than energy inputs required per ton of alumina to be smelted, so the level of use within the existing capital stock can be more readily varied. Given this categorization, it is apparent that personal consumption includes a high ratio of discretionary to process energy use while this ratio for service activity is a little lower, for manufacturing lower still and for electricity generation lowest of all. This ordering is precisely that observed in the sectoral response to the increase in energy prices.

More specifically, the input-output coefficients in table 6.16 show the processes of adjustment to the tax-induced increases in energy prices. Two types of adjustment can be seen. First, there is a substitution of the now relatively less expensive nonfuel inputs for the relatively more expensive fuel inputs. This is reflected in the total energy input coefficients which, for each sector, decline as the energy tax increases. The manufacturing input-output coefficients illustrate the outcome of this substitution process: energy inputs decline, as do inputs of materials and inputs of capital with inputs of labor services increasing to replace the three reduced inputs. Thus, in manufacturing, energy-capital-materials complementarity means that adjustments to economize on the expensive energy input lead to the use of energy, capital and materials all being reduced and more labor-intensive production techniques adopted.

The shift away from energy in manufacturing is relatively small in terms of changes in input-output coefficients, but it represents a substantial amount of energy. A similar process of substitution away from energy takes place in all sectors. The overall result, however, is a little different from that in manufacturing. The total reduction in energy use is made possible by an increase in inputs of both capital and labor. That is, on an economy wide basis, energy-capital substitutability, such as the use of insulation to save energy, dominates the complementarity relation that characterizes manufacturing. The net effect is that the 7.2 percent fall in energy input is accommodated by a 0.7 percent increase in the demand for labor and a 0.5 percent increase in capital use. These structural changes allow the decline in energy input to be absorbed without a comparable reduction in potential output.

The second set of adjustments occur within energy input as interfuel substitution takes place. The tax has the effect of increasing different fuel prices by different extents, depending on the energy content of each fuel. Coal prices are increased to the greatest extent, with gas prices next, then petroleum, with electricity prices being increased the least. The input-output coefficients for fuel use in manufacturing, shown in table 6.16, illustrate the resulting substitutions. Coal use declines only slightly for, despite the sharp price increase, coal remains the cheapest source of energy as well as being, for technical reasons, used in some production, such as iron and steel, regardless of the price changes. The petroleum and gas coefficients both decline more noticeably. Electricity use, however, increases since electricity has become a relatively less expensive fuel and since its flexibility in use permit it to substitute for petroleum and gas.

6.6.3 Tax Impact

The impact of the Btu tax on the price and consumption of each fuel is shown in table 6.17. Coal prices increase by the largest proportion, with the average increase of 28 percent, for the $0.5 tax rate, comprising a 70 percent increase in price to nonfuel purchasers and virtually no increase in price in fuel production or export uses. The gas price increases by 24 percent for the highest tax rate, with the wholesale price of refined petroleum products increasing by 23 percent and electricity prices rising by only 7 percent. The small price increase for electricity leads to a correspondingly small demand decline, only 2 percent. This small decline also implies that coal input into electricity, the main use of coal, declines by only a small proportion. The only

Table 6.17
Impact of Btu taxes on energy consumption and prices; 1980

Tax rate ($/million Btu)	0	0.1	0.3	0.5
1. Fuel consumption (quadrillion Btu)				
Coal	14.304	14.249	14.117	13.987
Petroleum	39.195	38.628	37.431	36.343
Electricity	8.853	8.827	8.758	8.690
Gas	26.800	26.105	24.818	23.710
2. Change in consumption from base (percent)				
Coal		−0.38	−1.31	−2.22
Petroleum		−1.45	−4.50	−7.28
Electricity		−0.29	−1.07	−1.84
Gas		−2.59	−7.40	−11.53
3. Average fuel prices				
Coal ($/ton)	16.89	17.85	19.76	21.67
Refined petroleum ($/barrel, wholesale)	12.80	13.38	14.55	15.73
Electricity ($/kilowatt hours)	0.0263	0.0266	0.0273	0.0279
Gas ($/thousand cubic feet)	1.54	1.61	1.77	1.91
4. Change in prices from base				
Coal		5.68	16.94	28.33
Refined petroleum		4.57	13.71	22.85
Electricity		1.32	3.96	6.30
Gas		4.87	14.62	24.36
5. Price of energy to taxed users ($/million Btu)				
Coal	0.73	0.83	1.03	1.23
Petroleum	2.39	2.49	2.69	2.89
Electricity	7.66	7.76	7.96	8.16
Gas	1.48	1.58	1.78	1.98

other sizeable domestic use of coal is in the manufacturing sector, but this use is relatively insensitive to price. The price of gas increases substantially and this, with the opportunities to economize in its use and to substitute other fuels for it, leads to a decline of 12 percent in its use. Similarly, petroleum prices rise substantially, causing a decline of 7 percent in the consumption of petroleum. (The average price elasticities implied by these consumption responses are: −0.10 for coal, −0.46 for petroleum, −0.28 for electricity and −0.47 for gas.)

The effects of the Btu tax are not restricted to the energy sectors. There are also effects on the input structure of other production, as have been outlined above, on the costs and prices of these other goods, on the demand for these goods in intermediate uses, and on the level and composition of real final demand. These effects are summarized in table 6.18 which gives the tax-induced changes in nonenergy prices and quantities demanded. All prices are increased as the effects of the higher fuel price work through the production cost structure. The process of substitution towards the relatively less expensive inputs lessens the impact of the fuel price increases on average costs, but the net effect is still an upward movement in costs, and in prices in general.

The price increases by sector are in line with the importance of energy in the sector's inputs: transport prices increase the most,

Table 6.18
Impact of Btu taxes on nonenergy prices and quantities; 1980 (percentage change from base case)

	Price			Quantity		
Tax rate ($/million Btu)	0.1	0.3	0.5	0.1	0.3	0.5
1. Gross output						
Agriculture	0.19	0.51	0.82	−0.16	−0.48	−0.77
Manufacturing	0.16	0.50	0.82	−0.10	−0.30	−0.48
Transport	0.23	0.67	1.09	−0.15	−0.44	−0.71
Services	0.06	0.18	0.31	−0.06	−0.16	−0.30
2. Final demand						
Consumption	0.28	0.79	1.17	−0.12	−0.33	−0.53
Investment	0.16	0.48	0.78	−0.08	−0.31	−0.51
Government	0.12	0.38	0.56	−0.08	−0.22	−0.36
GNP	0.24	0.68	1.07	−0.10	−0.26	−0.42

followed by agriculture and manufacturing, with service prices rising the least; this ranking is the same as the ranking of these sectors in terms of energy input-output coefficients. The price increases are not, however, very sizeable. Even for the $0.5 tax rate, the price increases range from 0.31 percent for services to 1.09 percent for transport. Similarly, the aggregate consumption price index and the GNP price deflator increase by only about 1 percent since the small nonenergy price rises dominate the larger fuel price increases in these price indices. The quantity changes induced by the energy tax are correspondingly small. The new prices, and the decline in real incomes, lead to a reduction and redirection of real final demand, but the resulting change in total real consumption and real GNP are very small, only of the order of 0.5 percent.

This section illustrates the structure of the inter-industry energy model and its application to problems of energy policy. The consideration of the Btu tax shows several important features of the model:

(a) The energy and nonenergy sectors of the economy are treated as interdependent components of the economic system, permitting the effects of energy changes of the rest of the economy to be systematically included in any consideration of energy policy.

(b) The model incorporates interfuel substitution, permitting, within certain production constraints, the substitution of relatively less for relatively more expensive fuels.

(c) The model incorporates interinput substitution in general. This recognizes the full set of complementarity-substitutability relations that exist between capital, labor, energy and material inputs. This substitution, together with interfuel substitution, is a known empirical fact and its inclusion is a critical feature of the model, from both theoretical and empirical points of view. (Also, if this substitutability were not included, it would imply that any reduction in energy input would cause a proportionate reduction in GNP, obviously a tenable assertion.)

(d) The role of the price system in securing resource allocation is explicitly modeled, as is the formation of prices themselves.

(e) In short, the model bases energy analyses on a simultaneous analysis of the behavior and interaction of the various parts of the economic system. This provides a sound foundation for the appraisal of national energy policies, building on the actual causal processes involved, and not dependent, as are many other energy models, on partial analysis or mechanical extrapolation of energy trends.

6.7   Alternative Oil Prices

6.7.1   Introduction

This section examines the level and composition of demand for energy under three different crude oil price assumptions. The three crude prices are in constant 1975 prices, $4, $7, and $11 a barrel. For the 1975–2000 forecast period simulations were run on each of these oil prices to find the demand for each type of fuel and the demand for each fuel by each category of consuming sector.

Changes in the price of crude oil, whether they result from actions of the U.S. government, or other governments or from market forces, have the power to induce significant changes in U.S. demand for energy. The principal impact is on the demand for petroleum itself. However, there is some degree of substitutability between petroleum and other fuels in each consuming sector and this results in a redirection of energy demand towards, for high oil prices, or away from, for low oil prices, these other fuels. The net result is that the entire pattern of fuel use is affected by changes in the price of petroleum. (The fact that demand for fuels other than petroleum changes in the opposite direction to petroleum demand means that the change in total energy input is always less than the change in petroleum consumption.)

6.7.2   Energy Utilization

The aggregate pattern of fuel use under the three different oil prices is shown, for 1975 to 2000, in tables 6.19 and 6.20. In each year the change in oil price produces a substantial change in petroleum demand, together with small changes, in the opposite direction, in the consumption of each other fuel-coal, gas, hydro and nuclear, and electricity. Consider first the case of $4 oil compared to $7 oil. The increase in petroleum consumption caused by the price decrease ranges from 2.680 quadrillion Btu, or 7.9 percent, in 1975, increasing over time, to 12.040 quadrillion Btu, or 19.6 percent, in 2000. Demands for other fuels are reduced as a result of substitution of the now cheaper petroleum, but these decreases are comparatively small, e.g., 0.746 quadrillion Btu in 1975. The overall effect of the reduction in oil prices is that total energy input increases, from 1.734 quadrillion Btu, or 1.9 percent, in 1975, rising to 10.046 quadrillion Btu, or 6.2 percent, in 2000.

Table 6.19
Summary of energy effects of alternative crude oil prices; 1975–2000

	1975	1977	1980	1985	1990	2000
1. Total energy input (quadrillion Btu)						
Crude price $4	78.964	85.152	94.209	111.180	130.360	173.429
Crude price $7	77.230	82.386	90.414	105.804	122.897	163.383
Crude price $11	75.802	80.241	87.553	101.469	116.279	155.422
Changes in total input from $7 crude (quadrillion Btu)						
Crude price $4	1.734	2.766	3.795	5.376	7.463	10.046
Crude price $11	−1.428	−2.145	−2.861	−4.335	−6.618	−7.961
Changes in total input from $7 crude (percent)						
Crude price $4	2.25	3.36	4.20	5.08	6.07	6.15
Crude price $11	−1.85	−2.60	−3.16	−4.10	−5.39	−4.87
2. Petroleum consumption (quadrillion Btu)						
Crude price $4	36.463	39.407	43.571	51.235	59.191	73.472
Crude price $7	33.783	36.046	39.195	45.031	50.783	61.432
Crude price $11	31.711	33.577	35.699	39.754	43.113	51.443
Changes in petroleum consumption from $7 crude (quadrillion Btu)						
Crude price $4	2.680	3.361	4.376	6.204	8.408	12.040
Crude price $11	−2.072	−2.469	−3.496	−5.277	−7.670	−9.989
Changes in petroleum consumption from $7 crude (percent)						
Crude price $4	7.93	9.32	11.16	13.78	16.56	19.60
Crude price $11	−6.13	−6.85	−8.92	−11.72	−15.10	−16.26

Table 6.20
Energy demands under alternative crude oil prices; 1975–2000 (quadrillion Btu)

Crude price ($1975/barrel)		Coal	Petroleum	Gas (incl. synth. gas)	Electricity	Hydro, nuclear	Total input
1975	4	13.044	36.463	24.230	6.627	5.228	78.964
	7	13.219	33.783	24.753	6.713	5.475	77.230
	11	13.296	31.711	25.110	6.751	5.685	75.802
1977	4	13.466	39.407	25.573	7.535	6.706	85.152
	7	13.553	26.046	25.995	7.600	6.792	82.386
	11	13.601	33.577	26.228	7.652	6.835	80.241
1980	4	14.124	43.571	26.484	8.773	10.030	94.209
	7	14.304	39.195	26.800	8.853	10.115	90.414
	11	14.585	35.699	26.991	9.101	10.278	87.553

Table 6.20 (continued)

Crude price ($1975/barrel)		Coal	Petroleum	Gas (incl. synth. gas)	Electricity	Hydro, nuclear	Total input
1985	4	16.528	51.235	28.176	11.324	15.932	111.180
	7	16.741	45.031	28.712	11.478	16.010	105.804
	11	16.944	39.754	29.262	11.666	16.199	101.469
1990	4	19.714	59.191	29.762	14.798	23.489	130.360
	7	19.887	50.783	30.408	14.984	23.616	122.897
	11	20.132	43.113	31.011	15.116	23.820	116.279
2000	4	25.759	73.472	31.530	23.200	46.308	173.429
	7	26.160	61.432	32.279	23.720	47.152	163.383
	11	26.636	51.443	32.948	24.183	48.035	155.422

The change in oil prices from $7 to $11 a barrel produces similar results. The increase in oil prices, both absolutely and relatively, leads to a reduction in oil demand which is partially offset by an increase in the demand for other fuels, with the overall result of a substantial decline in total energy input. In the 1975 simulations, the higher oil price leads to a decline of 2.072 quadrillion Btu (6.1 percent) in petroleum consumption and a smaller decline of 1.428 quadrillion Btu (1.9 percent) in total energy input. The magnitudes of these changes increase gradually over time with the energy use reductions in 2000 being 9.989 quadrillion Btu (16.3 percent) for petroleum and 7.961 quadrillion Btu (4.9 percent) for total energy input.

The figures for the response of energy consumers to changes in fuel prices show that the relative magnitude of the response is greater for a price increase than for a price decrease. This is caused by the greater ease with which energy use can be expanded than with which it can be contracted. For example, people apparently find it easier to turn the heating thermostat up rather than down, or to turn the cooling thermostat down rather than up, or to move up to more power and options in an automobile than down to less, and so on.

A second feature that can be noted from the projections is that the relative magnitude of the response to a change in oil prices increases over time. This is due to the time lags involved in adjusting levels and patterns of energy use to changes in fuel prices. A substantial amount of change can be made immediately after a fuel price change just by changing operating levels of existing energy using capital stock, e.g., adjusting thermostats, driving speeds or number of miles driven. But, given the complementarity between energy and capital, a significant proportion of energy use is locked in to existing capital stock and a change in the use must await the replacement of existing capital or the introduction of new capital. Some capital can be changed relatively rapidly, e.g., the stock of automobiles, some can be modified relatively easily, e.g., thermal insulation can be installed in existing buildings, but some take longer to replace. The overall result is that there is a graduated response of energy use to energy price changes. The greater part of the response occurs rapidly, but thereafter several years are required for the full effects to become evident.

6.7.3 Composition of Energy Use

The impact of the different oil prices on the sectoral demand for the various fuels is shown in table 6.21. The detailed pattern of response to different oil prices is similar in each forecast year; so, to examine the nature of these responses, only one year, 1975, is studied in detail. (Due to the increasing response, over time, of energy use to the petroleum price changes, the changes in 1975 are smaller than those that can be expected in later years.) The changes are examined in two steps, first those resulting from a reduction, from \$7 to \$4, of the oil price and second those resulting from an increase of the oil price from \$7 to \$11.

Coal is a competitor to petroleum, declining when petroleum becomes cheaper, increasing when it becomes more expensive. The only sectors using significant amounts of coal are manufacturing and electricity generation and each shows a similar response to the oil price change, with consumption decreasing by about 1.5 percent when oil prices fall and increasing by about 0.5 percent when oil prices rise. Thus, the total effect of the substitution between coal and oil is not very large. Gas shows a slightly greater degree of substitutability for oil. Total gas consumption declines by 2 percent when oil prices fall and increases by 1.4 percent when oil prices rise. Gas used in electricity generation shows the greatest changes of any of the sectors, with 5 percent changes for each of the oil price movements. Household and commercial and industrial sectors show a smaller degree of response with each reducing their gas use by around 1.5 percent when oil prices decline and each increasing use by about 1 percent when oil prices rise. Electricity is also a substitute fuel for gas, although the responses shown by the only two significant consuming sectors—household and

Table 6.21
Impact of alternative oil prices on composition of energy use; 1975 (percentage difference in energy use from $7 crude)

	$4 oil	$11 oil
Coal into manufacturing	−1.5	0.8
Coal into electricity	−1.3	0.5
Petroleum into household, commercial	6.1	−5.1
Petroleum into industrial	6.2	−5.2
Petroleum into transportation	8.5	−5.7
Petroleum into electricity	13.2	−14.6
Gas into household, commercial	−1.3	1.1
Gas into industrial	−1.7	0.7
Gas into electricity	−5.3	5.0
Electricity into household, commercial	−0.3	0.7
Electricity into industrial	−2.8	0.4
Coal consumption	−1.3	0.6
Petroleum consumption	7.9	−6.1
Electricity consumption	−1.3	0.6
Gas consumption	−2.1	1.4
Hydro, nuclear consumption	−4.5	3.8
Consumption by household, commercial	1.5	−1.2
Consumption by industrial	0.4	−0.9
Consumption by transportation	8.1	−5.5
Consumption electricity	−1.3	0.6
Total U.S. energy input	2.2	−1.9

commercial, industrial—indicate the the degree of substitution is rather small. Total use of electricity declines by 1.3 percent when oil prices fall and rises by 1.6 percent when oil prices increase.

The principal impact of changes in oil prices is on petroleum consumption itself. Total use increases by 8 percent when oil prices decline and decreases by 6 percent when prices rise. These changes are spread fairly uniformly over all four consuming sectors. Electricity generation shows the greatest response (with gas, hydro and nuclear inputs making compensating changes) with changes of around 14 percent for either oil price change. Transportation shows the next largest response, with its purchases of petroleum increasing by 8 percent when oil prices fall and declining by 6 percent when prices rise. Household and commercial and industrial uses of petroleum show similar changes, each moving by around 6 percent in response to the oil prices changes.

The transportation sector, which relies almost entirely on petroleum input, shows the greatest changes in energy use due to the oil price changes. The oil price decline induces an 8 percent increase in the total consumption of energy in transportation which the price rise leads to a 5 percent decline. The household and commercial sector shows the next largest response but, with changes in energy use of the order of 1.5 percent, is much less affected than transportation. Industrial demand shows the least sensitivity to oil price changes with changes of less than 1 percent resulting from the oil price variation.

6.8 Alternative Tax Policies

6.8.1 Introduction

This section considers three energy tax systems designed to achieve an objective defined in terms of upper limits to fuel imports. The purpose of this analysis is (a) to find whether these taxes do offer the potential of demand reductions sufficient to reduce dependence on fuel imports to the target levels, (b) to find the tax rates required to achieve these targets, (c) to find the effects of each tax on the level and composition of energy use, and (d) to compare these taxes in terms of their effectiveness in meeting the import targets and their costs in so doing. The definition of the import targets is given in table 6.24. The primary objective is taken to be the reduction in imports of petroleum from current levels to only nominal amounts (less than 0.5 million barrels a day) by 1985 and the continued requirement of only these small import quantities thereafter. A secondary objective is the elimination of the need for any natural gas imports by 1980.

Three general types of systems of taxing the use of energy are considered. Many different tax systems are possible but the two tax bases that are most feasible, from an administrative viewpoint, are the value of energy transactions (i.e., dollars) and the energy content (i.e., Btu) of these fuel transactions. Within each of these two categories there are many different tax schemes depending on which tax rates are applied to which fuels and which users. To analyze the general properties of these classes of tax systems, this section examines three representative types of taxes: (a) a uniform rate sales tax levied on all energy sales from the fuel-producing sectors (denoted the energy sales tax), (b) a uniform rate petroleum sales tax levied on all petroleum products sold to nonenergy-producing sectors (denoted the petroleum tax), and (c) a uniform rate energy tax levied on the Btu content of all sales of fuels to nonenergy-producing sectors (denoted the Btu tax). These taxes are applied only to energy as it emerges from the fuel sectors of the economy so that fuel purchased by the energy extraction and processing sectors—coal mining, petroleum and gas extraction, petroleum refining, electricity generation and gas utilities—is not taxed, but fuel sales from these sectors to any domestic user, whether an intermediate producer or final consumer, are subject to the tax.

A sales tax is added to the price charged the purchaser of energy. Since output prices are already at average costs in the inter-industry model the tax is not borne by the seller but is passed on to the fuel purchaser in the form of higher prices. Thus, the tax increases prices to the buyer but leaves prices received by the seller unchanged. This means that the tax has no direct effect on supply; the entire import-reducing force arises from the effect of the tax on reducing U.S. energy demand. For simulation, the tax can be entered directly into the inter-industry model as a markup of the purchaser's price over the seller's price for each transaction affected. A resimulation of the model incorporating these markups then gives a picture of the level and pattern of energy use after buyers have adjusted to the new set of fuel prices. The reference case used in these simulations is the set of projections for $7 oil, i.e., the taxes are imposed on the system of economic transactions and energy flows corresponding to a $7 crude oil price. The markups are uniform for the energy sales tax but vary between fuels for the Btu tax. The reason for this is that the price of energy, in terms of dollars per Btu, varies between fuels so that a uniform dollar tax rate per Btu translates into a different percentage price markup for each fuel. The ranking of the markups is opposite to the dollar cost of energy in each fuel, being highest for coal, next highest for gas, then lower for petroleum products and lowest for electricity.

6.8.2   Tax Impact

The results of the energy simulations under the three different tax programs are presented in table 6.22. The impact of the taxes on fuel
import requirements are summarized in table 6.23. These show that
any of the three taxes is sufficient to achieve the specified petroleum
import objectives; in fact the tax rates were chosen so that this objective would be achieved. The second objective, that of eliminating gas
imports, is largely incidental in this approach; there is no necessity
that the gas import target be reached. In fact, the petroleum tax fails
to achieve the gas imports objective. The reason for this is that a
petroleum tax contains no mechanism for reducing gas demand,
rather it increases this demand as users substitute gas for petroleum,
and so increase the need for imports of gas. Thus, a petroleum tax can
satisfy the petroleum import objective but cannot satisfy the gas
import goal. The sales and Btu taxes, however, tax energy use in general and thus do contain a mechanism for reducing demand for gas.
The result is that either an energy sales tax or a Btu tax sufficient to
meet the petroleum objective also reduces gas imports to nominal levels and removes the need for any gas imports after 1980.

    The tax rates required to meet the specified petroleum import tar-
gets are shown in table 6.24. It can be noted that, in each year, the
required rates of energy sales tax and of petroleum sales tax are the
same. This is due to the fact that objectives are defined in terms of
petroleum demand only so the critical parameter is the tax on
petroleum sales. It emerges that the substitutability between
petroleum and other fuels, although nonnegligible, is not sufficiently
strong that increasing the price of petroleum relative to other fuels, as
caused by a petroleum tax, reduces petroleum demand significantly
more than a rise in all fuel prices, as caused by an energy sales tax.
The required tax rate rises from 21 percent in 1975, to 70 percent in
1990 and then declines to 52 percent in 2000. The reduction in the rate
at the end of the period is due to changes in the domestic petroleum
supply-demand situation reducing the need for oil imports in the base
case—supply is boosted by increasing quantities of shale oil while
demand rises only slowly due to slower population and economic
growth, and to the saturation of much petroleum using equipment.
Also, it can be noted that an energy tax must be instituted as a permanent policy if continued independence from oil imports is to be
achieved—demand must continually be held down to domestic

Table 6.22a
Effects of alternative energy taxes on fuel prices and quantities; 1975

	Coal	Petroleum	Electricity	Gas	Hydro, nuclear	Total U.S. energy input
1. Energy consumption (quadrillion Btu, including synthetic products)						
Base case	13.219	33.783	6.713	24.753	5.475	77.230
Petroleum tax	13.326	31.637	6.734	24.875	5.480	75.318
Energy sales tax	12.905	31.669	6.285	23.075	5.109	72.757
Btu tax	12.914	31.705	6.628	21.898	5.389	71.906
2. Consumption, percentage change from base case						
Petroleum tax		−6.35	0.31	0.49	0.09	−2.48
Energy sales tax	−2.38	−6.26	−6.38	−6.78	−6.68	−5.79
Btu tax	−2.30	−6.15	−1.27	−11.53		−6.89
3. Fuel prices (average sales price, $/physical unit)						
Base case[a]	11.49	10.02	0.0210	0.99		
Petroleum tax	11.49	11.85	0.0211	0.99		
Energy sales tax	12.52	11.91	0.0250	1.14		
Btu tax	13.95	11.89	0.0223	1.26		
4. Fuel prices, percentage change from base case						
Petroleum tax	0	18.25	0.45	0		
Energy sales tax	8.96	18.91	19.05	15.15		
Btu tax	21.41	18.69	6.19	27.27		

[a] Average sales prices; average wholesale price for petroleum products.

Table 6.22b
Effects of alternative energy taxes on fuel prices and quantities; 1977

	Coal	Petroleum	Electricity	Gas	Hydro, nuclear	Total U.S. energy input
1. Energy consumption (quadrillion Btu, including synthetic products)						
Base case	13.553	36.046	7.600	25.995	6.792	82.386
Petroleum tax	13.766	32.726	7.643	26.241	6.812	79.544
Energy sales tax	13.145	32.792	6.860	23.471	6.102	75.511
Btu tax	13.241	32.906	7.452	21.818	6.633	74.598
2. Consumption, percentage change from base case						
Petroleum tax	1.57	−9.21	0.57	0.95	0.29	−3.45
Energy sales tax	−3.01	−9.03	−9.74	−9.71	−10.16	−8.34
Btu tax	−2.30	−8.71	−1.95	−16.07	−2.34	−9.45

Table 6.22b (continued)

	Coal	Petroleum	Electricity	Gas	Hydro, nuclear	Total U.S. energy input
3. Fuel prices (average sales price, $/physical unit)						
Base case[a]	13.40	11.05	0.0230	1.19		
Petroleum tax	13.40	13.91	0.0231	1.19		
Energy sales tax	15.13	14.03	0.0293	1.45		
Btu tax	16.94	13.93	0.0249	1.65		
4. Fuel prices, percentage change from base case						
Petroleum tax	0	25.85	0.44	0		
Energy sales tax	12.89	26.95	27.31	22.02		
Btu tax	26.38	26.05	8.37	38.53		

[a] Average sales prices; average wholesale price for petroleum products.

Table 6.22c
Effects of alternative energy taxes on fuel prices and quantities; 1980

	Coal	Petroleum	Electricity	Gas	Hydro, nuclear	Total U.S. energy input
1. Energy consumption (quadrillion Btu, including synthetic products)						
Base case	14.304	39.195	8.853	26.800	10.115	90.414
Petroleum tax	14.544	34.592	8.904	27.027	10.149	86.312
Energy sales tax	13.669	34.649	7.779	23.574	8.853	80.744
Btu tax	13.763	34.651	8.574	22.087	9.763	80.264
2. Consumption, percentage change from base case						
Petroleum tax	1.68	−11.74	0.58	0.85	0.34	−4.54
Energy sales tax	−4.44	−11.60	−12.13	−12.04	−12.48	−10.70
Btu tax	−3.78	−11.60	−3.15	−17.59	−3.48	−11.23
3. Fuel prices (average sales price, $/physical unit)						
Base case[a]	16.89	12.80	0.0263	1.54		
Petroleum tax	16.93	17.06	0.0265	1.54		
Energy sales tax	19.94	17.28	0.0355	1.95		
Btu tax	22.96	17.26	0.0294	2.16		
4. Fuel prices, percentage change from base case						
Petroleum tax	0.24	33.28	0.78	0		
Energy sales tax	18.07	34.97	35.16	26.35		
Btu tax	35.96	34.88	11.72	40.54		

[a] Average sales prices; average wholesale price for petroleum products.

Table 6.22d
Effects of alternative energy taxes on fuel prices and quantities; 1985

	Coal	Petroleum	Electricity	Gas	Hydro, nuclear	Total U.S. energy input
1. Energy consumption (quadrillion Btu, including synthetic products)						
Base case	16.741	45.031	11.478	28.712	16.010	105.804
Petroleum tax	17.086	36.203	11.557	29.123	16.086	97.809
Energy sales tax	15.359	36.238	9.263	23.465	12.867	87.238
Btu tax	15.644	36.351	10.737	21.679	14.926	87.911
2. Consumption, percentage change from base case						
Petroleum tax	2.06	−19.60	0.69	1.43	0.47	−7.56
Energy sales tax	−8.26	−19.53	−19.30	−18.27	−19.63	−17.55
Btu tax	−6.55	−19.28	−6.46	−24.49	−6.77	−16.91
3. Fuel prices (average sales price, $/physical unit)						
Base case[a]	22.49	16.35	0.0317	2.07		
Petroleum tax	22.65	25.11	0.0321	2.07		
Energy sales tax	29.06	25.73	0.0501	3.04		
Btu tax	37.58	25.52	0.0383	3.46		
4. Fuel prices, percentage change from base case						
Petroleum tax	0.70	53.56	1.33	0		
Energy sales tax	29.23	57.35	58.14	46.70		
Btu tax	44.87	56.09	20.93	67.01		

[a] Average sales prices; average wholesale price for petroleum products.

Table 6.22e
Effects of alternative energy taxes on fuel prices and quantities; 1990

	Coal	Petroleum	Electricity	Gas	Hydro, nuclear	Total U.S. energy input
1. Energy consumption (quadrillion Btu, including synthetic products)						
Base case	19.887	50.783	14.984	30.408	23.616	122.897
Petroleum tax	20.261	39.945	15.079	30.982	23.722	113.115
Energy sales tax	17.918	39.878	11.604	24.095	18.224	98.320
Btu tax	18.402	40.160	13.644	22.264	21.441	100.471
2. Consumption, percentage change from base case						
Petroleum tax	1.88	−21.34	0.63	1.89	0.45	−7.96
Energy sales tax	−9.90	−21.47	−22.56	−20.34	−22.83	−20.00
Btu tax	−7.47	−20.92	−8.94	−26.78	−9.21	−18.25

Table 6.22e (continued)

	Coal	Petroleum	Electricity	Gas	Hydro, nuclear	Total U.S. energy input
3. Fuel prices (average sales price, $/physical unit)						
Base case[a]	28.65	20.88	0.0377	2.79		
Petroleum tax	28.90	33.49	0.0382	2.79		
Energy sales tax	37.39	34.57	0.0625	4.35		
Btu tax	40.66	34.06	0.0474	4.94		
4. Fuel prices, percentage change from base case						
Petroleum tax	0.87	60.38	1.44	0		
Energy sales tax	30.49	65.56	65.71	55.89		
Btu tax	41.91	63.13	25.65	77.19		

[a] Average sales prices; average wholesale price for petroleum products.

Table 6.22f
Effects of alternative energy taxes on fuel prices and quantities; 2000

	Coal	Petroleum	Electricity	Gas	Hydro, nuclear	Total U.S. energy input
1. Energy consumption (quadrillion Btu, including synthetic products)						
Base case	26.160	61.432	23.720	32.279	47.152	163.383
Petroleum tax	26.449	50.136	23.791	32.748	47.255	152.949
Energy sales tax	23.923	50.083	18.799	26.324	37.309	133.999
Btu tax	24.291	50.029	21.269	24.821	42.220	137.721
2. Consumption, percentage change from base case						
Petroleum tax	1.10	−18.39	0.30	1.45	0.22	−6.39
Energy sales tax	−8.55	−18.47	−20.75	−18.45	−20.88	−17.98
Btu tax	−7.14	−18.56	−10.33	−23.10	−10.46	−15.71
3. Fuel prices (average sales price, $/physical unit)						
Base case[a]	44.54	34.07	0.0532	5.34		
Petroleum tax	44.88	49.79	0.0539	5.34		
Energy sales tax	54.51	51.04	0.0800	7.74		
Btu tax	57.59	51.15	0.0662	8.52		
4. Fuel prices, percentage change from base case						
Petroleum tax	0.77	46.14	1.39	0		
Energy sales tax	22.40	49.81	50.40	44.91		
Btu tax	29.30	50.13	24.40	59.48		

[a] Average sales prices; average wholesale price for petroleum products.

Table 6.23
U.S. oil and gas demand and supply under alternative energy taxes;
1975–2000

	1975	1977	1980	1985	1990	2000
1. Petroleum (million barrels a day)						
U.S. crude output (incl. shale oil)						
Base case	10.6	11.1	13.9	17.6	19.8	24.9
Petroleum tax	10.6	11.1	13.9	17.6	19.8	24.9
Energy sales tax	10.6	11.1	13.9	17.6	19.8	24.9
Btu tax	10.6	11.1	13.9	17.6	19.8	24.9
U.S. oil imports						
Base case	6.4	7.1	5.8	5.0	5.6	5.7
Petroleum tax	5.3	5.4	3.5	0.5	0.3	0.2
Energy sales tax	5.3	5.4	3.5	0.5	0.3	0.2
Btu tax	5.3	5.4	3.5	0.5	0.3	0.2
2. Gas (trillion cubic feet)						
U.S. gas output (incl. synth. gas)						
Base case	21.862	22.556	22.512	24.231	25.737	27.302
Petroleum tax	21.862	22.556	22.512	24.231	25.737	27.302
Energy sales tax	21.862	22.556	22.512	22.698	23.277	25.384
Btu tax	21.307	21.218	21.405	20.974	21.511	23.935
U.S. gas imports						
Base case	2.210	2.704	3.444	3.526	3.621	3.814
Petroleum tax	2.328	2.940	3.662	3.921	4.173	4.264
Energy sales tax	0.586	0.263	0.331	0	0	0
Btu tax	0	0	0	0	0	0

supply capacity. The required Btu tax rates show similar characteristics. The rates themselves rise steadily but this is due to the effects of continuing inflation as the nominal rates must rise merely to represent the same fuel price markups. When the trend in prices is removed, however, it can be seen that the real Btu tax rate peaks in the 1980s and then declines a little in the 1990s as the domestic oil supply deficit is projected to become less severe.

The impact of each tax on fuel use is shown in detail in table 6.25. The pattern of the changes in each year is the same, so to study these changes we focus on one just year, 1980. The specification of each tax is, in effect, to reduce petroleum demand by a predetermined amount from the base case. Therefore, petroleum demand under each tax is virtually identical; the differences in energy use arise from the impact of the tax on other fuels.

Table 6.24
Summary of economic effects of alternative energy taxes; 1975–2000

	1975	1977	1980	1985	1990	2000
1. Tax rates required for import objective						
Petroleum tax (%)	21	30	38	62	70	52
Energy sales tax (%)	21	30	38	62	70	52
Btu tax ($/million Btu)	0.36	0.55	0.85	1.73	2.48	3.37
Btu tax ($ 1975/million Btu)	0.36	0.50	0.67	1.13	1.35	1.28
2. Tax revenue resulting from						
Petroleum tax ($ bn)	11.657	20.072	33.520	81.138	134.198	203.129
Energy sales tax	23.685	41.516	69.995	175.744	294.120	460.889
Btu tax	19.615	30.674	49.902	106.314	166.924	292.634
3. Effect on average prices[a]						
Petroleum tax	0.68	1.10	1.12	1.41	1.55	1.43
Energy sales tax	1.32	1.88	2.27	3.44	3.88	3.11
Btu tax	1.26	1.69	2.17	3.24	3.56	2.95
4. Change in total U.S. energy input[b]						
Petroleum tax	−2.48	−3.45	−4.54	−7.56	−7.96	−6.39
Energy sales tax	−5.79	−8.34	−10.70	−17.55	−20.00	−17.98
Btu tax	−6.89	−9.45	−11.23	−16.91	−18.25	−15.71
5. Definition of oil import objective						
No tax imports (Mbd)	6.4	7.1	5.8	5.0	5.6	5.7
Desired imports (Mbd)	5.3	5.4	3.5	0.5	0.3	0.2

[a] Percentage change of GNP price deflator compared to the no tax case.
[b] Percentage change of total U.S. energy input compared to the no tax case.

The petroleum tax increases the sales price of petroleum but, apart from indirect effects through production costs, does not change other fuel prices. The results is an increase in petroleum prices relative to all other prices. This increase is over 33 percent in 1980. The effects on the prices of other fuels are negligible. This increase in petroleum prices has its principal effect in inducing a reduction in petroleum use. This consumption decline is 11.7 percent from the base case. Simultaneously, the comparative price of other fuels declines, leading to some substitution of these fuels for petroleum. These substitution effects are small individually but add up to a not insignificant total. Thus,

Table 6.25
Summary of energy effects of alternative energy taxes; 1975–2000

	1975	1977	1980	1985	1990	2000
1. Total U.S. energy input (quadrillion Btu)						
Base case	77.230	82.386	90.414	105.804	122.897	163.383
Petroleum tax	75.318	79.544	86.312	97.809	113.115	152.949
Energy sales tax	72.757	75.511	80.744	87.238	98.320	133.999
Btu tax	71.906	74.598	80.264	87.911	100.471	137.721
Change from base (%) under						
petroleum tax	−2.48	−3.45	−4.54	−7.56	−7.96	−6.39
energy sales tax	−5.79	−8.34	−10.70	−17.55	−20.00	−17.98
Btu tax	−6.89	−9.45	−11.23	−16.91	−18.25	−15.71
2. U.S. petroleum consumption (quadrillion Btu)						
Base case	33.783	36.046	39.195	45.031	50.783	61.432
Petroleum tax	31.637	32.726	34.592	36.203	39.945	50.137
Energy sales tax	31.669	32.792	34.649	36.238	39.878	50.083
Btu tax	31.705	32.906	34.651	36.352	40.159	50.029
Change from base (%) under						
petroleum tax	−6.35	−9.21	−11.74	−19.60	−21.34	−18.39
energy sales tax	−6.26	−9.03	−11.60	−19.53	−21.47	−18.47
Btu tax	−6.15	−8.71	−11.60	−19.28	−20.92	−18.56
3. U.S. gas consumption (quadrillion Btu)						
Base case	24.753	25.995	26.800	28.712	30.408	32.279
Petroleum tax	24.875	26.241	27.027	29.123	30.982	32.748
Energy sales tax	23.075	23.471	23.574	23.465	24.095	26.324
Btu tax	21.898	21.818	22.089	21.679	22.264	24.821
Change from base (%) under						
petroleum tax	0.49	0.95	0.85	1.43	1.89	1.45
energy sales tax	−6.78	−9.71	−12.04	−18.27	−20.34	−18.45
Btu tax	−11.53	−16.07	−17.59	−24.49	−26.78	−23.10

the decline of 4.603 quadrillion Btu in petroleum use is partially offset by an increase of 0.501 quadrillion Btu in the use of other inputs to leave a 4.102 quadrillion Btu decline in total energy inputs. Coal use shows the largest proportionate increase—of 1.7 percent—with gas use up 0.9 percent and electricity use increasing by 0.6 percent.

The energy sales tax increases the price of all fuels by the same proportion, to those uses that are taxed. Therefore, the principal effect of this tax is to increase the price of energy relative to other inputs rather than changing the relative prices of fuels themselves. The reduction in energy use caused by this tax arises, then, from the substitution of other inputs for energy. The price increases shown in tables 6.22 refer to average prices, a combination of taxed and nontaxed prices, so these increases understate the rise of each fuel to taxed users. The rate of tax is 0.38, so this is the increase in fuel prices facing the nonenergy sectors. The result is that use of each fuel is sharply curtailed, coal by the least, 4 percent, petroleum by 11.6 percent, gas input by 12.0 percent, hydro and nuclear input by 12.5 percent, and electricity demand by 12.1 percent. (The reductions in the use of electricity, gas, hydro and nuclear by more than the petroleum decline shows that, even within the general decline in energy use, petroleum is being substituted for some uses of these fuels.) The overall result is that total U.S. energy input declines by 10.7 percent from the base case.

The third of the taxes considered is that based on the Btu content of each fuel. This produces a very different pattern of price increases than the energy sales tax. Coal is the cheapest form of energy and, therefore, its price is increased the most by the tax. Even after averaging in coal used in electricity generation, and exempt from the tax, the increase in coal prices is 36 percent. Gas is taxed at a lower dollar markup than coal but, since more of its use is subject to tax, its average price increases by a greater proportion—by 41 percent. Average petroleum prices increase by less, with a 35 percent increase. Finally, electricity prices increase by very little, 12 percent, since the Btu content of a dollar of electricity purchased is low and the resulting tax markup is correspondingly low. In the Btu tax then, the tax increases energy relative to other prices but also results in substantial changes in relative fuel prices. The result is that electricity use declines by very little, only 3 percent, with a correspondingly small decline in hydro and nuclear and coal inputs into electricity. (This is the reason for the reduction in coal use being less for the Btu tax than for the energy sales tax, despite the much greater price increase, for the coal reduction in the latter case is caused by the large fall in electricity demand.) Gas demand, however, is reduced markedly, by almost 18 percent. The overall effect on energy use is for a decline of 11.2 percent (equal to 10.150 quadrillion Btu, made up of a 4.544 quadrillion Btu decline in petroleum use, a 4.713 quadrillion Btu in gas use and a 0.893 quadrillion Btu fall in the use of other inputs).

6.8.3   Import Independence

The above discussion has been concerned with the effects of each tax on the level and composition of energy demand. We turn now to a comparison of these effects as between taxes in order to compare the cost, in total energy use, of achieving the stipulated reduction in petroleum demand. Each tax achieves the same reduction in petroleum use; their differences lie in their effects on the other fuels. The petroleum tax produces the smallest decline in total energy use, indeed, use of other fuels increase slightly under this tax. This is advantageous for the objective of reducing petroleum imports with the least disruption elsewhere, but is disadvantageous from the point of view of the secondary objective of reducing gas imports. The energy sales tax and the Btu tax each cause about the same total reduction in energy input (although the decline under the Btu tax is slightly greater). Thus, in terms of the total energy cost of achieving the petroleum use decline, each of these policies is more costly than the petroleum use tax, but, as between the two, there is little difference. There is more difference, however, in terms of the composition of the reduction in the use of nonpetroleum fuels: the decline under the energy sales tax is spread evenly over electricity, gas and hydro and nuclear whereas the fall in the Btu tax case is concentrated largely in gas (and with coal demand being similar in each). Additional criteria, including the desirability of limiting the depletion of domestic gas reserves and the desirability of limiting the use of nuclear power, have to be brought into consideration in making this detailed comparison between the energy sales tax and the Btu tax.

Table 6.24 shows two other pieces of information that are useful in comparing the three types of energy tax: the tax revenue generated by the tax, and the impact of the tax on prices in general. The petroleum sales tax is the most restricted in its impact and, consequently, raises the smallest amount of tax revenue. The Btu tax raises more revenue and the energy sales tax the most. The revenue involved is substantial in 1980 for example, ranging up to $70 billion under the energy sales tax, and the differences between the revenues produced by the taxes is also large. Thus, the differences in costs of the three taxes, as measured by the taxation required to achieve the same objective, are nontrivial and, on this criterion, a definite ranking can be given: the petroleum tax is the least costly, followed by the Btu tax with the energy sales tax the most costly. The opposite side of this cost is the effect of the taxes on prices, measured, for example, by the GNP price deflator. The petroleum tax involves the least tax cost to energy purchasers and, therefore, results in the smallest increase in overall prices. The Btu tax involves the next largest cost and the next largest increase in prices with the energy sales tax causing the largest price increase. The magnitude of these price increases in the whole economy is not, however, very large as the energy sectors form a relatively small component of the economic system. In the 1980 simulations, for example, the increases in the level of the GNP price deflator, compared to the base case with no energy taxes, are 1.1 percent, 2.2 percent, and 2.3 percent for the petroleum tax, energy sales tax and the Btu tax, respectively.

The overall comparison of the three types of energy tax is a policy problem requiring the aggregation of the different costs of each tax. Each tax clearly has the power to secure by 1985, and maintain thereafter, the stipulated target for petroleum import independence. But, the side effects of each tax vary greatly. Table 6.26 presents a summary of the comparative costs of each of the three taxes on the basis of four of the criteria that have been discussed above—gas import independence, reduction in nonpetroleum energy use, tax revenue resulting from the program and increase in overall prices caused by the

Table 6.26
Comparison of total effects of alternative energy taxes (all taxes meet the petroleum import objective; ranking is 1 for most desirable, 2 for intermediate, and 3 for least desirable)

	Tax system		
Criterion	Petroleum tax	Energy sales tax	Btu tax
Gas import objective	3	2	1
Reduction in nonpetroleum energy use[a]	1	2[a]	2[a]
Tax revenue required[b]	1	3	2
Increase in average prices[c]	1	3	2

[a] The least reduction forced in the use of energy other than petroleum is considered as being least disruptive and, hence, most desirable.
[b] The least tax revenue extracted from fuel purchasers is taken as being the least disruptive and, therefore, the most desirable.
[c] The smallest increase in prices, measured by the GNP price deflator, is taken as being the most desirable.

taxes. Additional considerations such as impact on gas depletion or on the scale of nuclear power use have been indicated in the text. In addition, there will be many microeconomic differences that cannot be ascertained within the framework of a macroeconomic analysis.

On the basis of the macro criteria discussed above, the petroleum tax appears to be clearly preferable to the energy sale tax and the Btu tax. This is not surprising for the fundamental objective, that of reducing petroleum demand, is a specific objective that requires the same amount of tax power in this one area, no matter which tax is used. The petroleum tax is specific to this one area and only indirectly affects other areas. The energy sales tax and Btu taxes, however, are general instruments so that accompanying the required rate of tax on petroleum is a significant amount of tax on other activities. Thus, it is unavoidable that these general taxes have direct effects over a broad range of activity and that the total effects of these taxes are much wider and much more severe than the effects of the petroleum tax. Other criteria may introduce other considerations into the evaluation, but, from the point of view of the petroleum import independence objective, it can be concluded that (a) each type of energy tax can secure this objective, and (b) the petroleum sales tax is, of the taxes considered, the least costly way of securing independence.

6.9   Conclusion

We conclude with a brief overview of our methodology, comparing our framework for the analysis of energy policy with alternative approaches. Our model replicates each of the components of the over-all transactions flow—purchase of primary inputs, sales of goods and services between sectors, formation of product prices and purchase of output by final users. These aspects of economic activity are brought into consistency by means of simulated market processes. All decision units react to the same set of prices and prices and quantities adjust so that all markets are cleared and each production sector covers its costs. The heart of the model lies in a series of submodels of production behavior, one for each of the nine domestic producing sectors. This set of production relationships provides the basic information used to determine relative output prices and the corresponding set of input patterns.

The sectoral production models are based upon price possibility frontiers. Within each sector, the price frontier expresses output price in terms of the prices of inputs and the production efficiency of that sector. Each frontier contains first- and second-order terms, so that both the average requirements for each input and the interrelationships between inputs are captured. Thus, although the specification is in terms of prices, it captures the same information concerning input requirements, complementarities and substitutabilities as the more traditional production function.

The primary input prices are generated within our macroeconometric growth model. Productivities are exogenous to the producer submodels so the nine sectoral output prices can be solved from the nine price frontiers. The simultaneous determination of prices permits the derivation of a set of prices for all produced output which not only takes account of production constraints and interrelationships and primary input prices but also integrates all these price determinants into a consistent framework so that all sectors are simultaneously charging the minimum price that covers all their costs, including a return to capital. In short, given primary input prices and underlying production information, the model finds the equilibrium price system for the economy.

This approach to prices and production also permits the input pattern for each sector that is best suited to the prevailing set of prices and costs to be chosen from the infinity of patterns that are possible. Thus, producers can react to the prevailing structure of relative prices by adjusting their input patterns and substituting, within the limits set by the complementarity and substitutability information contained in the price frontiers, relatively less expensive for relatively more expensive inputs. In this way, a critical feature of the economy, the response of input patterns to prices, is systematically included in our model. This feature of the model is very important from a practical point of view in accommodating the detailed operation of the price system. Conceptually, it frees input-output analysis from the assumption of fixed coefficients, and extends input-output analysis by making the coefficients variable and by making them fully endogenous and linking them to price behavior.

After the analysis of production relationships has been completed, the next step in implementing our model is to examine the components of final demand. These components are produced by three final demand submodels. The initial inputs into these submodels are the prices charged for the output of each of the domestic producing sectors, the prices of primary inputs that enter directly into final use, and the total current dollar expenditures in three of the final demand categories—personal consumption, private investment and government purchases. These expenditure totals are produced by the use of our macroeconometric model of U.S. economic growth. Our growth model provides levels of relative prices of consumption, investment, capital and labor within the framework employed to generate final demand in real terms. The model represents a major extension of macroeconometric model building to incorporate elements of both aggregate demand and aggregate supply.

We begin with the set of prices that is consistent with equilibrium demand and supply and with the levels of prices and primary inputs. We find the pattern of input-output coefficients associated with this price regime. We determine the level and composition of final demand that is associated with these prices. The input-output coefficients have been determined already, so the balance equations of input-output analysis are sufficient to find, in constant dollar terms, the total sectoral outputs and the pattern of industry purchases and sales necessary to sustain the final demand. This step imposes a final set of market clearing relationships in our simulated economy with the condition of equality between real demand and supply of every commodity being added to the condition of equality between value of demand and supply and of equality between receipts and expenditures for every sector.

The output from the inter-industry model comprises prices for each of the supplying sectors, the matrix of constant-dollar transactions for the entire structure, and, by combining these two elements, the matrix of current-dollar transactions. The transactions matrices cover the whole economic structure—energy as well as nonenergy sectors. The energy information contained in these transactions matrices is already extensive, covering both volumes and prices. It can readily be extended, however, to produce the data forms traditionally used in energy analysis—energy flows in British Thermal Units, energy flows in physical units, and energy prices in terms of physical units. This further information for Btu can be generated by inserting known values of the Btu content per constant dollar of each fuel, the volume in physical units can be obtained by using known physical unit per constant-dollar ratios, and fuel prices can be generated by applying the base period prices to the price indices simulated in the model.

We conclude this overview of our framework for energy policy analysis by comparing the conceptual properties of our model with those of the traditional energy balance approach to energy analysis. The fundamental advantage of our approach is that, rather than viewing energy in isolation, it is viewed as one of the many interacting parts that make up the economic system. This perspective permits the systematic analysis of all the factors that influence energy on both demand and supply sides and, equally important, it permits the explicit linkage of energy developments to those variables, such as employment, incomes and consumption, that are the ultimate ends to which energy use is only a means.

More specifically, our model incorporates the influence of fuel prices on the level and composition of energy use and, further, it incorporates the effects of the level and pattern of nonenergy activity on energy use as well as the reverse linkage of energy prices and supplies to nonenergy price input, output and consumption patterns. These interrelationships are critical and it is essential, for both forecasting and policy purposes, to recognize them. Some examples of these linkages are the severe impact of the recent oil shortages on the output of and the incomes generated by the automobile and tourist industries, the implications for energy use of the secular trend of demand towards service activities, and the economies in fuel use induced by the recent increases in fuel prices.

One aspect of these linkages in which our model represents a particularly important advance over energy balance procedures is the variation of input patterns in response to relative prices. This is of great importance in energy analysis in view of the widespread ability to substitute between fuels, for example between coal and oil in electricity generation, between oil and gas in industrial heating, between gas and electricity in home cooking and so on. This substitution is not merely a matter of switching fuels for the associated capital stock must also be changed to permit the use of a different fuel. Our production models, by treating all inputs simultaneously, take account of the possibilities for both interfuel substitutions and substitutions of fuel for nonfuel input, but do this in such a way that the constraints implied by complementarities between inputs are recognized, so that a consistent analysis of the entire input picture is obtained.

Our investigation of the effects of a Btu tax serves to demonstrate the usefulness of our framework for energy policy analysis. The basic properties of the model are illustrated by the result that, in the 1980 simulations for example, energy input can be reduced by 8 percent at the cost of only a 1 percent increase in average prices and a 0.4 percent decrease in real income. In other words, the flexibility of the economy in adapting to changing resource availabilities and the power of the price system in securing this adaptation, mean that substantial reductions in energy use can be achieved without major economic cost. The analytical property of our model that incorporates this flexibility is the endogenous formation of prices and the endogenous determination of the response of production patterns and final demand to these prices. Also, the integration of the various components of the model by means of inter-industry analysis secures an overall consistency in the simulation of the market process. These features, permitting price formation and the reaction of producers and consumers to price changes, combined in a simultaneous model of the entire economy, represent a major advance over traditional inter-industry and energy balance analysis.

Notes

1. The seminal contribution to macroeconometric modeling of the U.S. economy is the Klein-Goldberger (1955) model. For a recent review of macroeconometric models of the United States, see Hickman (1972).
2. For the original development of input-output analysis, see Leontief (1955). A recent compendium of research on input-output analysis is Carter and Brody (1970).
3. A more detailed presentation of our approach is contained in Jorgenson, Berndt, Christensen and Hudson (1973).
4. In the Klein-Goldberger model the determination of prices can be completely suppressed with a resulting improvement in forecasting accuracy for real magnitudes. See Suits (1962) and Goldberger (1959).
5. The energy balance framework has been employed by Dupree and West (1972) and the National Petroleum Council (1971, 1972).
6. Energy imports are significant only for crude and refined petroleum products, and natural gas. For the period 1958–1972, petroleum imports were subject to a system of quotas. Natural gas imports are subject to regulation by The Federal Power Commission. For a discussion of the petroleum import quota system, see Burrows and Domencich (1970).
7. For a detailed interpretation of the price possibility frontier, see Christensen, Jorgenson and Lau (1973), esp. pp. 32–33.
8. See Samuelson (1966).
9. For further discussion of the model of producer behavior, see section 6.3 below.
10. The idea of treating input-output coefficients as functions of prices can be traced to Walras (1954), esp. pp. 382–392; this approach has been extensively discussed by Samuelson (1966, pp. 513–536), and Morishima (1964, pp. 54–92). A more influential idea is to model trends in input-output coefficients without treating them as part of a model of producer behavior. This alternative approach has been employed by Leontief (1953), Carter (1970) and Almon et al. (1974). Comparisons of input-output coefficients for 1947, 1958 and 1961 are given by Carter (1970) and Vaccara (1970).
11. For a detailed discussion of the indirect utility function, see Christensen, Jorgenson and Lau (1975).

12. This section is based on Berndt and Jorgenson (1973).

13. See Christensen, Jorgenson, and Lau (1973), pp. 29–32.

14. See Leontief (1947).

15. A KLEM model for total U.S. manufacturing based on the translog price possibility frontier has been developed by Berndt and Wood (1974). Berndt and Christensen (1973a,b, 1974) have developed models of capital-labor substitution for U.S. manufacturing based on the translog production function.

16. Methods for imposing convexity restrictions have been developed by Lau (1974).

17. These data were compiled by Jack Faucett Associates (1973).

18. The minimum distance estimator for nonlinear simultaneous equations is discussed by Malinvaud (1970), pp. 325–373.

19. See, for example, the discussion of the neoclassical two-sector growth model by Burmeister and Dobell (1970) and the references given there. A more detailed discussion of our model is presented in Hudson and Jorgenson (1973); see also Jorgenson, Berndt, Christensen and Hudson (1973), chapter 2.

20. Detailed projections are presented by Hudson and Jorgenson (1974b).

21. Our model of the household sector was originated by Christensen and Jorgenson (1968). Our model of the business sector was originated by Christensen, Jorgenson and Lau (1973).

22. The data are presented in a series of articles by Christensen and Jorgenson (1969, 1970, 1973a,b).

23. The conversion process is discussed in the following section.

24. See footnote 5.

25. See National Petroleum Council (1972).

26. See Chapman, Mount and Tyrrell (1972); a detailed report on the econometric model underlying these projections is given by Mount, Chapman and Tyrrell (1973).

27. This section is based on Hudson and Jorgenson (1974a), presented as testimony at hearings by the Senate Finance Committee, January 16, 1974.

7

Economic Analysis of Alternative Energy Growth Patterns, 1975–2000

Edward A. Hudson and
Dale W. Jorgenson

This study presents the results of simulations of U.S. economic growth over the 1975–2000 period under different energy supply and demand conditions. The economic impacts of moves from *Historical Growth* patterns to a *Technical Fix* growth path, and from this to a *Zero Energy Growth* path are examined. The main conclusions are:

- Substantial economies in U.S. energy input are possible within the existing structure of the economy and without having to sacrifice continued growth of real incomes.

- This energy conservation does have a nontrivial economic cost in terms of a reduction in real income levels *vis-à-vis* the *Historical Growth* position; in 2000, real income under *Technical Fix* and *Zero Energy Growth* are both about 4 percent below the *Historical Growth* figure.

- Adaptation to a less energy intensive economy will not have a cost in terms of reduced employment; in fact, it will result in a slight increase in demand for labor. This, with the reduced real output, means that labor productivity is reduced and, correspondingly, real wages are slightly lower in *Technical Fix* or *Zero Energy Growth* than in *Historical Growth*.

- Adaptation to a less energy intensive economy will not have a cost in terms of total capital requirements; in fact, *Technical Fix* or *Zero Energy Growth* should require slightly less total capital input than *Historical Growth*.

- The shift to reduced energy use will result in an increase in rates of inflation from a predicted 3.8 percent a year under *Historical Growth* to 4.1 percent under *Zero Energy Growth*.

  The quantitative economic changes involved in the move to *Technical Fix* or *Zero Energy Growth* are summarized in table 7.1.

Table 7.1
Summary of differences between growth paths (percentage difference in the level of each variable between growth paths)

	Historical Growth vs. Technical Fix		Historical Growth vs. Zero Energy Growth		Technical Fix vs. Zero Energy Growth	
	1985	2000	1985	2000	1985	2000
Real GNP	−1.64	−3.78	−1.61	−3.54	0.03	0.25
Price of GNP	2.00	4.81	2.26	6.03	0.25	1.17
Employment	0.90	1.52	1.25	3..32	0.35	1.77
Capital input	−1.02	−1.83	−0.88	−1.17	0.15	0.67
Energy input	−16.60	−37.70	−19.30	−46.10	−3.20	−13.40

7.1   Introduction

This report examines and compares the general economic environment corresponding to the three alternative energy growth patterns
being studied by the Energy Policy Project. These growth patterns
are: *Historical Growth* where past energy supply and demand patterns
are assumed to continue into the future; *Technical Fix* growth, where
energy conservation practices and known energy-saving technologies
are incorporated into production and consumption patterns to the
extent possible within existing life styles and economic organization;
and *Zero Energy Growth* (ZEG) where, in addition to the technical fix
measures, changes in life styles and economic structure are introduced
in order to move towards a situation of constant *per capita* energy consumption. Economic growth paths under each of these three scenarios
were simulated using the DRI energy model. The DRI energy model
simulates production, transactions and consumption aspects of the
economy to generate predictions of sectoral output levels, sectoral
prices and patterns of energy use. These data can then be used to
obtain a broad picture of the economic system along each of the alternative growth paths and, most importantly, to assess the differential
impact of the two energy conservation programs *vis-a-vis* the *Historical
Growth* path. Information on the differential impacts of *Technical Fix*
and *ZEG* is extremely important as it provides the basis for ascertaining the nature and magnitudes of the economic costs of the two con-

servation programs so that, as a basis for energy policy decisions, costs can be compared to the benefits resulting from reduced energy consumption.

The conclusion of this study is that the transition to *Technical Fix Growth,* or even to *Zero Energy Growth,* can indeed be accomplished within the current economic structure without major economic upheaval or collapse.

A final purpose of this report is to complement other technically oriented studies of energy consumption being conducted by the Energy Policy Project. The present economic approach, conducted at an aggregate level and incorporating observed patterns of economic complementarity, substitutability and adjustment, provides a broad-based measure of the impact of reduced energy use on production and prices. The engineering approach examines the possibilities for energy conservation at a detailed, process level by ascertaining which conservation measures would be cost-effective, given current technology and given projected energy prices. Both approaches incorporate the same motivating force—cost minimization in production or consumption activities. Also, each approach is based on similar information concerning technically feasible adjustments in the economy with the difference being that the macro data are more aggregated and reflect adjustment patterns actually observed, whereas the micro data incorporate adjustment possibilities predicted by the process analyst. Thus, there is no inherent conflict between the two approaches; they just view the same problem from different perspectives. In fact, the two approaches do yield consistent results. This means that each reinforces the other, for it establishes first, that the economic adjustments predicted by the macro approach on the basis of observed behavioral responses do have a valid technical basis at the process level, and second, that the adjustments predicted by the process approach have a valid economic basis in the senses of being mutually consistent within the broad system of economic interdependence and of being consistent with observed patterns of business and consumer adjustments to changes in the availability and price of energy.

7.2   The Data Resources Inc. Energy Model

The Data Resources Inc. (DRI) energy model has already been presented in detail in the DRI report to the Energy Policy Project: "Energy Resources and Economic Growth," DRI, September 30, 1973. This section presents a brief outline of the model with the intention of illustrating the general derivation of the results presented below. The starting point in the projections is provided by a macro econometric model of U.S. economic growth. This model integrates both the demand and supply sides of macro economic activity into a single framework. This is used to project the general economic environment within which the energy simulations can be conducted. Specifically, the macro model is used to define the prices and availability of capital and labor inputs and the total levels of final expenditures, variables that are used as inputs in the detailed energy simulations. The energy analysis is then based on an inter-industry model of the U.S. economy in which production and consumption are broken down in the following pattern:

• Production is classified into nine sectors, each of which is represented by a production submodel. These nine sectors are agriculture (together with nonfuel mining and construction), manufacturing, transport, services (together with trade and communication), coal mining, crude petroleum and natural gas extractions, petroleum refining, electric utilities, and gas utilities.

• The nine producing sectors purchase inputs of primary factors imports, capital services and labor services;

• The nine producing sectors must also purchase inputs from each other; for example, manufacturing makes purchases from transport and the transport sector makes purchases of manufacturing output;

• The nine producing sectors then sell their net output to final users— personal consumption, investment, government and exports.

These components are then integrated within an inter-industry, or input-output, model. The feature of input-output analysis is that transaction flows are brought into consistency so that each sector produces exactly that amount needed to meet final demands as well as the intermediate demands from other producing sectors. The critical feature of the DRI energy model is that the patterns of input into the producing sectors, as well as the final demand levels, are functions of, *inter alia*, prices. This means that the model allows for production to substitute, within the bounds of given technical parameters, relatively less expensive for relatively more expensive inputs. This feature is of central importance in energy analysis for it captures the fact that producers and consumers react to higher energy prices by economizing on energy use by substitutions between different fuels, and by substitutions between fuel and nonfuel purchases, as well as by cutting back on "nonessential" energy input without accompanying substitutions.

The actual solution of the model moves through the following steps:

1. prices are determined endogenously in terms of production coefficients, efficiency levels, primary input prices and other information,

2. these prices are then used to solve for the pattern of inputs into each producing sector that is most economical in terms of these prices,

3. these prices are also fed into final demand submodels to obtain final demands for each type of output,

4. the input-output system is then solved to find the primary inputs and the inter-industry transactions that are required to satisfy these final demands. Thus the model simulates, on the base of exogenous parameters characterizing the general economic environment, the entire flow of transactions in the economy—transactions from factors to producers, producers to producers, and producers to consumers. Specifically, the model generates transactions flows and totals in current dollars and real terms (constant dollars) together with the corresponding sectoral price levels and energy usages.

The parameters of the production models were obtained by econometric estimation of the models on the basis of U.S. inter-industry transactions over the 1947–1971 period (these data were prepared by the Energy Policy Project).

The approach uses information about production relationships that have actually occurred in the past as the basis for predicting future production responses to price changes. In particular, the projected reaction to energy price increases is based upon the observed patterns of past production responses. This requires the assumption of reversibility in the sense that producers' reactions to the very substantial declines in real energy prices in the past will apply, but in reverse, to the adjustment to increasing real energy prices in the future. In fact, this assumption is likely to be rather conservative in estimating the scope for energy conservation. The predicted responses are based on behavioral adjustments within existing technical knowledge and within advances in this knowledge along past trends. In fact, substantial future technical knowledge is likely to be of an energy-conserving nature which would permit even greater conservation than that predicted from historical relationship. Therefore, the projections

presented below probably err on the side of underestimating the
potential for future energy conservation.

7.3   Methodology

The simulations of the alternative energy scenarios were made in two
steps. First, the DRI energy model was calibrated so as to produce the
Energy Policy Project *Historical Growth* path of economic development. This involved selecting and inserting into the model initial
assumptions covering productivity advance, fuel imports, income
growth, primary input prices, energy supply conditions and so on, in
such a way that the predicted energy demand growth path exhibited
the same general characteristics and trends as observed in the *Historical Energy* growth patterns. Once the model was calibrated in this
way, the exogenous assumptions were fixed and only those parameters corresponding to a move from *Historical Energy* use patterns to a
Technical Fix situation and then from *Technical Fix* to a *Zero Energy
Growth* situation were varied. In other words, the general specification of the model was held unchanged in the three different energy
scenarios; only energy-specific parameters were varied to secure the
move between the three alternative growth paths.

The simulations focused on three years: 1975, which was used as
the common starting point for all three alternative growth paths; 1985,
when the three growth paths had clearly diverged; and 2000, by which
time the full effects of each energy conservation program had been felt
and the differential impacts of the energy conservation programs were
most clearly visible. Thus three economic growth paths, starting from
the same initial position in 1975, are examined at two points in
time—1985 and 2000. The differences between the growth paths can
still be examined in detail: limiting the comparison to two years has
no cost but saves the complexity involved in simulating every year
from 1975 to 2000. The solution presupposes that the economy has
had time to make the adjustment from its initial to its equilibrium configuration. The use of 1985 and 2000 as comparison years is entirely
consistent with this assumption since the time lags to these years are
more than sufficient to cover the transition period needed for the
economy to adapt to policies and conditions implemented in the near
future.

The predictions are based upon an economic model which simulates aggregate production, expenditure and consumption relationships. Since the model is a simplified and idealized representation of

actual processes, its forecasts cannot be considered as pin-point accurate predictions of future economic events. Actual future developments will vary from those predicted in this study because the assumptions made about future exogenous developments may not be completely accurate, and also because the model does not replicate economic processes with perfect accuracy. However, the focus of this report is on the differences in economic performance under different energy conditions rather than on future levels of economic indicators. The model does give meaningful estimates of these: first, because differencing itself eliminates any systematic bias introduced into the forecasts through incorrect assumptions and through biases in the model itself; second, because extensive testing of the model suggests that it does produce reasonable estimates of the changes in aggregate economic behavior produced by changes in exogenous parameters.

7.4 Historical Growth

The pattern of economic growth and energy consumption corresponding to the *Historical Growth* scenario is summarized in table 7.2. This growth pattern is, by design, essentially a continuation of recent trends so that, even in 2000, the forecast composition of the economy is similar to that of the 1975 starting point.

Production increases at rates similar to, although slightly below, recent growth rates. The decline in growth rates is expected to become significant only in the 1980s in response to the low fertility rates currently being experienced. The assumption is made that the fertility rates experienced over the 1970–1973 period, rates which imply an eventually constant population size, will continue so that when today's infants begin to enter the labor force in the late 1980s, the rate of labor force expansion slows, leading to a general reduction in the rate of increase of real GNP. *Per capita* income and output is not reduced, but a smaller labor force means a smaller total output.

The composition of production does change somewhat over the forecast period; in terms of gross output—that is, total sales of each sector—transport expands the most rapidly, followed by the energy industries, then manufacturing, then services. These trends in composition reflect developments that can be discerned today:

• increased demand for transport for business and vacation travel, and to service increasingly dispersed economic activity, together with some increase in the relative importance of public transport, result in a continued rapid increase in transport activity;

Table 7.2
Historical Growth path

	1975	1985	2000	Growth rates (% per annum)	
				1975–1985	1985–2000
Output (gross) (billion 1971 $)					
Agriculture	306.8	387.9	532.2	2.4	2.1
Manufacturing	848.6	1228.4	1966.1	3.8	3.2
Transport	94.4	140.2	244.8	4.0	3.8
Services	976.6	1364.7	2109.5	3.4	2.9
Energy	97.8	144.3	249.6	4.0	3.7
Demand (billion 1971 $)					
Consumption	838.3	1211.8	1990.9	3.8	3.4
Investment	309.7	430.5	670.4	3.3	3.0
Government	275.0	388.4	604.9	3.5	3.0
Net exports	19.2	33.2	78.8	5.6	5.9
GNP (billion 1971 $)	1442.2	2064.0	3345.0	3.6	3.3
Output (value added, billion 1971 $)					
Agriculture	135.8	186.6	290.1	3.2	3.0
Manufacturing	345.1	459.2	662.5	2.9	2.5
Transport	52.3	64.3	82.7	2.1	1.7
Services	703.3	1011.2	1669.6	3.7	3.4
Energy	63.1	101.3	190.4	4.9	4.3
Services of durables	142.6	226.6	446.8	4.7	4.6
Employment (billion manhours)					
Agriculture	16.478	19.696	26.006	1.80	1.87
Manufacturing	41.689	48.049	59.807	1.43	1.47
Transport	6.927	7.524	8.683	0.83	0.96
Services and government	105.452	129.834	168.061	2.10	1.74
Total	173.115	205.103	262.557	1.71	1.66
Energy (quadrillion Btu)					
Coal	13.15	18.54	34.40	3.49	4.21
Petroleum	34.87	39.48	58.91	0.36	2.70
Electricity	6.81	13.16	27.37	6.81	5.00
Gas	24.47	34.51	42.23	3.50	1.35
Nuclear, other	5.55	22.50	51.25	15.02	5.64
Total energy input	78.03	115.03	184.71	3.96	3.21

Table 7.2 (continued)

	1975	1985	2000	Growth rates (% per annum) 1975–1985	1985–2000
Energy consumption (quadrillion Btu)					
Personal consumption	23.165	31.606	48.359	3.2	2.9
Services and government	10.936	15.480	26.743	3.5	3.7
Electricity generation	21.080	40.739	84.716	6.8	5.0
Industry	26.900	36.900	49.476	3.2	2.0
Transport	2.672	3.469	4.867	2.6	2.3
Total input	78.032	115.031	184.706	4.0	3.2
Prices					
Agriculture				4.70	5.09
Manufacturing				3.04	3.68
Transport				2.03	2.56
Services				3.88	4.23
Coal				1.78	5.72
Crude petroleum				4.76	4.44
Refined petroleum				5.74	4.54
Electricity				−0.90	2.53
Gas				5.96	4.94
Consumption				3.63	3.98
Investment				3.58	4.08
Government				3.79	4.16
GNP				3.61	3.98

- energy output also grows rapidly in large part because of the rapid growth of electricity usage which, since electricity is a secondary energy form suffering large energy conversion losses, places great demands on the primary energy sources;
- manufacturing output grows in line with total production, driven both by demand for manufactured goods as an input into the other producing sectors as well as by continuing growth in final use demands for manufacturing output;
- services grow less rapidly than manufacturing in terms of total output for, although final demand for services in current dollars is rising more rapidly, the faster rate of price increase for services converts this to a slower rate of increase in real output. The his-

torical forecast implies a continuation of the relative increase in the importance of service activities, but services prices increase more rapidly than those of manufacturing, leading to real service output growing less rapidly than real manufacturing output;

• agriculture and construction real output grows at the slowest rate, primarily because demand for these types of output is linked to population more than income so that increasing consumption demand flows more to the other producing sectors.

The value added in each production sector moves a little differently from the growth pattern of real output. Services of consumer durables show the fastest increase; that is, the imputed flow of services to consumers from owner-occupied housing, automobiles and other home and personal appliances increases more than the market-transacted output. The greatest rate of increase in value added in marketed output occurs in energy production; the rapidly growing demand for energy sources along with the increasingly difficult supply conditions in fuel production result in inputs being drawn into these sectors relative to other production. Services show the next most rapid increase and are predicted to continue to increase relative to real GNP. This increase is due to the continuing rapid growth of final demand for services, along with the very low rate of productivity advance expected in service activitites, drawing capital and labor services into service occupations faster than the general rate of increase in the supply of these inputs. This process is reflected also in the increasing share of services in total employment. Agriculture and construction value added increases less rapidly than GNP, mainly because total demand for output from these activities is not growing as rapidly as GNP. Manufacturing and transport value added increases least rapidly of all sectors. The reason for this is the continued high rate of productivity advance expected in these activities since this allows their output to increase without a correspondingly rapid increase in primary inputs.

The employment pattern changes in a similar way to changes in the pattern of value added, with services, agriculture and construction increasing, and manufacturing and transport declining in relative importance. Services and government increase their share of total employment from 60 percent to 64 percent over the forecast period. Total employment (which includes a labor quality improvement index) increases at around 1.7 percent a year although this rate of increase declines over time due to the effect of low fertility rates in slowing labor force growth.

Prices are projected to increase at around 3.75 percent a year which is, although not as rapid as the inflation currently being experienced, still substantially faster than average inflation rates of the last 10 or 15 years. On the demand side, consumption, investment and government purchase price indices all rise at about the same pace. One the production side, however, there is more substantial variation in rates of price increase. Fuel prices, apart from electricity, rise the fastest of any prices as it becomes increasingly difficult to produce the fuel to meet the rapidly growing demand. Electricity prices show much less increase. The reason for this lies in the productivity assumptions upon which the *Historical Growth* forecasts are based. The past rapid growth in electricity use has been, in large part, due to the past steadiness, and even decline, in electricity prices which, in turn, have been made possible by a very rapid rate of productivity increase in the electricity generation sector. This productivity advance has moderated in the past four years due, apparently, to short run influences; but, in line with the historical conditions objective of the *Historical Growth* forecast, this slowdown is assumed to be temporary, with productivity advance in electricity generation returning to typical past rates. This efficiency permits fuel, capital and labor price increases to the electricity generation sector to be absorbed without comparable increases in electricity sales prices.

Nonfuel prices also show differences in their growth rates. Productivity advance in manufacturing and transport allows these sectors to absorb some input price increases with the result that their output prices increase a little less rapidly than the general rate of inflation. Service, agricultural and construction activity, however, does not exhibit such rapid productivity growth and this, together with their relative intensity of use of an input—labor—whose price is rapidly increasing, causes their prices to rise more rapidly than general inflation.

Energy use continues broadly along past trends. The dominant feature in energy is the rapid increase in the consumption of electricity. This increase is partially due to the productivity and price behavior of electricity generation already discussed. The growth in electricity production leads to rapid growth in the use of primary fuels used in the generation of electricity, with this growth being evidenced primarily in nuclear generation, but also in the demand for coal. Petroleum and gas consumption, on the other hand, increases more slowly, for here the price increases resulting from demand facing a restricted supply lead to some moderation in the demand for these fuels. Total U.S. energy input increases by around 3.5 percent a year which is close to past average rates of increase.

This *Historical Growth* projection approximates a continuation of the conditions, especially those relating to energy supply, existing in the 1960s. Developments of the recent past, such as limitations on fuel imports, restrictions on construction of nuclear electricity plants, slower productivity growth in electricity generation, restrictions on oil and gas exploration and production, major increases in fuel prices and so on are not incorporated in the *Historical Growth* projections. In other words, these projections assume no significant price or regulatory pressure to alter energy demand and no serious problems in obtaining the fuel resources to satisfy these demands.

Recent events have shown the set of assumptions underlying the *Historical Growth* forecast to be unrealistic. Thus, although this forecast is extremely useful as an analytical reference point, we need to supplement it by alternative forecasts which incorporate the recent energy developments. Therefore, we proceed to examine the *Technical Fix* and *ZEG* alternative growth paths, both of which incorporate less favorable conditions concerning the availability of energy or which, alternatively, could be viewed as projections of economic growth under policies designed to restrict energy demand.

7.5   Technical Fix Growth

The growth path of the economy under *Technical Fix* conditions is summarized in table 7.3. Also, this table shows the difference between the *Historical* and the *Technical Fix* growth paths. The summary information is that in 2000, a reduction of 38 percent in total energy input can be accommodated with only a 3.8 percent decrease in real GNP, a small increase in the rate of inflation and no increase in unemployment. That is, the economy can adjust to a substantial decline in energy use without major dislocation. The differences between the *Historical Growth* and the *Technical Fix* growth paths are now considered in more detail.

The motivating forces introduced into the energy model to secure the move from the *Historical Growth* path to the *Technical Fix* growth path were increases in petroleum products prices and in electricity prices. These price increases, when their impact on other prices, on input patterns and on demand levels has been solved through in the

Table 7.3
Technical Fix Growth

	1975	1985	2000	Growth rates (% per annum) 1975–1985	Growth rates (% per annum) 1985–2000	Difference from Historical Growth level (%) 1985	Difference from Historical Growth level (%) 2000
Output (gross) (billion 1971 $)							
Agriculture	306.8	381.3	512.3	2.2	2.0	–1.70	–3.74
Manufacturing	848.6	1214.3	1906.1	3.6	3.1	–1.15	–3.05
Transport	94.4	138.3	236.6	3.9	3.6	–1.36	–3.35
Services	976.6	1347.8	2045.5	3.3	2.8	–1.24	–3.03
Energy	97.8	115.4	144.0	1.7	1.5	–20.03	–24.31
Demand (billion 1971 $)							
Consumption	838.3	1188.2	1904.5	3.5	3.2	–1.96	–4.35
Investment	309.7	425.9	652.2	3.2	2.9	–1.07	–2.71
Government	275.0	383.1	585.5	3.4	2.9	–1.36	–3.21
Net exports	19.2	33.0	76.7	5.6	5.8	–0.60	–2.66
GNP (billion 1971 $)	1442.2	2030.2	3218.5	3.5	3.1	–1.64	–3.78
Output (value added, billion 1971 $)							
Agriculture	135.8	185.5	285.1	3.2	2.9	–0.59	–1.72
Manufacturing	345.1	456.3	650.8	2.8	2.4	–0.63	–1.77
Transport	52.3	63.5	80.8	2.0	1.6	–1.24	–2.30
Services	703.3	1010.6	1658.8	3.7	3.4	–0.06	–0.65
Energy	63.1	76.5	96.2	1.9	1.5	–24.50	–49.50
Services of durables	142.6	226.6	446.8	4.7	4.6	0.0	0.0

Table 7.3 (continued)

	1975	1985	2000	Growth rates (% per annum)		Difference from Historical Growth level (%)	
				1975–1985	1985–2000	1985	2000
Employment (billion manhours)							
Agriculture	16.478	19.696	25.962	1.80	1.86	0.00	-0.17
Manufacturing	41.689	47.914	59.454	1.40	1.44	-0.28	-0.59
Transport	6.927	7.452	8.488	0.74	0.86	-0.96	-2.25
Services and government	105.452	130.262	168.532	2.13	1.74	0.33	0.28
Total	173.115	206.949	266.548	1.80	1.70	0.90	1.52
Energy (quadrillion Btu)							
Coal	13.15	17.37	25.13	2.82	2.49	-6.31	-26.95
Petroleum	34.87	31.58	37.30	-0.99	1.12	-20.01	-36.68
Electricity	6.81	9.43	13.51	3.31	2.43	-28.34	-50.64
Gas	24.47	32.36	32.04	2.83	-0.07	-6.23	-24.13
Nuclear, other	5.55	14.62	22.57	10.17	2.94	-35.02	-55.96
Total energy input	78.03	95.92	115.00	2.09	1.22	-16.61	-37.74
Energy consumption (quadrillion Btu)							
Personal consumption	23.165	26.085	27.264	1.2	0.3	-17.5	-43.6
Services and government	10.936	13.548	17.836	2.2	1.9	-12.5	-33.3
Electricity generation	21.080	29.198	41.506	3.3	2.4	-28.3	-51.0
Industry	26.990	33.295	39.787	2.1	1.2	-9.8	-19.6
Transport	2.672	3.232	4.161	1.9	1.7	-6.8	-14.5
Total input	78.032	95.924	115.005	2.1	1.2	-16.6	-37.7

Table 7.3 (continued)

	1975	1985	2000	Growth rates (% per annum)		Difference from Historical Growth level (%)	
				1975–1985	1985–2000	1985	2000
Prices							
Agriculture				4.85	5.20	1.48	3.20
Manufacture				3.13	3.81	0.89	2.67
Transport				2.13	2.63	1.00	2.05
Services				3.98	4.31	1.00	2.31
Coal				2.63	7.52	8.59	40.30
Crude petroleum				3.85	4.60	-8.37	-6.15
Refined petroleum				8.38	6.11	27.98	59.98
Electricity				4.33	5.66	67.27	162.56
Gas				6.12	6.41	1.50	25.05
Consumption				3.88	4.22	2.46	5.95
Investment				3.69	4.19	1.07	2.80
Government				3.94	4.30	1.39	3.31
GNP				3.82	4.17	2.00	4.81

model, lead to a new economic configuration requiring a reduced energy input. The critical output from this analysis is the economic changes that are produced by these price increases; the underlying cause of the price increases is not directly relevant. In fact, the initial price increases in the model were secured by assuming unfavorable domestic petroleum supply conditions and restrictions on imports of petroleum, which served to produce a dramatic increase in petroleum product prices, and by assuming a continuation of recent slow productivity advance in electricity generation, which served to increase electricity prices. (The corresponding *Historical Growth* assumptions were that domestic oil production and/or imports could expand to accommodate petroleum demand growing at historical rates, and that electricity generation productivity advance returned to its rapid, historical trends after the slowdown of the past four years). Alternatively, the price increases might be viewed as being produced by taxes on petroleum and electricity sales with the revenue being returned to the private sector by decreases in income taxes; or the results might just be viewed as showing the effect of petroleum and electricity prices on the rest of the economy, without specifying the cause of the price rises. The main results concern the economic differences between the *Historical* and the *Technical Fix* growth paths and it is these differences which we now examine.

The *Technical Fix* growth path involves an increase in energy input at a little less than half the rate associated with *Historical Growth*, specifically at 1.6 percent a year instead of at 3.5 percent. The comparative reduction in energy use is 17 percent in 1985 and 38 percent in 2000. This reduction is concentrated in electricity and petroleum use. In 1985, electricity and petroleum consumption are each reduced by over 20 percent while the reduced electricity output leads to a reduced level of coal use and to a substantial reduction in nuclear input. But, higher petroleum and electricity prices lead to an increase, due to interfuel competition and substitution, in the price of gas. This produces a decline in use of all fuels, although the gas and coal use reduction is of a smaller order of magnitude than the reduction in petroleum and electricity use. Similarly, in 2000, electricity consumption (and nuclear input) are reduced by 50 percent, with petroleum use down by 37 percent and coal and gas use down by 25 percent.

Higher petroleum and electricity prices lead to a general upward pressure on prices due both to the consequent increase in production costs and to the redirection of demand and input patterns which places more demand pressure on other production. Thus, in 2000 for example, the electricity price more than doubles and the petroleum products price goes up by 60 percent; this leads to smaller, but still substantial, increases in coal and gas prices, as well as to increases in prices of nonfuel products, by about 2 to 3 percent over the period 1975 to 2000.

On the demand side, the higher energy prices have a substantial and immediate impact on the price index of consumption goods and services, and this increase is further boosted by the rise in prices of nonfuel goods and services. Thus, the rise in consumption prices is double the rise in prices of investment and government purchases. However, the overall impact on prices is not catastrophic; the GNP price deflator is increased by about 4 percent which corresponds to a 0.2 percentage point higher rate of inflation under *Technical Fix* than under *Historical Growth*—that is, inflation increases from 3.8 percent to 4.0 percent.

Output and real incomes are reduced slightly by the reduction in energy use but here, too, the reduction, although significant, is not catastrophic: real GNP under *Technical Fix* is 1.6 percent lower in 1985 and 3.8 percent lower in 2000 than the corresponding *Historical Growth* path levels. Energy output suffers the greatest reduction, a fall of 42 percent in constant dollar terms in 2000, for example. But other output is not drastically affected. Services output is reduced the least with agriculture output reduced the most; but the reductions, even in 2000, are only of the order of 3 percent. In terms of value added, service output is hardly affected while other output is reduced by about 2 percent in 2000. On the final use side, personal consumption suffers the greatest reduction, but even in 2000, real consumption is only 4.4 percent below the *Historical Growth* level. Total output, as measured by real GNP, is reduced by 3.8 percent in 2000 which corresponds to a reduction in real growth rates of 0.15 percentage points, from 3.42 to 3.26 percent a year.

The relatively small impact of such a large reduction in energy use on real output is a striking and important result. Its economic explanation lies in the following considerations:

• Final demand energy use is curtailed as a result of higher energy prices. This may take the form of turning down thermostats, switching to smaller cars, installing home insulation and so on. (These avenues for energy conservation mean that, after a transition period, lower energy input is consistent with the original level of effective energy-based personal and household services.) This reduction has very little impact on the rest of the economy, for the demand reduction corresponds to only a part of the output of what is, in economic terms, a relatively small sector of the economy. Even in the 2000 *Historical Growth* projection, the energy-producing sectors represent only 4.2 percent of the entire economy in terms of gross output and 5.7 percent in terms of value added. Since, in turn, personal consumption of energy absorbs only about one third of total fuel output, it can be seen that the direct impact of reduction of personal energy consumption on the total output of the economy is not very large.

• Use of energy in the producing sectors can be reduced somewhat without reducing output merely by reducing waste and by adopting more energy-efficient techniques. Further, there exists significant scope for substitutions between inputs into production, and the emergence of higher fuel prices stimulates use of nonenergy-intensive inputs. One area where this is important concerns capital input; capital and energy are complementary; so higher energy prices lead to reduced use of capital services and to the substitution of other inputs, particularly labor, for these services. The results of this substitution process are illustrated by the behavior of capital and labor inputs under *Technical Fix* growth: in 2000 for example, capital input is reduced by 1.8 percent from the *Historical Growth* level, whereas labor input increases by 1.5 percent. Also, substitutions between capital and materials, between capital and services and between other inputs are possible. The net result is that producing sectors can achieve substantial economies in energy use at the expense of comparatively small reductions in output.

• Any saving in the use of electricity by final consumers or by producers, even if offset by increased use of other energy services, leads, due to the conversion losses in electricity generation, to approximately three times the reduction in primary energy input. Further, to the extent that the input of uranium into electricity generation is reduced, the energy saving is even greater since the enrichment of uranium by present technologies is a heavy user of energy. Thus, increases in electricity prices, and the consequent reduction in electricity use, are a powerful instrument in reducing total energy input.

The relative magnitudes of each of these forms of energy saving are shown in table 7.3. In 2000, for example, the total reduction in energy input between *Historical Growth* and *Technical Fix* is 38 percent (69.7 QBtu). Energy use in electricity generation is reduced by the largest proportion, 51 percent (43.2 QBtu), while personal consumption use is reduced by 44 percent (21.1 QBtu), service and government use by 33 percent (8.9 QBtu), industrial use by 20 percent (9.7 QBtu) and transport (which excludes private automobiles) use by 15 percent (0.7 QBtu). This indicates that significant economies in energy use are possible in all forms of energy consumption, with personal consumption, service and government economies particularly significant. The greatest Btu savings are achieved through a reduction in the inputs absorbed in electricity generation. Electricity use is reduced due to economizing in fuel use in general as well as by the partial substitution of other fuels for electricity. The net result is that electricity conservation releases 62 percent of the total energy savings achieved in the move to *Technical Fix* growth.

The share of energy in total real personal consumption expenditure is shown in table 7.4. In *Historical Growth* conditions, energy purchases constitute an increasingly important component of consumption purchases, increasing from 5.54 percent in 1975 to 6.99 percent in 2000. The economies in personal energy use achieved under *Technical Fix* conditions are, however, sufficiently large to reverse this upward trend so that energy purchases in 2000 represent only 3.75 percent of real consumption expenditure. This is a significant reduction in the energy share but nonetheless, energy remains an important component in consumption spending and *per capita* personal consumption of energy is still higher than in 1975. The composition of personal energy use is also changed in response to the relative price changes. Electricity is clearly the major energy source in both *Historical Growth* and *Technical Fix* conditions, but the increase in the relative price of electricity under *Technical Fix* results in the partial substitution of both petroleum products and gas for electricity use.

Manufacturing and services also redirect their input patterns to economize on energy in response to the increase in energy prices under *Technical Fix* growth. These input patterns are shown in table 7.4. Energy input into manufacturing remains stable in *Historical Growth* but, under *Technical Fix*, the input proportion is reduced in 2000, from 2.08 to 1.68 percent. The overall reduction in energy use is accompanied by a redirection of energy purchases towards the relatively inexpensive fuels, particularly petroleum. In services, the trend to the increasing relative importance of energy input under *Historical*

Table 7.4
Energy use in consumption, manufacturing and services
Real expenditure on energy in proportion to total real expenditure (percent)

	1961	1971	1975	1985	2000
Personal consumption					
Historical Growth	4.74	5.53	5.54	5.96	6.99
Technical Fix			5.54	4.59	3.75
ZEG			5.54	4.43	3.23
Manufacturing					
Historical Growth	1.88	2.14	2.07	2.16	2.08
Technical Fix			2.07	2.08	1.68
ZEG			2.07	2.05	1.54
Services					
Historical Growth	1.30	1.76	1.85	2.14	2.58
Technical Fix			1.85	1.61	1.40
ZEG			1.85	1.55	1.21

Composition of energy input in 2000

	Personal consumption		Manufacturing		Services	
	HG	TF	HG	TF	HG	TF
Coal	—	—	11.8	13.2	—	—
Petroleum	16.9	21.0	23.4	27.8	41.1	39.9
Electricity	73.6	62.5	42.0	40.8	48.4	48.8
Gas	9.4	16.4	22.8	18.2	10.4	11.3
Total energy use	100.0	100.0	100.0	100.0	100.0	100.0

Note: HG = Historical Growth path energy use pattern; TF = Technical Fix growth path energy use pattern.

Growth is reversed under *Technical Fix* so that, in 2000, energy forms 1.40 percent of total real inputs compared to 2.58 percent.

The composition of energy input in *Technical Fix* is a little different from that in *Historical Growth*; energy conservation in services takes the form of general reduction in fuel use rather than substitutions between fuels. Technical considerations in services use of energy, and to a lesser extent in manufacturing, constrain the possibilities for substitution between energy forms, but those substitution possibilities that do exist, together with economy in energy input in general, permit significant reduction in service and manufacturing energy use.

The substitution between inputs and adjustment in input patterns that result from higher energy prices is shown for the manufacturing

Table 7.5
Composition of inputs into manufacturing and services (percentage that specified input represents in total input, based on constant dollar purchases)

	1961	1971	1975	1985	2000
(a) Manufacturing					
Capital input					
Historical Growth	10.2	10.6	11.6	12.4	13.6
Technical Fix			11.6	12.4	13.5
ZEG			11.6	12.4	13.4
Labor input					
Historical Growth	33.4	28.2	30.0	28.1	26.0
Technical Fix			30.0	28.3	26.6
ZEG			30.0	28.4	26.9
Energy input					
Historical Growth	1.9	2.1	2.1	2.2	2.1
Technical Fix			2.1	2.1	1.7
ZEG			2.1	2.1	1.5
Materials input					
Historical Growth	54.5	59.1	56.3	57.3	58.3
Technical Fix			56.3	57.2	58.2
ZEG			56.3	57.1	58.2
(b) Services					
Capital input					
Historical Growth	26.5	29.6	32.7	35.6	41.4
Technical Fix			32.7	35.9	42.1
ZEG			32.7	35.9	42.3
Labor input					
Historical Growth	47.3	42.6	39.0	35.9	30.4
Technical Fix			39.0	36.5	31.4
ZEG			39.0	36.6	31.6
Energy input					
Historical Growth	1.3	1.8	1.8	2.1	2.6
Technical Fix			1.8	1.6	1.4
ZEG			1.8	1.6	1.2
Materials input					
Historical Growth	24.9	26.0	26.5	26.4	25.6
Technical Fix			26.5	26.0	25.1
ZEG			26.5	25.9	24.9

Note: Materials are all nonfuel inputs that are purchased from other intermediate sectors and from imports.

and service sectors in table 7.5. The forces at work are initially illustrated by the input patterns along the *Historical Growth* path for the increasing relative use of capital and decreasing use of labor resulting from the increasing relative price of labor. This induces producers to substitute, within technical limits, capital for labor. Also, the relatively inexpensive energy available in *Historical Growth* leads to the continuing increase in the share of energy input. The move from *Historical Growth* to *Technical Fix* or *ZEG* paths with their causal and induced price changes leads to a further set of adjustments being superimposed on these. The price increases primarily relate to energy but these cause, in turn, a smaller change in the structure of other prices. The induced changes in input proportions in manufacturing and services can be followed from the input proportions given in table 7.5. The reduction in energy input has already been outlined. But, all inputs are affected by the change in prices. In manufacturing, capital-energy complementarity leads to capital input being reduced, although not to the same extent as energy. The small degree of complementarity between energy and inputs of materials leads to the material input proportion being reduced. The reduction in capital, energy and materials input into manufacturing is offset by increased use of the nonenergy-intensive and now relatively less expensive, input—labor services. Thus in 2000, for example, labor input which is already 26 percent of total input under *Historical Growth* increases to 27 percent of input under *Zero Energy Growth*. Similar forces are at work in the service sector although with slightly different results. In services, capital and energy are substitutes rather than complements, so increased energy prices lead to a slight increase in capital input (for example, capital might be absorbed in energy saving uses such as increased insulation, installation of more efficient heating and air-conditioning equipment, and so on). Some complementarity exists between materials and energy, so the rise in energy prices leads to a reduction in the proportion of materials inputs. Use of labor, the nonenergy-intensive input, increases to replace the reduction in energy and materials inputs and to permit service production to absorb these reductions without a comparable reduction in output.

The changes in input proportions in manufacturing and services involved in the shift from *Historical Growth* to *Zero Energy Growth* conditions are significant. But these shifts are well within the range of recent experience. Thus, the largest changes in input proportions involve energy input, but even these changes correspond only to reversing the *Historical Growth* trend to increasing energy inputs so that energy input proportions in 2000 are in the region of the actual 1961 proportions.

7.6   Zero Energy Growth

The economic and energy information describing *Zero Energy Growth* is presented in table 7.6. The move from *Technical Fix* growth to ZEG was simulated by imposing an energy sales tax (a uniform tax rate applied to each dollar of sales from the energy sector) with the tax revenue then being spent by the government on health, education and transport services (the revenue was allocated as follows: 75 percent to purchases of labor and services, 20 percent to purchases of manufactures and 5 percent to purchases from the transport sector). This is a dual mechanism: energy use is directly discouraged by taxes, and demand is further redirected by a change in spending patterns towards nonenergy-intensive production, which is superimposed on an economy which already has adapted to the energy-efficient *Technical Fix* position.

The move from *Technical Fix* to ZEG involves a reduction in energy input of 3 percent in 1985, and of 13 percent in 2000. The uniform energy tax discourages all energy use with the result that consumption of each energy source is reduced by comparable proportions; in 2000, ZEG consumption of nuclear power is reduced by 11 percent from the *Technical Fix* position, consumption of coal is down 12 percent, that of petroleum and electricity 13 percent, and of gas 16 percent. When compared to the *Historical Growth* energy consumption pattern, the ZEG energy consumption in 2000 is reduced by 46 percent with electricity and nuclear down by around 60 percent, and other fuels down by around 40 percent. The reduction in energy consumption varies between uses. The move from *Technical Fix* to ZEG in 2000 involves a 13 percent (15.4 QBtu) reduction in total energy input with final demand use reduced by 15 percent (4.2 QBtu), electricity generation use down by 13 percent (5.5 QBtu), and industrial use, including use of electricity, down by 12 percent (7.3 QBtu).

The tax rate required to produce the move between *Technical Fix* and ZEG is 3.3 percent in 1985 and 15 percent in 2000. The 1985 shift is comparatively small and the tax revenue is similarly small, but the 2000 shift is more substantial and the revenue raised by the energy sales tax is $131 billion ($50 billion in today's prices). This substantial

Table 7.6
Zero Energy Growth

| | 1975 | 1985 | 2000 | Growth rates (% per annum) | | % difference from level of | | | |
| | | | | 1975–1985 | 1985–2000 | Historical Growth | | Technical Fix | |
						1985	2000	1985	2000
Output (gross) (billion 1971 $)									
Agriculture	306.8	380.5	507.8	2.2	1.9	-1.91	-4.58	-0.21	-0.88
Manufacturing	848.6	1213.2	1898.2	3.6	3.0	-1.24	-3.45	-0.09	-0.41
Transport	94.4	138.4	237.9	3.9	3.7	-1.28	-2.82	0.07	0.55
Services	976.6	1350.1	2066.8	3.3	2.9	-1.07	-2.02	0.17	1.04
Energy	97.8	111.7	124.9	1.3	0.7	-22.6	-49.9	-3.21	-13.3
Demand (billion 1971 $)									
Consumption	838.3	1185.3	1885.4	3.5	3.1	-2.19	-5.30	-0.24	-0.99
Investment	309.7	424.9	643.8	3.2	2.8	-1.30	-3.97	-0.23	-1.29
Government	275.0	387.8	623.3	3.5	3.2	-0.15	3.04	1.23	6.46
Net exports	19.2	32.8	74.3	5.5	5.6	-1.20	-5.71	-0.61	-3.13
GNP (billion 1971 $)	1442.2	2030.8	3226.7	3.5	3.1	-1.61	-3.54	0.03	0.25
Output (value added, billion 1971 $)									
Agriculture	135.8	185.4	284.7	3.2	2.9	-0.64	-1.86	-0.05	-0.14
Manufacturing	354.1	456.5	652.8	2.8	2.4	-0.59	-1.46	0.04	0.31
Transport	52.3	63.5	80.4	2.0	1.6	-1.24	-2.78	0.00	-0.50
Services	703.3	1013.2	1682.7	3.7	3.4	0.20	0.78	0.26	1.44
Energy	63.1	74.7	79.3	1.7	0.4	-26.3	-58.4	-2.35	-17.6
Services of durables	142.6	226.6	446.8	4.7	4.6	0.0	0.0	0.0	0.0

Table 7.6 (continued)

	1975	1985	2000	Growth rates (% per annum)		% difference from level of			
				1975–1985	1985–2000	Historical Growth		Technical Fix	
						1985	2000	1985	2000
Employment (billion manhours)									
Agriculture	16.478	19.706	26.063	1.81	1.89	0.05	0.22	0.05	0.39
Manufacturing	41.689	47.982	60.028	1.42	1.50	-0.14	0.37	0.14	0.97
Transport	6.927	7.452	8.562	0.74	0.93	-0.96	-1.39	0.00	0.87
Services and government	105.452	130.652	179.691	2.17	2.15	0.63	6.92	0.30	6.62
Total	173.115	207.667	271.274	1.84	1.80	1.25	3.32	0.35	1.77
Energy (quadrillion Btu)									
Coal	13.15	16.90	22.01	2.54	1.78	-8.45	-36.0	-2.71	-12.4
Petroleum	34.87	30.64	32.59	-1.28	0.41	-22.4	-44.7	-2.98	-12.6
Electricity	6.81	9.15	11.73	3.00	1.67	-30.5	-57.1	-2.97	-13.2
Gas	24.47	31.07	27.04	2.42	-0.92	-9.97	-36.0	-3.99	-15.6
Nuclear, other	5.55	14.25	20.00	9.89	2.29	-36.7	-61.0	-2.53	-11.4
Total energy input	78.03	92.87	99.60	1.76	0.47	-19.3	-46.1	-3.18	-13.4
Energy consumption (quadrillion Btu)									
Personal consumption	23.165	25.170	22.340	0.8	-0.8	20.4	-53.8	-3.5	-18.1
Services and government	10.936	13.104	16.441	1.8	1.5	-15.3	-38.5	-3.3	-7.8
Electricity generation	21.080	28.319	36.298	3.0	1.7	-30.5	-57.2	-3.0	-12.5
Industry	26.990	32.245	34.448	1.8	0.4	-12.6	-30.4	-3.2	-13.4
Transport	2.672	3.177	3.844	1.8	1.3	-8.4	-21.0	-1.7	-7.6
Total input	78.032	92.865	99.600	1.8	0.5	-19.3	-46.1	-3.2	-13.4

Table 7.6 (continued)

| | | | | Growth rates (% per annum) | | % difference from level of | | | |
| | | | | | | Historical Growth | | Technical Fix | |
	1975	1985	2000	1975–1985	1985–2000	1985	2000	1985	2000
Energy consumption (quadrillion Btu)									
Personal consumption	23.165	25.170	22.340	0.8	−0.8	20.4	−53.8	−3.5	−18.1
Services and government	10.936	13.104	16.441	1.8	1.5	−15.3	−38.5	−3.3	−7.8
Electricity generation	21.080	28.319	36.298	3.0	1.7	−30.5	−57.2	−3.0	−12.5
Industry	26.990	32.245	34.448	1.80.4	−12.6	−30.4	−3.2	−13.4	
Transport	2.672	3.177	3.844	1.8	1.3	−8.4	−21.0	−1.7	−7.6
Total input	78.032	92.865	99.600	1.8	0.5	−19.3	46.1	−3.2	−13.4
Prices									
Agriculture				4.85	5.27	1.69	4.36	0.22	1.13
Manufacturing				3.16	3.89	1.13	4.10	0.23	1.39
Transport				2.15	2.68	1.21	3.10	0.21	1.03
Services				3.99	4.34	1.09	2.76	0.09	0.44
Coal				3.06	8.56	13.22	68.50	4.26	20.33
Crude petroleum				3.86	4.62	−8.31	−5.87	0.06	0.30
Refined petroleum				8.74	6.92	32.25	85.28	3.33	15.81
Electricity				4.67	6.54	72.71	207.0	3.25	16.93
Gas				6.57	7.39	5.95	49.68	4.39	19.70
Consumption				3.91	4.29	2.77	7.33	0.30	1.31
Investment				3.72	4.27	1.30	4.13	0.23	1.30
Government				3.95	4.32	1.51	3.75	0.12	0.43
GNP				3.85	4.24	2.26	6.03	0.25	1.17

revenue affords the opportunity to divert a significant amount of final demand from energy-intensive to nonenergy-intensive types of expenditure. (In fact, revenues of this size are of the order of magnitude required to sustain currently mooted national health insurance programs). The energy tax does result in substantial increases in energy prices; fuel prices in 2000 under *ZEG* are about 18 percent higher than under *Technical Fix*. Nonfuel product prices also increase, but by much smaller proportions, generally of the order of 1 percent. In total, therefore, *ZEG* involves only small increases in prices above those forecast for *Technical Fix* growth—the increase in the rate of inflation (of the GNP price deflator) is only 0.05 percentage points, from 4.03 to 4.08 percent a year.

Real incomes and real output are not reduced by the move from *Technical Fix* to *ZEG*, despite the reduction in energy consumption. The reason for this lies in the redirection of final demand caused by governmental purchases in services financed by the energy tax revenues. Reduced energy use without an exogenous change in spending patterns would lead to a reduction in real incomes and real output, as in the move from *Historical Growth* to *Technical Fix* growth, but the increase in demand for services caused by increasing government purchases creates sufficient new demand to offset the reduction in real output and, as the new demand is relatively energy-nonintensive, the restoration of output and incomes can be sustained at the new lower level of energy consumption. The net effect is that, in 2000 for example, real output rises by 0.25 percent in *ZEG* compared to the *Technical Fix* position, despite the 13 percent reduction in energy use. The gain in real output is, in itself, trivial, but the critical result is that energy consumption can be reduced without any cost in terms of total real output and total real income. The mechanism that secures this result is differential government policy—specific discouragement of energy use by means of taxes, and specific encouragement of nonenergy-intensive production and consumption by means of increased government provision of service activities.

The composition of production differs in *ZEG* from the *Technical Fix* pattern, due primarily to the impact of the new government expenditure. Agricultural and manufacturing output is reduced, transport and service output is increased. On the final use side, the net result of of the energy taxation and higher government expenditure is a relative increase in the proportion of government purchases in real GNP with an equal decrease in the share of personal consumption expenditure; investment and net exports are not affected. Real output and real income growth rates remain almost identical in *ZEG* and in *Technical Fix* growth. The composition of primary inputs does change, however. The energy tax and increased service purchases lead to an increase in labor input relative to capital input, although both inputs show an increase in *ZEG* compared to *Technical Fix* growth.

The increase in labor input associated with *ZEG* is the result of energy-capital complementarity. Higher fuel prices lead to the substitution of labor for capital. Increased purchases of services lead to an increase in primary inputs, again with emphasis on labor input. Labor input in all nonfuel sectors increases, reflecting labor-capital substitution, while employment in service and government sectors rises substantially since increased activity in labor intensive sectors is superimposed on labor-capital substitution. Thus, total employment (labor input in man-hours) is 1.8 percent higher in 2000 under *ZEG* than under *Technical Fix* growth. If all the increase in labor input were supplied by those previously unemployed, the unemployment rate would fall to 1.4 percent. But the decrease in unemployment would probably be less as the additional labor would be supplied partly from longer work-weeks, partly from higher participation rates and partly from decreased unemployment.

7.7   Conclusions

The basic result of these economic analyses is the qualitative finding that substantial reduction in U.S. energy input, compared to the *Historical Growth* energy demand patterns, can be secured without major economic cost in terms of reduced total real output or reduced real incomes or increased inflation or reduced employment. The scope for interinput substitution, for economizing on energy use and for redirection of demand patterns is such that the rate of growth of energy input over the remainder of this century can be more than halved without requiring fundamental changes in the structure of the economy and without requiring major sacrifices in real income growth.

Energy conservation, as represented by *Technical Fix* and *ZEG* conditions, will have an economic cost that is nontrivial. At the aggregate level the costs are that total real incomes and output are reduced; thus the level of real GNP, in 2000, for example, is 3.5 percent lower under *ZEG* than under *Historical Growth*; and that the rate of inflation is increased. The real GNP deflator increases at 3.8 percent a year under

Historical Growth but at 4.1 percent a year under *ZEG*. However, energy conservation leads to increased employment, so fears of widespread unemployment due to energy shortages are unfounded. Once the economy has had time to adjust to more expensive and less plentiful energy, employment will actually increase as labor is substituted for capital and material inputs. There are also costs of energy conservation at the microeconomic level; new input patterns in production will require a relocation of some people and jobs in both geographical and occupational terms, and people will have to adapt to new ways of doing things. The model does not spell out these very detailed effects, but it does show that, on the basis of economic responses observed in the past, such adaption is well within the bounds of practicability within the economic system as it is presently constituted.

The opposite side of these economic costs is the marked reduction in energy usage that is possible over the remainder of the century. The benefits from reduced energy usage are reduced environmental degradation, reduced pollution, reduced dependence on foreign sources for a critical economic input, reduced need for nuclear and other energy sources whose full implications are, as yet, incompletely known, slowing the rate of depletion of U.S. fuel resources and so on. These benefits are fully explored in other Energy Policy Project studies. The present study demonstrates that these benefits can be obtained, admittedly at a cost, but not at the cost of major economic dislocation. In fact, the present projections indicate that economic activity can grow along a broadly similar pattern to that experienced in the past while simultaneously achieving major economies in energy consumption.

We conclude this study by pointing out that:

• energy conservation along the lines of *Technical Fix* or *ZEG* ideas is possible within the existing structure of the economy;

• the cost of reduced energy use in terms of higher inflation and reduced real incomes and output are significant but not catastrophic;

• these costs have been quantified above so that the costs and benefits of energy conservation can be explicitly faced and compared. This information can provide the basis for a rational choice regarding energy policy in the United States.

8 The Integration of Energy Policy Models

Ben Bernanke and
Dale W. Jorgenson

8.1 Introduction

A wide variety of alternative econometric models is now available for the study of the impact of energy policies in the United States. These models differ considerably in scope and in the detailed representation of the production and distribution of energy. The models range from economy-wide models with a schematic representation of the energy sector to detailed models that incorporate regional and product detail for particular types of energy.

Economy-wide and sectoral energy models are complementary rather than competitive in the evaluation of alternative energy policies. Policies that can be assessed in terms of their impact on aggregate economic activity require the use of economy-wide models. Policies that can be assessed in terms of their impact on a particular energy sector can be studied only through the use of sectoral energy models. The problem that remains is to provide a basis for assessing the impact of energy policies that must be evaluated in terms of their effects both on a particular sector and on the economy as a whole.

A natural solution to the problem of assessing energy policies in terms of both sectoral impact and economy-wide impact is to combine economy-wide models with models of particular energy sectors. Each model can be used for policy assessments by itself; integrating the models, policy impacts can be studied for a particular energy sector, for the energy sector as a whole, and for the entire U.S. economy. Different combinations of energy policy models can be employed for different purposes, providing greater flexibility than that available through the application of any single model.

The purpose of this chapter is to test the feasibility of integrating energy policy models by combining an economy-wide model that incorporates the energy sector with a detailed model of the natural gas industry. Each of these models has been employed in isolation to study the impact of specific energy policies. We propose to combine the models into a single integrated model for the assessment of policies with a direct impact on the natural gas sector and important ramifications for the rest of the energy sector and for the U.S. economy as a whole.

The first model we consider is an economy-wide model that incorporates inter-industry transactions between energy and nonenergy sectors. The model includes separate models of production for each of the sectors included in the model. It determines the distribution of energy and nonenergy products among the industrial sectors included in the model and between the industrial sector and the components of final demand—personal consumption, government purchases, and net exports. The model also determines the prices of energy and nonenergy products, taking account of the interrelationship between the supply price for each producing sector and the prices that determine demand for the product by other producing sectors and by final demand categories.

The main advantages of the economy-wide model is that it determines the impact of energy policy on the production and distribution of energy and energy prices together with the impact on production and distribution of nonenergy products and nonenergy prices. By summarizing the activities of both energy and nonenergy sectors into a set of national income and product accounts, the impact of energy policy on aggregative economic activity can also be assessed. Variations in national product can be separated into price and quantity components to permit the assessment of policy impacts in terms of inflation and real growth.

For the analysis of energy policy the economy-wide model has two important disadvantages. First, investment in new reserves of petroleum and natural gas is exogenous to the model. Resource depletion through production from existing reserves is implicit in the models of production for each of the energy sectors. However, the effects of depletion are also exogenous to the model, so that the impact of higher or lower rates of production on future supply of energy is not incorporated into the model. Second, the model treats all sectors uniformly, so that the impact of government regulation of the price of natural gas is omitted.

The natural gas model we consider incorporates the production, distribution, and consumption of natural gas, broken down by twenty-nine producing regions and forty consuming regions. For each of the producing regions the model determines the level of exploration and development of new reserves as well as production from existing reserves. Resource depletion is modeled explicitly through additions to new reserves as a result of exploration and development and reductions of reserves through production. The model also incorporates the structure of interregional trade in natural gas by allocating the demand for each of the consuming regions among producing regions.

The natural gas model makes it possible to determine production, distribution, and consumption of natural gas by region within the United States, together with the prices of natural gas at the well-head in the producing regions and prices of natural gas delivered to each of the consuming regions. The well-head prices are exogenous to the model, so that the impact of alternative regulatory policies by the Federal Power Commission can be analyzed. If the ceiling prices for natural gas are below the market clearing prices, demand exceeds supply and shortages of natural gas result. The model can be used to study the regional distribution of shortages and the impact of regulation on investment in new exploration and development.

For the assessment of energy policies the main disadvantages of the natural gas model are those of any sectoral model. The model can be used to assess the impact of changes in regulatory policy on the natural gas industry. Since the model is limited to this sector, it cannot be used to assess the impact of changes in regulatory policy on the energy sector as a whole, on the level of aggregate economic activity, or on the rate of inflation. Shortages of natural gas have important implications for demand for other types of energy that are not incorporated into the model. Similarly, the elimination of ceiling prices on natural gas may have an important impact on the rate of inflation; it is impossible to assess this impact by means of a model of the natural gas sector alone.

Since the main disadvantages of the economy-wide model are precisely the advantages of the natural has model and *vice versa*, a model that integrates the two provides much greater flexibility in making policy assessments. In section 8.2, below, we present a detailed description of the economy-wide model and an outline of the computational techniques employed in implementing the model. In section 8.3 we describe the natural gas model and the details of its implementation. In section 8.4 we outline the integration of the two models into a single energy policy model. Many of the techniques for model integration can be applied both to the natural gas model and to models of other energy sectors.

The final section of this chapter provides an illustration of the application of an integrated energy policy model to the assessment of alternative policies. In particular, we compare the impact of phased deregulation of the well-head prices of natural gas and the impact of a quota in imports of oil. For each of these policies and for both policies together we assess the impact of policy changes on the natural gas sector, the energy sector as a whole, and the U.S. economy.

8.2   Inter-Industry Model

8.2.1   Introduction

An econometric model of the U.S. economy that incorporates explicit models of energy and nonenergy sectors has been constructed by Edward A. Hudson and Dale W. Jorgenson (1974a). The model includes the determination of deliveries of energy and nonenergy products to intermediate demand and final demand. Deliveries to intermediate demand are deliveries to other industrial sectors, so we will refer to the model as the Inter-Industry Model (IIM). The model also includes the supply of inputs into each sector, including deliveries from other sectors, deliveries of primary inputs, capital and labor, and deliveries of imports. The prices of both energy and nonenergy products are determined in such a way that supply and demand are equal for each product. The model determines the price and distribution of each type of energy and the price and distribution of nonenergy products through the equilibration of supply and demand.

8.2.2   Inter-Industry Production

The Inter-Industry Model divides the private domestic sector of the U.S. economy into nine sectors:

1. Agriculture, nonfuel mining, and construction
2. Manufacturing, excluding petroleum refining
3. Transportation
4. Communications, trade, and services
5. Coal mining

6. Crude petroleum and natural gas
7. Petroleum refining
8. Electric utilities
9. Natural gas utilities

For each of these nine sectors, the purpose of the model is to determine (1) the equilibrium quantity of output, broken down by use, (2) the equilibrium price of output, and (3) the quantities of inputs used in the sector's production processes, including intermediate goods supplied by all nine sectors, capital, labor, and imports. The model embodies two important innovations that provide flexibility in modeling production. These are: (1) the use of production functions based on the translog form, a mathematical structure of great generality,[1] and (2) a production structure with *endogenous* input-output coefficients. The endogeneity of the coefficients means that, instead of assuming fixed proportions in input use, as in input-output analysis, the model is able to incorporate the shift to cost-minimizing technologies as input prices to the sectors change.[2]

The Inter-Industry Model contains an econometric model of producer behavior for each of the sectors. These "models" are derived from the production functions for each sector. To simplify estimation and the computation of equilibrium prices, the production functions are not estimated directly. Estimation is based on the price possibility frontier, giving the price of sectoral output as a function of the prices of the sector's inputs. The mathematical form of these price possibility frontiers is transcendental logarithmic or translog; that is, the price of output is an exponential function of the logarithms of the prices of inputs (Berndt and Jorgenson, 1973).

A further simplification is introduced by taking the arguments of the estimated price possibility frontiers of four aggregate input groups, namely, capital (K), labor (L), energy (E), and materials (M). Thus, the form used in estimation is:

$$\ln AI + \ln PI = a_0^I + a_K^I * \ln PK + a_L^I * \ln PL + a_E^I * \ln PE + a_M^I * \ln PM$$

$$+ 1/2 * (b_{KK}^I * (\ln PK)^2 + b_{KL}^I * \ln PK * \ln PL + \dots),$$

$$(I = 1, 2 \dots 9),$$

where AI is interpreted as a sectoral index of technology, PI is the sectoral price, and $PK, PL, PE,$ and PM are the aggregate input prices.[3]

Additional equations are estimated relating the prices of aggregate input groups to the prices of the individual inputs in each group. The division of the price possibility frontiers into two stages simplifies the estimation procedure and the computation of equilibrium prices. Furthermore, it leads to little loss of flexibility from the theoretical point of view. The two-stage procedure requires the condition that the price possibility frontier is separable and homogeneous in the prices of inputs within each aggregate. This amounts to saying that the marginal rate of substitution between inputs within an aggregate must be independent of the levels of inputs outside of the aggregate (Berndt and Jorgenson, 1973).

It must be noted, however, that the advantages to be gained by replacing ordinary production functions with price possibility frontiers are not without cost. It is not the same thing to say that the physical *quantities* of outputs and inputs are related as to say their *prices* are. To say the latter, one must assume that the nature of demand is affecting firm pricing only through its effects on the price of inputs. This assumption is tantamount to an assumption of perfect competition in all sectors. A second assumption implicit in the existence of the price possibility frontiers is that production within each of the sectors is governed by constant returns to scale.

These two assumptions together permit the *independent* calculation of sectoral equilibrium prices and sectoral equilibrium quantities. Under these two assumptions the equilibrium prices for sectoral output and the relative demands for factor inputs are independent of the level or composition of final demands.[4]

Given these basic elements, the operation of the Inter-Industry Model side proceeds in two stages:

(1) Taken together, the estimated sectoral price possibility frontiers form a complete system of simultaneous equations. The solution of this system is found using Newton's method. The solution vector is the equilibrium set of nine mutually consistent sectoral prices. Prices for capital, labor, and imports are taken from elsewhere in the model to complete the array of prices.

(2) Given a complete set of relative prices, the endogenous cost-minimizing input-output coefficients can be determined. The relative share of the Jth intermediate input is given by the identity:

$$\frac{\partial \ln PI}{\partial \ln PJ} = \frac{PJ * XJI}{PI * XI} = \frac{PJ}{PI} * AJI \, ,$$

$$(I = 1, 2, \ldots, 9; \ J = 1, 2, \ldots, 9, K, L, R)$$

where PI and PJ are sector prices, XJI is the quantity of J input into sector I, XI is the output of sector I, and AJI is the input-output coefficient for the Jth input into sector I. The relative shares are divided by PJ/PI to obtain the input-output coefficients, so that we have a complete set of coefficients, each of which is responsive to all sectoral prices and the prices of capital, labor, and imports. Similarly, coefficients are found to represent the usage pattern of nonsectoral inputs, K, L, and R, where R is the level of imports.

The actual computation of sectoral input-output coefficients is done in two stages in a manner analogous to the two-step structure of the price possibility frontiers. The coefficients for the aggregate input groups are calculated first, then the coefficients for the individual inputs into the aggregate input groups. These two sets of coefficients are multiplied together to obtain the final input-output matrix.

8.2.3   Inter-Industry Demand

The demand side of the Inter-Industry Model has two major components. The first of these is a macroeconometric growth model, a model of long-term U.S. economic growth.[5] The principal purposes of this model are to project the prices (PK, PL, PR) that are exogenous to the supply side and to project future levels of U.S. aggregate demand. The second component of the demand side of the Inter-Industry Model is the model for the allocation of consumer demand among sectoral outputs. Total consumer demand is, of course, fixed, having been taken as the difference between the growth model's estimate of national income and the sum of government, investment, and trade balance as projected exogenously. The basis for this allocation is an indirect utility function of the form:[6]

$$\ln V = \ln V \left(\frac{P1}{PC * C} \ \frac{P2}{PC * C} , \ldots , \frac{P11}{PC * C} \right)$$

where V is utility, the PI are sectoral prices, and $PC * C$ represents total consumption expenditures. Note that there are eleven prices in the equation; these correspond to eight of the inter-industry sectors (crude petroleum and natural gas are excluded), plus housing, services of consumer durables, and noncompetitive imports.

The indirect utility function is assumed to be linear in the logarithms of the ratios of prices to total consumption expenditures. This implies that the income elasticities of demand for each class of expenditures are assumed to be equal to unity, while the price elasticities of demand are assumed to be equal to minus unity. This assumption can be replaced by alternative assumptions about income and price elasticities of demand. The linear logarithmic specification has the advantage that with constant relative prices, the components of the consumer budget grow at the same rate as total consumption expenditures. Furthermore, the demand for individual components is responsive to price changes, so that the effect of variations in price on the composition of final demand are partly endogenous.

To summarize: The volume of final demand for the output of each sector is determined in four steps. (1) Total nominal demand is set equal to C from the growth model, plus investment, government, and export demand. (2) The prices of domestic availability for sectoral production are determined, as described in the section on supply. (3) The value of expenditures for each sector is found by dividing total projected expenditure into the fixed-ratio shares. (4) By dividing expenditure in each sector by the price of domestic availability, the physical volume of demand for each class of commodities is calculated.

By working through supply and demand in a sequential manner, one is able to derive the necessary ingredients for a classical input-output system, namely, a set of cost-minimizing input-output coefficients and a vector of sectoral final demands. Let A be the 9 by 9 matrix of input-output coefficients, and y the 1 by 9 vector of final demands. Let x be the 1 by 9 vector of equilibrium sectoral supplies. Then intermediate demand, in equilibrium, is equal to the vector

$$Ax = \begin{bmatrix} A11 * X1 & + & A12 * X2 & + \ldots + & A19 * X9 \\ A21 * X1 & + & A22 * X2 & + \ldots + & A29 * X9 \\ \vdots & & & & \vdots \\ A91 * X1 & + & A92 * X2 & + \ldots + & A99 * X9 \end{bmatrix}.$$

Setting supply equal to demand (the sum of intermediate and final demands), we arrive at the equilibrium condition

$$x = Ax + y.$$

The domestic availability of the output of each sector thus can be found by solving the system of equations

$$x = (I - A)^{-1} y.$$

8.2.4   Computational Scheme

The Inter-Industry Model requires solutions of simultaneous equation systems in several places. No external source or package is called for this purpose; instead, the program contains its own algorithm, based on Newton's method (Ortega and Rheinboldt, 1970, pp. 181–188). Newton's method for finding the zero points of a function or system of functions (equivalent to a system of equations) is based on the numerical calculation of approximate partial derivatives. Given functions in N variables of the form

$$FI(X1, X2, \ldots, XN) = 0, \qquad (I = 1, 2, \ldots, N),$$

the problem is to find the intersection of the kernels $(\overline{X1}, \overline{X2}, \ldots, \overline{XN})$. The algorithm begins by evaluating each of the FI at some initial point; this "initial guess" is supplied by the programmer, and is usually just the origin. This first evaluation generally finds at least some of the FI yielding values different from zero by more than some prespecified distance. Thus a second approximating guess is required.

To construct the second point guess, the program evaluates the system of functions $2N$ more times, once each for small positive and negative changes in each variable, $X1, X2, \ldots, XN$. Dividing the change in the function values induced by perturbing the XI by the absolute value of the perturbations, the program makes a numerical estimate of the values of the functions' N^2 first partial derivatives at the initial guess point. Figure 8.1 illustrates this procedure for the partial derivative of $F1$ with respect to $X1$.

Given the vectors of the approximate partial derivatives, the new guess for the system's zero point is taken as the intersection of the approximating plane (made up of the partials) and the zero plane. Figure 8.2 shows this in two dimensions. The new guess is evaluated to determine if it yields values suitably close to zero for all the FI. If not, the algorithm is repeated, ending when a solution is found or a specified maximum number of iterations is reached.

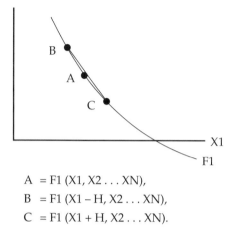

A = F1 (X1, X2 . . . XN),
B = F1 (X1 – H, X2 . . . XN),
C = F1 (X1 + H, X2 . . . XN).

Figure 8.1
The numerical derivative is the slope of the segment *BC*.

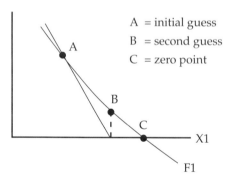

Figure 8.2
New guess.

As noted, this algorithm is used in several places—for the simultaneous solution of the price possibility frontiers and the solution of the input-output system, among others. As the algorithm is a long and complex one, it would be inconvenient to write it into the program each time it must be used. An efficient program can be designed to store the most general part of the algorithm separately from that part which sets up the simultaneous system of functions.

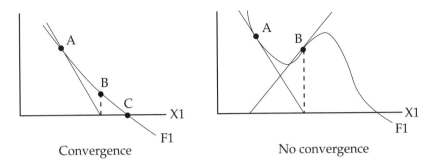

Figure 8.3
Convergence vs. no convergence.

8.3   Natural Gas Model

8.3.1   Introduction

An econometric model of the natural gas and, secondarily, the petroleum sectors of the economy has been constructed by Paul W. MacAvoy and Robert S. Pindyck (1973). The wealth of microeconomic detail in the Natural Gas Model (NGM) provides a valuable complement to the more aggregative Inter-Industry Model. The Natural Gas Model contains detailed representations of both supply and demand for natural gas and petroleum as functions of exogenously given prices. There is no process of convergence or equilibration; supply and demand operate independently in the model.

8.3.2   Natural Gas Supply

Supply in the Natural Gas Model is modeled for both oil and gas for eighteen regions of the country, plus offshore Louisiana; ten more regions are sketchily included for gas alone (see table 8.1). Except for the offshore district, where special features are worked out in a distinct manner, the regions where both oil and gas are modeled are handled in parallel fashion. The general approach to parameter estimation is based on a time series at cross sections with the resulting coefficients uniform for the eighteen key districts.

  Each of the fully modeled districts contains both short-term and long-term components of supply, which are distinguished by their assumptions about oil or gas reserves. In the short run, one year,

Table 8.1
Natural Gas Model supply districts

Districts modeled for oil and gas		M-P prefix
1.	California	CA
2.	Colorado-Utah	COUT
3.	Kansas	KA
4.	Louisiana north	LN
5.	Louisiana south (excl. offshore)	LS
6.	Mississippi	MS
7.	Northern New Mexico	MN
8.	Permian	PE
9.	Oklahoma	OK
10.	Texas District 1	T1
11.	Texas District 2	T2
12.	Texas District 3	T3
13.	Texas District 4	T4
14.	Texas District 6	T6
15.	Texas District 9	T9
16.	Texas District 10	T0
17.	West Virginia-Kentucky	WK
18.	Wyoming	WY
	Louisiana offshore	LX
Districts with gas supply only		
19.	Arkansas	AR
20.	Michigan	MI
21.	Missouri	MO
22.	Nebraska	NB
23.	North Dakota	ND
24.	New York	NY
25.	Ohio	OH
26.	Pennsylvania	PA
27.	Texas District 5	T5
28.	Texas District 7	T7

The enumeration of these districts corresponds to their index numbers in the FORTRAN version of the Natural Gas Model.

reserves are taken as unresponsive to economic incentive and as technical constraints on current production. In the long run, the effect of price changes on well drilling patterns and the level of exploratory and developmental effort in general changes the reserve base and, therefore, supply conditions in later years.

The basic supply equation, the one that ultimately determines current availability, is the *production from reserves equation*. At this stage, unfortunately, this equation is fully specified only for natural gas, and in the eighteen main supply districts; production in the eighteen oil districts and in the other ten gas supply districts is driven by an assumption of a constant reserves-to-production ratio. Short-term supply of oil, therefore, is perfectly inelastic. Where it is fully specified, current production of gas in each district is taken as a function of the district well-head price, and of the fixed level of reserves which have been proved in the district. This specification is based on alternative functional forms representing the long-term cost structure of the industry, and on the assumption of marginal cost pricing.[7]

In the long run, each district's reserves of oil and gas are permitted to vary, thus affecting the position and shape of later years' current production curves. In the case of oil, then, although supply is inelastic in the short run, it is price-responsive over multiyear periods. Variations in reserves are explained through the individual components in the identity:

Net additions to reserves = New discoveries + Extensions

+ Revisions − Current production

where extensions are developments of existing fields and revisions represents changes in geologists' estimates of recoverable reserves. Of these components, current production has already been mentioned; it remains to outline the treatment of discoveries, extensions, and revisions.

Following Franklin Fisher's earlier work (1964), the Natural Gas Model writes the total of new discoveries as identically equal to the product of three other quantities:

$\text{Discoveries}_{gas} = (\text{Wildcats drilled}) * (\text{Success ratio}_{gas})$
$* (\text{Average size of discovery}_{gas})$
$\text{Discoveries}_{oil} = (\text{Wildcats drilled}) * (\text{Success ratio}_{oil})$
$* (\text{Average size of discovery}_{oil})$

The reason for this particular decomposition have to do with the possibly contradictory effects of a change of the price level on the quantity of new discoveries; in particular, it is intended to explain why the price elasticity of the supply of new discoveries will tend to be lower than the price elasticity of drilling effort (see below). This tautology gives rise to five equations for each district, which are used in the model to describe district new discovery response to economic incentives. These are:

1. A *wildcats equation* that predicts the amount of exploratory activity in the district as a function of potential revenue, risk, and costs.

2–3. *Average size of discovery equations*, one each for oil and natural gas, which depend mainly on price (the contract price for natural gas), the district's geologic history, and the degree of field depletion.

4–5. *Success ratio equations*, also both for oil and gas, which predict the proportion of successful oil or gas wells to total wildcats as a function of prices, drilling activity, and geologic history.

Underlying the wildcats specification is a portfolio theory approach to the choice of prospects to be drilled. The prospects in drillers' "portfolios" are classified as extensive or intensive. Extensive drilling reaches out beyond well-developed areas to open up new geographical locations or previously unexplored deeper strata in oil fields; this may result in large average discoveries, but extensive drilling is generally perceived as riskier. Intensive drilling takes place in familiar, well-exploited fields; here, the probability of a given well making a discovery is high, but the size of the find is likely to be small. The driller who has options on both extensive and intensive prospects faces a risk-return tradeoff similar to the one confronting the holder of a financial portfolio. His propensity to undertake a given project depends on the information he can find about this and alternative prospects and on the shape of his utility map (his relative desires for return and risk-aversion).

Both the "objective" inputs to the decision-making process and the preferences which control the choice are part of the drilling equation. The "objective" inputs include prices, costs, historical find rates, expected risk (variance of discovery size), the degree of depletion: these are the independent variables. The estimate of the relationship between this information and drilling activity in a given region and year gives a measure of the drillers' average subjective weighting of the various incentives and disincentives.

Depending on incentives, preferences, and the resulting distribution of drilling effort (among supply regions, in this model), some reaction can be expected in the nature of aggregate discovery statistics. There effects are simulated by the success ratio and average discovery size equations for each region. If the wildcats equations project stepped-up activity in old, familiar producing regions (the intensive margin), these variables capture the aggregate tendencies toward higher success rates and smaller discovery size. If the bulk of drilling is in relatively unexplored areas, the simulations of discovery characteristics will show the opposite effect. Overriding these tendencies in the long run is the general trend of depletion, also represented by these variables.

The foundation for the explicit specification of the success ratio and average discovery size equations is the statistical analysis of the discovery process by Kaufman, Baker and Kruyt (1974).[8] Using postulates suggested by geologic experience and other studies, Kaufman was able to derive and test expressions for the size distribution of reservoirs in a homogeneous subpopulation and for the probabilistic behavior of drilling success and discovery size when exploration begins. MacAvoy and Pindyck adapted these formulations to the specification of discovery size and success ratio equations for individual supply regions. The chief difficulty with this adaptation is the high probability that the large supply regions will contain not just one homogeneous subpopulation of reservoirs, but many; this is partly corrected by the inclusion of a price term to represent economic choices between subpopulations within a region. The use of Kaufman also does not provide a means of predicting the discovery characteristics of totally new fields; however, this is a problem that no has solved.

As noted, the products of the regional predictions for new wildcats, success ratio, and average discovery size give regional projections for total new discoveries, and the price elasticity of discovery is the product of the price elasticities of the three variables. We expect the product of the price elasticities of average discovery size and the success ratio to be less than one, since the model includes a secular trend of depletion and a corresponding declining expected average find per well. When this is the case, we see that the price elasticity of discovery is less than the price elasticity of exploratory effort—an empirical phenomenon which Fisher was trying to capture with his original disaggregation of the discovery variable.

The other components of net additions to reserves, extensions, and revisions, are more random in their behavior than discoveries, and are modeled in a more *ad hoc* manner. *Gas extensions* are a function of drilling (lagged) and of gas discoveries (also lagged); *oil extensions* also depend on drilling and discoveries. *Revisions equations*, for both oil and gas, include as arguments the reserve levels, drilling activity, and the rate of depletion.

An important fact to note about the structure of the additions to reserves equations is that it includes numerous dynamic linkages, so that much more than price enters into the determination of reserve formation. One finds, for example, that annual reserve levels, average sizes, success ratios, discoveries, and current production all feed, as lagged values, into subsequent projections; still other links arise from potential reserve estimates, depletion rates, and indices of drilling activity.

Because of its unique characteristics, one important production district, Louisiana offshore, is modeled independently.[9] Louisiana offshore's primary differentiating attributes include a less exploited potential, purely extensive as opposed to intensive drilling, higher costs, and different leasing procedures. The offshore subprogram, set up by Philip Sussman, is built of three sequential blocks (MacAvoy and Pindyck, 1975): (1) In the first block, the amount of acreage to be made available by the Bureau of Land Management is determined, thus circumscribing the opportunity set for offshore drillers; key variables are the amount of new acreage leased in a given year, and the amount of acreage forfeited because of insufficient productivity. (2) Next, given total available "supervised" acreage, total producing acreage is determined. (3) Finally, given producing acreage, costs, prices, and available drilling rigs, total offshore additions to reserves the production are found in a manner roughly analogous to the onshore model.

One additional point completes this brief overview of supply in the Natural Gas Model. The model, with its admirable and characteristic passion for institutional detail, includes a large array of different prices. Prices differ not only be geographical area, but by institutional character. At least two different gas prices, for example, are relevant to the supply of crude gas in this model; these are the *well-head price* and the *contract price*. The relationship of these two prices is an intriguing one. No uniform price covers the sale of all crude natural gas. Instead, since gas in contracted long in advance of delivery at a fixed price (the contract price), and since contracts are not necessarily coterminous, a given producer may be selling different parts of his production at different prices. The producer's overall average price (the weighted average of the contract prices) is his average well-head price. It is the new contract price that is regulated by the Federal Power Commission, and which is relevant to wildcatters and explorers (since it is at the new prevailing contract price that they will be able to sell what they find); the well-head price, on the other hand, is more closely related to current production.

8.3.3   Natural Gas Demand

The demand side of the Natural Gas Model plays only a minor role in the first stage integration of the two models. In all, three general characteristics of the demand side should be noted: First, comprehensive demand equations, estimated from a time series of cross sections, as on the supply side, are provided for forty demand regions of the country. This disaggregation all the way down to approximately the state level is intended to allow for analysis of interdistrict flows of gas and oil. Second, the demand for natural gas (more scrupulously modeled than the demand for oil) is broken down in each demand region into a number of components. The most important of these are residential-commercial demand and industrial demand; these are estimated in a manner closely following Balestra (1967) and Balestra and Nerlove (1966). The demand structure is run off a complex set of both estimated (wholesale prices, field prices) and exogenous (alternate energy source prices) price variables, as well as a number of exogenous projections of regional growth, and development.

To link supply and demand in the Natural Gas Model a conceptually simple but statistically detailed representation of the flow structure of domestic natural gas from producer to consumer is included in the model. Flows are determined mainly by the placement of existing pipeline networks and are not responsive to changes in relative demand prices. Using this assumption, a static flow matrix gives the gas available to each demand region group as a fixed proportion of the gas produced in the appropriate supply districts. By comparing the projections of regional demand with those of regional supply derived from this structure, regional excess demand, projected demand minus projected supply, can be calculated.

8.3.4   Computational Scheme

A simulation run for the Natural Gas Model consists, first, of the entry of a time series of exogenous crude oil well-head and natural gas contract prices. The latter tends to correspond to the particular (actual or proposed) FPC natural gas regulation policy the modelers wish to study. Given these prices and lagged reserve figures, a calculation of current oil and gas production is made. Additions to reserves of oil and gas are also calculated for each district; this will enter into the short-run supply curves for the next "year" of simulation. Next, "markup equations" are used to find regulated wholesale and retail prices, which feed into the determination of the various components of demand for each of the demand regions. Finally, an estimate of supply availability for each consuming region is made, based on the level of production by the supplying regions and on the historical pattern of interregional pipeline flows. The ultimate output—the output to which the model's developers seem to ascribe normative significance—is "regional excess demand."

An important objection that can be made to this type of procedure is that it lacks an equilibration process; excess demand is simply left hanging at the end of the year. Excess demand for gas would not disappear, but would be reflected in higher oil prices, which would mean more drilling and, consequently, a higher energy supply than predicted. This is exactly the kind of feedback the Inter-Industry Model incorporates. If the current production functions of the Natural Gas Model were used as the supply curves for oil and gas in the Inter-Industry Model, the level of imports being given, the combined model would determine prices that clear all markets. Excess demand for gas is erased by generally higher prices and shifts to alternate sources; no demand would be left over.

It was not necessary to translate all of the Natural Gas Model into a form appropriate for integration with the Inter-Industry Model. Only small parts of the demand structure were employed; the offshore model was made exogenous. The problem of converting the National Gas Model into FORTRAN was carried out in two stages. It was uneconomical to do the necessary debugging on a comparatively bulky integrated model, so that the first step was to establish a FORTRAN replica of Natural Gas Model supply. After this program was checked out and shown able to duplicate the model's projections on a region-by-region basis, the program was incorporated into the integration of the Natural Gas Model and the Inter-Industry Model.

The notational and organizational simplifications provided by FORTRAN is a great programmer's convenience. FORTRAN's advantage is due largely to more flexible variable subscripting in conjunction with the use of DO loops. By the use of subscripting, FORTRAN adds a great deal of compactness to the nomenclature. The general array for the wildcats variable, for instance, would be denoted by

$WXT(II, J)$, where II is the year index and J is the district index. This feature is important when the programmer wants a similar operation performed with reference to all of the districts; for example, the statements

DO 10 J = 1, 18

10 $WXT(II, J)$ = $A0 + A1 * (PW(II, J))$,

which gives a hypothetical equation predicting the number of wildcats drilled in each district as a function of that district's well-head price.

The second advantage of the FORTRAN version of the Natural Gas Model is superior efficiency with regard to machine time usage. This is due to the fact that, working in FORTRAN, the programmer is able to eliminate a great deal of spurious simultaneity. The Natural Gas Model is almost entirely recursive, i.e., equations may usually be solved sequentially rather than simultaneously. Using FORTRAN, then, the programmer can treat the model's equations as consecutive data processing statements, calling in Newton's method for another subroutine when true simultaneities occur.

8.4   Integrated Model

8.4.1   Introduction

We have described the Inter-Industry Model constructed by Hudson and Jorgenson and the Natural Gas Model constructed by MacAvoy and Pindyck. We next proceed to describe the integration of the two models. The first step is to incorporate long-term supply functions for petroleum and natural gas into the Inter-Industry Model. We have developed a methodology for incorporating supply functions into the Inter-Industry Model that can be used for any econometric model of primary energy supply. We describe this methodology and its implementation for the Natural Gas Model in the following section.

The second step in integration of the Inter-Industry Model and the Natural Gas Model is to incorporate the regulation of well-head prices for natural gas by the Federal Power commission.[10] If the regulated ceiling price is below the market clearing price, demand exceeds supply and supply must be allocated to consuming sectors by the regulatory agency. Shortages of natural gas will affect demand for other

Table 8.2
Block summary of the free-standing FORTRAN version of Natural Gas Model supply

Lines	Description
1–31	COMMON statements (transmit variable values to other subroutines) DIMENSION statements (set up variable arrays)
32–134	READ in initial data from punched cards
135–175	Sets up Natural Gas Model dummy variables
176–232	Enter equation parameters from Natural Gas Model
233–247	Calculate values of those lagged variables which must be found from variables previously read in
248–257	Enter exogenous price series
258–324	Loop through all 18 districts, calculating values of following variables from regression equations or identities

QG	Current gas production
QO	Current oil production
CQG	Cumulative gas production
GAGE	Gas depletion variable
OAGE	Oil depletion variable
CQO	Cumulative oil production
SZG	Average size of gas discovery
SZO	Average size of oil discovery
SRG	Success ratio, gas
SRO	Success ratio, oil
WXT	Wildcats drilled
WXG	Gas wells
WXO	Oil wells
GD	Gas discoveries
OD	Oil discoveries
WXGREF	Index of drilling activity, gas
WXOREF	Index of drilling activity, oil
XT	Gas extensions
RT	Gas revisions
OX	Oil extensions
OR	Oil revisions
OY	Oil reserves
YT	Gas reserves

Lines	Description
326–328	Add QG and YT, districts 19–28
329–365	Aggregate to national totals, under matrix US(I,J)
366	END

types of energy and for nonenergy inputs into each sector. We have developed a methodology for incorporating the effects of regulation, based on an application of the theory of rationing. This methodology and its implementation are described in section 8.4.3, below.

8.4.2 Resource Supply

The Inter-Industry Model is a static model and does not include resource depletion or the discovery and development of new primary energy resources as endogenous elements in the model. To overcome this deficiency, long-term supply curves for primary resources must be introduced into the model. Whatever supply curves were to be introduced, they had to be made fully consistent with the production structure of the Inter-Industry Model. There are three requirements: (a) The input requirements of the energy production sectors must be derivable and must represent production combinations consistent with their endogenous prices and the translog structure. (b) The inputs of energy products into other sectors must be consistent, given prices, with the translog price possibility frontiers of those sectors. (c) The supply and use of each type of energy must be in balance.

To solve the problem of making the new supply curves consistent with the Inter-Industry Model the levels of technology in the price possibility frontiers were made endogenous, as follows:

(1) Consider any econometrically estimated sectoral supply function, $XI = F(PI)$, that we want to introduce into the Inter-Industry Model.

(2) Assume that the appropriate form of the production function underlying the supply function is represented by the price possibility frontier, as before

$$\frac{PI}{AI} = PI(PK, PL, PE, PM).$$

(3) The level of technology AI is chosen so that

$$XI = F(PI),$$

where XI and PI are determined as solutions to the Inter-Industry Model.

The Inter-Industry Model can incorporate any observed supply function or set of supply functions by the procedure given above. The supply functions are allowed to dictate the equilibrium market conditions for sectoral output, while the price possibility frontiers determine demands for sectoral inputs. The only additional assumption required is that the relative use of inputs by energy sectors is a function of input prices only, and is not related to the scale of production or the extent of resource depletion.

If the level of technology could be determined so that the supply predicted by the translog production structure and the supply function are the same, the internal consistency of the complete model is assured. The technique of solution for the complete model is based on the same algorithm discussed previously, Newton's method. Recall that this algorithm searches for the intersection of kernels of a system of functions by perturbing each argument separately, then calculating numerical approximations to the vectors of partial derivatives; these approximations are used to construct new "guesses" closer and closer to the simultaneous solution. In this situation, Newton's method was used to find the equilibrium solution for the generalized model, given exogenously determined supply curves for N sectors.

For equilibrium in the complete model, the supply and demand for the output of each sector in the model must be balanced. Balance is already assured in sectors that have no exogenous supply curves; we are concerned, then, only with the N sectors that are externally modified. If SI and DI represent, respectively, the total supply of and demand for the outputs of the Ith sector, then the N functions whose (simultaneous) zeros are to be found are $F1, F2, \ldots, FN$, where $FI = SI - DI$. Supply and demand in this model are functions of disposable income, prices, and input-output coefficients, which in turn are dependent on the scale coefficients, the parameters of the translog production and utility functions, and the income projections of the growth model. Taking the translog parameters and the income projections as fixed, the FI can be evaluated with reference to only N endogenous variables—the N scale coefficients, $A1, A2, \ldots, AN$. The search for an equilibrium solution can be conducted through iterations on the AI.

To summarize: The estimated coefficients of utility and production functions are given; the macroeconometric growth model has projected a level of national product; supply functions are introduced along with initial guesses for the scale factors AI corresponding to the N exogenous supply curves. The overall Newton's method begins by evaluating $F1, F2, \ldots, FN$, the differences between sectoral supply and demand. This is done in the manner outlined above: First, a set of interconsistent prices, based on the initial guesses for the scale coefficients and the translog parameters, are calculated. Note that this requires a Newton's method *within* a Newton's method. Cost minimizing input-output coefficients are found for these prices (another Newton's method) and, given the predetermined level of final demands, total (final plus intermediate) sectoral demands (DI) are derived. Given the sectoral price and the exogenous supply function, it is easy to find the level of sectoral supply (SI). FI is then equal to the Ith sector supply-demand discrepancy.

Presumably the initial evaluation will find most of the FI different from zero. Thus, the laborious process of perturbing each of the N scale coefficients (AI) and evaluating the whole model twice for each perturbation begins. New guesses for the scale coefficients are found, and the process is repeated until all supplies and demands differ by only miniscule amounts.

The whole procedure can be visualized in an intuitive way. For each of the sectors in which constant returns is not assumed, there is implicitly a downward-sloping demand curve DI, derived from the Inter-Industry Model, and a presumably upward-sloping supply curve introduced from some other source, $SEXOGI$. Superimposed on this graph is the horizontal supply curve resulting from the translog price possibility frontier. Call this line $SIIMI$.

The equilibrium price for the Ith sector's output is determined by the intersection of DI and $SEXOGI$. The interactions over which the translog scale factor AI is modified have the effect of moving the hori-

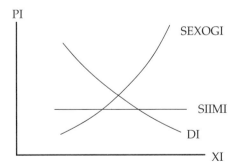

Figure 8.4
Supply and demand curves.

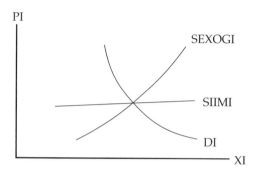

Figure 8.5
Equilibrium price.

zontal *SIIMI* curve up and down, until it passes through the intersection of *DI* and *SEXOGI*; at this juncture the point on *SEXOGI* is now also on *SIIMI*. Thus input demand becomes consistent with both the translog production structure and the empirically observed level of output.

In principle, this procedure could be used for any number of exogenous supply functions.[11] In actual practice, it would likely be too expensive to introduce more than three or four. It must be remembered that, every time the program evaluates the system of functions, it must work through the entire Inter-Industry Model plus whatever complementary model provides the supply curves. The required number of evaluations is $(2N + 1) * I * T$, where N is the number of exogenous supply functions, I is the requisite number of iterations to gain convergence (usually three or less), and T is the number of years to be simulated. This number grows quickly with added functions, since I as well as N tends to react to extra variables. This limit of three or four, however, is neither hard and fast nor a serious drawback if observed. This is because exogenous supply curves must be introduced only in primary energy sectors.

8.4.3   Well-head Price Regulation

The remaining problem to be solved is that the Inter-Industry Model relies on the movement of all prices to bring about market clearing. The Natural Gas Model, however, incorporates price regulation and the resulting shortages of natural gas. Its equations are estimated over

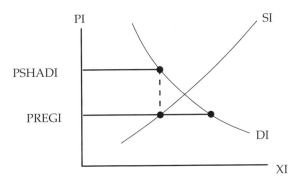

Figure 8.6
Shadow price.

a period of tight regulation of new gas contract prices by the Federal Power Commission, and it is intended to simulate over a period when this control presumably will be maintained. Regulated pricing must be effectively modeled in the Inter-Industry Model in order to incorporate the Natural Gas Model.

The solution to this problem is to introduce a shadow price, also called a virtual or scarcity price, *PSHADI*. When a price is held below the market-clearing level by regulation, say *PREGI*, there is more of the good demanded at that price than will be supplied at that price; the difference of supply and demand is called "excess demand" or "shortage." In this situation the relevant shadow price was defined as the price at which the amount of the good actually supplied at the real price would be the amount of the good actually demanded.[12] Graphically, this is the price at which a vertical line through the intersection of the regulated price and the supply curve would cut the demand curve.

The value of this shadow price for modeling the regulation situation is twofold: Given a fixed supply (determined by the fixed supply price), the replacing of the real (fixed) price of gas with a flexible, endogenous shadow price (1) allows the model to achieve supply-demand consistency, and (2) forces the input-output coefficients into a cost-minimizing configuration. This can be seen as follows:

(1) *The consistency problem.* If current supply of natural gas is a function only of own price and lagged quantities, if there is a ceiling (regulated) price, and if that ceiling price is below equilibrium so that

the ceiling price is the effective price, then supply in the short run depends on the regulated price. Since the regulated price is assumed to be below the equilibrium price, however, supply and demand are not equal; there is a "shortage" or "excess demand." However, *given* the supply of gas as a function of the regulated price, there is a market clearing shadow price, that is, a price that would have to exist to bring demand down to the fixed supply. Tautologically, the use of this price in the demand side, creating a price wedge between supply and demand, provides for consistency of supply and demand in the regulated sector.

Note that, although the shadow price is used to determine demand, the real (regulated) price must be employed in the calculation of (money) transactions levels. Otherwise, a high shadow price for natural gas would inappropriately reduce residual income and the level of demand for other commodities. This is particularly true for the final demand sector, with its fixed income constraint; the intermediate sectors, which calculate only relative demands as a function of prices, pose no difficulty.

(2) *The cost-minimization problem.* In the Inter-Industry Model, given estimated production functions and relative equilibrium input prices, subroutine *COEFF* is set up to find the input-output coefficients that minimize the total cost of output. If these input-output coefficients were to be calculated on the basis of nonequilibrium input prices (prices that do not reflect scarcity values), they would set up nonattainable cost-minimization path. The problem, then, is to have the program find a cost-minimizing solution when supply in one sector is perfectly inelastic, rather than perfectly elastic. The solution to this problem is to replace the regulated (nonequilibrium) price with the endogenous shadow price in the determination of optimum input-output coefficients: Since the final shadow price arises out of an equilibration process, it is clear that this price, not the regulated price, reflects the real scarcity value of gas as an input. By using the shadow price in its perfect markets context, the program is able to equate the ratios of marginal productivities to scarcity values of all inputs. This implies that total costs are minimized.

The sectoral breakdown employed in the Inter-Industry Model raises one further difficulty in the application of the shadow price concept. Given the regulated price and the supply function, we know how much natural gas is available to the economy *as a whole*. But the Inter-Industry Model is subdivided into sectors, all of which would presumably demand more gas at the real price than would be readily available; there is also final demand.

There are two basic approaches to this problem that are consistent with both the mode of operation of the Inter-Industry Model and the Natural Gas Model. The first possibility is the *uniform shadow price method*. This method involves a single shadow price that insures consistency of supply and demand for the economy as a whole. No explicit sector-by-sector allocation is to be made. The steps in the procedure are:

1. Take current supply of the regulated sector's output as a function of the fixed ceiling price.

2. Use the normal iteration method to find the shadow price that brings demand for that output down to the available supply, all the while keeping final demand as a function of the *real* price.

3. Take as the correct usage patterns those dictated by the shadow price.

4. Replace the shadow price with the real price in the calculation of actual transactions levels. Final demand is independent of the shadow price in order to avoid an income effect and a resulting inconsistency between income and expenditure.

Note that while no explicit sectoral allocation is made prior to this method's operation, a sectoral allocation of a very specific nature does result. First, final demand absorbs none of the shortage, but gets its full allotment at the real price. Second, among intermediate demanders, those sectors with the most elastic demands suffer the greatest loss in supply since they are most responsive to changes in the shadow price.

An alternative approach is the *sectoral shadow price method*. This approach is based on the hypothesis that geographic location, not elasticity of demand, is the main determinant of allocation decisions. It is a more flexible technique than the other because it allows the programmer to make explicit, and to vary, the type of allocation he is modeling.

The steps of this method are as follows:

(1) The model is run first without an equilibration, in the manner of the Natural Gas Model, to find the initial amounts of excess demand for gas in each of five major consuming regions.

(2) By explicit policy assumption, a division of the excess demand is made in each region between final and intermediate users. Total expenditure from the final demand sector for gas can be calculated, the difference between the expenditure and expenditure on natural gas estimated from the Inter-Industry Model being allotted over other final demands. The supply of gas available to each individual production sector is found by determining the percentage of the sector's value added produced in each geographical demand region, allotting to that portion of the sector the percentage shortage for industrial users in that region, and summing up over all regions for all sectors.

(3) Given an explicit allocation of supply to each sector, independent shadow prices, one for each sector, bring each sector's demand down to its allotted supply. The result will have consistency between demand and supply and sector by sector cost minimization. In addition, the initial allocation can be changed and the economy-wide effect of different allocation mechanisms can be evaluated.

The sectoral shadow price method is more expensive to use in simulation than the uniform shadow price method. For this reason the uniform shadow price method is currently being used in the integrated model.

8.4.4   Model Integration

There are but three details left to discuss, and the exposition of the integration of the two models will be complete.

(1) An incomplete element in the translation of the Natural Gas Model into FORTRAN is omission of the production and exploration model for offshore Louisiana. The absence of the submodel has no effect on oil production, since offshore oil is modeled along with the onshore component. In order to make the prediction for natural gas supply consistent, however, it was necessary to introduce into the integrated model the offshore gas production projections, one for each year and for each gas price scenario, as output by simulation runs. Offshore gas discoveries do not reflect differential cross-price effects arising from different endogenous paths for domestic oil prices.

(2) In an effort to achieve as complete an integration of the two models as possible, the demand sides were carefully surveyed and compared. It was apparent that the intermediate demand structures of the two were irreconcilable: Intermediate demand in the Inter-Industry Model is derived from the endogenous input-output struc-

ture, while the Natural Gas Model's industrial demand is a function of the usual demand determinants. The final demand totals used in the Inter-Industry Model are exogenous and have no connection with the inter-industry component of the model. Accordingly, it was possible to introduce the residential demand estimates from the Natural Gas Model.

(3) Finally, the original sectoral breakdown of the Inter-Industry Model included raw natural gas and crude petroleum in the same sector, sector 6. The operation of the integrated model, however, requires the independence of oil and gas prices. Sector 6, therefore, has been broken down into sector 6, crude oil, and sector 10, raw natural gas. All subroutines were appropriately modified for the resectorization; it was assumed that the new sectors 6 and 10 have the same price possibility frontiers as the original sector 6.

8.5   Applications

8.5.1   Introduction

In order to provide further insight into the working of the integrated model, this section presents the results of four policy simulations. The options explored include two basic alternatives facing energy policymakers—the "status quo" vs. "controlled deregulation" approaches to natural gas price regulation, and the "current policy" vs. "reduction by quota" approach on oil imports. These policies are simulated in the four possible combinations. They are then compared with respect to some key variables and finally evaluated in their effect on general economic performance.

8.5.2   Policy Alternatives

The possible combinations of the two gas price regulation and two oil import policies to be examined give a total of four cases. These are as follows:

Case 1. The *base case.* This case assumes what MacAvoy and Pindyck call "status quo" regulation of the natural gas contract price, i.e., the four-cent-a-year increase currently in effect. Oil imports are assumed to remain at approximately their 1974 levels, something over six-and-one-half million barrels a day (crude plus refined). Oil from unconventional sources is assumed to go from 0.5 mb/d in 1978 to 1.0

mb/d in 1980; Alaskan oil (exogenous, nonprice-responsive) begins at
0.2 mb/d in 1977 and progresses linearly to 2.0 mb/d in 1980. The
inputs from the macroeconometric growth model and the demand
side in general are similar to the base case in Hudson and Jorgenson
(1975a); the supply side is not comparable to Hudson-Jorgenson, however, since it includes the "exogenous" supply sectors.

Case 2. The *oil quota case*. "Status quo" regulation of natural gas
prices is maintained, but it is assumed that a quota or equivalent measure reduces oil imports permanently to a level one million barrels a
day below that of 1974. The purpose of this option is presumably to
stimulate domestic production.

Case 3. The *controlled deregulation case*. In this case the Federal
Power Commission maintains its control of gas contract prices, but is
assumed to allow a more liberal six-cents-a-year average increase in
the price ceiling. Oil imports are assumed to remain constant at 1974
levels. We will want to see if this policy can stimulate domestic
energy production without raising the general price level.

Case 4. The *combined case* (oil import quota plus controlled deregulation of natural gas prices). This option is the strongest attempt to
stimulate domestic production of fossil fuels.

Six-year simulations (1975–1980) were carried out for each case.
Multi-year simulation was important, of course, because of the
dynamic aspects of the Natural Gas Model supply side. The following
section compares the effects of the different policy combinations on
some important output variables.

8.5.3   Simulation Results

The most striking differential effect of the alternative policies is upon
the price of oil. As table 8.3 shows, the crude oil price ranges from
7.59 to 9.32 in 1976 (depending on the policies used); from 10.00 to
12.44 in 1978; and from 10.65 to 13.21 in 1980. Predictably, the higher
prices occur when the imposition of a quota drives down the supply
of imports. The highest price results in Case 2, where "status quo"
natural gas price regulation holds down the gas supply, placing further pressure on oil. In the controlled deregulation case (Case 3), the
greater availability of natural gas resulting from the higher ceiling
price and the absence of a quota permit a relatively low oil price.

Projections of oil prices in this version of the model must be viewed
in the light of two weaknesses in the representation of domestic oil

Table 8.3
Effects of alternative policies on energy prices

	Base case	Oil quota	Controlled deregulation of gas prices	Controlled deregulation plus oil quota
1976				
Price of crude oil ($/bb)	8.05	9.32	7.59	9.09
Price of gas ($/th cu ft)	0.33	0.33	0.41	0.41
Price of coal ($/short ton)	14.57	14.58	14.56	14.58
Price of electricity ($/kw hr)	0.0244	0.0246	0.0240	0.0243
1978				
Price of crude oil	10.61	12.44	10.00	11.96
Price of gas	0.41	0.41	0.53	0.53
Price of coal	18.14	18.16	18.12	18.14
Price of electricity	0.0275	0.0278	0.0268	0.0270
1980				
Price of crude oil	11.38	13.21	10.65	12.89
Price of gas	0.49	0.49	0.65	0.65
Price of coal	22.15	22.17	22.14	22.16
Price of electricity	0.0300	0.0302	0.0288	0.0292

price formation: (1) The equilibrium solution is confined to the domestic market; imports are taken as exogenous, and there is no direct link between domestic and import prices. (2) The effect of price controls on "old" oil is not explicitly considered. More recent versions of the model have been modified to deal more satisfactorily with these problems.

Natural gas prices vary a good bit by case, but this is due only to the assumptions about the nature of FPC price regulation. Coal and electricity prices exhibit the same secular trend as the oil price, but are not affected much by the change of policies. Supply of these inputs can expand without the strong upward price pressure seen with oil. The small variations that do occur in coal and electricity prices under different policies arise because the coal and electricity generation sectors face varying input prices as policies change. The highest prices for both coal and electricity for example, always occur in the oil quota case, when oil is the most expensive.

Corresponding to the energy prices are energy consumption patterns, summarized in table 8.4. The oil quota option forces down domestic oil consumption, sending up the equilibrium price. The Natural Gas Model supply side predicts a strong supply response for

Table 8.4
Effects of alternative policies on energy consumption

	Base case	Oil quota (% change)	Controlled deregulation of gas prices (% change)	Controlled deregulation plus oil quota (% change)
1976 Fuel consumption (Tr Btu)				
Coal	15811	1.8	-2.7	-0.4
Petroleum	33517	-5.1	1.1	-5.0
Electricity	6895	0.7	-0.5	0.3
Natural gas	23577	0.2	5.1	5.2
1978 Fuel consumption				
Coal	16281	2.3	-4.1	-2.0
Petroleum	32831	-6.4	0.0	-6.1
Electricity	7632	0.7	-0.5	0.2
Natural gas	25494	0.0	12.5	10.3
1980 Fuel consumption				
Coal	15952	1.9	-5.8	-3.5
Petroleum	34077	-5.5	0.2	-6.8
Electricity	8290	0.6	-0.6	0.1
Natural gas	28045	0.0	17.8	17.8

natural gas under the liberalized regulation options (3 and 4). Coal and electricity tend to compensate for the effects of policy on the remaining energy sectors.

It is instructive to break down these aggregate consumption figures and analyze their sectoral components. By considering output and price variations for each sector along with changes in sectoral energy consumption patterns, we can better understand the impacts of the various policies on the individual sectors.

Table 8.5 contains this information for the agricultural sector. The most important numbers in this table are the natural gas usage figures under the controlled deregulation policies (numbers 3 and 4); in both cases we see an increase in consumption of over 70% by 1980. Apparently the agricultural production function is such that natural gas, were there enough of it, could be highly productive, substituting for electricity, and even oil to some extent. In Case 3, for example, a large rise in gas input coupled with a small growth in oil usage increases agricultural output by 0.4% over the base case by 1980. Simultaneously, because of increased efficiency in input use, agricultural prices are trimmed a significant 0.4% below the base case. Case 4 shows us,

Table 8.5
Impact of alternative policies on agricultural sector

	Base case	Oil quota (% change)	Controlled deregulation of gas prices (% change)	Controlled deregulation plus oil quota (% change)
1976				
Coal use (Tr Btu)	0	0.0	0.0	0.0
Petroleum use (Tr Btu)	3772	−6.3	2.1	−5.6
Electricity use (Tr Btu)	134	3.0	−3.7	0.0
Natural gas use (Tr Btu)	465	1.3	26.9	25.2
Output ($ 1971 Bn)	294.8	−0.3	0.2	−0.2
Price of output (1971 = 1)	1.5108	0.3	−0.2	0.2
1978				
Coal use	0	0.0	0.0	0.0
Petroleum use	3731	−8.0	1.1	−6.6
Electricity use	152	3.3	−5.9	−2.6
Natural gas use	486	−0.6	52.1	51.9
Output	326.2	−0.4	0.3	−0.1
Price of output	1.6887	0.5	−0.3	0.1
1980				
Coal use	0	0.0	0.0	0.0
Petroleum use	3901	−6.9	1.7	−7.2
Electricity use	157	3.2	−8.3	−4.5
Natural gas use	599	−0.5	72.6	73.5
Output	350.2	−0.4	0.4	0.0
Price of output	1.8748	0.4	−0.4	0.1

however, that the substitutability of gas for petroleum is limited; when oil supplies are diminished by a quota, large infusions of gas are not enough to improve agricultural performance over the base case.

Manufacturing also responds quite well to the increased availability of natural gas resulting from controlled deregulation. As table 8.6 shows, manufacturing does not increase its gas consumption in Cases 3 and 4 to anything resembling the extent that agriculture does. Yet the extra gas has even a more salutary effect on this sector; with normal oil imports and controlled deregulation of gas prices, manufacturing output in 1980 is 0.6% better than the base case, and manufacturing prices are 0.5% lower. This sector is also better able than agriculture to substitute natural gas when oil becomes short: when an oil quota is combined with more liberal gas prices (Case 4), for example, manufacturing is able to reduce oil usage greatly—but, by adding more natural gas, it still improves its performance over the base case.

Table 8.6
Impact of alternative policies on manufacturing sector

	Base case	Oil quota (% change)	Controlled deregulation of gas prices (% change)	Controlled deregulation plus oil quota (% change)
1976				
Coal use (Tr Btu)	3435	3.1	−4.0	0.0
Petroleum use (Tr Btu)	4547	−5.6	−0.2	−6.7
Electricity use (Tr Btu)	1761	1.8	−2.1	0.2
Natural gas use (Tr Btu)	11531	1.7	6.6	7.6
Output ($ 1971 Bn)	863.4	−0.2	0.3	0.0
Price of output (1971 = 1)	1.3701	0.2	−0.3	0.0
1978				
Coal use	3882	3.8	−5.9	−2.3
Petroleum use	4565	−7.1	−2.5	−9.1
Electricity use	1994	2.1	−2.9	−0.8
Natural gas use	12798	0.9	12.3	13.3
Output	966.8	−0.3	0.4	0.1
Price of output	1.4965	0.3	−0.4	−0.1
1980				
Coal use	3914	3.3	−8.5	−4.4
Petroleum use	4714	−6.1	−3.5	−10.9
Electricity use	2116	1.8	−4.0	−1.7
Natural gas use	14349	0.5	19.0	20.2
Output	1652.3	−0.3	0.6	0.2
Price of output	1.6235	0.3	−0.5	−0.2

Also, here, as in the agricultural case, we see the flexibility of coal as an input; when oil usage is cut back, coal takes up much of the slack.

Tables 8.7 and 8.8 contain the energy consumption patterns of the transportation and services sectors, respectively. As might be expected, we see that the availability of oil is as crucial for transportation as it is unimportant for services. In the two oil quota case (2 and 4), the transportation sector is unable to reduce its petroleum use nearly as much as the others. Even this smaller cut has serious effects on the sector's output and, especially, its prices. Like agriculture and manufacturing, transportation fares best under the controlled deregulation option. But, unlike the first two sectors, this is not because transportation can use large additions of natural gas. Rather, the high gas prices help through their indirect stimulation of the oil supply.

Of all the portions of the economy, the services sector is the least susceptible to changes in energy policy (table 8.8). This sector is able

Table 8.7
Impact of alternative policies on transportation sector

	Base case	Oil quota (% change)	Controlled deregulation of gas prices (% change)	Controlled deregulation plus oil quota (% change)
1976				
Coal use (Tr Btu)	0	0.0	0.0	0.0
Petroleum use (Tr Btu)	2576	−3.0	1.4	−2.3
Electricity use (Tr Btu)	15	0.0	0.0	0.0
Natural gas use (Tr Btu)	254	0.8	−0.4	0.0
Output ($ 1971 Bn)	94.4	−0.3	0.2	−0.2
Price of output (1971 = 1)	1.2955	0.4	−0.3	0.2
1978				
Coal use	0	0.0	0.0	0.0
Petroleum use	2617	−4.2	1.5	−2.6
Electricity use	16	0.0	0.0	0.0
Natural gas use	263	0.0	−1.1	−1.5
Output	105.6	−0.4	0.2	−0.1
Price of output	1.3779	0.6	−0.4	0.2
1980				
Coal use	0	0.0	0.0	0.0
Petroleum use	2791	−3.8	2.3	−2.4
Electricity use	17	0.0	5.9	5.9
Natural gas use	270	−0.4	−1.1	−2.2
Output	115.8	−0.3	0.3	−0.1
Price of output	1.4558	0.5	−0.6	0.1

Table 8.8
Impact of alternative policies on services sector

	Base case	Oil quota (% change)	Controlled deregulation of gas prices (% change)	Controlled deregulation plus oil quota (% change)
1976				
Coal use (Tr Btu)	143	0.7	−0.7	0.0
Petroleum use (Tr Btu)	3956	−7.7	3.1	−6.5
Electricity use (Tr Btu)	1940	−0.5	1.1	0.4
Natural gas use (Tr Btu)	2301	−0.6	10.2	7.9
Output ($ 1971 Bn)	941.1	−0.1	0.1	0.0
Price of output (1971 = 1)	1.4172	0.1	−0.1	0.0

Table 8.8 (continued)

	Base case	Oil quota (% change)	Controlled deregulation of gas prices (% change)	Controlled deregulation plus oil quota (% change)
1978				
Coal use	111	0.9	−0.9	0.0
Petroleum use	3689	−9.7	2.4	−7.2
Electricity use	2116	−0.8	2.0	1.3
Natural gas use	2430	−2.0	18.0	15.7
Output	1037.9	−0.1	0.1	0.0
Price of output	1.5499	0.1	−0.2	0.0
1980				
Coal use	91	1.1	−2.2	−1.1
Petroleum use	3809	−8.4	3.5	−7.4
Electricity use	2324	−0.6	3.0	2.2
Natural gas use	2285	−2.0	27.6	24.9
Output	1128.9	−0.1	0.2	0.1
Price of output	1.6897	0.1	−0.2	−0.1

to cut back on oil use during a quota or step up utilization of gas when it becomes available. In any situation, its performance differs little from the base case.

Finally, table 8.9 surveys the electricity generation sector. Again, as in the case of the transportation sector, output figures reveal the importance of oil as an input. Like agriculture, however, the electricity generation sector shows the capacity for a substantial absorption of natural gas input, when it becomes available.

If output and price figures are taken as the basis for judgment, these simulation runs seem to indicate controlled deregulation without a quota as unambiguously the best policy combination of the four. This is clear in each sector individually; table 8.10 gives the aggregate figures. The oil quota alone (Case 2) seems to be the worst policy, while the base case and Case 4 are similar in the aggregate. In the next subsection we will consider why the model makes this ranking; to what extent the ranking holds under different assumptions; and what alternate criteria for choosing among policies might be used.

Table 8.9
Impact of alternative policies on electricity generation sector

	Base case	Oil quota (% change)	Controlled deregulation of gas prices (% change)	Controlled deregulation plus oil quota (% change)
1976				
Coal use (Tr Btu)	8928	1.6	−2.7	−0.6
Petroleum use (Tr Btu)	2456	−6.9	0.5	−7.7
Electricity use (Tr Btu)	660	0.9	−1.5	−0.3
Natural gas use (Tr Btu)	4572	−1.8	16.8	12.6
Output ($ 1971 Bn)	41.1	−5.1	1.1	−5.0
Price of output (1971 = 1)	1.4214	0.7	−1.5	−0.5
1978				
Coal use	9001	2.0	−4.3	−2.4
Petroleum use	2170	−8.6	−1.7	−9.9
Electricity use	638	1.1	−2.0	−1.0
Natural gas use	4563	−3.2	31.9	28.4
Output	40.3	−6.4	0.0	−6.1
Price of output	1.6027	1.1	−2.6	−1.6
1980				
Coal use	8785	1.7	−5.8	−3.9
Petroleum use	2127	−7.5	−2.2	−11.5
Electricity use	614	0.8	−2.6	−1.5
Natural gas use	5244	−2.4	46.6	43.2
Output	41.8	−5.5	0.2	−6.8
Price of output	1.7467	1.0	−3.7	−2.6

Table 8.10
Effects of alternative policies on national product and inflation, 1976–1980

	Base case	Oil quota (% change)	Controlled deregulation of gas prices (% change)	Controlled deregulation plus oil quota (% change)
1976				
GNP ($ 1971 Bn)	1256.6	−0.1	0.2	0.0
Price level (1971 = 1)	1.3577	0.5	−0.2	0.4
1977				
GNP	1330.7	−0.2	0.2	0.0
Price level	1.4183	0.5	−0.2	0.3

Table 8.10 (continued)

	Base case	Oil quota (% change)	Controlled deregulation of gas prices (% change)	Controlled deregulation plus oil quota (% change)
1978				
GNP	1396.6	−0.2	0.2	0.0
Price level	1.4920	0.6	−0.3	0.2
1979				
GNP	1465.1	−0.2	0.3	0.1
Price level	1.5550	0.5	−0.4	0.2
1980				
GNP	1523.1	−0.2	0.3	0.1
Price level	1.6270	0.5	−0.4	0.1

8.5.4   Policy Evaluation

That the integrated model would rank the oil quota as a generally inferior energy policy is no surprise, given the model's scope and structure. Trade restriction is inefficient, and the model picks this up. The advantage of the model over abstract theory is that the model provides an estimate of the *magnitude* of the inefficiency, thereby giving the policymaker an economic cost against which to weigh whatever benefits he perceives in the quota.

The cost that the model assigns to the oil quota is significant, as can be seen by comparing Case 1 with Case 2, or Case 3 with Case 4, in either the sectoral or aggregated tables. Any of the comparisons will show the oil quota causing prices to rise (due to higher energy input prices) and output declining (because of a lower energy availability). The size of these effects is large enough to be judged serious.

We must ask, however, if the model's estimate of the cost of an oil quota is realistic. It could be argued that the weakness of the domestic oil supply response is overstated in this model, and that the higher oil prices created by the quota might lead to stepped-up secondary and tertiary recovery, increased development in Alaska and offshore, the use of shale, etc.—none of which is adequately accounted for in these simulations. If such a strong supply response did occur, the quota-induced efficiency losses might be sharply reduced.

This argument may be answered in several ways. First, while the model may overstate the cost of this policy by assuming too weak a supply response, it simultaneously understands the real costs because of its middle- to long-term equilibration period. As the Arab oil embargo demonstrated, the costs of an oil reduction in the short term may exceed those of the longer term because of fixed technologies, bottlenecks, and other rigidities; these costs are not captured by the model. A quota is presumably imposed more gradually than an embargo; still, it cannot be too gradual and still hope to accomplish its aims.

Second, the model does not include the real costs of using domestic oil rather than foreign oil. A policy that emphasizes domestic supply incurs the environmental costs associated with offshore drilling, wilderness pipelines, and the excavation of shale. Such policies also contribute to the depletion of the domestic reserve base.

Finally, while there are a number of potential sources for new domestic supply, our experience with the industry and our knowledge of the technological difficulties involved suggests that supply response is likely to be relatively inelastic, even if it is stronger than assumed in these simulations. Yet, no matter how strong domestic supply turns out to be, a quota logically must raise the price and reduce the supply of oil available to domestic consumers, other things being equal. Thus the policymaker must ask: What are the other problems with which an oil quota is supposed to deal? Is this solution worth the real costs? What alternative approaches exist?

This is not the place to discuss these questions in detail, but a few comments can be made. If the quota is for security purposes, to reduce dependence on foreign oil, then it seems misdirected. How is dependence to be reduced by encouraging the speedy depletion of our resource base? To avoid dependence we should continue to import while it is possible, simultaneously stockpiling and engaging in the development of reserves, but not increasing current production. If the balance of payments is thought important, then should't the present international monetary system be considered before defending it at such cost? Finally, if cartel-breaking is the object, we should ask if there are not better ways; and, if the marginal effectiveness of an American quota in weakening the cartel would produce significant benefits compared to the costs.

In contrast to the oil quota, the policy of "controlled" liberalization of natural gas contract prices gets strong support from these simulations. In 1980, for example, the controlled deregulation case (Case 3) yields 0.3% higher output and 0.4% lower prices than the base case.

Here, apparently, is one of those rare policy options that is unambiguously beneficial, increasing output and weakening inflation.

Again, as in the oil quota simulations, the model is estimating a magnitude for a result that is generally predicted by economic theory. In the "status quo" situation, the gas price is being held below the market equilibrium (judging by the persistent and growing shortages). A higher price, theory says, must help output, by making more gas (and more oil) available instead of less productive resources. Theory also predicts that the higher price for gas should help the general price level. The model finds both of these results. The model also makes clear the mechanisms by which the second, seemingly paradoxical proposition becomes true: The additional gas takes pressure off alternative energy sources, lowering their prices; it also permits more productive input combinations, lowering the required number of Btu's per dollar of output. All of these effects can be seen by studying sectoral consumption and output patterns.

There are some complications that might cause trouble for the position that liberalization of gas prices would have unambiguously beneficial effects. For example, the initial increase in gas prices coupled with an expansionary monetary policy might generate cost-push pressures; or, at the beginning of a series of large price rises, owners of gas reserves might withhold production in order to realize a greater return later. There might be rigidities in the markets for energy inputs or problems in the adaptation to gas-intensive technologies to add pressure to the price level.

Still, if the Natural Gas Model supply side is correct and controlled deregulation would stimulate natural gas production, then in the long term the salutary effects of this policy would surely be felt. Moreover, unlike the case of the oil quota, there are here no external criteria for judgment such as dependence; the support of the integrated model for controlled deregulation need not be qualified by such considerations.

Notes

1. The translog form for representation of technology was introduced by Christensen *et al.* (1971, 1973).
2. Input-output analysis, based on fixed input-output coefficients, was introduced by Leontief (1951).
3. The separation of inputs into four aggregate groups—capital, labor, energy, and materials—was introduced by Berndt and Wood (1974).
4. The recursive decomposition of the determination of prices and quantities is a consequence of the nonsubstitution theorem, due to Samuelson (1966).

5. The macroeconometric growth model employed in the Inter-Industry Model was constructed by Hudson and Jorgenson (1974b).

6. For further discussion of the indirect utility function, see Jorgenson and Lau (1975).

7. The authors argue that the assumption of marginal cost pricing is reasonable, since it is true either if the industry is competitive (MacAvoy, 1974) or it regulation is sufficiently effective (MacAvoy and Pindyck, 1973).

8. G.M. Kaufman, Y. Baker, and D. Kruyt, A probabilistic model of the oil and gas discovery process—part I. Unpublished memorandum, Sloan School of Management, MIT, March (1974).

9. The model was constructed by Sussman (1974).

10. For a detailed discussion of well-head price regulation for natural gas, see Breyer and MacAvoy (1974), A.E. Kahn (1960), MacAvoy (1962, 1974).

11. For alternative econometric models of the supply of petroleum and natural gas, see Barouch and Kaufman (1974), Erickson (1970), Erickson and Spann (1971), Kaufman (1973), Khazzoom (1973), and Uhler and Bradley (1970).

12. This analysis is standard in the economic theory of rationing. See, for example, Tobin (1952).

9

Economic and Technological Models for Evaluation of Energy Policy

Kenneth C. Hoffman and Dale W. Jorgenson

9.1 Introduction

The Arab oil embargo of 1973 and the extraordinarily cold winter of 1977 are part of a series of events that have elevated energy policy in the United States to the highest level of social priority. A new Federal government agency, the Federal Energy Administration, was established to administer price controls and associated allocation mechanisms adopted in the face of higher world oil prices. A second agency, the Energy Research and Development Administration, was established to coordinate research, development, and demonstration projects for the energy sector. These agencies have now been incorporated into a new cabinet-level Department of Energy. Energy research and development in the private sector has expanded with increased financial support from both government and private sources.

The guidelines of a national energy policy for the United States have emerged; detailed programs are being developed and implemented. To preserve flexibility in the face of uncertainty a continuous assessment of existing programs is required. Analysis is needed for likely impacts of such policy measures as price controls, taxes, and regulation to stimulate energy conservation in the private sector, government support to generate additional conventional energy supplies, and government sponsored research and development programs, directed toward providing new technology for energy production, conversion, and utilization. The evaluation of new and existing energy policies must incorporate information from detailed engineering studies of specific technologies emerging from research and development programs and must include the assessment of policy impacts on the structure of the energy sector and on the overall level and composition of economic activity.

Alternative models for energy policy assessment have been developed on the basis of both process analysis and econometrics. In the process analysis approach energy flows and energy conversion processes are described in physical terms. The description need not be limited to a particular technology, but can encompass the entire system for the production and utilization of energy. In the econometric approach the representation of technology is based on behavioral and technical responses of production patterns to alternative prices; a similar approach can be employed for the representation of consumer preferences. Flows of economic activity, including energy flows, are described in terms of economic accounts in current and constant prices.

The process approach provides for the incorporation of explicit information on anticipated technological change in the energy system and in the economy based on detailed engineering studies, including studies of technologies that are under development and consideration for future implementation. This approach is well adapted to the description of the energy sector; however, the representation of aggregate consumer behavior and economic activity by means of process analysis is infeasible. The econometric approach including appropriate exogenous variables to represent new policy initiatives is well adapted to the description of aggregate economic activity in summary form and provides for the analysis of policy impacts on the overall level of economic activity and its distribution among industry groups or groups of consumers. However, this approach is infeasible for the study of technologies that are not already in use or for the study of consumer preferences for commodities not already in existence.

A satisfactory framework for the assessment of the full range of alternative energy policies requires an approach that encompasses both process analysis and econometrics. Since the output of the energy producing industries is largely consumed by other industries rather than by final consumers such as households, governments, and the rest of the world, a natural focal point for the study of the impact of energy policy is the matrix of inter-industry transactions, representing flows of commodities, including energy, among industrial sectors. For the energy sector these transactions can be expressed in economic terms, in current and constant prices, to provide a link with econometric models. These energy sector transactions can also be expressed in physical terms, in British thermal units, to provide a link with process analysis models. By using both forms for the expression of energy flows, process analysis and econometric modeling can be combined.

The purpose of this chapter is to present a new approach for the assessment of energy research, development, and demonstration policy, integrating process analysis and econometric models that have already been used extensively in energy policy analysis and technology assessment. The first component of the approach is an econometric model of inter-industry transactions together with a macroeconomic model, presented in section 9.2, developed for the Energy Policy Project. The second component is a process analysis model of the energy sector, also presented in section 9.2, developed for the Energy Research and Development Administration. We present the combined econometric and process analysis approach in section 9.3; a preliminary model based on this approach has been employed by the Energy Research and Development Administration in the construction and analysis of a national research, development, and demonstration plan. In section 9.4 we employ the results of a policy analysis prepared for the national plan to illustrate the application of this approach to energy policy assessment.

The methodology for our combined econometric and process analysis model is illustrated in figure 9.1. The econometric model reflects economic impacts at the aggregate level, including changes in final demand and employment, that result from changes in energy policy. The process analysis model determines the optimal use of resources for a given energy policy and a given economic environment. Our methodology can be applied to a wide range of national policy questions where the technological component is significant. In any policy area involving technology it is necessary to make explicit the relationships between choice of technology and the economic and social environment. Process analysis is the most appropriate methodology for describing alternative technologies; econometrics provides a basis for describing consumer behavior in the economy as a whole. With this combined approach, provision is made to allow for structural changes in the energy system and economy arising from technological change and specific policy actions. Our model represents the first attempt to implement a model that combines the advantages of both methodologies.

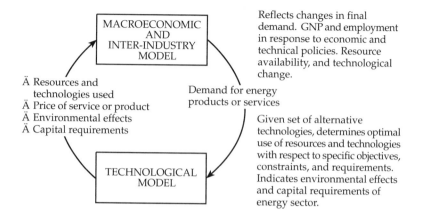

Figure 9.1
Combined econometric and process analysis model.

9.2 Econometric and Process Analysis Models

The first component of our model for the analysis of energy research, development, and demonstration policy is an econometric model of inter-industry transactions, developed by Hudson and Jorgenson (1974a). This model is based on a system of accounts for the private domestic sector of the U.S. economy, including final demand, primary input, and inter-industry transactions in current and constant prices. By means of this accounting system we can trace the process of production for energy and nonenergy products from the purchase of primary inputs through all stages of intermediate processing to deliveries to final demand. The accounts in constant prices correspond to commodity flows in physical terms. For energy sectors (or industries) these flows can be measured in physical units such as tons of coal, barrels of petroleum, and thousands of cubic feet of natural gas, or, alternatively, in energy units such as British thermal units (Btu).[1] The accounts in current prices correspond to flows in financial terms and can be used to generate financial accounts for each industry group included in the model. For energy and nonenergy sectors the prices can be expressed as index numbers; for energy sectors the prices can also be given in terms of physical or energy units.

In our system of accounts the private domestic sector of the U.S. economy is divided among nine industry groups, including five groups within the energy sector—coal mining, crude petroleum and natural gas, petroleum refining, electric utilities, and gas utilities. Our representation of the energy sector provides for an analysis of the impact of energy research, development, and demonstration policy on the industrial sectors directly affected by changes in energy technology. By incorporating final demand and four industry groups making up the nonenergy sector we can assess the impact of changes in energy technology on the sectors that consume energy products. Our complete system of accounts is represented in diagrammatic form in figure 9.2. The nine industry groups included in the accounting system are listed in figure 9.2. In this figure we also list three categories of primary inputs—capital services, labor services, and imports—and four categories of final demand—consumption, investment, government purchases, and exports.

In our system of accounts for inter-industry transactions, each industry group purchases primary inputs and intermediate inputs produced in each of the nine industrial sectors. These purchases are represented as columns of the matrix of inter-industry transactions in figure 9.2. Intermediate inputs include five types of energy—coal, crude petroleum and natural gas, refined petroleum, refined natural gas, and electricity—and four types of nonenergy products. The output of each industry is distributed to final demand and to intermediate demand by each of the nine industrial sectors. These deliveries are represented as rows of the matrix of inter-industry transactions in figure 9.2. The rows corresponding to the five industries that make up the energy sector include deliveries of energy products to energy and nonenergy sectors and to final demand. Similarly, the rows corresponding to the four industries of the nonenergy sector include deliveries of nonenergy products.

Our econometric model of inter-industry transactions includes balance equations between supply and demand for the products of each of the nine industrial sectors included in the model.[2] These balance equations state that the output of each sector in constant prices must be equal to deliveries of this output to all nine industrial sectors and to all four categories of final demand. For energy products the balance equations assure that for each form of energy, the energy units produced must be equal to the energy units consumed by all industrial groups and by final demand. Similarly, our econometric model includes balance equations stating that the output of each sector in current prices must be equal to the value of deliveries of this output to

Input to Sectors:

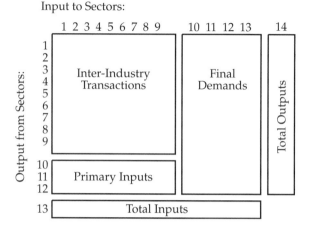

INDUSTRY SECTORS:
1. Agriculture, nonfuel mining, and construction
2. Manufacturing, excluding petroleum refining
3. Transportation
4. Communications, trade, and services
5. Coal mining
6. Crude petroleum and natural gas
7. Petroleum refining
8. Electric utilities
9. Gas utilities

PRIMARY INPUTS:
10. Imports
11. Capital services
12. Labor services

FINAL DEMANDS:
10. Personal consumption expenditures
11. Gross private domestic investment
12. Government purchases of goods and services
13. Exports

Figure 9.2
Inter-industry transactions in the econometric model.

all nine industrial sectors and to final demand. These equations assure that differences between prices received by producers and prices paid by consumers reflect excise and sales taxes paid on the value of each product.

Our econometric model of inter-industry transactions includes models of producer behavior for each industrial group included in the model.[3] Producer behavior in each industrial sector can be characterized by a system of technical coefficients, giving primary and intermediate inputs per unit of output of the sector. The model of producer behavior gives the technical coefficients as functions of the prices of output and of primary and intermediate input. For each sector the technical coefficients as functions of the prices are generated from the price possibility frontier, giving the minimum price of output of the sector attainable for given prices of primary and intermediate inputs and for a given level of productivity of the sector. The minimum price of output depends on the technological possibilities for substitution among primary and intermediate inputs, including the substitution between energy and nonenergy inputs and the substitution among different forms of energy. The price possibility frontier for each sector provides a representation of the technology of that sector. This representation assures that the value of output of the sector is equal to the sum of the values of all primary and intermediate inputs into the sector.

Finally, our econometric model of inter-industry transactions includes a model of consumer behavior that allocates personal consumption expenditures among the commodity groups included in final demand.[4] Consumer behavior can be characterized by a system of quantities purchased *per capita*. The model of consumer behavior gives the quantities purchased as functions of total personal consumption expenditures *per capita*, prices of the products of the nine industrial sectors, and prices of capital services and noncompetitive imports. The quantities purchased as functions of total expenditure and the prices can be generated from the indirect utility function, giving the maximum level of utility attainable for given total expenditure and given prices. The maximum level of utility depends on the substitutability of alternative goods and services in consumption, so that the indirect utility function provides a representation of consumer preferences. This representation assures that the sum of the values of all quantities purchased is equal to total personal consumption expenditures.

Starting with prices of primary inputs—capital services, labor services, and imports—and levels of productivity in each of the nine industrial sectors, the prices of both energy and nonenergy products are determined by the nine price possibility frontiers. With prices of primary inputs and prices of energy and nonenergy products determined from our model of production, we can generate the matrix of technical coefficients, giving primary and intermediate inputs per unit of the output of each of the nine industrial sectors. Similarly, with total personal consumption expenditures, the prices of capital services and noncompetitive imports, and the prices of energy and nonenergy products, we can generate the quantities purchased *per capita* of the products of the nine industrial sectors, capital services, and noncompetitive imports. Given the level of population, we can convert these quantities *per capita* to quantities of personal consumption expenditures as a component of final demand. To obtain final demand for the output of each of the nine industrial sectors we add personal consumption expenditures to gross private domestic investment, government purchases of goods and services, and exports.

From the quantities of final demand for the output of each of the nine industrial sectors and the matrix of technical coefficients, providing intermediate input per unit of output of each sector, we can determine the quantities of output of both energy and nonenergy sectors. We can also determine the distribution of the output of each sector between intermediate and final demand and the distribution of intermediate demand among intermediate inputs to each of the nine industrial sectors. The output of energy sectors and its distribution can be expressed in constant prices, physical units such as tons of coal or barrels of petroleum, or energy units such as Btu. From the matrix of technical coefficients of primary input per unit of output, we can determine the quantities of primary input into each sector. Finally, given the nine industrial prices and the prices of primary inputs, we can express the flow of primary input, inter-industry transactions, and final demand in current prices. We can generate the complete system of inter-industry accounts in current and constant prices from the prices of primary inputs, the levels of productivity in each inter-industry sector, total personal consumption expenditures, and the quantities of final demand for the output of each sector for investment, government purchases, and exports.[5]

The second component of our model for the analysis of energy policy is a process analysis model of the energy sector, developed at the Brookhaven National Laboratory (1973). This model is based on the Reference Energy System presented in figure 9.3. This description of the U.S. energy system provides a complete physical representation of the technologies, energy flows, and conversion efficiencies from extraction of primary energy sources through refining and various stages of conversion from one energy form to another, and through

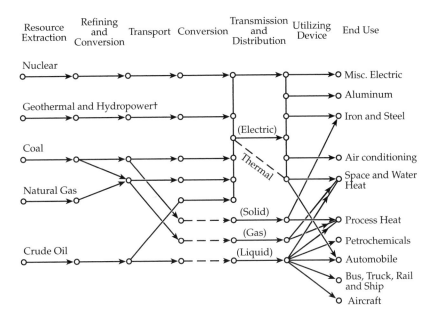

Figure 9.3
Reference Energy System.

transportation, distribution, and storage of energy.[6] In the Reference Energy System energy supplies such as nuclear fuels, fossil fuels, and hydropower are allocated to energy demands defined on a functional basis, such as space heating, industrial process heat, and automotive transportation. The characteristics of utilizing technologies, which are important in the identification of conservation and fuel substitution options, are included at the same level of detail as supply technologies. The allocation of energy resources to specific demands depends on the energy technologies that are available for the production, transportation, distribution, and storage of energy and on the cost and efficiency of these technologies. The allocations may be determined by a judgmental or optimization approach. Conversion losses are represented by the efficiency of each conversion process in physical terms. In the Reference Energy System all energy flows are measured in British thermal units (Btu).

In the Reference Energy System energy supplies and demands are linked by energy conversion processes, such as steam generation of electricity from coal. This process converts a primary energy supply, coal, into an intermediate form of energy, electricity. Electricity can be used to satisfy demands for a variety of energy products, such as base, intermediate, and peak load electricity, space heat, air conditioning, and water heat. For each process we can specify the efficiency of conversion of primary energy supplies into intermediate forms of energy and the efficiency of conversion of the intermediate forms into final energy services or products. For the coal steam electric process the conversion loss from the primary to the intermediate form of energy is associated with the generation of electricity. Similarly, the conversion loss from intermediate to final form of energy is associated with transmission and distribution losses for electric energy and the conversion efficiency of the end use device. The supply efficiency for a given energy source is defined as the product of the supply efficiencies on a path from the primary resource to the intermediate form of energy. Similarly, the demand efficiency is defined as the product of the demand efficiencies on a path from the intermediate form to the final energy product.

The Brookhaven Energy System Optimization Model (BESOM) is based on the allocation of energy supplies to energy demands to minimize cost.[7] The minimization of cost can be formulated as a linear programming problem of the transportation type. Sources in the transportation problem can be identified with energy supplies; in the optimization model there are eleven types of energy supplies, including underground and strip-mined coal, domestic, shale, and imported oil, domestic and imported natural gas, and hydro-electric, nuclear, geothermal, and solar energy. Uses can be identified with energy demands, including base, intermediate, and peak load electricity, low, intermediate, and high temperature thermal, ore reduction, petrochemicals, space heat (including heat pumps as well as electric resistance heat), air conditioning, and water heat, and air, truck and bus, rail and automobile transportation. Energy storage and synthetic fuels including hydrogen are also incorporated in the model.

The optimization model is designed around the Reference Energy System. Each trajectory through the system from a resource to a specific end use is represented by a single activity. The input data for the model are:

1. The level of demand for energy services for energy products, consistent with those determined in the integrated model.

2. Annual production constraints on supply of energy resources and availability constraints on new technologies.[8]

3. Characterization of energy supply and use technologies in terms of conversion efficiency, capital, and operating cost, and emissions to the environment (air, water, and land).

4. Definition of objective function.[9] This can be based on annual cost, including the cost of energy resources, or on alternative objectives that include utilization of primary resources, capital requirements, environmental impact, and dependence on imports.

5. Definition of any special constraints required to reflect policies or market forces that result in departures from an unconstrained optimum.

Given these data, the optimization determines resource utilization, technology, and fuel mix employed to satisfy the energy product requirements. Activity levels are given in terms of the quantity of fuel or energy delivered from a supply trajectory to the end use.

In BESOM each energy supply-demand combination is associated with costs of extraction, refining and conversion, transportation and storage, and final utilization. Annual costs per unit of operation of an energy conversion process include both capital costs and operating costs. Capital costs are converted into annual form and are conceptually equivalent to the capital service prices that enter into the econometric model of inter-industry transactions. Constraints on the supply of energy resources and the degree of implementation of new technologies are based on geological information, market surveys, and engineering judgment. A version of BESOM has been developed which incorporates supply elasticities to relate annual resource production levels to the shadow prices on resources determined in the model. Each energy conversion process produces environmental pollutants as well as intermediate forms of energy. Constraints can be imposed on the level of environmental pollution as well as on the level of energy demand and supply. Capacity limitations on energy conversion processes can be included as separate constraints in the optimization model; additional constraints corresponding to balance requirements between peak and off-peak electricity generation are also included.

The energy sector optimization model determines a set of energy conversion levels that minimizes the cost of satisfying energy product demands from energy resource supplies. The dual to this linear programming problem is to maximize the value of energy products less the value of primary energy supplies by choosing a set of energy product and energy resource shadow prices. These shadow prices assure that the value of the output of each conversion process in actual use is equal to the value of input, including the input cost of primary energy supplies and any scarcity shadow prices and costs of extraction, conversion, and transportation, just as in the econometric model of inter-industry transactions. Any energy resource with a positive price is fully utilized; similarly, the demand for any energy product with a positive price is exactly satisfied. For energy products and resources with positive shadow prices, supplies and demands are balanced in both physical terms and in current prices, as in our econometric model of inter-industry transactions.

The solution of the dual to the energy sector optimization model determines the shadow prices associated with energy products and energy resources. The assignment of energy supplies to energy demands through energy conversion processes determined by the model can be represented in physical terms in the Reference Energy System format. Given the prices of resources and the costs associated with energy conversion processes, BESOM also provides a complete description of the energy sector in financial terms. We can generate the resultant energy system scenario in the format of the Reference Energy System in both physical and financial terms from the costs of energy conversion processes, the availability of energy resources, the requirements for energy products, and any additional constraints associated with conversion capacities and environmental restrictions.

In appraising alternative energy research, development, and demonstration policies we first associate with each policy the resulting technology for the energy sector; changes in energy research and development policy are associated with changes in dates of commercial implementation, costs, and technical characteristics of specific energy technologies.[10] We can introduce the corresponding changes in energy technology into the Reference Energy System in two ways. First, the introduction of new technologies provides new energy conversion processes in addition to those that already exist. Accelerated research, development, and demonstration programs may make it possible to accelerate the introduction of new technologies. Second, the improvement of existing technologies may increase the efficiency of energy conversion or may reduce the costs of extraction, conversion, or transportation. More extensive research, development, and demonstration may speed the increase in efficiency or the reduction in cost. The introduction of new energy technology or the improvement of existing technology may reduce the costs associated with meeting given demands for energy products from given energy resource supplies. For any change in the technology options resulting from new policy initiatives we can assess the effects on the energy sector in both physical and financial terms, using the energy sector optimization model. We can also assess the environmental impact of the changes, using the environmental impact associated with alternative energy conversion processes.

9.3 Model Integration

We have presented the two models utilized for the analysis of energy research, development, and demonstration policy. The first is an econometric model of inter-industry transactions providing a representation of the technology of the energy sector through models of producer behavior for five industrial groups that make up that sector. In addition, the econometric model provides a representation of the nonenergy sector through models of producer behavior for four industrial groups making up that sector and a model of consumer behavior for the personal consumption expenditures component of final demand. The second model for the analysis of energy policy is an optimization model for the energy sector providing a much more detailed representation of the technology of that sector through the specification of characteristics of energy conversion processes linking energy resource supplies with energy resource demands. The energy sector optimization model includes existing technologies, such as steam generation of electricity from coal, and technologies that can be developed through research, development, and demonstration programs, such as the liquid metal fast breeder reactor for the generation of electricity.

Although both components of our energy policy model can be used to generate a description of the energy sector in physical and financial terms, the energy sector optimization model provides a far more detailed characterization of technology and permits the analysis of the effects of introducing new technologies. The econometric model also provides a description of the nonenergy sector and generates a complete description of the U.S. economy, including flows of primary input, inter-industry transactions, and final demand in current and constant prices. The energy sector optimization model is especially well suited to the assessment of the impacts of alternative research, development, and demonstration policies on the energy sector. The econometric inter-industry model is well suited to the assessment of the impact of these policies on the economy as a whole. By integrating the two models we can combine the detailed characterization of technology available from the energy sector optimization model with the complete representation of the economy, including energy and nonenergy sectors, available from the econometric inter-industry model. This section describes the conceptual basis for the integration of the models. A preliminary version of the integrated model has been implemented and applied by Behling, Dullien, and Hudson (1976).

Our integrated model is based on an expanded system of inter-industry accounts for the private domestic sector of the U.S. economy. In our expanded system of inter-industry accounts the energy sector is divided into energy resource sectors, energy conversion processes, and energy product sectors. The remaining components of our original system of inter-industry accounts—inter-industry transactions in nonenergy products, primary inputs, and final demands—are also included in the expanded system. The expanded system of inter-industry accounts is presented in diagrammatic form in figure 9.4.[11] The nonenergy industry sectors of our expanded system correspond to industry groups that can be found in a conventional inter-industry accounting system. Similarly, primary inputs such as capital and labor services and final demands such as personal consumption expenditures and gross private domestic investment occur in a conventional system.

To incorporate a detailed physical representation of the energy sector we have introduced categories of transactions involving energy resources, energy conversion processes, and energy products that do not correspond to industry sectors in a conventional inter-industry accounting system. The activities of the five industry groups comprising the energy sector in our econometric model are allocated among energy resources, energy conversion processes, and energy products in the integrated model. For example, the electric utility sector in the original system converts fossil fuels and other energy resources into base load, intermediate load, and peak load electricity and into other energy products such as space heat and air conditioning. In our integrated model energy flows are represented in energy units (Btu) as

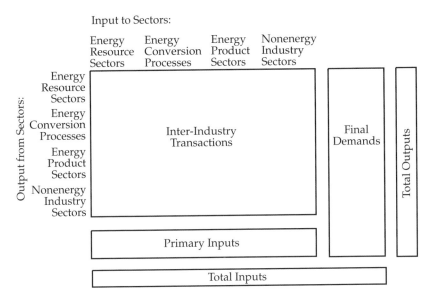

Figure 9.4
Inter-industry transactions in the integrated model.

in the Reference Energy System. Nonenergy flows are represented in constant dollars, as in our econometric model of inter-industry transactions. Given a set of energy product and energy resource prices and prices for nonenergy products and primary inputs, our expanded system of inter-industry accounts can also be represented in current prices.

In the integrated model energy resources are delivered to energy conversion processes and to final demand for inventory accumulation and for exports. Energy resources are also used in the production of energy resources; for example, coal is used as a fuel in the coal mining industry. However, energy resources are not delivered to energy products, to nonenergy sectors of our integrated model, to personal consumption expenditures, or to government purchases of goods and services. The corresponding entries in our expanded system of inter-industry accounts are equal to zero. Similarly, in the integrated model energy conversion processes deliver their output to energy product categories such as miscellaneous electric demand and rail transportation. The outputs of energy conversion processes are used in energy conversion; for example, production and distribution of electricity require electric energy. There are no direct deliveries to energy resource sectors, to nonenergy sectors, or to final demands in our integrated model; the corresponding inter-industry accounting entries are zero. Finally, energy products are delivered to nonenergy industrial sectors and to final demand. There are no deliveries of energy products to energy resource, energy conversion, or energy product sectors, so that the corresponding inter-industry accounting transactions are zero.

All final demands for energy in our integrated model, except for inventory accumulation and exports of energy resources, are supplied by deliveries of energy products. Similarly, all demands for energy by nonenergy producing sectors are supplied by deliveries of energy products. The first step in the construction of our expanded system of inter-industry accounts is to disaggregate flows of energy from the five industry groups that make up the energy sector in our econometric Inter-Industry Model. Flows from these groups to the four nonenergy industry groups and the four categories of final demand are distributed among energy product categories in our integrated model on the basis of historical data. For example, deliveries from the electric utility sector to nonenergy industry groups and final demand categories are divided among base load, intermediate load, and peak load miscellaneous electric and among the other energy products that can be supplied by electric energy. Not all energy products can be supplied by means of electricity. Miscellaneous thermal, air transportation, and truck and bus transportation are examples of energy products supplied by nonelectric energy sectors in our econometric model of inter-industry transactions.

The energy sectors in our integrated model employ inputs of capital and labor services, nonenergy intermediate goods, and energy. The energy inputs are represented in the same way as in the Reference Energy System. Energy resources are delivered to energy conversion processes and energy products receive deliveries from energy conversion processes. Inputs of labor services and nonenergy intermediate goods are components of operating cost in the objective function of the energy sector optimization model. To obtain total operating cost in current prices we evaluate labor services and nonenergy intermediate goods given a system of prices for primary inputs and nonenergy products. Similarly, inputs of capital services are a component of capital cost in the objective function of the optimization model. Capital cost in current prices is expressed in annual form. The second step in construction of our expanded system of inter-industry accounts is to disaggregate flows of nonenergy products and primary inputs in the energy sector optimization model. For each energy resource, energy conversion process, and energy product these flows must be distributed among the four nonenergy industry groups, capital services, and labor services.

Our integrated model is based on an expanded system of accounts for inter-industry transactions. The integrated model includes balance equations between supply and demand for products of each of the fifty-one sectors included in the model—eleven energy resource sectors, twenty energy conversion processes, sixteen energy products, and four nonenergy industrial sectors. The model incorporates a process analysis representation of the technology of the energy sectors of the model and an econometric representation of the technology of the nonenergy industry groups. It also incorporates an econometric model for personal consumption expenditures. The integrated model can be used to generate a complete system of inter-industry accounts in current and constant prices. The integrated model can also be used to generate energy flows in physical terms for the forty-seven categories of energy included in the model.

A flow chart of the integrated model is presented in figure 9.5. The first step in solving the model is to solve the econometric model of inter-industry transactions and the energy sector optimization model separately. From these initial solutions we determine the final demands for the nonenergy industrial sectors and the demands for the five energy industrial sectors in the econometric model. Using a fixed distribution of final demands for the products of the five energy sectors to energy product categories, we can determine final demands for sixteen energy products and for inventory accumulation and exports of energy resources. We obtain technical coefficients for the four nonenergy industrial sectors from the econometric model. Using a fixed distribution of intermediate demands for the products of the five energy sectors to energy product categories, we allocate demands for energy by the four nonenergy industrial sectors among the sixteen energy products. We obtain technical coefficients for the forty-seven energy sectors of the integrated model from the energy sector optimization model. Given the technical coefficients and the final demands, we can determine levels of output for all fifty-one sectors of our integrated model. Given the prices of primary inputs and nonenergy industrial products from the econometric model, energy resource

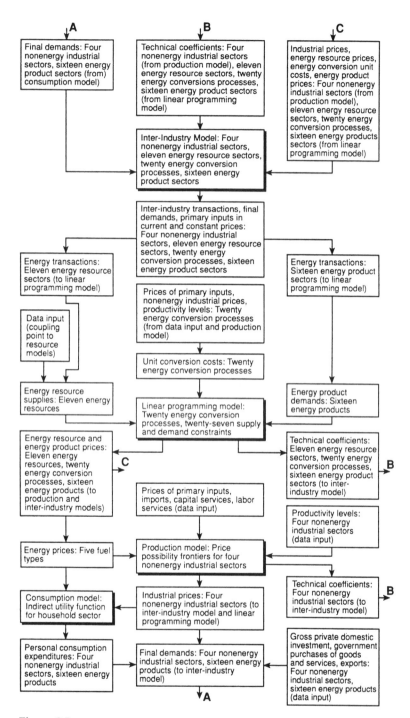

Figure 9.5
Flow chart of the integrated model (starting with inputs to the Inter-Industry Model).

prices, energy conversion costs, and energy product prices from the energy sector optimization model, we can convert the array of inter-industry transactions, final demands, and primary inputs into current prices.

The second step in solving the integrated model is to generate input data for the energy sector optimization model. The eleven energy resource supplies correspond to levels of energy resource output in the integrated model. The sixteen energy product demands correspond to levels of energy product output in the model. Unit conversion costs for the twenty energy conversion processes are the sums of unit operating and capital costs for the conversion processes of the model. Operating costs include costs of labor services and costs of intermediate goods employed in the conversion processes.[12] Capital costs correspond to costs of capital services in the model. These data define a linear programming model that is identical to the energy sector optimization model. Given the unit costs, the energy product demands, and the energy resource supplies, the energy sector optimization model generates cost minimizing levels for the energy conversion processes and value maximizing prices associated with energy supplies and demands.

The third step in solving the integrated model is to determine prices for products of each of the five energy sectors that appear in the econometric Inter-Industry Model. Prices of domestic petroleum, natural gas, and coal correspond to energy resource prices from the energy sector optimization model. The prices of gas delivered by gas utilities, electricity, and refined petroleum products are determined as a weighted average of the corresponding energy product prices. The weights are based on the proportions of deliveries of each fuel to each energy product in the total of all deliveries of the fuel. Given the prices of the products of the five energy sectors that appear in the econometric model, the prices of primary inputs, and the levels of productivity in each of the four nonenergy industrial sectors, we can determine prices for the products of the four nonenergy sectors from the four price possibility frontiers for these sectors from the econometric model. From energy and nonenergy prices and the prices of primary inputs, we can generate the technical coefficients for the nonenergy industrial sectors of the integrated model. On the basis of these prices we can allocate total personal consumption expenditures among the products of the nine sectors of the econometric model and primary inputs.

We have outlined three steps in the solution of the integrated model. At the completion of these steps we have generated a new set of data to initiate the process of solution. We repeat the sequence of three steps until the data employed to initiate the process are generated as a solution of the integrated model. The integrated model includes technical coefficients for the energy sector from the energy sector optimization model, technical coefficients for the nonenergy sector from the production models for the four nonenergy industrial sectors from the econometric Inter-Industry Model, and final demands for energy and nonenergy products from the econometric Inter-Industry Model, allocated among the energy products of the energy sector optimization model. The expanded Inter-Industry Model assures that supplies and demands are balanced for energy resources, energy conversion processes, energy products, and nonenergy products.

To summarize: A solution of the integrated model consists of a solution of the expanded Inter-Industry Model for which the following conditions hold:

1. The energy conversion levels minimize cost for the corresponding levels of energy demands and supplies and for the corresponding unit costs of the energy conversion processes.

2. The prices of energy products and energy resources maximize the value of the products less the value of the resources.

3. The prices of the five fuel types in the econometric Inter-Industry Model are generated by dual solution of the LP model.

4. The prices of the four nonenergy products are consistent with the energy product and fuel prices and the exogenously given prices of primary inputs.

5. The unit costs of the energy conversion processes are consistent with nonenergy product prices and the given prices of primary inputs.

6. The technical coefficients for the energy sectors are those associated with the cost minimizing solutions of the energy sector optimization model; the technical coefficients for the nonenergy sectors are those associated with the prices for primary inputs, the four nonenergy products, and the five fuel types.

7. The final demands for energy and nonenergy products are those associated with the prices for these products.

Under these conditions the value of the output of each sector of the expanded Inter-Industry Model is equal to the value of the input of that sector.

9.4 Application

We next present an application of the preliminary version of the model to the analysis of energy research, development, and demonstration policy.[13] Our first step is to establish a base case, representing a projection of the U.S. economy and the energy sector through 1985, that meets the following specifications:

1. Real gross national product will grow at 4 percent per year from 1975 to 1985.

2. Energy prices will grow relative to the implicit deflator of the gross national product at 1.3 percent per year over the same period.

3. Energy supplies for 1985 are similar to the "calibration case" presented in *1976 National Energy Outlook* (1976), as modified for the purposes of this analysis.

4. The availability of new energy technology for 1985 is given by the "combination scenario," in *A National Plan for Energy Research, Development and Demonstration* (1975).

Under these assumptions imports rise from 8.6 percent of total U.S. energy supply in 1967 to 18.4 percent of total supply in 1985.

The dramatic increase in the proportion of energy resource supplies that must be imported under the base case assumptions for 1985 suggests that energy policy may have to be modified to meet national security objectives. Accordingly, we have examined the implications of a reduction of imports from 18.4 percent of total energy supply in 1985 to no more than 10 percent of total supply in that year. This objective requires the introduction of a tariff on imported petroleum at the rate of 51.8 percent; we have also introduced taxes on domestic supplies of oil and gas so as to leave the prices received by domestic suppliers unchanged. Energy product and conversion levels under the base case assumptions and under our alternative case for 1985 are presented in table 9.1. The results of the proposed change in policy are presented in table 9.2. Energy prices rise by an average of 11.6 percent with the greatest increase in the price of refined petroleum products. New technologies such as oil from shale, direct use of solar

Table 9.1
Energy products and conversion levels, base case and alternative case 1985
(quadrillion Btu)

	Base case	Alternative case	Percentage change
1. Energy products			
Air conditioning	2.14	2.01	−6
Private ground transportation	3.04	2.75	−10
Air transportation	0.85	0.78	−8
Truck, bus, and diesel RR	0.95	0.84	−12
Space heat	12.73	11.96	−6
Water heat	1.79	1.67	−7
Process heat	10.91	10.64	−2
Misc. electric (incl. elec. RR)	5.39	5.09	−6
Coke for iron production	1.64	1.56	−5
Petrochemicals	4.83	4.70	−3
2. Electricity generation			
Coal steam	10.71	11.53	+8
Coal steam comb. cycle	0.00	0.00	0
Solvent refined coal steam	0.00	0.00	0
Oil steam	3.71	2.21	−40
Gas turbine	1.57	1.73	+10
Gas steam	4.39	2.70	−38
Total energy systems	0.00	0.02	—
LWR	9.55	10.51	+10
HTGR	0.00	0.25	—
Hydroelectric	3.38	3.38	0
Geothermal	0.69	1.66	+141
Solar	0.00	0.00	0
Total electricity inputs	34.00	34.00	0
Other inputs	66.00	62.70	−5

Source: Behling, Dullien, Hudson (1976), table V.4, p. 84; table V.8, p. 96.

Table 9.2
Alternative case 1985

1. Energy prices (percentage change from base case 1985)	
Coal	0.0
Refined petroleum	35.3
Refined gas	4.6
Electricity	2.4
Energy	11.6
2. New technology (change from base case 1985 in quadrillion Btu)	
Oil shale	1.00
Direct solar	0.20
Geothermal electric	0.97
Coal gasification and liquefaction	1.42
LWR	0.96
HTGR	0.25
Electric car	0.09

Source: Behling, Dullien, and Hudson (1976), table V.3, p. 81; table V.1, p. 77.

energy, generation of electricity from geothermal sources, and coal gasification and liquefaction are introduced in greater quantities under the alternative energy policy. In addition, there is greater reliance on nuclear energy through use of both light water reactors and high temperature gas-cooled reactors for generation of electricity. Finally, electric automobiles are introduced on a modest scale to conserve gasoline.

The reduction in oil and gas imports resulting from the energy policy underlying our Alternative Case for 1985 is analyzed in table 9.3. Of the total reduction in imports of 8.42 quadrillion Btu in 1985, reduced demand accounts for 3.30 quadrillion Btu; increased supplies account for an additional 2.17 quadrillion Btu; the substitution of alternative forms of energy for oil and gas accounts for the remaining 2.72 quadrillion Btu of import reduction. We recall that domestic supplies of oil and gas remain unchanged under the assumptions of our alternative case. The economic impact of the alternative case for 1985 is analyzed in table 9.4. Higher prices of imported oil result in higher prices for the output of the agricultural, manufacturing, transportation, and service sectors of the U.S. economy with the greatest increase in transportation prices. In table 9.4 we also present the resulting changes in technical coefficients for each of the four non-

Table 9.3
Reduction in oil and gas imports, alternative case 1985 (quadrillion Btu)

1. Reduced demand	3.30
2. Increased supplies	
Oil shale	1.00
Direct solar	0.20
Geothermal electric	0.97
3. Substitution	
Coal gasification and liquefaction	1.42
LWR	0.96
HTGR	0.25
Electric car	0.09
Other	0.23
4. Total reduction	8.42

Source: Behling, Dullien, Hudson (1976), table V.2, p. 78.

Table 9.4
Economic impact, alternative case, 1985

	Base case	Alternative case	Percentage change
1. Nonenergy prices (percentage change from base case, 1985)			
Agriculture			1.10
Manufacturing			0.62
Transportation			1.33
Services			0.26
2. Technical coefficients			
Agriculture			
Capital	0.1755	0.1753	
Labor	0.2515	0.2542	
Energy	0.0148	0.0125	
Nonenergy	0.5582	0.5580	
Manufacturing			
Capital	0.1143	0.1140	
Labor	0.2959	0.2977	
Energy	0.0194	0.0189	
Nonenergy	0.5705	0.5694	

Table 9.4 (continued)

	Base case	Alternative case	Percentage change
Transportation			
Capital	0.1831	0.1814	
Labor	0.4074	0.4082	
Energy	0.0390	0.0344	
Nonenergy	0.3706	0.3761	
Services			
Capital	0.3197	0.3201	
Labor	0.4025	0.4036	
Energy	0.0166	0.0161	
Nonenergy	0.2612	0.2603	
3. Final demand (percentage composition)			
Agriculture	11.66	11.62	
Manufacturing	33.58	33.61	
Transportation	2.48	2.46	
Services	49.19	49.41	
Energy	3.09	2.91	
4. Output (percentage composition)			
Agriculture	11.94	11.91	
Manufacturing	38.40	38.44	
Transportation	4.50	4.44	
Services	40.44	40.78	
Energy	4.73	4.43	

Source: Behling, Dullien, Hudson (1976), table V.14, p. 110; table V.17, p. 118; table V.15, p. 111; table V.16, p. 115.

energy sectors and changes in the composition of final demand and total output for these sectors and for the energy sector as a whole.

9.5 Conclusion

We have presented an assessment of the impact of energy research, development, and demonstration policies in combination with tax and tariff policies to reduce imports of energy resources for the year 1985. A complete evaluation of alternative energy policies requires assessments for a wider range of policies over a longer period of time. In addition to the impact of energy policy on the structure of the energy sector and the level and composition of overall economic activity, assessments must also be made of the impact on levels of well-being, life styles, and environmental pollution in the United States; international repercussions of alternative policies must also be considered.

These assessments must be combined into an overall evaluation of energy policy.[14]

The application of the preliminary version of the model for the analysis of energy research, development, and demonstration policy involves the creation of base case projections for the U.S. economy for additional years along the lines of our base case for 1985. The assessment of alternative energy policies requires the development of alternative case projections for each policy. Our model can be used to analyze the impact of energy policy on the energy sector and on overall economic activity. In addition, the energy system optimization model and other closely related models can be used to assess the environmental impact of alternative energy policies, to estimate capital requirements associated with the implementation of new technologies, and to evaluate the effect of changes in energy prices on the domestic supply of primary energy resources such as uranium, coal, oil, and gas.[15]

While the successful integration of process analysis and econometric models of energy policy is an important step in the development of a framework for the evaluation of energy policy, we must emphasize the limitations of our current approach. A fully satisfactory data base requires the development of Inter-industry transactions accounts for energy flows in physical terms as well as current and constant prices. It would be very useful to incorporate these accounts into the U.S. national income and product accounts on an annual basis. It would also be useful to disaggregate the nonenergy sectors of our model and to extend our modeling effort to incorporate primary factor input supplies and supplies of primary energy resources. Finally, additional research is required on the most efficient techniques for solution of our model.

Ultimately, projections for different years over a planning horizon could be developed within a dynamic version of our integrated process analysis and econometric model. In a dynamic model capital requirements and investment costs, together with the prices of capital services and labor services, would be generated endogenously by incorporating the supply of primary factors of production along with the demands included in our existing framework. Such a dynamic model could be extended to encompass the development of reserves of primary energy resources, production from reserves, and the pricing of current supplies of these resources for each period of time. Research is now under way that will enable us to extend our existing model in the direction of a dynamic model for the assessment of alternative energy policies.[16] Our objective has been to present a model that integrates a process analysis model of the energy sector with an econometric model of inter-industry transactions for application to policy analyses where the technological component is significant. We have illustrated the use of this model for assessment of the impact of energy policy. We have not attempted a comprehensive evaluation of alternative energy policies in order to focus on the methodology we have developed for model integration. Integration of process analysis and econometric models, using an extended accounting framework for inter-industry transactions, has proved to be feasible. A great deal of additional research will be required to develop the most appropriate framework for evaluation of alternative energy policies.

Notes

1. The data are described in more detail in a report by Jack Faucett Associates (1973). Inter-industry accounts for the year 1967 have been compiled for a more detailed industry breakdown by Bullard and Herenden (1973a,b). The corresponding Inter-Industry Model has been linked to the Brookhaven Energy System Optimization Model discussed below by Hoffman, Palmedo, Marcuse, and Goldman (1973) and by Behling, Marcuse, Swift, and Tessmer (1975). Energy flows for six years have been compiled for the Federal Energy Administration by Jack Faucett Associates (1975).
2. The model of inter-industry transaction is described by Hudson and Jorgenson (1974a), especially pp. 467–474.
3. The model of producer behavior is described by Berndt and Jorgenson (1973). See also Christensen, Jorgenson, and Lau (1973) and Berndt and Wood (1975).
4. The model of consumer behavior is described by Jorgenson (1975). See also Christensen, Jorgenson, and Lau (1975) and Jorgenson and Lau (1975).
5. Applications of the econometric model to policy analysis are given by Hudson and Jorgenson (1974 a,b,c; 1975 a,b) and Jorgenson and Wright (1975).
6. The Reference Energy System is described in Beller et al. (1975).
7. The Brookhaven Energy System Optimization model is described by Hoffman (1973) and Cherniavsky (1974).
8. The constraints of the optimization model are described by Cherniavsky (1974), pp. 9–18.
9. The objective function of the optimization model is described by Cherniavsky (1974), especially pp. 18–23.
10. Methodology for application of the optimization model for assessment of alternative energy research, development, and demonstration policies is described by Hoffman and Cherniavsky (1974) and Cherniavsky (1975). This methodology was applied in a series of twelve scenarios for 1985 and 2000 in *A National Plan for Energy Research, Development, and Demonstration* (1975).
11. The sectors in this expanded system of accounts include: (a) energy resource sectors: (1) underground coal, (2) strip-mined coal, (3) domestic oil, (4) shale oil,

(5) imported oil, (6) domestic natural gas, (7) imported natural gas, (8) hydro-energy, (9) nuclear energy, (10) geothermal energy, and (11) solar energy.

(b) energy conversion processes: (12) coal steam electric, (13) coal steam combined cycle, (14) oil steam electric, (15) oil steam combined cycle, (16) gas turbines, (17) gas steam electric, (18) total energy systems, (19) LWR electric, (20) LMFBR electric, (21) HTGR electric, (22) hydro-electric, (23) geothermal electric, (24) solar electric, (25) pumped storage, (26) synthetic gas from oil, (27) synthetic gas from coal, (28) electrolytic hydrogen, (29) methanol, (30) hydrogen from coal, and (31) synthetic oil from coal.

(c) secondary energy forms and energy product sectors: (32) base load miscellaneous electric, (33) intermediate load miscellaneous electric, (34) peak load miscellaneous electric, (35) storage and synthetic fuel, (36) miscellaneous thermal, low temperature, (37) miscellaneous thermal, intermediate temperature, (38) miscellaneous thermal, high temperature, (39) ore reduction (iron), (40) petrochemicals, (41) space heat, (42) air conditioning, (43) water heat, (44) air transport, (45) truck, bus, (46) rail, and (47) automobile.

(d) nonenergy industry sectors: (48) agriculture, nonfuel mining, and construction, (49) manufacturing, excluding petroleum refining, (50) transportation, and (51) communications, trade, and services.

(e) primary inputs: (52) imports, (53) capital services, and (54) labor services.

(f) final demands: (55) personal consumption expenditures, (56) gross private domestic investment, (57) government purchases of goods and services, and (58) exports.

12. This link between prices and costs has not been included in the initial implementation of our model. Research is now underway to complete this linkage.

13. This application is based on the research of Behling, Dullien, and Hudson (1976).

14. An overall evaluation of U.S. energy research, development, and demonstration policy, incorporating assessments of policy impacts based on our integrated econometric and process analysis model is given by the Energy Research and Development Administration (1976).

15. For a detailed discussion of the application of our model, see Behling, Dullien, and Hudson (1976).

16. A dynamic version of the Brookhaven Energy Systems Optimization Model has been developed by Marcuse, Bodin, Cherniavsky, and Sanborn (1975). A dynamic version of our econometric Inter-Industry Model has been developed by Dullien et al. (1976). Incorporation of models of primary resource supply into our econometric Inter-Industry Model is discussed by Bernanke and Jorgenson (1975).

10   Energy Policy and U.S. Economic Growth

*Edward A. Hudson and
Dale W. Jorgenson*

10.1   Econometric and Process Analysis Models

A satisfactory framework for analysis of the effect of alternative
energy policies requires an approach that encompasses both process
analysis and econometrics. Process analysis provides for a detailed
characterization of technology for energy conversion and energy utilization and permits the analysis of effects of introducing new energy
technologies. Econometrics provides for the incorporation of behavioral and technical responses of patterns of production and consumption to alternative energy prices and permits an analysis of the impact
of energy prices on the demand for energy, nonenergy intermediate
goods, capital services, and labor services. By representing energy
sector transactions in physical terms we can provide a link to process
analysis models. By representing these transactions in economic
terms, in current and constant prices, we can provide a link to econometric models. By using both forms for representing energy transactions, process analysis and econometric modeling can be combined
within the same framework.[1]

The first component of this framework is the Long-Term Inter-
Industry Transactions Model (LITM) developed by the authors.[2] In
LITM, the technology of each producing sector is represented by an
econometric model based on the price possibility frontier, giving the
supply price of output as a function of the prices of primary and intermediate inputs and the level of productivity.[3] Technical coefficients
giving primary and intermediate inputs per unit of output of the sector as functions of prices and productivity can be derived from the
price possibility frontier. Given the level of output of the sector, the
technical coefficients determine demand for intermediate and primary
inputs into production. The preferences of the household sector are
represented by an econometric model determining demand for consumption goods, demand for leisure, and supply of saving.[4]

The second component of our modeling framework is the Time-Phased Energy System Optimization Model (TESOM) developed at the Brookhaven National Laboratory by K.C. Hoffman and associates.[5] This model is based on the Reference Energy System, which provides a physical representation of technologies, energy flows, and conversion efficiencies.[6] Within each period TESOM allocates energy supplies to energy demands so as to minimize cost. This is formulated as a linear programming model of the transportation type. Given levels of demand for energy services, available supplies of energy resources and conversion capacities, conversion efficiency and capital and operating costs of utilizing technologies, the energy sector optimization model determines the set of energy conversion activities and operating levels that minimizes total cost. Between periods, investment changes the capacities of the conversion processes.

The combined LITM-TESOM framework models inter-industry transactions as a result of a dynamic general equilibrium of the U.S. economy.[7] In each period the relative prices of all commodities are determined by balance between demand and supply; technical coefficients for inputs of intermediate goods and primary factors of production are determined simultaneously; final demands are calculated and these with the technical coefficients, determine demands for the output of each sector of the economy and for primary factors of production. In each period the supply of capital is fixed by past investments. Variations in demand for capital services affect the price but not the quantity of these services. Similarly, the available labor time in each period is fixed by past demographic developments. Variations in demand for labor time by the producing sectors and by the household sector for consumption in the form of leisure affect the price of labor and the allocation of labor time between market and nonmarket activity. Finally, the supply of saving by the household sector must be balanced by final demand for investment by the producing sectors. Dynamic adjustment to changes in energy policy is modeled by tracing through the impact of investment on future levels of capital stock.[8]

10.2   Alternative Energy Policies

The starting point for our analysis of the impact of alternative energy policies is a base case projection of future energy and economic growth with no change in energy policy. We assume that any quantity of petroleum imports is available at the world price, where the world price of petroleum rises at a rate of 1 percent per year relative to the rate of growth of the U.S. GNP price deflator. The annual rate of growth or real GNP is projected to average 3.2 percent from 1977 to 2000. This growth rate is considerably below the 3.8 percent average annual growth experienced between 1950 and 1973. The decline is partly due to a reduction in population and labor force growth, and partly due to a reduction in productivity growth resulting from higher energy prices. Primary energy input is projected to rise from 76 quadrillion Btu in 1977 to 139 in 2000, an average annual growth rate of 2.6 percent, also below the average annual growth rate between 1950 and 1973 which was 3.5 percent. Part of the reduction is due to decreased economic growth and part is due to the conservation induced by regulation and by a continuing increase in real energy prices.

We consider four sets of energy policies intended to reduce energy growth and to reduce dependence on imported energy sources:

Policy 1: Taxes are imposed on U.S. petroleum production to bring domestic petroleum prices to world levels; natural gas prices are increased but price controls are retained; energy conservation is stimulated by taxes on use of oil and gas in industry, restriction of oil and gas use by electric utilities, subsidies for insulation of structures, and mandatory performance standards for energy-using appliances.

Policy 2: The measures included in Policy 1 are combined with tariffs on imported oil rising to $7.00/barrel in 2000 and with corresponding taxes on natural gas.

Policy 3: Policy 2 is combined with excise taxes on delivered energy sufficient to reduce total primary energy input in 2000 to 90 quadrillion Btu.

Policy 4: Policy 2 is combined with excise taxes on delivered energy sufficient to reduce total primary input in 2000 to 70 quadrillion Btu.

Delivered energy prices under each policy in 2000 are presented in table 10.1. Under Policy 1, the average price of delivered energy is only 1.7 percent higher than the base case, while in Policy 4 the increase is 187 percent. Extensive nonprice conservation measures explain the small indicated price rise between the base case and Policy 1. The average annual rate of increase in real energy prices between 1977 and 2000 is 1.6 percent in the base case and Policy 1, 2.1 percent in Policy 2, 4.4 percent in Policy 3, and 6.3 percent in Policy 4. The

Table 10.1
Energy prices and quantities in the year 2000

	Base case	Policy 1	2	3	4
Prices[a]					
Coal	1.64	1.71 (4.3)	1.71 (4.3)	4.07 (148)	6.12 (273)
Refined petroleum	4.47	4.79 (7.2)	5.84 (30.6)	8.77 (96)	13.67 (206)
Natural gas	3.47	4.06 (17.0)	5.12 (47.6)	8.33 (140)	12.99 (274)
Electricity	10.54	10.89 (3.3)	10.99 (4.3)	18.30 (74)	27.11 (157)
Average price of delivered energy	5.21	5.30 (1.7)	5.86 (12.5)	9.78 (88)	14.97 (187)
Quantities[b]					
Coal	32.7	40.2 (23)	41.3 (26)	27.3 (–17)	20.0 (–39)
Petroleum	48.8	35.1 (–28)	28.2 (–42)	24.0 (–51)	19.4 (–60)
Natural gas	19.0	17.4 (–8)	14.9 (–22)	15.0 (–21)	13.2 (–31)
Nuclear	28.5	23.7 (–17)	21.7 (–24)	18.1 (–36)	13.0 (–54)
Other	9.6	10.2 (6)	10.2 (6)	5.5 (–43)	4.3 (–55)
Total	138.5	126.6 (–9)	116.3 (–16)	89.9 (–35)	69.9 (–50)
Imports as percent of total input	20.4	10.7	3.0	1.9	0.0

[a]Delivered prices in \$1975/million Btu; percentage difference from base case levels in parenthesis.
[b]Primary energy in quadrillion Btu; percentage difference from base case levels in parenthesis.

policies also change the structure of energy prices with petroleum and natural gas becoming more expensive relative to other fuels. The level and pattern of primary energy input in 2000 for each policy scenario are also presented in table 10.1. Policies 1 and 2 have similar impacts on energy input, leading to reductions of 9 percent and 16 percent, respectively, from the base case; Policies 3 and 4 are more drastic, involving reductions of 35 percent and 50 percent. The policies change the pattern of energy input, decreasing the relative importance of petroleum and increasing that of coal. The reduced demand for petroleum and natural gas leads to large reductions in the degree of dependence on imported energy.

Increases in energy prices and energy conservation measures have a widespread and significant impact on the structure and growth of the economy. The initial step in this process of adjustment is the restructuring of relative prices of goods and services. Table 10.2 shows the changes in output prices in 2000. Output prices rise in line with the energy content of each type of product—delivered energy

Table 10.2
Sectoral prices and quantities in the year 2000

	Base case	Policy 1	2	3	4
Prices[a]					
Agriculture		1.1	1.3	2.3	5.5
Manufacturing		0.1	−0.2	1.1	5.9
Transportation		3.1	4.6	7.8	13.3
Services		−0.3	−0.9	0.6	2.2
Energy		1.7	12.5	87.7	187.3
Final output		0.7	1.0	5.1	11.0
Quantities[b]					
Agriculture	8.4	8.3	8.2	8.2	8.2
Manufacturing	30.5	30.5	30.4	30.3	29.6
Transportation	3.6	3.5	3.4	3.3	3.2
Services	54.1	54.7	55.1	56.0	57.2
Energy	3.4	3.0	2.8	2.2	1.7
Quantities[c]					
Agriculture	8.6	8.5	8.5	8.4	8.2
Manufacturing	35.9	35.9	35.8	36.0	36.0
Transportation	5.0	4.9	4.9	4.8	4.7
Services	45.7	46.1	46.5	47.4	47.8
Energy	4.8	4.6	4.3	3.4	3.2

[a] Percentage change in output price index from base case.
[b] Percentage composition of real final demand.
[c] Percentage composition of real output.

prices rise the most, services prices the least. Producers respond to higher energy prices and energy conservation regulations by altering input patterns so as to minimize unit costs in the face of the new price structure, subject to government regulations on energy use. These adjustments in input patterns involve reduced intensity of energy use, greater intensity of labor input, less use of nonenergy intermediate materials in most sectors, and, apart from services where capital input increases, a reduction in the relative importance of capital services. Final demand patterns alter in response to the policy measures, partly as a result of the changing price structure and partly as a result of government regulations on energy use patterns. Table 10.2 also shows the effects of energy policy in final demand patterns for 2000. As a result of final demand patterns and the structure of inputs into production both shifting away from energy-intensive goods and services, the pattern of gross output also shifts away from energy; these changes are also summarized in table 10.2.

10.3 Economic Growth

Finally, we consider the effects on economic growth of restrictions on energy consumption. Table 10.3 summarizes the aggregate economic effects of the four policies in the year 2000. The level of real GNP in 2000 is reduced, relative to the base case, by 1.5 percent for Policy 1, 3.2 percent for Policy 2, 7.2 percent for Policy 3, and 11.9 percent for Policy 4. Both consumption and investment are reduced; the reduction in consumption is greater than that in investment in Policy 1 but the reverse is true for the other policies, that is, the more stringent the policy, the greater the relative impact on investment. The investment impact is particularly important since it leads to a slowing of the rate of growth of productive capacity and of output. By 2000, capital stock in Policy 4 is 11 percent below the base case level. This reduction in capital inputs accounts for 3.2 of the 11.9 percent reduction in real GNP. In subsequent years the relative importance of this dynamic effect is still larger. We conclude, then, that policies to restrict the growth of energy consumption have the potential to achieve the specified objectives of reduced energy growth, reduction in dependence on imported energy sources, and increased use of relatively abundant domestic energy sources, but that these changes involve possibly large economic cost in terms of slowed economic growth and output foregone. Reduction in energy growth is not a desirable social objective in itself. The benefits assigned to this reduction must be balanced against these costs.

Table 10.3
Economic impact of energy policies in the year 2000

	Base case	Policy 1	2	3	4
GNP ($1972 billion)	2721.7	2679.8	2634.9	2524.6	2397.0
Percentage difference		−1.5	−3.2	−7.2	−11.9
Average annual growth rate, 1977–2000 (percent)	3.2	3.1	3.0	2.8	2.6
Consumption ($1972 billion)	1763.5	1733.1	1706.4	1622.2	1520.3
Percentage difference		−1.7	−3.2	−8.0	−13.8
Investment ($1972 billion)	401.1	394.7	381.4	359.0	335.8
Percentage difference		−1.6	−4.9	−10.5	−16.3

Notes

1. Annual inter-industry accounts for the U.S. for the period 1947–1971 in physical and economic terms have been prepared by Jack Faucett Associates (1973). Inter-industry accounts for the year 1967 have been compiled for a more detailed industry breakdown by Bullard and Herendeen (1973a,b).

2. The model of inter-industry transactions is described by the authors (Hudson and Jorgenson, 1973, 1974a, 1977).

3. The model of producer behavior is described by Berndt and Jorgenson (1973). See also Christensen, Jorgenson, and Lau (1973) and Berndt and Wood (1975). A comparison of econometric and process analysis models of energy consumption is given by Berndt and Wood (1977).

4. The model of consumer behavior is described by Jorgenson (1975). See also Christensen, Jorgenson, and Lau (1975), and Jorgenson and Lau (1975).

5. The Brookhaven optimization models are described by Hoffman (1973), Hoffman and Cherniavsky (1974), and Cherniavsky (1975). A comparison of these models and alternative process analysis models of the U.S. energy sector is given by Koopmans in Kantorovich and Koopmans (1976).

6. The Reference Energy System is described in Beller (1975).

7. The integration of the Hudson-Jorgenson model with the Brookhaven Energy System Optimization Model (BESOM) is discussed in detail by Hoffman and Jorgenson (1977). A dynamic version of our econometric model of inter-industry transactions is discussed in detail by Hudson and Jorgenson (1977). A dynamic version of BESOM has been developed by Marcuse et al. (1975). A comparison of the combined model with alternative models for analyzing the relationship of energy and economic growth is given by Hogan (1977b).

8. A theoretical analysis of this dynamic adjustment process is presented by Hogan (1977a).

11

The Role of
Energy in the
U.S. Economy

Dale W. Jorgenson

11.1 Introduction

The purpose of this chapter is to analyze the relationship between energy and the outlook for U.S. economic growth over the next decade.[1] Our main conclusion is that reduced rates of growth are in prospect as a consequence of the four-fold increase in world petroleum prices resulting from the establishment of the OPEC cartel in late 1973 and early 1974. Slower economic growth will be accompanied by a reduction in the growth of real disposable income, a shift away from capital formation toward consumption, and a sharply reduced "fiscal dividend" available for disposal by the government through tax cuts or increased expenditures.

Adjustment of the U.S. economy to higher world petroleum prices has been delayed by continued price controls on domestically produced petroleum and natural gas. Any energy bill now in prospect will reduce or eliminate the effects of policies shielding large sectors of the U.S. economy from the full impact of higher prices for petroleum and natural gas. The difficult political issue confronting the Congress and the Administration is to decide on a redistribution of the substantial gains to domestic producers from higher prices. The re-distribution of these gains will have an important effect on the distribution of economic welfare, but the impact on economic growth will be insignificant by comparison with the effects of higher energy prices.

11.2 Background

A little background will be useful in putting the relationship between energy and economic growth in historical perspective. From 1950 to 1973 the real price of energy to the consumer, the price of energy adjusted for inflation, declined at a rate of 1.8 percent per year. While real gross national product grew at 3.7 percent per year, the consumption of primary energy sources—mainly petroleum, natural gas, and coal—was increasing at 3.5 percent per year. The ratio of energy consumption to real GNP declined very gradually over the period. The decline in real energy prices through 1973 continued a historical trend dating back at least two centuries to the beginning of the Industrial Revolution.[2] This decline was an important facilitating factor in the relatively high rates of economic growth in the U.S. during the postwar period.

Although government policy has been very important to domestic producers of petroleum and natural gas, energy policy was not a significant national political issue before 1973. Between 1959 and 1972 the Federal Government administered a program of import quotas on crude petroleum in order to maintain domestic petroleum prices above world levels. In 1954 the Federal Power Commission was given the power to set well-head prices for natural gas entering interstate commerce. Over time well-head price controls generated a separate intrastate market for natural gas with prices well in excess of the regulated prices for interstate gas. What Congress gave the domestic oil industry through the oil import program, the FPC took away, at least in part, through well-head price regulation of natural gas.[3]

In late 1973 and early 1974 world petroleum prices underwent a four-fold increase, following the Arab oil embargo of October 1973. At the time of the embargo a system of price and wage controls was in effect in the United States, dating from the New Economic Policy of 1971. The response to the increase in world petroleum prices by the Republican Administration was to view this increase in terms of the war against inflation. The resulting energy policy rapidly evolved into a complex system of price controls on domestically produced crude petroleum and refined products that had the effect of maintaining the prices of domestic petroleum products below world levels.

From historical evidence it is now abundantly clear that the Arab oil embargo had very little impact on the supply of petroleum products in the United States. However, uncontrolled prices for petroleum products in Europe reached levels that have been seen neither before nor since. The continuation of price controls on domestically produced petroleum products gave producers and consumers an opportunity for successful speculation on an increase in petroleum prices. This led to a massive increase in demand for purposes of inventory accumulation. While lines formed at the gas pumps, producers, distributors, and consumers of petroleum products added to inventories, creating the need for a Federal program to allocate petroleum products under a regime of continued price controls.[4]

The dramatic rise in petroleum prices in late 1973 and early 1974 has given rise to an interpretive literature that is growing daily. Among the alternative explanations for higher prices we can identify at least the following three strands of thought:

1. *Resource exhaustion.* According to this thesis the world began to run out of oil in October 1973. The date has been pushed back as the discussion has proceeded; current thinking among proponents of this thesis is that the world will begin to run out of oil in 1985. My prognosis is that this date will continue to recede, perhaps indefinitely.

2. *Scarcity rents.* This explanation is a sophisticated version of the resource exhaustion thesis. Given the fact that the world will run out of petroleum beginning in 1985, there was a speculative increase in petroleum prices beginning in October 1973 to reflect the coming scarcity. The best available estimates of scarcity rents range from seventeen cents in 1970 to forty-six cents in 1980 per barrel of petroleum, dampening the enthusiasm of some economists for this explanation of the rise in petroleum prices.[5]

3. *The OPEC cartel.* The third explanation is that the Organization of Petroleum Exporting Countries (OPEC) succeeded in late 1973 and early 1974 in establishing an effective cartel in petroleum. This cartel raised prices four-fold and has settled back to enjoy the fruits of a well-entrenched monopoly position. At first some economists refused to believe that a successful cartel could be established and, if established, that it could persist. History appears to be on the side of those who believe that a cartel has been established and that it can persist.

The establishment of the OPEC cartel elevated energy policy from a matter of parochial concern, discussed among well-heeled special interest lobbies, to a matter of intense national concern appropriate for televised Presidential addresses. In response to the cartel action then-President Richard Nixon appeared on television to announce Project Independence, a program designed to deal with the threat of future oil embargoes by cutting back imports while continuing price controls. The system of price controls involved averaging the price of imported crude with that of domestic crude in the pricing of refined products so that, in effect, foreign producers received a subsidy paid by means of a corresponding tax on domestic producers. The result was that demand was allowed to rise more rapidly than it would have risen in the absence of price controls. The effective tax on domestic producers permitted domestic supply to fall more rapidly than it would have fallen in the absence of controls. The impact of Project Independence was a dramatic increase in petroleum imports.[6]

The stated objective of the oil import program in force from 1959 to 1972 was to maintain national security by keeping petroleum prices above world levels. The objective of Project Independence was to maintain national security by keeping prices below world levels. Conflicts between alternative objectives—maintaining high prices of petroleum and low prices of natural gas before 1972—and conflicts between alternative means of attaining a given objective like national security—high prices before 1972 and low prices prices after 1972—are typical of U.S. energy policy rather than temporary aberrations. Contradictory objectives and conflicting approaches to attaining a given objective have continued up to the present and can be expected to continue for the foreseeable future.

It is interesting to speculate on the number of times we have heard that this country needs a national energy policy. Perhaps a majority of U.S. voters would agree with Mobil Oil on the need for a national energy policy. The reason this country does not have a national energy policy is that energy policy means different things to different people. To the producers of energy the objective of national energy policy must be to provide incentives for energy production, that is, higher prices to producers. To the consumers of energy the objective of policy must be to provide plentiful energy at a cost we can afford, that is, lower prices to consumers. The reconciliation of these two mutually inconsistent objectives is the main problem now confronting the Congress and the current Administration in enacting new energy legislation.

11.3 The Carter Program

On April 20, 1977 President Jimmy Carter elevated energy policy from a matter of national concern to the moral equivalent of war. Carter offered a plan for national energy policy[7] involving four significant features:

1. Over time the U.S. price for petroleum products is to be allowed to rise to world levels. This would eventually eliminate the effective subsidy to foreign production of petroleum and the effective tax on

domestic production. It would also increase the domestic price of petroleum products so as to curtail demand and promote energy conservation. Similarly, the price of domestically produced natural gas is to be allowed to rise to its "replacement cost" level, based on petroleum prices, possibly through eventual deregulation; this will also curtail demand and promote conservation. In its final days last summer the Federal Power Commission announced its own program to subsidize foreign production of natural gas by taxing domestic producers. This will be brought about by averaging the prices of imported liquefied natural gas (LNG) with controlled prices of domestic natural gas in determining the price of natural gas to consumers. Secretary of Energy James Schlesinger has announced his opposition to this approach to pricing for future LNG projects.

2. To provide an added spur to energy conservation a system of taxes on the use of petroleum products and natural gas is to be imposed on industrial and utility users of these fuels. These taxes will amount to as much as six dollars per barrel of petroleum for users affected by the tax. A great scramble is on to find ways to qualify various interest groups for exemption from the six dollar levy. Small users are to be exempted along with transportation, farming, apartment houses, commercial buildings, the oil and gas industry, and gas used as a feedstock or raw material. The Senate has exempted all users who are unable to switch to coal, while the House version exempts only certain categories of nonconverters.

3. To provide a further incentive to convert from petroleum and natural gas to coal, solar energy, wind energy, and other more plentiful energy sources, the Administration has proposed a system of tax credits for the purchase of equipment required for conversion. Under the leadership of Senator Russell Long the Senate has taken up the President's initiative and has proposed a vast expansion of the program of tax credits. At last reading the incentives will cover electric cars, tricycles, and bicycles, but will exclude electric golf carts. Available estimates of the revenue loss to the Treasury upon full implementation of the Senate's program of tax credits range up to forty billion dollars.

4. The Administration plan would add regulatory measures over and above the system of taxes on fuel use and tax credits for conversion to coal. The regulations on fuel efficiency of automobiles are the best publicized of these measures. The President originally proposed a system of escalating taxes on gas guzzlers, more familiarly known as

family automobiles. In addition, there will be mandatory standards for energy efficiency of appliances of all types.

The combined effect of the four sets of measures proposed in the Administration plan would be to raise the effective price of petroleum and natural gas to consumers well above world market levels. First, the phased decontrol of prices for petroleum and natural gas would permit prices to rise to world market levels. The tax on the use of petroleum and natural gas, if anyone ends up paying it, will raise prices paid by users of petroleum and natural gas well above world market levels. Tax credits on the use of facilities for conversion to energy sources other than petroleum and natural gas would have the effect of reducing the cost of using competing fuels. Finally, regulations restricting the use of petroleum and natural gas would reduce consumption to levels associated with much higher prices of these fuels.

The most bitter controversy over the Administration program has involved the President's proposed crude oil equalization tax, designed to transfer gains on existing petroleum deposits from the proposed price increases to the Federal treasury. Much of the controversy over the proposed tax on crude petroleum has centered on the distribution of the proceeds. In the Administration proposal the proceeds are to be turned back to consumers. Alternative beneficiaries of the program have been proposed, including mass transit, the highway trust funds, and an energy development corporation to promote the development of exotic energy sources. The *Wall Street Journal* has suggested darkly that the money will be allowed to accumulate in the Federal treasury rather than dispersed to the populace at large. The oil industry has recommended that part of the tax be "plowed back" or returned to the industry in order to provide additional incentives for production. This has brought forth harsh language from President Carter, who has characterized the industry's proposals as "ripoffs."

It remains to be seen where the balance between the Administration energy plan, the House energy plan, and the Senate energy plan will be drawn. The House-Senate Conference Committee is proceeding slowly and cautiously to the formulation of a final package of energy legislation. It has yet to confront the difficult issue of redistributing the gains to domestic producers of petroleum and natural gas from higher prices. Whatever the final redistribution of these gains, the primary impact of new energy legislation will be to reduce or eliminate the effects of price controls that now shield large sectors of the U.S.

economy from the full impact of higher world petroleum prices resulting from the OPEC cartel. Redistribution of the gains from higher
energy prices will have a substantial effect on the welfare of energy
producers and consumers, but the impact of such a redistribution on
economic growth will be insignificant.

So far as energy policy is concerned, it is quite possible that something like the following will eventually land on the President's desk:
There will be taxes on U.S. crude petroleum production designed to
bring prices up to world levels over time. There will be a sizeable
immediate increase in prices for newly discovered natural gas that
will be phased in over time with eventual deregulation of the well-
head prices on newly discovered gas. There will be modest taxes on
the use of petroleum and natural gas by industrial users and utilities
with myriad exemptions and special provisions. Most of the tax credits proposed by the Senate will be bargained away in the negotiations
over redistribution of the gains from higher domestic prices for
petroleum and natural gas but some may be retained and could provide several new sections for the Internal Revenue Code and may
show up on your Form 1040. Finally, there will be mandatory performance standards for automobiles and appliances.

The impact of the energy bill, if signed by President Carter, will be
to bring about a relatively modest reduction in the growth of primary
energy input. The cutback will fall within the range of three or four
percent over the next decade; this would correspond to a reduction of
three-tenths of a percentage point in the annual growth rate. At the
same time coal will rise from twenty to twenty-five percent of primary
energy input and imports of petroleum will be reduced from twenty-
four percent to eighteen percent. Overall, the new national energy
policy will move toward the announced objectives of increased energy
conservation and reduced energy imports at a relatively modest cost
in reduced economic growth. Conversion to coal will be stimulated.
In addition, stockpiling of petroleum provided by existing legislation
will give needed protection from future oil embargoes.[8]

There is a real possibility that tax measures included in the Carter
energy plan will be considered by Congress as part of the Administration tax bill rather than as part of the energy bill. This would have the
effect of eliminating the crude oil equalization tax, the use taxes on
petroleum and natural gas, and the system of tax credits proposed by
the Senate from the energy bill. Consideration of these measures
could be postponed indefinitely, leaving the existing system of subsi-

dies for foreign producers of petroleum and natural gas paid by taxes on domestic producers in place until as late as 1981 for petroleum and even longer for natural gas. In this eventuality the Administration might be tempted to impose a tariff or quota on imports of crude petroleum. OPEC officials have indicated that they would be pleased to assist the Administration's efforts by raising prices for petroleum above currently prevailing world market levels.

Petroleum prices have not increased in real terms since 1975, despite continuing calls for price increases by some members of OPEC. Higher prices for petroleum have created a glut on world markets as the *London Economist* predicted in 1974. Members of OPEC, like members of the U.S. Congress, have a problem of distributing the proceeds of higher petroleum prices. An increase in prices would increase the present petroleum glut, raising the problem: Who is willing to absorb the production cutbacks that will be required? This problem accounts for some of the lack of enthusiasm for price increases by the larger producers, such as Iran and Saudi Arabia. The smaller producers would be perfectly happy to raise prices and to have the Iranians and the Saudis cut back on production, thereby redistributing cartel profits.

Although the OPEC cartel is not a perfect monopoly, it comes sufficiently close that it is useful to consider the consequences of an optimal monopoly price policy.[9] Such a policy would involve an initial increase in prices, followed by a long and very gradual decline. Unfortunately, the costs of deviations from the optimum are small; OPEC could miss the optimal monopoly price by ten or twenty-five percent and hardly feel the consequences. By removing the effective subsidies to OPEC through the present system of price controls in the United States, the Carter energy program would help to increase the world petroleum glut. This would put pressure on the smaller members of OPEC to support the policies of price moderation espoused by Sheik Yamani, the Saudi Minister of Petroleum, and the Shah of Iran. Leaving these subsidies in place would reduce the downward pressure on U.S. petroleum imports and on world petroleum prices. In either case the intermediate term prospects for an increase in the world price of petroleum in excess of the rate of inflation are rather limited.

Our assessment of the likely course of world petroleum prices differs substantially from the widely publicized views of the Central Intelligence Agency, espoused by President Carter and by Administration energy planners as part of the rationale for the National Energy Plan.[10] According to the CIA assessment the world petroleum glut will disappear in the early 1980s as a result of a switch by the Soviet Union, currently the world's largest producer of petroleum, from the position of net exporter to the position of a substantial net importer of petroleum. Disappearance of the petroleum glut, according to the CIA, will result in a substantial increase in petroleum prices on the pattern of 1973 and 1974. This thesis has been greeted with considerable skepticism by specialists on Soviet energy developments on the grounds that there is no obvious way for the Soviet Union to pay for imports of the magnitude projected by the CIA.[11] Recently, the Russians have announced that their own energy plans for the 1980s involve no net imports of petroleum.

The Administration has continued to place heavy reliance on the CIA assessment in formulating energy policy. On Sun Day the President announced a Phase II energy plan, intended to emphasize the development of alternative energy supplies to replace imported petroleum. Repeated technology assessments of solar energy, oil from shale, and synthetic fuels based on coal have revealed very limited opportunities for commercialization at current real prices for petroleum. The Phase II energy plan would require real prices at least double current levels for successful implementation by private industry. The Administration also announced on Sun Day that a decision had been made not to fund the programs recommended by the Department of Energy to implement the Phase II plan. An effective energy policy must allow for the possibility that the world petroleum market will go "over a cliff" in the 1980s, but it should also allow for the possibility of a continuing decline in real prices of petroleum.

11.4   The Recovery

Before turning to the economic outlook, we can set the stage by recalling a few features of the great recession and recovery that have accompanied the dramatic changes we have described in the world market for petroleum. For comparison it is also useful to characterize the recovery from 1970 to 1973. Beginning with the earlier recovery, recall that the longest period of continuous economic expansion in U.S. postwar history was brought to an end by the Nixon Administration in 1969. Military expenditures associated with the Vietnam War were cut back and the investment tax credit was repealed, leading to a sizeable slowdown in investment spending in 1970 and 1971. The policy of deflation was reversed in late 1971 and early 1972 under the New Economic Policy, leading to a recovery that turned into a boom in 1972 and 1973. The boom was accompanied by a jump in the prices of food and and other raw materials and by a staggering increase in petroleum prices associated with the establishment of the OPEC cartel.

In the wake of higher energy prices and renewed efforts to deflate the economy, the boom of 1972 and 1973 gave way to the great recessions of 1974 and 1975. This downturn was the most severe of the postwar period and resulted in a collapse of investment in 1975 with a drop of 13.2 percent in real terms.[12] We are well into the recovery from the great recessions of 1974 and 1975. However, the recovery of 1976 and 1977 has some features that set it apart from prior cyclical experience. Some of the salient features of the current recovery are summarized in table 11.1.

1. Real growth, as measured by the growth rate of gross national product, is a little less than in the last recovery, but is about average in comparison with the past five recoveries.

2. The recovery of capital spending has been very weak. After the collapse of investment in 1975 the growth of investment in 1976 and 1977 has been just about sufficient to bring the level of spending up to prerecession levels.

3. The growth of employment was slowed by the downturn in business activity, but has continued at levels well above those that characterized the recovery of 1970 to 1973.

Table 11.1
Two postwar recoveries

	Growth rate Real GNP (%)	Growth rate Real BFI (%)	Employment change (millions)	Growth rate Productivity (%)	Own rate of return (%)
1970–73 (turning point, 1970 IV):					
1970	−0.4	−3.6	2.0	−1.2	3.7
1971	3.3	−0.6	1.4	−0.3	4.0
1972	6.2	9.1	1.6	3.7	4.6
1973	5.9	12.8	2.2	4.3	5.5
1974–77 (turning point, 1975 I):					
1974	−2.1	−0.4	2.3	−3.5	3.8
1975	−2.9	−13.2	1.6	2.2	3.6
1976	6.0	3.6	2.1	4.0	4.2
1977	4.9	8.6	3.5	2.2	4.6

4. The growth of productivity, defined as output per hour worked for the nonfarm business sector, has lagged behind the rate of growth of productivity in the previous recovery.

5. The rate of return for the economy as a whole, corrected for inflation, has been drifting steadily downward relative to levels at corresponding stages of the earlier recovery.

The problem that must be solved in any analysis of the recovery in 1976 and 1977 is to account for the slowdown of capital formation and the relatively rapid growth of employment. The key to this analysis is the impact of dramatically higher energy prices. *At any given level of output* higher energy prices drive down the demand for energy. The impact of higher energy prices can be summarized by means of the elasticity of demand for energy, that is, the percentage change in the demand for energy corresponding to each percent change in the price of energy. The short run impact of changes in energy prices is rather modest. However, the long-run elasticity of demand for primary energy sources—crude petroleum, natural gas, and coal—is of the order of magnitude of three-tenths or four-tenths, so that a ten percent increase in the price of energy results in a three or four percent decrease in energy demand.

Similarly, at any level of output higher energy prices have effects on the demand for other productive inputs employed in the economy—capital, labor, and nonenergy intermediate goods. To simplify our terminology for purposes of this discussion, we will refer to nonenergy intermediate goods as "materials" although some of them are semifinished manufactured goods or even services rather than raw materials. Again, we can summarize the impact of higher energy prices by means of the cross-elasticities of demand for capital, labor, and materials, that is, the proportional changes in these demands with respect to a proportional change in the price of energy. The key cross-elasticities are those with respect to capital and labor, which affect levels of investment and employment.

To characterize the cross-elasticities of demand for capital, labor, and materials it is useful to think about the price effects in qualitative terms. We say that energy and one of the other productive inputs are substitutes if the effect of an increase in the price of energy is to increase the demand for the other input. Alternatively, we say that energy and one of the other productive inputs are complements if the effect of an increase in the price of energy is to decrease the demand for the other input. Recent empirical research has shown that an increase in energy prices has a positive impact on the demand for labor, so that energy and labor are substitutes.[13] Similarly, higher energy prices have a positive impact on the demand for materials; again, energy and materials are substitutes. However, higher energy prices have a negative impact on the demand for capital, so that energy and capital are complements. The impact of higher energy prices is to drive down the demand for energy and capital and to drive up the demand for labor and materials at any given level of output. Complementarity of energy and capital is not surprising, since the space provided by structures must be heated or cooled and lighted through the use of energy. Similarly, the work performed by machinery and equipment requires energy as motive power.

Energy-capital complementarity is not inconsistent with the fact that more capital in the form of added insulation or greater instrumentation can be used to conserve energy. Again, an example may be useful in clarifying ideas. Suppose that we employ refrigeration services, involving capital and energy, in producing food. We also use labor and agricultural raw materials in the process. Now, suppose we increase energy prices, this will give food producers an incentive to conserve energy by using more capital in the form of better insulated and more carefully instrumented refrigeration equipment. However, it will also give food producers an incentive to conserve refrigeration services, which are now more costly, thereby using less capital as well as less energy. If the demand for refrigeration service is reduced enough to offset the increased demand for capital for energy conservation, the demand for capital will be reduced along with the demand for energy. This example illustrates complementarity between capital and energy in the production of food along with substitution between capital and energy in the production of refrigeration services.

Up to this point we have described the demand side of the impact of higher energy prices. What will happen on the supply side of the labor market as workers face greater demands for their services? In the short run wage rates will rise and employment will increase. This is precisely what has happened in the course of the current recovery; most of the impact has been to increase employment. Higher wages and enhanced prospects for employment have accelerated the growth of the labor force. Rapid growth of the labor force has contributed to the persistence of high levels of unemployment in the face of rapidly expanding employment opportunities.

Turning to the owners of capital, the supply of capital is fixed in the short run, so that reduced demand for capital depresses the rate of return without affecting supply. In the course of the current recovery rates of return have deteriorated steadily relative to levels at corresponding stages of earlier recoveries. For any given level of output a fall in the rate of return results in a fall in the level of capital formation and a rise in consumption. Again, this is precisely what has happened in the course of the current recovery. The recovery of investment spending has been disappointingly sluggish, while a boom in consumer spending has led the recovery. The failure of investment to develop its expected momentum at the present phase of the recovery has been the source of great anxiety on the part of economic forecasters. Concern has surfaced that we may be on the verge of a new economic collapse. Our analysis suggests that capital formation will continue to play a diminished role in the growth of aggregate demand and consumption will continue to be unusually buoyant.

11.5   The Outlook

In analyzing the current recovery we have emphasized short-run impacts of past increases in energy prices. A key element in the long-run outlook is the course of future energy prices. Our analysis of Carter Administration energy policy suggests that the effective subsidy to foreign production of crude petroleum financed by an effective tax on domestic production through averaging of foreign and domestic prices will be eliminated. The stated objective of this policy change is to reduce petroleum imports; this objective will be realized through inducing energy conservation and stimulating domestic energy supplies by permitting petroleum prices to rise to world levels.

The initial impact of the Carter energy plan will be to raise prices for domestic crude petroleum. Domestic natural gas prices will follow with a delay due to lags in the regulatory process. The prices of coal and other primary energy sources are not now controlled, so that these prices can be expected to rise more rapidly to a "replacement cost" basis, keyed to the price of crude petroleum. Higher energy prices will have an important impact on energy demand through the elasticity of demand. Higher energy prices will also affect the demand for capital, labor, and materials through cross-elasticities of demand for these productive inputs. In short, the Carter energy plan will reinforce those tendencies in the U.S. economy that have set the current recovery apart from previous historical experience.

We have already considered the short run impact of an increase in energy prices. At any given level of output, the effect of higher energy prices will be to boost the demand for labor and materials and to further dampen the demand for capital. We can expect continued growth of employment at high levels, continued deterioration in the rate of return relative to levels at comparable stages of earlier recoveries, relatively weak growth of investment spending, and continued strength in consumer spending. To consider the long run impact of these developments, we find it useful to treat the long run as a sequence of short runs even if, as Keynes pointed out, we are all dead by the end of the process. In the long run, the level of capital formation is critical since the accumulation of capital provides the capacity for future growth of output.[14]

Historically, gains in U.S. productivity can be attributed about equally to increases in the capital intensity of production through the substitution of capital for labor and to increases in the level of technology.[15] A reduction in the level of capital formation will result in a slowdown in the rate of substitution of capital for labor over time. It is important not to confuse a slowdown in the rate of substitution with a reversal of the substitution process, that is, with the substitution of labor for capital. Lower capital formation corresponding to any level of output will result in a lower rate of substitution with a reversal of the substitution process, that is, with the substitution of labor for capital. Lower capital formation corresponding to any level of output will result in a lower rate of substitution of capital for labor over time; there will be no tendency to substitute labor for capital. A reduction in the rate of substitution of capital for labor over time will result in a reduction in the rate of productivity growth.

The rate of economic growth is the sum of the rate of growth of productivity and the rate of growth of hours worked. Although hours worked may fluctuate with the state of aggregate demand in the short run, the long run growth in hours worked is determined by demographic developments, largely resulting from variations in fertility that have already taken place. A reduction in the level of capital spending at any given level of output will reduce the rate of growth of productivity and the rate of economic growth. Our conclusion is that the outlook for the U.S. economy over the next decade is for reduced rates of economic growth. This reduction in growth rates can be traced to higher energy prices resulting from the establishment of the OPEC cartel in late 1973 and early 1974 and the four-fold increase in world petroleum prices that resulted.

In the short run higher energy prices may result in relatively rapid growth of personal disposable income through rising wages and rapid growth in employment. In the long run the rate of growth of disposable income is determined by the rate of economic growth, so that the long run outlook is for disappointing gains in real personal disposable income and for an end to the boom in consumer spending that has fueled the current recovery. Capital formation will be relatively weak in the short run, but can be expected to recover slowly over time as normal rates of return are reestablished. There is nothing in the short run outlook that suggests an imminent downturn in the economy; similarly, there is nothing in the long run outlook that suggests a realistic possibility of returning to high rates of economic growth.

Both short run and long run prognoses for the U.S. economy are dismal, at least by the standards of that great but brief Golden Age of modern economics, the early and middle 1960s. The unsatisfactory character of economic performance during the current recovery has given rise to a great yearning for a return to the Golden Age. Some members of the current Administration are advocating tax changes to bring about a revival of the investment boom of the middle 1960s. The Carter Administration has proposed an energy program that will further dampen investment spending, so that the Golden Age scenario would require new tax incentives for investment considerably in excess of those adopted during the period 1962 to 1964.

According to one popular scenario, investment would have to grow at ten percent per year for four years in order to produce President Carter's promised economic nirvana of a balanced budget, an end to inflation, and full employment—all by 1981. An investment tax credit in the range of twenty to twenty-five percent would be needed to generate an investment boom of the required dimensions.[16] Proposed tax changes under discussion within the Administration are far less dramatic and would be hardly sufficient to offset the depressing effects of the changes in energy policy that are now in prospect. Our conclusion is that the Golden Age is behind us rather than ahead of us. There are no realistic prospects that the Carter Administration will succeed in attaining its stated objectives for economic policy by 1981.

In closing, we can consider a few of the implications of the long-run outlook for fiscal policy. The prevailing perspective in Washington since the beginning of the Carter Administration has been that the current recovery presents opportunities like those of the early 1960s to get the country moving again. By holding to the illusion that nothing fundamental has changed in the economy, the Administration has held out a vision of good times ahead that has led to a large and growing credibility gap, diagnosed incorrectly as a lack of business confidence. Fiscal policy has been highly stimulative and the Administration has proposed to increase the full employment deficit at a time that the economy is approaching full utilization of capacity. The result has been an explosive increase in the rate of inflation that can be traced directly to a mistaken view of the state of the economy on the part of the makers of fiscal policy.

As the prospects for tax reform have given way to a proposal for an election-year tax cut, revenues have continued to rise at rates far below those required to balance the budget by 1981, as promised by President Carter. Any net revenue gain resulting from energy taxes is likely to be offset by a postponement of higher social insurance taxes, so that postponement of a tax cut is the only remaining fiscal weapon for the fight against inflation. Prospects for substantial expansion of expenditures are growing more remote with the passage of time. The task forces that have been hard at work drawing up grandiose plans for completion of the Great Society are up against the wall of fiscal reality. Welfare reform is dead; programs to "save the cities" will be severely limited; even defense spending is constrained, despite the reappearance of the missile gap of the early 1960s. The equivalent of an Apollo project to develop exotic energy sources or nationalized health care financed through the Federal budget are less and less likely.

It will be difficult to come to terms with the impact of the OPEC cartel at an intellectual level until much time has passed. The effects of higher energy prices are not easy to detect for quarter-to-quarter fluctuations in the national income and product accounts. In the short and intermediate term, we can expect that the full gamut of "special factors" will be brought into play by economic commentators in order to explain the growing departure between current economic developments and past historical experience. Business confidence will be seen to be declining, even as consumer confidence is seen to be rising. The ability of the American labor force to continue to perform according to the work ethic will be seriously questioned. Environmental regulations, occupational safety, the declining dollar—all these and other explanatory factors will appear in the commentator's lexicon. We are entering a Ptolemaic age of explanations built upon explanations. But in the long run, presumably when we are all dead, there is at least a modest probability that the most significant economic reversal since the Great Depression of the 1930s will be seen to be the slowdown in economic growth brought about by the establishment of the OPEC cartel.

Notes

1. This paper is a revised and updated version of Jorgenson (1977); some of the same ground is covered in Jorgenson (1976).
2. For further historical perspective and international comparisons of patterns of energy use, see Darmstadter, Dunkerley, and Alterman (1977).
3. An analysis of the oil import program is given by Burrows and Domencich (1970); well-head price regulation of natural gas by the Federal Power commission is analyzed by Breyer and MacAvoy (1974).
4. For further discussion of the Arab oil embargo, see Houthakker (1978).
5. These estimates are given by Nordhaus (1976), p. 554.
6. This analysis of the system of price controls as a tax-subsidy scheme has been advanced by Hall and Pindyck (1977).
7. See Executive Office of the President (1977). Assessments of the National Energy Plan have been published by the Congressional Research Service, the General Accounting Office, and the Congressional Budget Office. A review of these assessments is given by the Congressional Research Service (1978).
8. A more detailed analysis is presented by Hudson and Jorgenson (1978a).
9. For a discussion of optimal monopoly price policy for OPEC, see Pindyck (1978).
10. See Central Intelligence Agency (1977).
11. For further details, see Goldman (1977).
12. A very comprehensive analysis of the recessions of 1974 and 1975 is given by Eckstein (1978).
13. An exhaustive review of the evidence has been undertaken by Berndt and Wood (1977).
14. The relationship between energy prices and capital formation has been analyzed by Hogan (1977a) and by Hudson and Jorgenson (1978a).
15. For historical perspective and international comparisons of sources of economic growth, see Christensen, Cummings, and Jorgenson (1978).
16. The impact of alternative investment incentives is analyzed by Gordon and Jorgenson (1976), following the earlier study by Hall and Jorgenson (1971).

12

Energy Prices and the U.S. Economy, 1972–1976

Edward A. Hudson and
Dale W. Jorgenson

12.1   Introduction

The purpose of this chapter is to analyze the impact on the United States economy of higher energy prices resulting from the establishment of the OPEC oil cartel in late 1973 and early 1974. The year 1972 is the last year of the "old" regime of energy prices and provides the starting point for our study. The year 1976 is the most recent year for which detailed data on energy prices are available and it provides the termination point for our study. These years correspond to periods of vigorous expansion following the recessions of 1970 and 1974. However, they differ drastically with regard to the level of energy prices.

The main conclusions of our analysis of the impact of higher energy prices on the U.S. economy are the following:

1. *GNP*: Real GNP in 1976 was reduced by 3.2 percent because of the increase in energy prices from 1972 to 1976.

2. *Energy*: Total energy consumption in 1976 was reduced by 8.8 percent because of the increase in energy prices, resulting in a sizeable fall in the energy-GNP ratio.

3. *Capital*: The level of capital stock in 1976 was reduced by $103 billion in constant dollars of 1972 because of the increase in energy prices. This can be compared with 1976 gross investment of $165 billion in constant dollars.

4. *Labor*: Despite the reduction in GNP growth, employment in 1976 declined by only 0.5 million jobs as a result of higher energy prices. As a consequence, productivity growth fell substantially over the period 1972–1976.

Our overall conclusion is that higher energy prices have had a dramatic impact on the U.S. economy over the period 1972–1976. This impact is not limited to a reduction in the growth of energy consumption, but it has also resulted in a slowdown in economic growth, a weak recovery of capital spending, a substantial increase in employment and a decline in the growth of productivity. We now turn to a detailed examination of the mechanisms through which energy prices have affected the U.S. economy. We examine the shift in the composition of total spending away from energy and energy-intensive goods and services. We will next consider the impact of a reduction of energy and energy-intensive inputs into the production sectors of the economy. Finally, we will analyze the impacts of these changes on investment and capacity and on employment and labor productivity.

12.2   Analytical Framework

Our analysis of the effects of higher energy prices is based upon a dynamic general equilibrium model of the U.S. economy. The original form of the model was developed for the Energy Policy Project of the Ford Foundation.[1] Subsequent development of the model is outlined by Hudson and Jorgenson.[2] Production activity in this model is divided among ten sectors: agriculture and construction, manufacturing, transportation, services, and six energy sectors. There are thirteen inputs into each sector—intermediate inputs consisting of output from the ten producing sectors, together with three primary factors of production, including capital services, labor services and imports. Each producing sector supplies output to each of the ten intermediate sectors and to the four categories of final demand: personal consumption, investment, government purchases and exports.

The technology of each producing sector is represented by an econometric model giving the supply price of output as a function of the prices of primary and intermediate inputs and the level of technology.[3] Also, technical coefficients giving the use of each type of primary and intermediate input per unit of output for each producing sector are derived as functions of prices and productivity from these models of technology. Consumer preferences are represented by an econometric model giving the allocation of personal consumption expenditures among goods and services as a function of prices and income.[4] Given the final demands and the technical coefficients, the level of output from each sector can be determined. Then, using the levels of output and the technical coefficients, each sector's demand for intermediate and primary inputs, including energy, can be calculated.

In each period, the relative prices of all commodities are determined by the balance between demand and supply. Technical input coefficients are determined simultaneously with the prices. Final demands are also functions of these prices. Final demands and input coefficients together determine sectoral output levels and input purchases from the condition that there is balance between total demand and supply for each type of output. The condition that demands for capital and labor equal their supplies yields the prices of these primary inputs.

The supply of capital in each period is fixed by past investment. Variations in demand for capital services affect the price but not the quantity of these services. Similarly, the supply of labor time in each period is fixed by past demographic developments. Variations in demand for labor time by the producing sectors and by the household sector for consumption in the form of leisure affect the price of labor and the allocation of labor time between these market and nonmarket activities. Finally, the supply of saving by the household sector must be balanced by final demand for investment by the producing sectors. Dynamic adjustment to higher energy prices is modeled by tracing through the impact of investment on capacity expansion.[5]

Our dynamic general equilibrium model was used to simulate two economic growth paths over the 1972–1976 period. In the first simulation, actual values of the exogenous variables, including world oil prices, were employed as the basis for model solution. This simulation provides an estimate of the actual development of the U.S. economy between 1972 and 1976. In the second simulation, 1972 energy prices were employed over the whole 1972–1976 period; i.e., world oil prices were held at their 1972 real values. As world oil prices are the only set of exogenous variables to change between the two simulations, the differences in simulated economic activity can be attributed solely to the impact of the oil price increase. (Other energy prices are affected by the oil price change so all energy prices change between the simulations.) Therefore, comparison between the two simulations provides the basis for analyzing the impacts of the energy changes on energy use and on the level and structure of economic activity.

12.3   Overall Economic Impact

The energy price increases, and the associated changes in energy use, have significant impacts on both the quantity and the price aspects of overall economic activity. The level of real GNP is reduced, or the rate of economic growth is slowed as a result of the energy changes, while the structure of spending and production is also changed. The overall price level is increased, or the rate of inflation is raised from the energy changes, at the same time as the structure of relative prices is altered.

The rise in energy prices leads to a reduction in real GNP. The simulated level of real GNP for 1976 under actual energy price conditions was 3.2 percent lower than its simulated level under 1972 energy prices. There are two broad sets of reasons for this decline, one centering on input productivity and one centering on capital. Producers can economize on energy by substituting other inputs for energy. This substitution is not perfect, so that productivity is adversely affected. In addition, any additional input used as a substitute for energy must be taken from some other use, further detracting from overall productive potential. The result is that a given set of primary inputs can sustain a lower real GNP than would be possible without the restructuring of production patterns caused by the energy price increases.

A second result of the energy-induced changes is a reduction in the demand for capital services. The rise in energy prices leads to a decline in the rate of return on capital. This reduces the incentive for saving and investment, slowing the rate of capital formation. In addition, the energy price increase and the reduced level of real GNP lead to less saving and to a change in the allocation of income between consumption, on the one hand, and saving and investment on the other. This further slows the rate of capital formation. There is, then, a slowing of the rate of growth of productive capacity with the result that the level of potential GNP is lower than would have been the case at lower energy prices. The combination of substitution and capacity expansion effects results in an estimated reduction in 1976 real GNP of 3.2 percent.

The rate of economic growth, as well as the level of real GNP at any time, is affected by higher energy prices. The substitution or productivity changes affect the level of GNP; after the adjustment to the new spending and production patterns has been made there is no further pressure from this source tending to reduce GNP. This results in a

shift to lower economic growth path but it does not depress the underlying growth rate. The capacity expansion effect, however, can have a
longer lasting impact. At reduced GNP levels, under higher energy
prices and with the reduced rate of return, savings and investment
account for a smaller fraction of income. The resulting slowdown in
the rate of capacity expansion works to reduce the rate of economic
growth. Only in the long run will the rate of growth return to the
underlying trend. Since this new economic growth path is, at every
point, below the previous path, the loss of income or production
resulting from higher energy prices is permanent.

Inflation will be accelerated by the higher energy prices, since the
direct impact of higher energy prices is to raise the level of output
prices as the energy prices are passed through the whole cost structure. In addition, the shift from energy towards other inputs results in
some loss of productivity and some further increases in unit costs,
adding to inflationary pressures. The inflationary effects can be com-
plicated by the labor productivity changes. If wage and salary
demands are based on past trends, and if they are granted, then the
slowdown in labor productivity growth means that unit labor costs
will rise more rapidly than previously, giving further impetus to inflation. All of these effects, however, correspond to a transition to a
higher price level, not to a higher rate of price increase. They give
inflation only a temporary increase. It is only if some additional feedback mechanism such as a price-wage-price spiral comes into operation that these short-run inflationary impacts can be translated into a
permanent rise in the rate of inflation.

12.4   Effect on Economic Structure

The structure of economic activity, as well as the level of output,
changes as a result of the energy price increases. Higher energy prices
raise the whole price structure. In addition, the pattern of relative
prices is changed with the more energy intensive goods experiencing
the largest price increases. These price changes induce a shift in the
pattern of final demand spending away from the now more expensive
energy intensive products. Similarly, the pattern of inputs into production is altered with the role of energy being reduced. Since both
the mix of final demand and the way in which output is made are
adjusted away from energy, the composition of total output shifts

away from energy and energy-intensive sectors. Thus, the energy content of each dollar of GNP is reduced. Final demand patterns alter as a result of the energy price rises, partly in response to the price increases themselves and partly as a result of the associated reduction in income levels. The essence of the final demand changes is a movement away from energy intensive, and now more expensive, products. Table 12.1 shows the change in the pattern of final demand between the high and low energy price simulations. This gives the allocation of real final demand—personal consumption expenditure, investment, government purchases and exports—over the four nonenergy products and delivered energy. The principal change is the reduction in the relative importance of energy purchases.

The share of energy in total real final demand declines from 3.9 percent under low energy price conditions to 3.4 percent with higher energy prices. Purchases of transportation and of agriculture and construction show the next largest declines while the share of manufacturing is reduced slightly. Purchases of services are increased, absorbing the expenditure directed away from each other type of output. The services' share of total real final demand rises from 48.8 percent at the lower energy prices to 49.9 percent under the higher price conditions. In sum, final demand is redirected from energy to nonenergy products and, within the nonenergy group, it is redirected to the purchase of services.

Producers respond to higher energy prices in a way analogous to final demand. The motivation is to minimize unit costs in the face of the new price structure. The direction of adjustment is to economize

Table 12.1
Composition of real final demand in 1976 (percent of total real final spending)

	Simulated with 1972 energy prices	Simulated with actual energy prices
Agriculture, construction	12.3	12.0
Manufacturing	32.4	32.2
Transportation	2.6	2.5
Services, trade, communications	48.8	49.9
Energy	3.9	3.4
Total	100.0	100.0

on energy input and, given time to adjust, significant reductions in energy use are cost-effective under a regime of high energy prices. This reduction in energy use is not costless; it is achieved by increases in the use of labor services, capital services and other intermediate inputs. What is involved, therefore, is a redirection of input patterns away from energy, not a net reduction in input levels. The changes in input patterns can be represented by changes in input-output coefficients. These coefficients are given in table 12.2 for four input categories—capital services, labor services, energy, and materials (all other intermediate inputs)—into each nonenergy producing sector. Two sets of coefficients are given for each sector, one the simulated 1976

Table 12.2
Input-output coefficients for inputs into production (simulated coefficients for 1976)

	Coefficient corresponding to energy price for:		Difference[a] (percent)
	1972	1976	
Agriculture:			
Capital	0.2242	0.2222	−0.9
Labor	−0.2532	0.2591	2.3
Energy	0.0219	0.0204	−7.0
Materials	0.5007	0.4983	−0.5
Manufacturing:			
Capital	0.1059	0.1015	−4.1
Labor	0.2822	0.2909	3.1
Energy	0.0215	0.0181	−15.8
Materials	0.5904	0.5895	−0.2
Transportation:			
Capital	0.1777	0.1743	−1.9
Labor	0.4102	0.4135	0.8
Energy	0.0415	0.0380	−8.4
Materials	0.3706	0.3742	1.0
Services, trade, communications:			
Capital	0.2962	0.2995	1.1
Labor	0.4262	0.4347	2.0
Energy	0.0176	0.0143	−18.8
Materials	0.2599	0.2515	−3.2

[a] Percentage difference of the coefficients corresponding to 1976 energy prices relative to those based on 1972 energy prices.

coefficients, the other the coefficients simulated for 1976 on the basis of the 1972 energy prices.

The result of the adjustment from lower to higher energy prices is that for every sector the energy input coefficient is reduced. Thus, considerable energy savings are achieved in production activities. The greatest proportionate energy reductions are estimated to occur in services and in manufacturing, where the energy input coefficient is reduced by about 15 percent. Agriculture, construction and transportation obtain energy savings of half this amount. There are also considerable differences among the sectors as to how the other inputs are adjusted to compensate for reduced energy use. Labor input is increased in all sectors and capital input is decreased in all sectors other than services. Manufacturing shows particularly noticeable adjustments: the 16 percent reduction in the energy coefficient is accompanied by a 4 percent reduction in the capital coefficient, with both of these reductions being offset by the 3 percent increase in labor intensity of production.

Patterns of input into production in each sector move toward less energy use. Final demand patterns are adjusted away from energy-intensive goods and services. These two changes in combination mean that the pattern of gross sectoral outputs is altered and that the nature of this change is a shift away from energy and energy-intensive products. Table 12.3 summarizes these changes. The relative importance of the energy sector is reduced substantially, from 5.9 percent to 5.0 percent of total output. Transportation shows the next largest relative decline while agriculture, construction and manufacturing show smaller reductions. The role of services increases significantly. There is, then, a redirection of production in the economy away from energy, and to a lesser extent away from goods and towards service activities.

These changes in the structure of economic activity are significant. First, they imply that all aspects of the economy are affected by the energy price changes, despite the relatively small fraction that energy represents in total economic output. Thus the relative sizes of the different sectors of the economy are affected as well as spending patterns and production patterns. In addition, the use of capital and labor inputs will be affected throughout the economy. Second, these structural changes have the effect of reducing the energy content of spending and of production. This means that, under the higher energy prices, each dollar of GNP requires less energy input.

Table 12.3
Composition of real gross output in 1976 (percent of total real gross output)

	Simulated with 1972 energy prices	Simulated with actual energy prices
Agriculture, construction	10.2	10.1
Manufacturing	33.3	33.2
Transportation	4.0	3.9
Services, trade, communications	46.6	47.8
Energy	5.9	5.0
Total	100.0	100.0

12.5   Reductions in Energy Use

In 1972 the U.S. used 72.0 quadrillion Btu of primary energy input to sustain a real GNP of $1171 billion in constant dollars of 1972. This corresponds to an energy-GNP ratio of 61.4 (million Btu per dollar (1972)). In 1976, GNP had increased to $1275 billion in constant dollars but energy use had risen only to 73.7 quadrillion Btu,[6] giving a significantly reduced energy-GNP ratio. If the 1972 energy-GNP ratio still applied in 1976, the primary energy input required to sustain the actual 1976 GNP would have been 78.3 quadrillion Btu. Further, if GNP has not been reduced by 3.2 percent as a result of the energy changes, the required energy input would have been 80.8 quadrillion Btu. In these very aggregative terms, therefore, the changes in energy use patterns and economic structure induced by the rise in energy prices are shown to have resulted in an annual energy reduction of 7.1 quadrillion Btu by 1976. The mechanisms yielding this energy saving are now outlined.[7]

The composition of real final demand changed significantly between the high and low energy price simulations. These changes were presented above. They imply that the direct energy content of a given total of real final spending is reduced in response to the rise in energy prices. Between the two simulations there is a reduction of 0.45 percent in the share of spending going to energy. When applied to the simulated 1976 total real final spending of $1330 billion in constant dollars, this represents a reduction of $6.0 billion in constant dollars in the demand for energy.

The nonenergy component of real final spending accounts for the larger proportion of total final spending in 1976 as a result of higher energy prices. This shift in itself implies that more energy will be absorbed in satisfying nonenergy final demand. Also, composition of spending as between the nonenergy types of goods and services is altered. Services absorb a greater part of this spending while the other sectors decline in relative importance. Since services are the least energy-intensive type of production, this corresponds to a shift away from energy-intensive purchases. This shift works to reduce the energy content of final demand. These two types of adjustment work in opposite directions as far as energy use is concerned. The net change in the energy content of nonenergy final demand could there-fore, be either positive or negative.

The information needed to calculate the impact of the change in nonenergy final demand on energy utilization is presented in table 12.4. This table determines the direct energy requirements for 1976 nonenergy final demand spending, as well as the energy requirements of the same total spending allocated over commodities in the pattern associated with 1972 energy prices. Under the higher energy prices, there is a reduced requirement for direct energy for agriculture and construction, manufacturing and transportation. In contrast, spend-ing on services is increased and this additional energy demand is suf-ficient to offset the energy reduction in the other three sectors. The net effect is that the direct energy content of nonenergy final spending increases as a consequence of the higher energy prices. The increase is small, about $0.4 billion in constant dollars, but it does work to counter the energy reductions achieved by fewer direct final pur-chases of energy.

The pattern of inputs into each production sector also changes as a result of the energy price increases; these changes have been analyzed above in terms of adjustments in input-output coefficients. This restructuring of inputs means that the energy content of any set of total sectoral outputs is reduced. The implications of this reduction caused by energy saving are developed in table 12.5. This table gives the energy content of the 1976 gross sectoral outputs for input patterns simulated under the 1976 energy prices, as well as the energy content of this output given the input patterns simulated on the basis of the 1972 energy prices. The change in energy content is the energy saving achieved by producing a given set of outputs in a less energy-intensive way. These energy savings are substantial, corresponding to

Table 12.4
Change in direct energy content of 1976 real nonenergy final demand (real variables in billion dollars [1972])

	Real final demand in pattern for prices of[a]		Energy input coefficient[b]	Energy content for spending in pattern of[c]		Change in direct energy content[d]
	1976	1972		1976	1972	
Agriculture, construction	159.0	163.6	0.0219	3.48	3.58	–0.10
Manufacturing	428.4	431.0	0.0215	9.21	9.27	–0.06
Transportation	33.1	34.5	0.0415	1.37	1.43	–0.06
Services, trade, communications	663.5	649.0	0.0176	11.68	11.42	0.26
				25.75	25.70	0.04

a Total real final demand in the 1976 simulation allocated over sectors in the 1976 patterns and in the pattern simulated for 1976, based on 1972 energy prices.
b Input-output coefficients for energy into each producing sector as simulated for 1976, based on 1972 energy prices.
c Direct energy input into each of the two sets of final demand.
d Direct energy content of 1976 nonenergy final demand allocated in the pattern corresponding to 1976 energy prices, less direct energy content of this final demand allocated in the pattern corresponding to 1972 energy prices.

Table 12.5
Change in energy content of 1976 production due to input restructuring (real variables in billion dollars [1972])

	Total output[a]	Energy input coefficients for energy prices of[b]		Energy content with coefficients of[c]		Change in energy content[d]
		1976	1972	1976	1972	
Agriculture, construction	221	0.0204	0.0219	4.51	4.84	−0.33
Manufacturing	719	0.0181	0.0215	13.01	15.46	−2.45
Transportation	86	0.0380	0.0415	3.27	3.57	−0.30
Services, trade, communications	1004	0.0143	0.0176	14.36	17.67	−3.31
				35.15	41.54	−6.39

[a] Total real sectoral outputs in the 1976 simulation.
[b] Input-output coefficients for energy into the production sectors for the 1976 simulation, and for the simulation of 1976 under 1972 energy prices.
[c] Energy content of the given sectoral outputs under the two sets of energy input coefficients.
[d] Energy content of 1976 output, given input based on 1976 energy prices less energy content of this output under the coefficients based on 1972 energy prices.

$6.4 billion in constant dollars of 1972. The greatest energy savings are achieved in the manufacturing and the services sectors, reflecting the large size of these sectors and the substantial reductions in unit energy requirements achieved in these sectors.

The final type of energy saving is that due to a reduction in the overall level of economic activity. The rise in energy prices led to a reduction in 1976 real GNP, relative to its simulated level based on 1972 energy prices, of 3.2 percent. This reduction implies a decline of approximately 3.2 percent in energy use, even with no changes in economic structure. This yields an estimated $4.0 billion in constant dollars as energy saved from reducing the scale of economic activity.

These changes show the mechanism of economic adjustment to higher energy prices and the resulting energy saving. In brief, there are three general sources of energy saving: the scale of economic activity is reduced, final demand becomes less energy intensive, and methods of production become less energy intensive. Using the approximations that these three types of energy reduction add up to the total estimated 1976 energy saving of 7.1 quadrillion Btu, and that each constant dollar of energy purchases is equal to the same number of Btu, we can allocate the total energy saving over its sources. The results are presented in Table 12.6.

Final demand changes account for 35 percent of the total saving, and all of this saving is due to redirection of final demand away from energy purchases and towards purchases of nonenergy goods and services. Changes in input patterns, as represented by the input-output coefficients, account for 40 percent of the total energy saving. Reductions in energy used in service-oriented activities are the greatest single source of saving, at 21 percent of the total, with energy savings in the manufacturing sector, at 15 percent of the total, also being significant. Energy reduction in agriculture, construction and transportation provides a much smaller volume of saving, about 4 percent of the total. Reduction in the scale of economic activity resulting from higher energy prices yields the final 25 percent of energy saving. In terms of physical units of energy, the total saving of over 7 quadrillion Btu is achieved by a reduction of 2.5 quads in final demand energy use, a reduction of 1 quad in manufacturing, a decline of 1.5 quads in services, and a decrease of almost 2 quads due to the reduced level of economic activity.

Table 12.6
Sources of energy saving in 1976

	Energy reduction, percent of total		Energy reduction quadrillion Btu	
Changes in final demand				
Reduction in energy purchases	37.5		2.7	
Restructuring of nonenergy purchases	−2.5		−0.2	
Total		35.0		2.5
Changes in inputs to production				
Agriculture, construction	2.1		0.1	
Manufacturing	15.3		1.1	
Transportation	1.9		0.1	
Services, trade, communications	20.7		1.5	
Total		40.0		2.8
Reduction in economic activity		25.0		1.8
Total energy reduction		100.0		7.1

12.6   Reduction in Capital Stock

The adjustments in spending and production patterns that reduce energy utilization relative to GNP also affect capital, labor and other factors of production. Demand for capital is affected as a result of changes in the mix of final demand and changes in the pattern of inputs into each sector. In addition, any effect of the energy changes on the level of real GNP will affect the overall level of demand for capital services as an input to production. Each of these three sources of change in demand for capital services will now be examined and the implications of the energy changes for investment and capacity growth indicated.

The change in the composition of final demand will alter the demand for capital input. For example, a decline in the proportion of spending directed to energy and an increase in spending on services will result in a different overall level of demand for capital services, since the capital requirements of these two types of production are different. The magnitudes of these changes are calculated in table 12.7. This table presents the direct capital requirements of the simulated total 1976 real final demand when allocated over sectors in the 1976 patterns, and when allocated over sectors in the patterns corresponding to the 1972 energy prices. As a result of the higher energy prices,

Table 12.7
Change in direct capital input to 1976 real final demand (real variables in billion dollars [1972])

	Real final demand in pattern for prices of[a]		Capital input coefficient[b]	Capital content for spending in pattern of[c]		Change in direct capital content[d]
	1976	1972		1976	1972	
Agriculture, construction	159.0	163.6	0.2242	35.65	36.68	−1.03
Manufacturing	428.4	431.0	0.1059	45.37	45.64	−0.28
Transportation	33.1	34.5	0.1777	5.88	6.13	−0.25
Services, trade, communications	663.5	649.0	0.2962	196.53	192.23	4.29
Energy	45.7	51.6	0.2396	10.95	12.36	−1.41
Total	1329.7	1329.7		294.38	293.04	1.33

[a] Total real final demand in the 1976 simulation allocated over sectors in the 1976 patterns and in the pattern simulated for 1976, based on 1972 energy prices.
[b] Input-output coefficients for capital into each producing sector as simulated for 1976, based on 1972 energy prices.
[c] Direct capital input into each of the two sets of final demand.
[d] Direct capital content of 1976 final demand allocated in the pattern corresponding to 1976 energy prices, less direct capital content of this final demand allocated in the pattern corresponding to 1972 energy prices.

spending is directed away from energy and goods and towards services. The capital content of each type of production is held constant at the levels given by the input-output coefficients corresponding to 1972 energy prices. Under these conditions, the change in final demand composition leads to an increase in the direct requirement of capital services input of $1.3 billion in constant 1972 dollars. The central reason for this increase is the shift of spending towards services, which is relatively capital-intensive.

The demand for capital services also changes as a result of adjustments in the pattern of inputs to each producing sector. Specifically, the energy changes are accompanied by shifts in the capital input-output coefficients. In some sectors, production becomes more capital intensive; in other sectors it becomes less intensive. The overall change depends on the size of the shift in each sector and the magnitude of each sector. Estimates of the size of the overall change are presented in table 12.8. This table gives the input of capital services needed to sustain the simulated 1976 set of sectoral outputs under two sets of conditions: the 1976 input patterns and the input patterns simulated for 1976 based on 1972 energy prices. The difference in total demand for capital services, a reduction of $0.3 billion in constant dollars of 1972, is due to a change in methods of production. Under higher energy prices manufacturing uses less capital services, while the services sector demands a higher input of capital. These are almost offsetting, resulting in a small overall decline in demand for capital.

In addition, the energy price increases lead to a reduction in the simulated 1976 real GNP below the level estimated on the basis of a continuation of 1972 energy prices. The 1976 real GNP was 3.2 percent less than the level estimated for lower prices. As an approximation, this corresponds to a 3.2 percent reduction in the demand for capital services input. In constant dollars of 1972 this results in a $15.5 billion reduction in demand for capital services purely because the overall level of economic activity has been reduced.

The three types of changes in demand for capital services can now be brought together. Under the first order approximation that these components can be added to find the total change in capital demand, this yields the result that total demand for the input of capital services in 1976 is reduced by $14.5 billion in constant 1972 dollars, due to the increase in energy prices. Capital services are the effective input services, or the implicit rental value, of capital stock. In any year, each

Table 12.8
Change in capital content of 1976 production due to input restructuring (real variables in billion dollars [1972])

	Total output[a]	Capital input coefficients for energy prices of[b] 1976		Capital content with coefficients of[c] 1976		Change in capital content[d]
		1976	1972	1976	1972	
Agriculture, construction	221	0.2222	0.2242	49.11	49.55	-0.44
Manufacturing	719	0.1015	0.1059	72.98	76.14	-3.16
Transportation	86	0.1743	0.1777	14.99	15.28	-0.29
Services, trade, communications	1004	0.2995	0.2962	300.70	297.38	3.32
Energy	128	0.2418	0.2396	30.95	30.67	0.28
Total				468.73	469.02	-0.29

[a] Total real sectoral outputs in the 1976 simulation.
[b] Input-output coefficients for capital services into the production sectors for the 1976 simulation, and for the simulation of 1976 under 1972 energy prices.
[c] Capital content of the given sectoral outputs under the two sets of input coefficients.
[d] Capital content of 1976 output, given input based on 1976 energy prices less capital content of this output under the coefficients based on 1972 energy prices.

Table 12.9
Sources of reduction in capital stock in 1976

	Capital reduction, percent of total	Capital reduction $(1972) billion
Changes in final demand	−9.2	−9.5
Changes in inputs to production		
Agriculture, construction	3.0	3.1
Manufacturing	21.9	22.4
Transportation	2.0	2.0
Services, trade, communications	−23.0	−23.5
Energy	−1.9	−2.0
Total	2.0	2.1
Reduction in economic activity	107.2	110.7
Total reduction in capital stock	100.0	103.3

dollar of capital stock provides about $0.14 of capital services. Therefore, this reduction in demand for capital services corresponds to a reduction of $103.3 billion in constant dollars in the desired level of capital stock. The allocation of this reduction over its sources is given in table 12.9. The principal sources of change in demand for capital are the restructuring of inputs into manufacturing, which has a $22.4 billion reduction in constant dollars in demand for capital stock, the restructuring of inputs into services, which increases demand for capital stock by $23.5 billion in constant dollars, and the decline in the level of economic activity, which reduces demand for capital stock by $110.7 billion in constant dollars.

These are significant changes in the demand for capital. The overall decrease in demand for capital stock will be reflected by investment levels being lower than they would otherwise have been. If, as an illustration, all the capital adjustments were made in 1976, investment would be $103 billion less in constant dollars than would normally be expected. When this is compared to actual 1976 gross investment of $165 billion in constant dollars, it can be seen that the relative magnitude of the investment adjustment can be substantial.

12.7   Change in Employment

Demand for labor and employment is affected by the energy-induced adjustments through a restructuring of final demand spending, a restructuring of the pattern of inputs into production, and a reduction in the overall level of economic activity. Final demand is redirected, as a result of the higher energy prices, away from energy and energy-intensive products. The implications of this adjustment for labor demand are presented in table 12.10. The 1976 total real final demand is allocated over sectors in two patterns, one based on the 1976 energy prices, the other based on the lower 1972 energy prices. The direct energy content of these demands is calculated using one set of input-output coefficients. The result of the rise in energy prices is a substantial increase in labor demand. This increase of $2.9 billion in constant dollars of 1972 reflects the shift of final demand towards services and away from energy and goods. Since service activities have a higher labor content than any of these other sectors, the result of the shift is an increase in the labor content of each dollar of real final demand.

A restructuring of input patterns occurs in the producing sectors of the economy. In each sector increased labor input per unit of output results from the higher energy prices, so that the labor input for any given set of production outputs is increased. Table 12.11 presents the information necessary to make an exact calculation of this change in labor demand. In each sector, the labor input coefficient increases, leading to additional labor demand totaling $16.6 billion in constant dollars of 1972. The largest increases in labor demand occur in services and in manufacturing, although there is also a significant increase in the agriculture and construction sector.

These two structural shifts add substantially to the demand for labor. Together they amount to $19.5 billion in constant dollars of 1972, or 2.64 percent of the total demand for labor at the lower energy prices. If there had been no change in real GNP as a result of higher energy prices, the adjustment to these higher prices would greatly stimulate the demand for labor. If all of this increase were reflected in an increase in employment, it would imply a 2.6 percent reduction in the rate of unemployment as a result of higher energy prices. In the absence of an increase in energy prices, the rate of unemployment would have been 10.3 percent rather than the actual rate of 7.7 percent. In fact, the increase in energy prices reduced the level of GNP. This decreased the demand for labor and worked against the employment expansion which was resulting from high energy prices.

The estimated real GNP impact of the higher energy prices in 1976 is a reduction of 3.2 percent. This reduces the demand for labor by approximately 3.2 percent. Therefore, the overall impact on labor of the higher energy prices is a decrease in effective demand of 0.6

Table 12.10
Change in direct labor content of 1976 real final demand (real variables in billion dollars [1972])

	Real final demand in pattern for prices of[a] 1976	1972	Labor input coefficient[b]	Labor content for spending in pattern of[c] 1976	1972	Change in direct labor content[d]
Agriculture, construction	159.0	163.6	0.2532	40.26	41.42	-1.16
Manufacturing	428.4	431.0	0.2822	120.89	121.63	-0.73
Transportation	33.1	34.5	0.4102	13.58	14.15	-0.57
Services, trade, communications	663.6	649.0	0.4262	282.78	276.60	6.18
Energy	45.7	51.6	0.1329	6.07	6.86	-0.78
Total	1329.7	1329.7		463.58	460.66	2.92

[a] Total real final demand in the 1976 simulation allocated over sectors in the 1976 patterns and in the pattern simulated for 1976, based on 1972 energy prices.
[b] Input-output coefficients for labor into each producing sector as simulated for 1976, based on 1972 energy prices.
[c] Direct labor input into each of the two sets of final demand.
[d] Direct labor content of 1976 final demand allocated in the pattern corresponding to 1976 energy prices, less direct labor content of this final demand allocated in the pattern corresponding to 1972 energy prices.

Table 12.11
Change in labor content of 1976 production due to input restructuring (real variables in billion dollars [1972])

| | Total output[a] | Labor input coefficients for energy prices of[b] | | Labor content with coefficients of[c] | | Change in labor content[d] |
		1976	1972	1976	1972	
Agriculture, construction	221	0.2591	0.2532	57.26	55.96	1.30
Manufacturing	719	0.2909	0.2822	209.16	202.90	6.26
Transportation	86	0.4135	0.4102	35.56	35.28	0.28
Services, trade, communications	1004	0.4347	0.4262	436.44	427.90	8.54
Energy	128	0.1344	0.1329	17.20	17.01	0.19
Total				755.62	739.05	16.57

[a] Total real sectoral outputs in the 1976 simulation.
[b] Input-output coefficients for labor services into the production sectors for the 1976 simulation, and for the simulation of 1976 under 1972 energy prices.
[c] Labor content of the given sectoral outputs under the two sets of input coefficients.
[d] Labor content of 1976 output, given input based on 1976 energy prices less labor content of this output under the coefficients based on 1972 energy prices.

Table 12.12
Sources of reduction in employment in 1976

	Employment reduction percent of total		Employment reduction, millions of jobs
Changes in final demand		−71.1	0.3
Changes in inputs to production			
Agriculture, construction	−31.6		0.2
Manufacturing	−152.3		0.8
Transportation	−6.8		0.0
Services, trade, communications	−207.8		1.0
Energy	−4.6		0.0
Total		−403.1	2.0
Reduction in economic activity		574.2	−2.8
Total increase in employment		100.0	−0.5

percent. The GNP decline, then, more than affects the employment increase resulting from the changed economic structure, so the net result in 1976 of the higher energy prices is a slight decline in labor demand and in employment. The structural increase in employment is significant, however, in that it serves to minimize the loss of employment associated with the lower general level of economic activity.

This change represents a reduction of 0.5 million jobs. Table 12.12 shows the sources of this change in employment. The restructuring of the inputs into production, as labor substitutes for energy input, adds substantially to labor demand. In particular, there are large increases in the manufacturing and services sectors. The change in final demand patterns adds only slightly to labor demand. These increases are more than offset by the effects of the reduced level of economic activity. All told, restructuring of inputs provides about two million more jobs, changed final demand patterns lead to 0.3 million jobs, and the decline in real GNP causes a loss of 2.8 million jobs.

The adjustments of spending and input patterns in response to higher energy prices leads to a substantial increase in the demand for labor. This increase in labor input is beneficial for employment, reducing the loss of jobs in the face of the GNP reduction, but it has an adverse effect on productivity. More labor input per unit of output is equivalent to less output per unit of labor input. These adjustments, therefore, lead to a reduction in the average gross productivity of labor. Specifically, the economic restructuring that occurs between the high and low energy price simulations leads to a 2.57 percent reduction in average labor productivity. To place this change in perspective, it can be noted that the average annual rate of labor productivity increase between 1950 and 1970 was 1.44 percent. Against this norm, the reduction of 2.57 percent corresponds to the loss of two years of productivity improvement.

The decline in productivity growth implies that the rate of growth in real wages will not be as rapid as would otherwise have occurred. To the extent that real wages outstrip the slower growth of productivity, unit labor costs will increase and inflation will be accelerated. Lower productivity leads to slower real growth, slower growth of real wages, and more rapid inflation. It should be noted that these are one-time effects rather than permanent trends. Once the economy has adjusted to the new labor and productivity conditions, there will be no further energy-induced pressures for further changes. Continued changes will occur only if there is a secondary wave of induced price responses.

12.8   Conclusions

The oil price increases beginning in 1973 have had a significant impact on the U.S. economy. One direct effect of the higher oil prices has been to raise all energy prices and to induce a reduction in the intensity of energy use throughout the economy. This change in energy use patterns is estimated to have reduced 1976 energy input from about 81 quadrillion Btu, corresponding to historical energy use patterns, to the actual level of about 74 quadrillion Btu. Analysis of the sources of this energy saving suggests that about one third of the savings came from a redirection of final demand—consumption, investment, government, and export purchases—away from energy and energy-intensive goods and services; that almost half came from a restructuring of patterns of input into production away from energy; and that one fourth came from the reduced scale of economic activity. Four particular facets of these changes stand out: a substantial reduction in direct final demand purchases of energy, an increase in final purchases of services, substantial reductions in energy input to manufacturing, and substantial reductions in energy input to the service industries.

The effects of the energy changes have spread throughout the entire economy. Demand for capital input is reduced as a result of the higher energy prices. This leads to a reduction in investment levels and to a slowing in the rate of growth of capital stock and productive capacity. Equally important is the change in demand for labor input. The adjustment in economic structure, with final spending shifted towards labor intensive services and with labor substituting for energy as an input into production, results in an increase in the demand for labor, largely offsetting the adverse employment impacts of the reduced level of economic activity resulting from the higher energy prices. It is estimated that in 1976 employment under the higher energy price conditions was only 0.6 percent, or 0.5 million jobs less than would have been the case if 1972 energy prices were still in effect.

These structural effects are of interest in themselves, but they are also of great importance in interpreting recent economic developments. Two features of the current economic recovery stand out sharply from the pattern of virtually all previous business cycle upswings. The first feature is that employment has expanded much more rapidly, and unemployment has declined to a greater extent, than would have been anticipated from past cyclical upturns. The second feature is that investment has picked up more slowly than would have been anticipated. But both of these developments tie in closely with the predicted effects of the energy changes. This suggests that the observed changes are due at least in part to structural shifts, permitting adjustment to lower energy use, being superimposed on the normal cyclical patterns of recovery from recession. A related feature of the present economic situation that is at variance with the pattern of previous recoveries is the low level of advance in productivity. But again, at least part of the reason for this result lies in the structural shifts, in particular the greater intensity of labor use, resulting from the energy changes.

Finally, the energy price increases have significant impacts on the level and growth of real GNP. The estimated decline in 1976 real GNP between a situation characterized by 1972 energy prices and the actual present energy price situation is 3.2 percent. This means that the oil price increase amounted for part, though certainly not all, of the recession of the mid-1970s. Further, the entire future economic growth path has been shifted down as a result of the energy changes so that, even if long-term future growth rates are not affected, the level of real GNP will always be less than it would have been in the absence of the oil price increase. The oil price rise has, therefore, imposed a significant and continuing cost on the U.S. economy.

Notes

1. The original form of the model was presented in Hudson and Jorgenson (1973).

2. A comprehensive description of the current version of the model is given in Hudson and Jorgenson (1977). A related discussion of the model in the policy analysis context is given in Behling, Dullien and Hudson (1976).

3. The econometric model of production also is described in Berndt and Jorgenson (1973) and in Christensen, Jorgenson and Lau (1973). A related application of the production model is given in Berndt and Wood (1975).

4. The econometric model of consumption is described in Jorgenson (1977). The theory of this model also is developed in Christensen and Jorgenson (1975) and Christensen, Jorgenson and Lau (1975).

5. A theoretical analysis of the dynamic adjustment process, in a macroeconomic growth model context, is presented by Hogan (1977a).

6. U.S. primary energy input in 1976 is estimated to be 73.7 quadrillion Btu; see Energy Information Administration (1978).

7. The role of energy in the current recovery also is discussed in Jorgenson (1977). The impact of energy policy on future U.S. economic growth is considered in Hudson and Jorgenson (1978a).

13

The Economic Impact of Policies to Reduce U.S. Energy Growth

Edward A. Hudson and Dale W. Jorgenson

13.1 Introduction

The purpose of this chapter is to quantify the impact of alternative energy policies on future energy prices, energy utilization, and economic growth in the United States. Growth in energy consumption has become an important issue in U.S. economic policy as a result of the establishment of an effective international petroleum cartel by the Organization of Petroleum Exporting Countries (OPEC). The OPEC cartel has succeeded in raising world petroleum prices four-fold since 1973. This has resulted in rapid increases in the real price of delivered energy in the U.S.; the real price of delivered energy rose 7.0 percent annually between 1973 and 1977. To put these price increases in historical perspective, it can be noted that from 1950 to 1973 the real price of delivered energy in the U.S. declined at the rate of 1.8 percent per annum.

Since 1954, the Federal Power Commission has maintained a system of well-head price controls for natural gas entering interstate commerce. These controls have maintained prices below market clearing levels and have necessitated the development of a system for the quantitative allocation of interstate natural gas. A similar situation has developed in the petroleum market. The U.S. government responded to the increase in world petroleum prices beginning in 1973 with a system of controls on domestic crude oil prices and on prices of petroleum products. These controls have been maintained and have been accompanied by an increasingly complex system for the allocation of petroleum.

The system of price controls on petroleum products within the U.S. has involved averaging the price of imported crude with that of domestic crude in the pricing of refined products. In effect, foreign producers receive a subsidy paid by means of a corresponding tax on domestic producers. By maintaining petroleum prices below world levels, U.S. domestic demand for petroleum has been allowed to rise more rapidly than in the absence of price controls. The effective tax on domestic production has permitted domestic supply to fall more rapidly than in the absence of price controls. The net impact of price controls has been to increase imports of petroleum products dramatically in the face of higher world petroleum prices. The Federal Power Commission approved a similar pricing system for domestic natural gas and natural gas imported in liquefied form (LNG), creating a system of effective subsidies for imported natural gas.

Higher world energy prices have not been passed on to domestic energy consumers in full, due to continued price controls on domestically produced petroleum and natural gas. Energy policy measures now in prospect will reduce or eliminate the effects of these controls and will expose large sectors of the U.S. economy to the full impact of higher world energy prices. The Carter Administration has proposed that the prices of petroleum and natural gas be set on the basis of 'replacement cost' on the world petroleum market. In addition, the Administration has proposed taxes on the utilization of petroleum and natural gas and measures to promote conversion to coal and other fuels that would have the effect of raising prices for petroleum and natural gas above world market levels. Higher energy prices will result in a reduction in the growth of energy consumption. However, higher energy prices can also have an important impact on future U.S. economic growth.

13.2   Econometric and Process Analysis Models

A satisfactory framework for analysis of the effect of alternative energy policies on energy prices, energy utilization, and economic growth requires an approach that encompasses both process analysis and econometrics. Process analysis provides for a detailed characterization of technology for energy conversion and energy utilization and permits the analysis of effects of introducing new energy technologies. Econometrics provides for the incorporation of behavioral and technical responses of patterns of production and consumption to alternative energy prices and permits an analysis of the impact of energy prices on the demand for energy, nonenergy intermediate goods, capital services, and labor services. In the process analysis approach, energy flows and energy conversion processes can be described in physical terms. In the econometric approach, flows of economic activity, including energy flows, are described in terms of economic accounts in current and constant prices.

To analyze the effect of alternative energy policies, we employ a dynamic general equilibrium model of the U.S. economy. For each of the commodities endogenous to the model—energy resources, energy conversion processes, energy products, nonenergy products, capital services, and labor services—the model incorporates a balance between demand and supply that determines relative prices. In addition, the model includes a balance between saving and investment that determines the rate of return and the growth of capital stock. Economic growth is modeled as a sequence of one-period equilibria determining demand and supply and relative prices for all commodities. Investment in each period determines the level of capital stock available in the following period. Dynamic adjustment to changes in energy policy is modeled by tracing through the impact on future levels of capital stock.

Since the output of the energy producing industries is largely utilized by other industries rather than by final consumers, the matrix of inter-industry transactions, representing flows of commodities including energy among industrial sectors, is a natural focal point for the study of the impact of energy policy. By representing energy sector transactions in physical terms we can provide a link to process analysis models. By representing these transactions in economic terms, in current and constant prices, we can provide a link to econometric models. By using both forms for representing energy transactions, process analysis and econometric modeling can be combined within the same framework. This integration of process analysis and econometric approaches permits a detailed characterization of energy technology to be combined with a complete representation of the impact of energy prices on the economy as a whole.

The first component of our modeling framework is the Long-Term Inter-industry Transactions Model (LITM) developed by Hudson and Jorgenson.[1] This model is based on a system of inter-industry accounts for the private domestic sector of the U.S. economy, divided among ten producing sectors.[2] Six sectors cover energy conversion and extraction—coal mining, crude petroleum, crude natural gas, petroleum refining, electric utilities, and gas utilities; the remaining four sectors—agriculture, manufacturing, transportation, and services—cover the production of nonenergy products. Final demand is divided among four categories—personal consumption expenditures, gross private domestic investment, government purchases of goods and services and exports. Primary input is divided among capital services, labor services and imports.

In the LITM framework the technology of each producing sector is represented by an econometric model based on the price possibility frontier, giving the supply price of output corresponding to given prices of primary and intermediate inputs and a given level of productivity.[3] For any given set of prices technical coefficients giving primary and intermediate inputs per unit of output of the sector can be derived from the price possibility frontier. Given the level of output of the sector, the technical coefficients determine demand for energy, nonenergy intermediate goods, and primary factors of production. The preferences of the household sector are represented by an econometric model determining demand for consumption goods, supply of labor, and supply of saving.[4] This model allocates personal consumption expenditures among the outputs of the ten producing sectors, services of housing and consumers durables, and domestic labor services.

The second component of our modeling framework is the Time-Phased Energy Systems Optimization Model (TESOM) developed at the Brookhaven National Laboratory by Hoffman and associates.[5] This model is based on the Reference Energy System, which provides a complete physical representation of technologies, energy flows, and conversion efficiencies from extraction of primary energy sources, through refining and various stages of conversion from one energy form to another, and to transportation, distribution, and storage of energy sources.[6] In the Reference Energy System energy supplies such as nuclear fuels, fossil fuels, and hydropower are allocated to energy demands defined on a functional basis, such as space heating, industrial process heat, and automotive transportation. Energy supplies and demand are linked by energy conversion processes such as steam generation of electricity from coal.

Energy flows in TESOM are based on the cost-minimizing pattern of allocation of energy supplies to satisfy energy demands. The minimization of cost can be formulated as a linear programming model of the transportation type. Given levels of demand for energy services, available supplies of energy resources and conversion capacities, conversion efficiency and capital and operating cost of utilizing technologies, the energy sector optimization model determines a set of energy conversion levels that minimize cost; the dual to the linear programming problem determines shadow prices for energy demands, energy resources, and energy conversion capacities. In the time-phased version of this model the energy conversion capacities are the result of previous investments.

The combined LITM-TESOM framework models the U.S. interindustry transactions—flows of energy resources, energy conversion activities, energy products, nonenergy products, capital services, and labor services—as a result of a dynamic general equilibrium of the U.S. economy.[7] In each period the supply prices of all commodities are determined by price possibility frontiers for the nonenergy sectors and by processes selected for the energy sectors—given the prices of capital and labor services and exogenously given prices of imports. Given these prices and the supply prices for each product, technical coefficients for inputs of intermediate goods and primary factors of production are determined. Finally, given the technical coefficients, demands for the output of each sector of the economy are determined by final demands for all products. While the level of investment for the private domestic economy as a whole is endogenous to the model, the allocation of investment among producing sectors is given exogenously. Final demand for government purchases and exports is also determined exogenously.

We can complete the description of a dynamic general equilibrium analysis of the U.S. economy by describing the markets for capital and labor services. In each period, the supply of capital is fixed initially by past investments. Variations in demand for capital services by the producing sectors and household sector affect the price but not the quantity of capital services. Similarly, in each period the available labor time is fixed by past demographic developments. Variations in demand for labor time by the producing sectors and by the household sector for consumption in the form of leisure affects the price of labor and the allocation of labor time between market and nonmarket activity. Finally, the supply of saving by the household sector must be balanced by final demand for investment by the producing sectors. Investment generates the level of capital stock available at the beginning of the following period and creates the conditions for a new equilibrium of product and factor markets, given the time endowment available in that period.[8]

13.3   Alternative Energy Policies

The starting point for our analysis of the impact of alternative energy policies is a Base Case projection of future energy and economic growth with no change in energy policy. We assume that any quantity of petroleum imports is available at the world price, where the world price of petroleum rises at a rate of one percent per annum relative to the rate of growth of the U.S. GNP price deflator until 1990 and 2.5 percent annually, in real terms, thereafter. The annual rate of growth or real GNP is projected to average 3.2 percent from 1977 to 2000. This growth is considerably slower than the average annual growth rate of 3.8 percent between 1950 and 1973. The decline is partly due to a reduction in population growth and partly due to a reduction in pro-ductivity growth resulting from higher energy prices. Primary energy input is projected to rise from 76 quadrillion Btu in 1977 to 139 in 2000, an average annual growth rate of 2.6 percent. This growth is also slower than that experienced in the past—the average rate of growth of primary energy input between 1950 and 1973 was 3.2 percent per annum. Part of the reduction is due to decreased economic growth and part is caused by the continuing rise in real energy prices.

The increase in the relative price of petroleum over time leads to a steady decline in the relative importance of petroleum in total energy use. Natural gas is also projected to decline in relative importance due to supply constraints and price increases. Coal and nuclear sources sustain much of the growth in energy use; both direct use of coal and the use of electricity grow relatively rapidly. Imported petroleum accounts for approximately half of all petroleum use in 1977; in the Base Case projection this share rises to almost sixty per-cent by 2000. The Base Case projections therefore imply continued reliance on imports for a substantial fraction of energy supply.

The reduction of import dependence, in order to reduce the associ-ated economic and political risks, is an important objective underlying U.S. energy policy proposals. To analyze such policies, and their energy and economic effects, we consider the following set of policy packages:

Policy 1: Taxes are imposed on U.S. petroleum production to bring domestic petroleum prices to world levels; natural gas prices are increased but price controls are retained; energy conservation is stimu-lated by taxes on use of oil and gas in industry, restriction of oil and gas use by electric utilities, subsidies for insulation of structures, and mandatory performance standards for energy-using appliances.

Policy 2: The measures included in Policy 1 are combined with tariffs on imported oil rising to $4.50/bbl in 1985 and to $7.00/bbl in 2000, and with corresponding taxes on natural gas.

Policy 3: Policy 2 is combined with excise taxes on delivered energy sufficient to reduce total primary energy input in 2000 to 90 quadrillion Btu.

Policy 4: Policy 3 is combined with excise taxes on delivered energy sufficient to reduce total primary input in 2000 to 70 quadrillion Btu.

13.4   Overview of Economic Effects

The processes by which the economy adjusts to higher energy prices and reduced availability of energy involves many simultaneous changes and takes time to accomplish.[9] For expository purposes these processes can be represented as in fig. 1. The changes in the prices and availability of energy and induced changes affecting other inputs, give rise to changes in the pattern of prices of inputs into production. This leads to a changed pattern of output prices. This, in turn, induces a redirection of the pattern of final demand spending—in particular, consumption, but also investment, government and foreign purchases—away from the now more expensive energy-intensive goods and services. Simultaneously, producers react to the changed pattern of prices that they must pay for inputs by altering their operating procedures, processes and products to economize on expensive energy input. Both final demand and production patterns are restructured. Therefore, the pattern of sectoral output and the pattern of use of pro-

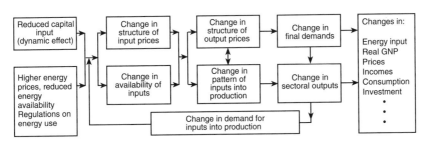

Figure 13.1
Overview of adjustment to reduced energy input.

ductive inputs are redirected away from energy and energy-intensive products. Finally, these changes are reflected in changes in summary measures of economic performance such as energy input and real GNP.

The adjustment processes involve shifts in the consumption of final spending and of production input patterns away from energy. While energy output will show the most noticeable changes, use of capital, labor, and intermediate materials can also be significantly affected. These changes occur both in each year and over time. Within each year, substitutions between products and processes will lead to a different mix of inputs being used. This restructuring will permit part of the energy reduction to be absorbed without loss of overall economic output. However, as these different inputs are only imperfect substitutes and as these other inputs must be diverted from other uses, some output will be lost through this restructuring. In addition there is a dynamic adjustment which operates through investment and capital. If saving and investment are reduced as a result of energy restrictions due to lower income or lower rates of return, the rate of accumulation of capital is slowed. This in turn slows the rate of growth of productive capacity and of output and incomes, providing an additional source of economic restructuring and economic cost.

The impact of energy changes on GNP reflects both the substitution and the dynamic effects. Table 13.1 indicates the aggregate nature of these effects for Policies 1 and 2 in the year 2000. Real GNP in Policy 2 is 3.2 percent less than in the Base Case. This decline is partly due to the dynamic effect operating through the capital stock—capital input is 3.0 percent lower than in the Base Case. This decline in capital input accounts for approximately a one percentage point reduction in real GNP or one-third of the total GNP reduction. At the same time, there are substitutions away from energy as an input into production. Of the 16 percent reduction in energy input, 3.2 percent is accounted for by reduced total economic output while approximately 13 percent is sustained by substitutions towards other inputs and towards nonenergy intensive products. Both capital and labor are partially substituted for energy; the energy-capital ratio is reduced by 14 percent, the energy-labor ratio by 16 percent. Labor and energy turn out to be substitutes in all production sectors. This leads to an increase in labor input relative to GNP. The level of gross labor productivity, or real GNP per unit of labor input, is therefore reduced; it declines by

Table 13.1
Capital, labor and energy inputs in 2000

	Base Case	Policy 1	Policy 2
Quantities of input			
Capital services[a]	831.5	821.9	806.3
Labor services[a]	1281.3	1281.2	1281.1
Energy[b]	138.5	126.6	116.3
Real GNP	2721.7	2679.8	2634.9
Input quantities, percent change from Base Case			
Capital		−1.12	−3.0
Labor		−0.0	−0.0
Energy		−8.7	−16.0
Real GNP		−1.5	−3.2
Gross input productivities[c]			
Gross capital productivity	1.0	0.9961	0.9984
Gross labor productivity	1.0	0.9846	0.9682
Gross energy productivity	1.0	1.0771	1.1529
Ratios between input quantities[d]			
Energy: Capital	1.0	0.9240	0.8606
Energy: Labor	1.0	0.9134	0.8406
Capital: Labor	1.0	0.9885	0.9698

[a] Measured in billions of 1972 dollars.
[b] Quadrillion Btu of primary energy input.
[c] Gross input productivity is real GNP per unit of the input in the policy case divided by this ratio in the Base Case.
[d] Ratios are divided by their Base Case values.

more than 3 percent from the Base Case level. This corresponds to lower real per capital incomes and is the counterpart of GNP reductions.

The relationship between capital and energy is more complex. In some sectors, such as services, capital and energy are substitutes so that increased investment in capital such as insulation is the pattern of response to higher energy prices and to requirements forcing energy reductions. In other sectors, such as manufacturing, capital and energy frequently move in a complementary fashion so that the response to higher energy prices is to reduce the rate of investment. In addition, the shift of spending patterns between sectors, each sector with a different capital intensity, results in a change in the relation between capital input and total output. The net result of these capital changes is that capital input rises relative to energy input, that capital input declines relative to labor input, and that capital input per dollar of real GNP rises, with a corresponding decline in capital productivity.

13.5   Adjustments in the Price Structure

The immediate point of impact of energy policy measures is in the structure of relative prices. Energy becomes more expensive relative to other goods and services. In the attempt to allocate purchases so as to minimize production costs, producers reduce energy use, moving towards less energy-intensive inputs and processes. Similarly, in the attempt to derive maximum value from their consumption budgets, households redirect their expenditure patterns to economize on the now expensive energy and energy-intensive goods and services. Thus, higher prices for energy, and so for energy-intensive products, lead to reductions in energy use and to slower growth in energy consumption. In addition, the nonprice energy conservation measures contained in the Policy 1 package add considerable further pressure to the shift towards less intensive energy use.

The price adjustments commence with the relative prices of inputs. Table 13.2 shows these changes for the simulations for 2000. The changes in capital, labor, materials and energy input prices feed through the production structure to alter the whole pattern of relative prices of produced goods and services. The price of capital services is taken as the numeraire in the model system, so the pattern of variation is for other prices to adjust relative to the prices of capital services. The variation involves an increase in the price of energy, an increase in the price of intermediate materials and a decrease in the price of labor services.

The rise in energy prices directly reflects the taxes and other policy measures. Two measures of the energy price increase are given. The first, referring to actual energy prices, relates to dollar prices paid for the purchase of energy. These increase, relative to the Base Case, by 0.2 percent for Policy 1 and by 187 percent for Policy 4. However, the effective cost of energy rises by more than this due to the effect of nonprice policy measures. Nonprice regulations which require the use of more capital equipment or of different production processes increase average costs of production. The estimate of these additional costs, together with the direct price increases, is given by the second measure, Effective Energy Cost. (Effective energy cost is calculated by the model as a shadow price for energy. It is the energy price that would

Table 13.2
Adjustments in input and output prices in 2000

	Policy 1	Policy 2	Policy 3	Policy 4
Input prices, percent change from Base Case				
Capital	–	–	–	–
Labor	−0.68	−2.04	−5.43	−9.90
Energy	15.73	29.74	108.24	217.01
Intermediate materials	0.24	0.80	1.12	2.61
Output prices, percent change from Base Case				
Agriculture, nonfuel				
mining, construction	1.07	1.31	2.29	5.54
Manufacturing	0.08	−0.23	1.14	5.91
Commercial transportation	3.11	4.57	7.83	13.38
Services, trade,				
Communications	−0.26	−0.87	0.56	2.24
Energy, actual prices[a]	0.19	10.75	87.71	187.33
Energy, effective costs[b]	15.73	29.74	108.24	217.01

[a] Actual energy prices refer to the average dollar cost of delivered energy in terms of dollars per Btu.
[b] Effective energy costs refer to the average cost of energy services to energy purchasers, allowing for both price and nonprice conservation measures, and calculated using a fixed weight quantity index.

induce purchasers to reduce their energy use to the levels required to satisfy government mandated energy standards.) For Policy 1 this overall measure of energy cost is 16 percent above the Base Case, for Policy 4 it is 217 percent higher. Thus, both price and nonprice measures contribute significantly to the pressure to reduce consumption of energy.

Labor prices show a relative decline. This means that labor prices under the policy simulations show a less rapid growth over the forecast period than under Base Case conditions. The reason for this slower growth lies in the employment constraint imposed on the simulations—the rate of unemployment is constrained to be the same as in the Base Case. As the energy measures lead to a reduction in the level of economic activity, the demand for labor is reduced. This reduction is more than enough to offset the additional labor use due to energy-labor substitution. A relative reduction in labor prices is required in order to stimulate labor use. Thus, labor prices in Policy 2 are 2 percent less than in the Base Case and are 10 percent less in Policy 4. Finally, the prices of intermediate materials show a small increase as a result of the policy measures. This is due to the effect of higher energy costs raising production costs for these materials to an extent greater than the cost reduction following the decline in labor prices.

These changes in input prices lead to adjustments in the level and pattern of output prices. The overall level of output prices is increased. However, since energy represents, compared to capital, labor and materials inputs, only a small component of total production costs in most industries, the higher energy prices lead to relatively small increases in average output prices. The pattern of relative prices is more substantially altered. Energy prices rise significantly, in Policy 3 for example, by 88 percent in terms of dollars per Btu and by 108 percent in terms of effective costs to purchasers. Other output prices change by smaller proportions—in Policy 3, transportation prices rise by 8 percent, agriculture, nonfuel mining and construction prices rise by 2.3 percent, manufacturing prices rise by 1.1 percent and services prices are 0.6 percent higher.

The pattern of price changes is closely related to the mix of inputs used in each sector. Energy output, of course, is highly energy-intensive and it shows a substantial price increase. Commercial transportation is the next most energy-intensive sector and its price also rises significantly. Agriculture, nonfuel mining and construction, and manufacturing are less energy intensive and show smaller price increases. Services, trade, and communications is the least energy-intensive sector, and is also relatively labor-intensive, so that these prices either decline or show only a small increase. The pattern of changes in prices and effective costs alters to make energy intensive goods and services relatively expensive. Together with the associated nonprice measures, this is the force motivating producers and consumers to redirect their expenditure patterns and to use less energy in production and consumption activities.

13.6 Changes in the Pattern of Final Demand

Final demand expenditure is a critical determinant of the overall level and consumption of activity in the economy. Final demand—personal consumption expenditure, private investment, government purchases and exports—dictate what is produced in the economy. Changes in final demand are therefore important in securing reductions in the energy intensity of economic activity. Reduction in final demand

Table 13.3
Final demand patterns in 2000

	Base Case	Policy 1	Policy 2	Policy 3	Policy 4
Composition of real final demand (%)					
Agriculture, nonfuel mining, construction	8.38	8.30	8.22	8.13	8.06
Manufacturing	30.48	30.48	30.45	30.30	30.02
Commercial Transportation	3.64	3.48	3.36	3.30	3.21
Services, trade, Communications	54.08	54.70	55.15	55.91	56.94
Energy	3.43	3.04	2.82	2.36	1.77
Total	100.0	100.00	100.00	100.00	100.00
Real Final Demand, percent change from Base Case					
Agriculture, nonfuel mining, construction		−3.1	−5.6	−10.6	−15.9
Manufacturing		−1.9	−3.9	−8.4	−13.9
Commercial Transportation		−6.2	−11.0	−16.6	−22.8
Services, trade, Communications		−0.8	−2.1	−4.7	−8.0
Energy		−13.1	−20.9	−36.5	−54.9
Total		−2.0	−3.9	−7.9	−12.6

purchases of energy directly result in energy saving. Also, reductions in final demand purchases of energy-intensive goods permit less energy to be used in production activities and so accentuate the overall saving in energy. Both these types of expenditure adjustments—less energy purchases and less use of energy-intensive products—are induced by the restructuring of output prices.

Table 13.3 summarizes the changes in final demand spending resulting from the energy policy measures. The broad pattern of spending is similar under all policies, with services absorbing a little more than half and manufacturing about one-third of total real final demand. However, there are some significant shifts in final spending induced by the price and nonprice energy policy measures.

The changes in the price structure and the other energy conservation measures lead to a substantial adjustment in real final demand. The overall level of real final demand is reduced; this in itself results in a significant reduction in energy use. For example, final demand for energy in Policy 1 is 13 percent below the Base Case. This energy saving is compounded by a redirection of spending patterns away from energy and energy-intensive goods and services. Nonenergy intensive output, particularly services, become relatively more important within the pattern of final spending.

13.7   Changes in Production Patterns

The patterns of inputs into each production sector also change in response to the energy policy measures. Higher energy prices create an incentive for producers to alter input patterns away from energy and thereby reduce production costs. The nonprice direct regulations concerning energy use provide additional pressure to reduce energy purchases. Also, the changes in labor prices and prices of other intermediate inputs provide incentives for further adjustments in the mix of inputs and processes. The net result of these pressures is to induce, or to force, producers to adjust their purchase patterns, economizing on energy use by changed production practices and processes, and to place greater reliance on nonenergy inputs. Thus, not only is energy input reduced but the entire pattern of inputs into each sector is changed. The estimated changes in input patterns are shown in table 13.4 which gives the aggregate input-output coefficients for each of the major nonenergy producing sectors—agriculture, nonfuel mining and construction; manufacturing; commercial transportation; and services, trade and communications. These coefficients measure the proportion of the total real input into the sector that is of the specified form, whether capital services, labor services, energy, or intermediate materials.

The unit input requirement of energy into agriculture, nonfuel mining and construction is reduced by the policy measures by 4 percent in Policy 1 and by up to 27 percent in Policy 4. Energy and capital show a complementary relationship in this sector; when energy prices increase the use of capital input is reduced. Therefore capital input is reduced as part of the adjustment process, although this change is not large. The reduction in energy and capital inputs must be compensated by an increase in other inputs. Labor is the key input that provides this compensating increase. The input-output coefficient of labor rises from 0.2542 in the Base Case to 0.2722 in Policy 4, a sufficient rise to offset the move away from energy, capital and materials. Finally, the input of intermediate materials is reduced slightly as part of the adjustment process.

Table 13.4
Input patterns in nonenergy production 2000 (input-output coefficients for aggregate input categories)

	Base Case	Policy 1	Policy 2	Policy 3	Policy 4
Agriculture					
Capital	0.1946	0.1938	0.1932	0.1921	0.1900
Labor	0.2542	0.2575	0.2598	0.2661	0.2722
Energy	0.0242	0.0232	0.0225	0.0200	0.0176
Materials	0.5271	0.5255	0.5245	0.5218	0.5193
Manufacturing					
Capital	0.1194	0.1176	0.1161	0.1143	0.1131
Labor	0.2815	0.2845	0.2881	0.2963	0.3046
Energy	0.0235	0.0231	0.0226	0.0193	0.0179
Materials	0.5756	0.5748	0.5732	0.5701	0.5644
Transportation					
Capital	0.1971	0.1956	0.1939	0.1920	0.1888
Labor	0.4016	0.4031	0.4049	0.4076	0.4100
Energy	0.0384	0.0373	0.0361	0.0327	0.0298
Materials	0.3629	0.3640	0.3651	0.3677	0.3714
Services					
Capital	0.3389	0.3405	0.3418	0.3456	0.3493
Labor	0.3526	0.3585	0.3627	0.3738	0.3864
Energy	0.0186	0.0180	0.0175	0.0151	0.0131
Materials	0.2899	0.2830	0.2780	0.2655	0.2512

The manufacturing sector follows a similar pattern of adjustments between inputs. The use of energy per unit of output is significantly reduced. Also, energy and capital show a strong complementarity relationship. This means that a reduction in capital input is associated with the higher energy costs and with reduced energy input. In contrast, labor is a substitute for both capital and energy. Consequently, the more expensive energy and capital input mix is partially replaced by the now relatively less expensive input of labor services. Input of intermediate materials declines slightly. Overall, energy saving in manufacturing is achieved by a reduction in energy and capital use accompanied by an increase in labor input.

The nature of the energy-capital link can be complex. Some types of capital have a direct complementary relationship with energy in that the more capital is used, the more energy input is required. This is true for many types of motive power uses of energy and capital and for some types of process uses. In other instances, however, there is a substitution relationship between capital and energy; energy can be saved by the use of more capital equipment. For example, energy required per unit of output can often be reduced by the use of more sophisticated and more expensive capital. However, even this energy-capital substitution relationship is consistent with an overall appearance of complementarity between energy and capital. The reason for this operates through a separate input, labor, which is typically a substitute for both capital and energy. A rise in the price of energy gives rise to the following adjustments; energy use is reduced; capital input tends to be increased (energy-capital substitutability); labor input is increased (energy-labor substitutability); capital input tends to be decreased (labor-capital substitutability). There are, then, pressures to reduce and to increase capital use. In manufacturing, the net result is that a reduction in capital use accompanies the reduction in energy input.

Transportation shows a substantial decline in energy intensity as a result of the policy measures; for example the input coefficient for energy falls from 0.038 to 0.036, an 11 percent decline, between the Base Case and Policy 2. Complementarity between energy and capital leads to a reduction in the input of capital services; the capital input coefficient falls by 2 percent for Policy 2. Both labor and intermediate materials can substitute for energy and capital in transportation and the coefficients for these inputs in Policy 2, rise by 0.8 percent and 0.6 percent, respectively.

The services, trade, and communications sector responds somewhat differently from the other nonenergy producing sectors. The extent of the energy reduction, 6 percent in Policy 2, is comparable to that achieved in the other sectors but the manner in which this reduction is achieved is different. The principal difference is in the role of capital. In services the relationship between energy and capital is one of substitutability; higher energy costs and reduced energy input are associated with greater use of capital services. The reduction in energy input is, in part, secured by an increase in capital input. A central reason for the different energy-capital relationship in this sector lies in the type of use made of energy. In services, a great deal of energy is used for space heating and for air conditioning. Reduction in this use of energy can be achieved through improved design and insulation of structures and more sophisticated heating and cooling equipment. Each of these changes uses additional capital. In Policy 2, for example, the reduction in the energy input coefficient is associated with a 0.9 percent increase in the capital input coefficient. Labor can also be substituted for energy; in fact, the degree of substitution is greater than that between energy and capital, and the labor input coefficient is increased by 2.9 percent. The final set of inputs, nonenergy intermediate goods, are reduced substantially, the input coefficient in Policy 2 being 4 percent less than in the Base Case. In sum, the input restructuring in services is to move away from energy and other produced inputs towards capital and labor inputs.

The economy-wide pattern of capital, labor, energy, and materials inputs is determined jointly by the pattern of these inputs in each sector and by the relative size of each sector in the economy. Higher energy prices and nonprice restrictions on energy use result in a restructuring of input patterns away from energy, away from capital (except in services), and towards labor. In addition, the sectoral composition of output shifts away from energy, transportation and agriculture, and towards services. The overall effect of these changes is to substantially reduce the overall energy intensity of production; the average labor intensity increases; and the average capital intensity shows a very small increase.

The interrelationships between inputs can be formalized by means of the Allen partial elasticity of substitution. This elasticity indicates the changes in the relative quantities in which two inputs are used, caused a change in their relative prices. The elasticities, for each pair of inputs into each sector and evaluated at the 1971 data point, are shown in table 13.5. It should be noted that the model system does not use these elasticities explicitly, rather it incorporates models of producers' behavior, some of whose characteristics can be summarized in numerical terms by means of these elasticities. The numerical values of these elasticities can be interpreted as follows: a value of zero means that the two inputs are used in fixed proportions; a negative value means that there is a complementary relationship between the inputs, a rise in the price of one input is associated with reduced use of the second input; a positive value implies a substitution relationship, a rise in the price of one input leads to increased use of the other. Also, the greater the absolute value of the elasticity, the stronger the relationship or interaction between the inputs. The own elasticity of substitution will be negative; this simply implies that when the price of this input rises, demand for the input will decline.

In agriculture, nonfuel mining, and construction there is a reasonably strong substitution relationship between energy and labor, and a

Table 13.5
Interrelationships between inputs: Allen partial elasticities of substitution

	Capital	Labor	Energy	Intermediate materials
Agriculture, nonfuel mining, construction				
Capital	−1.7673			
Labor	0.3553	−2.5018		
Energy	−0.0591	1.4148	−29.6499	
Intermediate materials	0.6134	1.0442	0.5987	−0.8289
Manufacturing				
Capital	−3.1820			
Labor	1.1004	−1.6181		
Energy	−1.4156	1.8900	−4.8410	
Intermediate materials	0.0963	0.5072	−0.4732	−0.2435
Commercial transport				
Capital	−1.4036			
Labor	0.1755	−1.0920		
Energy	−0.8577	−0.0574	−11.5998	
Intermediate materials	0.5747	1.1309	1.7739	−1.7267
Services, trade, communications				
Capital	1.6979			
Labor	1.0903	−0.8795		
Energy	1.2110	2.3065	−49.3616	
Intermediate materials	0.0660	0.0440	−1.8201	−0.0245

substantial response of energy demand to energy price. In manufacturing, there are three strong interactions: energy and labor, and capital and labor are substitutes while energy and capital are complements. The commercial transportation sector exhibits complementarity between energy and capital and a significant own price elasticity of demand for energy. In the services, trade, and communications sector, there are four strong interdependencies: energy and capital, energy and labor, and capital and labor are substitutes while energy and intermediate materials ar complements. In addition, there is a high own price elasticity of demand for energy.

13.8 Composition of Total Output

Total output from each sector depends both on final demands and on purchases as inputs into other producing sectors. Final demand expenditure and the pattern of input purchases are each adjusted

Table 13.6
Sectoral real gross output in 2000

	Base Case	Policy 1	Policy 2	Policy 3	Policy 4
Composition of total gross output (%)					
Agriculture, nonfuel mining, construction	8.59	8.53	8.46	8.39	8.37
Manufacturing	35.93	35.88	35.84	36.05	35.98
Transportation	5.04	4.93	4.90	4.77	4.74
Services	45.67	46.09	46.48	47.43	47.76
Energy	4.77	4.56	4.31	3.35	3.16
Total	100.00	100.00	100.00	100.00	100.00
Total gross output, percent change from Base Case					
Agriculture, nonfuel mining, construction		−2.9	−5.0	−9.7	−15.0
Manufacturing		−2.0	−3.8	−7.3	−12.6
Transportation		−4.0	−6.3	−12.6	−17.9
Services		−1.0	−1.8	−4.1	−8.7
Energy		−6.2	−12.8	−35.1	−42.2
Total		−1.9	−3.6	−7.6	−12.7

away from energy-intensive products as a result of the higher energy prices and associated nonprice conservation measures. Therefore, total demand for the output of each sector changes, with output in general declining and with the output of energy-intensive products declining most substantially. The patterns of changes in real gross outputs are shown in table 13.6. Gross output in the economy declines as a result of the energy policy packages. In 2000, total real gross output in Policy 1 is 1.9 percent less than in the Base Case while in Policy 4 the reduction is 12.7 percent. The energy sector is most affected, with its output, in constant dollar terms, declining by 6.2 percent in Policy 1 and by 42.2 percent under Policy 4. The next largest decline is in output from the transportation industry, the decline being 4.0 percent and 17.9 percent in Policies 1 and 4, respectively. Output from the agriculture, nonfuel mining and construction sector is also reduced, by 2.6 percent for Policy 1 and 15.0 percent for Policy 4. The manufacturing sector maintains its relative size in the economy; the reduction in the output of manufactured goods is almost identical to the overall reduction in economic output. Output from service, trade, and communications activity is reduced by less than average. The reduction in the output is only 1.0 percent in Policy 1 and 8.7 percent in Policy 4. Service types of activities therefore assume a greater importance within the overall productive structure of the economy.

These sectoral changes are closely related to the energy intensity of production. The largest reductions in output occur in those industries which are most energy-intensive. The smallest reductions occur in sectors, particularly services, that use relatively little energy per unit of output. The result is a shift of production towards those industries whose output is relatively nonenergy intensive. The average energy content of production is therefore reduced; the energy required per dollar of output from the economy is reduced under these new economic structures relative to the energy requirement in Base Case conditions.

13.9   Dynamic Adjustments Through Investment

The above analysis has focused on adjustments to spending and input patterns that were essentially substitution responses to changes in relative prices. These are the principal means by which the economy adjusts to a less energy-intensive structure. However, another very significant, and related, set of effects is through investment and the capital stock. Higher energy prices lead to a reduction in capital income and to a reduced rate of return on capital. Part of this reduction in the rate of return is related to the energy-capital complementarity observed in some sectors. Additional investment in energy conserving capital, particularly where it is forced by direct regulation and mandatory performance standards, can have low total productivity and can accentuate the decline in yield on capital. Lower rates of return lead directly to reduced saving and investment in the private economy. In addition, the income reductions due to the substitution adjustments considered above lead to further cutbacks in the volumes of private saving and investment. Thus, private investment is reduced below Base Case levels. This directly results in a slowing of the rate of growth of capital stock. In fact, the growth paths of capital stock under the energy policy measures are projected to be permanently below the Base Case growth path.

The significance of these reductions in investment and the capital stock is that one of the principal inputs into production, capital services, is reduced. Reduced investment and capital means that the productive capacity of the economy is reduced, relative to the Base Case, throughout the forecast period. Further, this lowering of productive

Table 13.7
Investment and capital stock

	1985	1990	2000
Investment, percent change from Base Case			
Policy 1	−0.4	−1.0	−1.6
Policy 2	−1.4	−3.0	−4.9
Policy 3	−1.8	−5.2	−10.5
Policy 4	−2.4	−6.7	−16.3
Capital Stock, percent change from Base Case			
Policy 1	−0.17	−0.47	−1.17
Policy 2	−0.49	−1.27	−3.03
Policy 3	−0.63	−1.85	−7.00
Policy 4	−0.81	−2.40	−10.75

potential becomes progressively greater over time. This capital reduction or dynamic effect is a fundamental mechanism through which the shift to a less energy-intensive configuration of spending and production can lead to slower growth and can impose output and income loss on the economy.

The magnitudes of the investment and capital effects are shown in table 13.7. Investment rises over time under the energy policies as well as in the Base Case, but the rate of growth of investment is less under the policy measures. The relative reduction in investment levels is not large—by 2000 it is 1.6 percent for Policy 1 and 4.9 percent for Policy 2—but the cumulative impact on the level of capital stock is significant. Under Policy 2 conditions, the level of capital stock in 1990 is 1.3 percent below the Base Case and by 2000 it is 3.0 percent below. This slowing in the rate of growth of capital directly implies that the productive potential of the economy grows less rapidly than in the Base Case.

13.10   Aggregate Economic Cost of Energy Reductions

Two types of adjustments of the economy to changes in energy conditions have been analyzed. The first involves the restructuring of production and spending patterns away from energy and energy-intensive inputs and production. The second adjustment operates through changes in savings and investment, and results in a slower growth of capital and aggregate productive capacity. Both of these adjustment mechanisms impose costs on the economy.[10] From an aggregate point of view, these costs take the form of a reduction in the volume of a final output that can be obtained from the economy, compared to that possible under Base Case conditions.

The substitution of labor, capital and nonenergy goods and services for energy input into production is not perfect; some output is lost as a result of the restrictions. In other words, additional labor and other inputs can help to compensate for less energy input but some reduction in net output is still probable. Also, additional labor and other inputs used to replace energy must be obtained from other uses, thus reducing the total volume of potential output. These same adjustments can be viewed in terms of factor productivities. The process of reducing intensity of energy use involves increasing the intensity of labor use and in some cases, capital use. The input-output coefficients for labor and, in an aggregate sense, capital increase. Thus, more labor and capital are used per unit of output. This is equivalent to saying that the average productivities of labor and of capital are reduced as a result of the energy adjustments. At any time these inputs are limited in supply, so reduction in their average productivities translates directly into reduction in the potential output of the economy. Real GNP declines, or its growth rate slows, as a result of the substitution away from energy input into production.

The dynamic costs of energy reduction follow in part from these substitution costs and in part from separate mechanisms. The reduction in output and income as a result of the substitution processes leads directly to a reduction in the aggregate level of saving and investment. In addition, the rate of return on capital can fall as a result of the higher energy prices and the greater input of capital per unit of output in the economy a a whole. A decline in rates of return leads to further reductions in saving and investment. Therefore, capital growth under the energy policies is lower than in the Base Case. This corresponds directly to a slowing of the growth of the productive capacity. At any point in time, this involves a lower real GNP than under Base Case conditions, compounding the economic cost caused by the substitution process.

The magnitudes of the economic costs of restrictive energy policies are shown in table 13.8 in terms of real GNP. For each of the four policy packages, real GNP is less than in the Base Case. Further, the reduction is larger, the more restrictive the policy measures. Also, the reduction under each policy becomes larger over time in both absolute and relative magnitude. For Policy 1, the economic cost in 1985 is 0.6

Table 13.8
GNP effects of energy policies

	1985	1990	2000
Change in real GNP from Base Case, $(1972) bn			
Policy 1	−10.6	−24.0	−41.9
Policy 2	−29.9	−53.5	−86.8
Policy 3	−36.9	−79.6	−197.1
Policy 4	−48.4	−107.3	−324.7
Change in real GNP from Base Case, percent			
Policy 1	−0.60	−1.18	−1.54
Policy 2	−1.69	−2.64	−3.19
Policy 3	−2.08	−3.91	−7.24
Policy 4	−2.73	−5.27	−11.93
Growth in real GNP (average percent per annum)			
Base Case	3.65	2.82	2.94
Policy 1	3.58	2.70	2.90
Policy 2	3.43	2.63	2.88
Policy 3	3.38	2.44	2.58
Policy 4	3.30	2.28	2.19

percent of real GNP while in 2000 the cost rises to 1.5 percent of GNP. Under Policy 4 the cost is 2.7 percent of GNP in 1985 rising to 11.9 percent in 2000. Economic growth is reduced under each policy but positive growth continues in all cases. For example, Policy 1 reduces the annual rate of economic growth by about 0.1 percentage points.

These economic costs are substantial. One way to calculate the overall cost is to find the present value of the real GNP loss over the entire 1977 to 2000 period. These present values (as at 1977 using a 5 percent discount rate) are $148(1972)bn for Policy 1, $350(1972)bn for Policy 2, $615(1972)bn for Policy 3, and $919(1972)bn for Policy 4. To place these in perspective it can be noted that U.S. real GNP in 1977 was about $1330(1972)bn. Thus, although energy reductions can be achieved, they do involve a substantial real cost in loss of potential income and output.

The GNP loss from energy policies can be separated into a part resulting from the substitution cost and a part resulting from the dynamic or capital cost. This separation is only approximate, since both costs arise from interdependent adjustment processes, but it does indicate the relative magnitudes of these two cost components. The GNP loss resulting from reduced capital input is calculated by using a result from the macroeconomic theory of growth which states that, if

Table 13.9
Substitution and dynamic effects in GNP reduction

	1985	1990	2000
Change in real GNP, percent change from Base Case			
Policy 1	−0.60	−1.18	−1.54
Policy 2	−1.69	−2.64	−3.19
Policy 3	−2.08	−3.91	−7.24
Policy 4	−2.73	−5.27	−11.93
Dynamic effect, change in real GNP due to capital reduction (percentage points)			
Policy 1	−0.05	−0.14	−0.35
Policy 2	−0.15	−0.38	−0.91
Policy 3	−0.19	−0.56	−2.10
Policy 4	−0.24	−0.72	−3.23
Change in real GNP due to substitution effects (percentage points)			
Policy 1	−0.55	−1.04	−1.19
Policy 2	−1.54	−2.26	−2.28
Policy 3	−1.89	−3.35	−5.14
Policy 4	−2.49	−4.55	−8.70
Proportion of real GNP change due to substitution effects (%)			
Policy 1	92	88	77
Policy 2	91	86	71
Policy 3	91	86	71
Policy 4	91	86	73

factor inputs are paid at rates equal to the value of their marginal products, a one percent change in capital input leads to an S_k percent change in real GNP, where S_k is the share of capital income in national income. This income share in the projections is approximately 0.35. The relative GNP loss arising from the dynamic adjustment mechanism is indicated by 0.35 multiplied by the percentage reduction in capital stock relative to the Base Case. The remaining GNP loss is attributed to the substitution effects of moving towards less energy intensive input patterns. Table 13.9 shows the separation of real GNP loss into substitution and dynamic effects. The greater part of the loss arises from the substitution effect. Thus, in Policy 2 in 1985, the 1.69 percent real GNP reduction comprises a 1.54 percent decline due to substitution effects and a 0.15 percent decline due to dynamic effects; over 90 percent of the reduction is due to substitution effects. Over time, however, the dynamic effect increases in relative importance. By 2000, the 3.19 percent GNP reduction in Policy 2 comprises a 2.28 percent substitution cost and a 0.91 percent dynamic cost; only 70 percent of the loss is now due to substitution effects. The cumulative and durable nature of capital means that the relative importance of the dynamic changes further increase in the more distant future.

13.11 Summary and Conclusion

Analysis of each of the four energy packages suggests that substantial reductions, relative to the Base Case, can be achieved in the volume of energy use. These reductions occur as a result of adjustments in the pattern of energy use and in the structure of economic activity. However, a consequence of these adjustments is a reduction in the level of real GNP relative to the Base Case. For example, real GNP in 2000 for Policy 2 is predicted to be 3.2 percent or $87(1972)bn below the Base Case while the loss in real GNP in Policy 4 is 11.9 percent or $325(1972)bn. Alternatively, the effects may be viewed in terms of growth rates—the growth of energy use can be slowed but at the cost of some decrease in the rate of aggregate economic growth. For example, the policies can reduce average annual real GNP growth rates by up to 0.7 percentage points. There is, then, predicted to be a significant economic effect and economic cost as a result of energy conservation policies.

However, a significant result of the analysis is that the economic impact as measured by the loss in real GNP is relatively less than the reduction in energy use. Adjustments in the pattern of energy use and of economic activity permit the energy intensity of spending and production to be reduced. This reduces the average energy content of each dollar of economic activity. Conversely, it means that the decline in real GNP caused by energy policy is less than the proportionate decline in energy use. Table 13.10 summarizes the relationship between the decline in real GNP and the reduction in energy input. On average, each percentage point reduction in energy input leads to only a 0.2 percentage point reduction in real GNP. Thus, in Policy 2 in 2000 for example, the 16 percent reduction in energy input is associated with a substantial improvement in the aggregate economic efficiency of energy use and requires only a 3 percent reduction in the total output of the economy. The relative economic cost of energy reduction becomes greater as the strength of the policy measures increases, since energy saving becomes progressively more difficult

Table 13.10
Aggregate relationship between energy input and real GNP (ratio of
percentage change in real GNP to percentage change in primary energy input,
changes relative to the Base Case)

	1985	1990	2000
Policy 1	0.18	0.18	0.18
Policy 2	0.19	0.19	0.20
Policy 3	0.19	0.20	0.21
Policy 4	0.20	0.21	0.24

and costly. Also, the relative cost increases over time, due to the
investment and capital reductions caused by restrictive energy policies.

This chapter has focused on the economic adjustment mechanisms
that provide the flexibility in energy use underlying the result that
energy reductions can be achieved with less than proportionate reductions in the level or growth of economic output. In particular, two features of this energy-economy relationship have been analyzed. The
first covers the nature of the adjustment mechanisms and the reasons
for partial rather than total flexibility in the relationship between
energy input and economic output. The second covers the reasons for
the variation in this relationship, particularly the increasing economic
impact over time of energy reductions.

Our empirical finding that there is a reasonable degree of flexibility
in the energy-economy relationship is highly significant. From a policy point of view it suggests that it is possible to implement energy
policies designed to restrict energy growth without having to suffer
comparably large economic costs in terms of reduced GNP and slower
economic growth. This makes it possible to contemplate restrictive
energy policies designed to reduce petroleum imports. At the same
time there is an economic cost associated with such policies. Only if
policy-makers judge this cost to be less than the benefits obtained
from promoting energy related objectives are the measures justified.
From a forecasting point of view, the finding provides important information for assessing the likely economic impacts of increases in
energy prices, whether due to government policy, to increasing relative scarcity of resources, or to external influence.

Notes

1. The original form of this model was presented in a report to the Energy Policy Project of the Ford Foundation, see Hudson and Jorgenson (1973, 1974a). The model has subsequently been revised and extended. A comprehensive description of the current version of the model is given in Hudson and Jorgenson (1977).

2. Annual inter-industry accounts for the United States for the period 1947 to 1971 have been prepared by Jack Faucett Associates (1973). These accounts, on the same sectoral basis as the LITM system, give transactions in both current dollar and constant dollar terms.

3. The model of production is also described in Berndt and Jorgenson (1973), and in Christensen, Jorgenson and Lau (1973). A related application of the production model for the manufacturing sector is given in Berndt and Wood (1975).

4. The econometric model of consumption is described in Jorgenson (1977). The theory of this model is also developed in Christensen, Jorgenson and Lau (1975), and in Jorgenson and Lau (1975).

5. The Brookhaven optimization models are described by Hoffman (1973), Hoffman and Cherniavsky (1974), and Cherniavsky (1975).

6. The References Energy System is described in Beller *et al.* (1975).

7. The integration of the LITM system with the TESOM framework is discussed in detail by Hoffman and Jorgenson (1977). An application of the integrated framework is given in Behling, Dullien and Hudson (1976).

8. A theoretical treatment of the dynamic adjustment process, in the context of a macroeconomic growth model, is given by Hogan (1977a).

9. The impact of energy policy on future U.S. economic growth, and the types of economic adjustments resulting from energy policy, are considered in Hudson and Jorgenson (1978a).

10. A detailed analysis of the reduction in productivity, capital, and real GNP resulting from higher energy prices (in this case the 1973 and subsequent rises in world oil prices) is given in Hudson and Jorgenson (1978b).

14

The Impact of Restrictions on the Expansion of Electric Generating Capacity

Edward A. Hudson,
Dale W. Jorgenson, and
David C. O'Connor

14.1 Introduction

14.1.1 The General Setting

Operating companies in the electric power industry must function within a complex environment of regulations, prices and technical constraints. Licensing requirements, emission regulations, tax laws, input prices, electricity price regulations, capital costs, interest rates, fuel prices fuel-use regulations and technical aspects of generation transmission and distribution are some of these external conditions. Within these constraints utilities must develop policies, defined over those variables that are under their direct control, to promote service and corporate objectives. Any change in these external conditions may lead to a change in the utilities' own decisions and will affect the overall performance of the electric power industry.

Changes initially involving the electric power industry can also have a marked effect on the entire energy system. Any changes in the price and availability of electricity will alter the competitive relation between electricity and other fuels and can lead to shifts in the market share of each fuel. Equally important, any redirection of demand for fuels as an input to electricity generation will directly affect the pattern of demand for energy resources. For example, shifts in base-load generation from nuclear to coal or to petroleum would cause a massive adjustment in the markets for nuclear fuel, coal and oil. Thus, changes in the electric power industry can have profound impacts on the energy system both in terms of delivered energy patterns and in terms of energy resource use.

Finally, changes in the energy sector can lead to adjustments and impacts throughout the economy. Changes in the quantity of electricity generated and in investment in capacity additions will lead to adjustments in the quantities of fuel, labor, materials, construction services and equipment absorbed into the energy system. These demand changes affect the prices and availability of capital, labor and other inputs to the rest of the economy. In addition, changes in the price and availability of electricity can affect the costs and the choice of inputs selected by producers and the expenditure patterns of consumers throughout the economy. The cost impacts in turn affect inflation, the changes in input and purchase patterns affect productivity and so incomes and production. In short, the level, structure and growth of economic activity can be impacted by changes in the conditions affecting the electric power industry.

There is, then, a complex set of interconnections linking the electric power industry, the energy system and the economy. Developments in the electric power industry not only affect the industry but also the energy and economic systems. Policies directed at or changes initially involving the electric power industry cannot be appraised only in terms of industry impacts—to do so would miss these potentially significant energy and economic impacts.

This study focuses on three sets of external constraints within which the electric power industry must operate—capacity expansion costs, capital costs and fuel costs. These constraints encompass the variables affecting the electric power industry that are subject to the greatest uncertainty. The remaining variables are subject to somewhat less uncertainty—operating the maintenance costs are closely correlated with labor and other prices in the economy and can be predicted reasonably well; electricity prices are set by regulatory agencies using established and generally predictable procedures. By contrast, government policy measures related to environmental, safety or energy policy goals, new cartel action on the part of energy suppliers, or market responses to changing energy resource and demand conditions are all possible, even likely, and each could result in major changes in the conditions facing electric utilities concerning capacity expansion and operations.

14.1.2   Capacity Expansion

Until a decade ago, utilities had considerable latitude in their capacity expansion decisions. This latitude applied to the timing of expansion, the type of fuel and generating technology to be used and, to a lesser extent, to the location of the new plants. However, utilities' discretionary powers in these areas have become increasingly circumscribed, primarily through government action. The area in which government action has most severely constrained utilities' planning is in the choice of fuel and generating technology. Public and political pressure has focused on these areas, through both regulatory and legislative processes, and has had major impacts on the planning decisions and actual policies of electric utilities.

Safety and environmental concerns have motivated most of the restrictions on capacity expansion. The use of oil has been restricted because of concern about sulfates in generating station emissions. Use of coal has been subject to restrictions based on the particulate and sulfate content of its emissions, although frequently these restrictions have been satisfied by equipment retrofits or add-ons. Nuclear energy has also been subject to significant restrictions based on arguments ranging from operating safety to spent fuel disposal and to heat discharge. These restrictions have frequently taken the form of delays in construction and changes in design, both of which add to costs, but on some occasions have taken the form of outright prohibition. Some states already have enacted legislation or have adopted regulations that amount to a ban on construction of nuclear facilities.

Another source of regulations about capacity use options and capacity expansion has been government energy policy. Recent policies have been concerned with altering the overall mix of fuel used in the United States. As part of government policy to reduce demand for oil and gas, use of oil and gas by utilities for steam generation is now severely restricted and the construction of new oil-steam or gas-steam generating plants is not possible. Recent government policy proposals have included measures designed to force utilities still further into coal use and away from oil and gas.

14.1.3   Capital Costs

Capital costs of new generating capacity have risen sharply in recent years. Part of this increase has been due to inflation but there has still been a large increase in costs even after inflation had been allowed for. Part of the cost increases have been due to the rise, relative to the general level of prices, in costs of equipment and construction. However, a large part of the cost increases can be attributed to government regulations. A whole set of new regulations has come into force concerning emission reductions in fossil-fueled plants and safety aspects of nuclear plants; these regulations have necessitated extensive new capital equipment as standard features of new generating plants and this has resulted in large increases in capacity costs.

An extensive set of regulations is already in force concerning the physical and chemical emissions from fossil-fueled plants. These requirements have, for example, led to the widespread use of stack gas scrubbers and fuel gas desulfurization equipment, equipment that has added greatly to capital costs. Additional safety features on nuclear stations has similarly increased the capital costs of these stations. There is a real possibility that emission and safety standards will continue to be tightened, leading, in all probability, to further increases in capital costs. For example, requirements that best available emission control technology be used or that tighter safety standards be applied to nuclear operation and nuclear fuel storage would lead to further rises in plant costs.

Licensing procedures for new generating plants are designed to consider representations by all interested parties. While this review process provides a framework for the evaluation of all points of view it can also result in long periods of time being required before the license decision is actually made. These delays can result in considerable additions to the total costs of new plants. A related source of cost increase is the need to change the nature of capital equipment, even after design or construction has started. This need might be based on stipulations by licensing authorities, by the necessity of conforming to court decisions, or by the requirement of satisfying new government regulations about the fuel, environmental and safety aspects of generation. Whatever the source, modifications are expensive at the design stage and still more expensive during the construction phase.

In sum, there are many reasons underlying the rise in capital costs in the past; the mechanisms, institutions and forces underlying each reason continue to exist and provide the potential for continued cost increase in the future.

14.1.4   Fuel Prices

The 1970s have seen large increases in energy resource prices. The most striking increase has been in the price of crude petroleum which, as a result of cartel action by the members of the Organization of Petroleum Exporting Countries (OPEC), rose by several hundred percent. These oil price increases induced, through the operation of the energy market, substantial increases in the prices of substitute fuels, particularly coal, gas and nuclear fuel. These price rises have been compounded by separate forces. Legislated changes affecting safety, reclamation and other aspects of coal mining has resulted in substantial increases in the costs and prices of coal. Partial deregulation of prices has raised natural gas and petroleum prices. A cartel-like operation by suppliers of uranium fuel has added to the upward pressure on prices of this energy source.

Similar kinds of forces could result in large increases in future energy prices. The conditions permitting the rapid increases in world oil prices still exist—the price elasticity of demand for oil is less than one so OPEC can increase its revenue by raising prices. The suppliers' cartel has remained cohesive, permitting OPEC to raise the oil price almost at will. Given this continuing power over prices and the existence of possible motivating factors to use it (whether the desire for additional revenue or the wish to exert political pressure on the western nations) the possibility of continuing oil price increases remains very real.

Policies within the United States can also force the fuel prices upward. Decontrol of oil prices, and of natural gas prices, will result in further price increases for these fuels. Government policy measures to reduce oil imports through promotion of synthetic fuels, tariffs on imported oil, or taxes on petroleum could add to these price pressures. Supply bottlenecks, for example, in the transportation system, could further increase the delivered price of coal. On top of these is the impact of resource depletion—particularly in oil and gas, depletion of low-cost domestic supplies may further raise the price of domestically produced petroleum and natural gas. In addition, the interaction between substitute fuels within the energy market will create spillover effects between fuel prices with a large rise in the price of any one fuel inducing upward adjustments in the prices of the remaining fuels.

For each of these reasons there is uncertainty about future trends in fuel prices. This uncertainty, however, appears to be mainly in one direction, about how rapidly prices will rise; the probability of prices moving in a downward direction is low. Therefore, electric utilities, and all energy users, are likely to face any one of many combinations of prices for their oil, gas, coal and nuclear fuel purchasers, each combination involving higher prices than today.

14.1.5   Purpose of the Analysis

This review has outlined three groups of external conditions that are of major relevance to the electric power industry. These areas are restrictions on capacity expansion, increases in capacity costs, and increases in fuel costs. These variables are of concern based on two criteria: they can have a major impact on the electric power industry, as well as the energy and economic systems; and there is considerable uncertainty characterizing future developments in these areas, including a significant probability that restrictions will become more stringent and that costs will increase. Therefore, each of these sets of variables assumes great importance in strategic planning in the electric power industry.

The first question addressed in this study concerns the impact on the electric power industry of capacity restrictions, higher capital costs, and higher fuel prices. For strategic planning in the industry it is essential to have estimates of the likely range of uncertainty and the relative impacts of changes in the external environment faced by the industry. For each of the sources of uncertainty, a range of variation is defined and the effects of changes over this range, alone or in combination with other changes, are estimated. The resulting estimates help to identify the strategic variables from the point of view of the industry and indicate the sensitivity of each variable to the capacity, capital cost, and fuel price changes.

A second set of issues centers on the broad impacts of government policy and of other changes external to the electric power industry. The analysis will trace out the effects of alternative government policies and other changes in the industry's environment on the industry itself, the energy system as a whole, and the U.S. economy. Government policies affecting the industry have impacts on the energy system and the economy that go far beyond the electric power industry. Restrictions on generating capacity, higher capital costs, and higher fuel costs affect the level and growth of income and production in the U.S. economy. Policy measures are frequently motivated by environmental, safety, and national security objectives. The benefits of these measures can be considered in conjunction with the associated costs. The availability of estimates of economic costs helps provide a sound basis for a full evaluation of the benefits and costs of alternative policies.

14.1.6   Methodology

The effects of capacity restrictions, higher capital costs and higher fuel costs are examined by means of simulations of an electricity-energy-economy model system. The analyses all start from a Reference Case set of electricity, energy and economic projections. This Reference Case incorporates current energy conditions, legislation and regulations and is intended as a possible outcome of energy and economic developments. The Reference projection is constructed using an electricity-energy-economy model system to incorporate the details and interactions in a consistent manner. Next, the capacity and cost changes are introduced into the model system and new projections obtained. The differences in assumptions between the Reference Case and the alternative model solutions are the known changes introduced into the assumption set. Therefore, the projected differences in electric power industry, energy and economic performance between the Reference and alternative projections can be attributed entirely to the specified changes in the underlying energy conditions.

The model system used for these analyses is the Long-term Inter-industry Transactions Model developed by Edward A. Hudson and Dale W. Jorgenson[1] combined with the regionalized Electricity Model of the electric power industry constructed by Martin L. Baughman and Paul J. Joskow.[2] The two models have been linked into a single program and are run simultaneously in the development of these projections.[3]

The Baughman-Joskow electricity model[4] has several principal components for each of the nine geographic regions for which it is specified.

a. Pricing is determined by an algorithm which takes account of regulatory practices in setting electricity prices allowing for the rate base and an allowed rate of return;

b. demand for electricity is estimated for each region; both the level and the shape of the load curve are explicitly identified;

c. existing capacity is used to meet this demand with existing capacity being dispatched to satisfy the load curve in a cost minimizing fashion;

d. demand trends are projected over a planning period; any capacity expansion required to satisfy this demand is translated into new investment of a type determined by cost considerations and by the length of time required until commissioning;

e. financial calculations take account of fuel costs, operating and maintenance costs, capital costs, investment outlays, and revenues in estimating the rate base and net income variables.

The Hudson-Jorgenson model covers the energy and economic systems.[5] Its features include:

a. Separation of production activities into six energy and four nonenergy sectors; the electric power industry is one of the energy sectors, the nonenergy sectors are agriculture and construction, manufacturing, transportation and services;

b. each producing sector is modeled in terms of output pricing and in terms of determining input patterns (input-output coefficients) in a cost-minimizing fashion given prevailing prices and subject to technical constraints on input adjustments;

c. the household sector is modeling in terms of the labor supply choice, the consumption-saving choice and the allocation of consumption spending over the different types of of goods and services;

d. industry output levels are determined on the basis of final plus intermediate demand subject to the production constraints imposed by capital and labor availability and productivity;

e. investment is constrained by private, government and foreign saving; growth in productivity capacity over time occurs through capital accumulation by investment, labor force growth and productivity change.

The electricity supply sector of this model is represented by the Baughman-Joskow model. The principal linkages are that electricity prices, as well as input requirements in the electric power industry, are calculated in the Baughman-Joskow model and inserted into the Hudson-Jorgenson system, while the U.S. demand for electricity, together with input prices, are calculated by Hudson-Jorgenson and introduced into Baughman-Joskow. The two models are solved iteratively until a consistent solution is obtained.[6]

This model system integrates detailed operating and investment aspects of the electric power industry into a consistent representation of the energy system and the economy. Thus competition and substitution between electricity, petroleum, gas and coal fuels is explicitly modeled as part of the delivered energy system[7] while demands originating in the electric power industry for coal, oil, gas and other fuel inputs are modeled as part of the primary energy system. Interaction, in most cases substitution but in some case complementarity, between energy and other inputs into production in the nonenergy sectors of the economy is explicitly treated; for example, as energy prices increase there will be partial replacement of energy as an input to production by capital, labor and other materials. Similarly, in consumer demand, there is interaction between energy and other goods and services as the prices and availabilities of fuels change.[8]

Electricity and energy changes affect the economy by leading to changes in producers' and consumers' demand patterns, hence to changes in industry output levels and to adjustments in capital and labor productivity. These can alter real output and incomes in the initial year and will also, particularly through changes in investment, capital growth and productivity, involve permanent impacts on the course and rate of economic growth in subsequent years. In sum, the integrated model system provides a consistent and comprehensive framework for the analysis of changes in energy conditions in terms of their impacts, both initially and over time, on the electric power industry, the energy system and the economy.

14.2   Reference Case Economy, Energy and Electricity Projections

14.2.1   Objectives

The Reference Case has two functions. First, it is intended to provide a meaningful projection in the sense of a feasible path of energy and economic growth that could emerge, given the existing structure of the economy and given present trends in energy and economic policies and conditions. It must be recognized that any projection is subject to error. Further, this Case is not intended as a representation of the most likely path of energy and economic growth. The second purpose of the projection is to serve as a reference point against which to estimate the effects of changes in policies and conditions. For such estimates, the critical information is the difference, between the Reference Case and alternative forecasts of the energy and economic systems, resulting from changes in the assumptions concerning energy conditions. Thus, the changes between projections, rather than the absolute magnitudes of the projections, are of central concern. In this case, many of the errors in the absolute magnitudes of projected variables can be expected to cancel out. The resulting information on changes depends very much on the structure of the model system and the interactions incorporated within the system. A feature of both economic and electricity models, and of the integration, is their incorporation of a complex set of interdependencies and feedbacks in explicitly analyzing the structure of the energy and economic systems. Therefore, the projected differences between Base Case and alternative projections should give a meaningful representation of the impacts of energy and policy changes.

14.2.2   Assumptions

A Reference Case is a projection of one feasible development path for the U.S. energy system and economy over the remainder of the century. The Reference Case is based largely on the continuation of existing trends and policies, incorporating also future trends in energy policies that are embodied in legislation. Energy supply possibilities are incorporated on a basis consistent with present expectations about the future availability and prices of energy resources; these expectations embody a steady upward trend in real energy prices.

The principal assumptions entering the Reference Case are as follows:

1. *General*

1.1. Fertility rates remain at recent levels corresponding to a fertility rate of 2.1; population growth follows Bureau of the Census, Population Projection Series II.[9]

1.2. Labor supply and participation rate patterns continue to exhibit behavior similar to that observed in the past; these labor supply features are econometrically modeled on the basis of observed behavior.

1.3. The current structure of government tax and expenditure programs continues; real government purchases increase approximately in line with real GNP.

1.4. While imports into the United States are computed endogenously within the model, a balance of trade constraint is imposed; this requires that the value of exports grows to sustain the projected imports. Adjustment of the value of the U.S. dollar is the mechanism for securing these changes.

1.5. Cyclical fluctuations in growth and employment are incorporated into the projection out to 1985. After 1985, the assumption of steady high employment is made. The implicit assumption is that government policies for management of the aggregate economy maintain this level of steady high employment. This assumption is made for analytical convenience, it is not intended to be a realistic representation of government policy. Since long-term cycles cannot accurately be forecast and since it is the trend rather than the cycle that is important for the forecast, attention is focused on the analysis of the trend growth path.

1.6. The future course of price inflation is exogenous to the model; the central calculations within the model are based on relative prices and on real or constant dollar magnitudes. To permit variables to be expressed in current dollars an inflation estimate is needed. It is assumed that inflation averages 7 percent annually until 1985, then 5 percent annually after 1985.

2. *Energy*

2.1. Coal supply can be significantly expanded without major increases in prices. Cost increases in coal extraction lead to some increase in real coal prices; this increase occurs at the rate of 2.5 percent annually.

2.2. U.S. oil production shows some response to higher prices but most additional oil supply is obtained from imports; the world price of oil in real terms rises steadily. The average price of crude petroleum available in the United States is assumed to increase at 2.5 percent annually.

2.3. U.S. natural gas production remains at approximately current levels. Gas price regulation is removed and gas prices then rise in line with oil prices at a 2.5 percent annual rate in real terms.

2.4. Uranium supply possibilities are based on the EPRI Technical Assessment Guide (1977) and on the EPRI Supply 77 (1977) publication: average prices of uranium (U $_3$O$_8$) rise from $(1977)24 per pound in 1977 to $(1977)41 per pound in 2000.

3. *Electricity*

3.1. Heat rates for generation from some types of new plants decline over time; the heat rates (in thousand Btu per kilowatt-hour) for 1977 and 2000 are 10.0 and 9.5 for coal steam, oil steam, gas steam and hydro, 15.0 and 12.5 for combustion turbines and other peaking plants, and a constant 10.5 for nuclear generation.

3.2. Usage factors for each type of plant are subject to maxima. These ceilings are, in percent:

Coal	77	
Oil steam	85	
Gas steam	85	
Nuclear	58	(rising to 66 by 1985)
Turbines, peaking	85	
Hydro	47	average (hydro differs between regions)

It can be noted that these are technical maxima; allowing for generation economics means that some of these ceilings, in particular for oil steam, gas steam and combustion turbines, will seldom be reached.

3.3. The nine regions specified in the model are: New England, Middle Atlantic, East North Central, West North Central, South Atlantic, East South Central, West South Central, Mountain and Pacific.

3.4. Fuel prices follow from the energy assumptions and the representations of the energy sector and the transportation system within the model.

3.5. Capital costs for generation, transmission and distribution remain unchanged, in constant dollar terms at the levels given in the EPRI Technical Assessment Guide (1977) and in the EPRI publication Supply 77 (1977). Government regulations on plants, including those concerning emission controls, remain as those in force or enacted into legislation in 1977.

3.6. Operating and maintenance costs increase in real terms of 0.5 percent annually, i.e., at 0.5 percent more rapidly than general inflation.

3.7. Electricity price setting is performed within the established regulatory framework; price setting procedures follow established patterns.

3.8. No restrictions on nuclear power expansion are introduced in the Reference Case (although there are severe restrictions in the alternative projections). This means that electric utility investment decisions regarding nuclear plants can be made on the basis of utility economics and are not constrained by regulatory factors.

14.2.3   Summary of the Economic Projections

The Reference projections for the U.S. economy are summarized in table 14.1, which gives the principal indicators of economic performance for the years 1977, 1985, 1990, and 2000.[10] Both energy and economic growth rates are projected to be positive but less rapid than historical trends. Over the 1977 to 2000 period, real GNP growth averages 3.1% per annum (compared to the 3.5% for the 1950–1973 period).

Part of the reason for the slower rate of future economic growth involves the slowing of labor force expansion. This, in turn, reflects the high birth rates of the 1950s and 1960s followed by the low birth rates of the 1970s. The labor force grows rapidly until the mid 1980s when its expansion slows to less than 1% per annum. Another major reason for slower economic growth involves productivity—output per person employed, or gross labor productivity, grows much less rapidly than in the past: at 1.7% per annum compared to an average annual growth of 2.1% between 1950 and 1973. This productivity change is due to several factors, three of which are explicitly incorporated in the model and the projections. First, increasingly expensive energy induces some substitution of other factors, particularly capital and labor, for energy as an input to production. Increased intensity of capital and labor input per unit of output corresponds to decreased productivity of capital and labor. Thus, the rate of productivity growth is slower than would otherwise have occurred. Second, there is some change in the composition of spending, for example with services becoming relatively more important. As productivity growth in services tends to be slower than in other industries, overall productivity advance slows. Third, there is some slowing in investment growth which slows the growth of capital, in turn reducing the growth in gross labor productivity and output.

The declining energy intensity of the economy reflects several forces, in particular steadily rising energy prices and changes in economic structure. Real energy prices in the Reference Case are projected to rise at an average annual rate of 2.2% (a reversal of the -1.8% annual change observed between 1950 and 1973). These price rises induce shifts of spending and production inputs away from energy and energy-intensive products. The evolving pattern of economic activity accentuates this trend—spending and production are projected to shift towards communications, trade and services which are

Table 14.1
Reference projection of economic growth, 1977–2000

	1977	1985	1990	2000
Real GNP[a]	1340.5	1810.2	2095.4	2725.7
Real GNP *per capita*[b]	6.19	7.77	8.61	10.47
Energy input[c]	75.8	97.4	112.0	139.5
Energy: GNP ratio[d]	56.5	53.8	53.5	51.2
Unemployment rate	7.0	5.0	4.8	4.8
Employment[e]	90.5	107.0	114.9	125.8
Population[f]	216.7	232.9	243.5	260.4
Rate of growth (average percent per annum)[g]				
Employment	1.6	2.1	1.4	0.9
Gross labor productivity[h]	2.1	1.7	1.5	1.7
Real GNP	3.7	3.8	3.0	2.7
Real GNL *per capita*	2.3	2.9	2.1	2.0
Energy input	3.5	3.2	2.8	2.2
GNP price deflator	3.0	7.0	5.0	5.0

[a] Real GNP in billions of 1972 dollars
[b] Real GNP *per capita* in thousands of 1972 dollars
[c] Primary energy input in quadrillion Btu
[d] Energy: GNP ratio in thousand Btu per 1972 dollar of GNP
[e] Employment civilian labor force, millions
[f] Population in millions
[g] Growth rates in the 1977 column refer to the 1950-1973 period
[h] Real GNP per member of the employed civilian labor force
Sources: Historical data on GNP and employment is from the U.S. Department of Commerce, *Survery of Current Business*; energy data is from Energy Information Administration, *Annual Report to Congress* (1977), vol. III.

generally less energy intensive than agriculture, manufacturing and personal transportation which were of greater relative importance in the past. These adjustments lower the energy input used for each dollar of output produced; the primary energy: real GNP ratio declines from 57 (thousand Btu per 1972 dollar) in 1977 to 51 to 2000.

The composition of spending is projected to remain broadly along present lines with personal consumption accounting for about 65% of real GNP, investment around 15% and government purchases around 19%. This investment share is slightly lower than historical averages (the implied slowing of capital growth accounts for some of the decline in productivity growth noted above). Although the government share of real GNP is steady, the share of current dollar output absorbed by government purchases steadily rises, reflecting the labor intensity of government services and the continuing rise in labor costs relative to the prices of goods and services.

The pattern of gross output is projected to show steady change. (Gross output includes all production from each industry, both that used as an input to production in some other industry and that used for consumption or some other component of final demand.) In terms of volume of production, the agriculture, construction and energy sectors show slower than average growth while manufacturing, commercial transportation, communications, trade and services increase more rapidly. In terms of the value of sales, the principal growth occurs in the communications, trade and services areas although rising energy prices result in rising relative importance of the energy industries. Manufacturing and commercial transportation show less than average growth in output value.

Changes in output prices and in final demand are summarized in table 14.2. There are distinct differences in the rates of price increase for each sector, corresponding to differences in input composition (in particular to the energy and labor content since the prices of these inputs are rising most rapidly) and to differences in the rate of sectoral productivity advance. Prices of manufacturing and of transportation are projected to rise less rapidly than average prices due to relatively rapid rates of productivity growth and relatively low labor content; slow productivity improvement accounts for the more rapid rise of prices of agriculture, nonfuel mining and construction output; services, trade and communications prices rise somewhat faster than average due to slow productivity gains and to relatively high labor content; and energy prices show the most rapid rate of increase of all the major output groups.

Final demand comprises personal consumption, investment, government purchases and exports, with consumption comprising about two-thirds of the total. In quantity or volume terms, the structure of final demand is projected to shift towards services, with purchases of goods decreasing in relative importance (although still increasing in absolute levels). Agriculture and construction falls from 12 to 9% of real final demand between 1977 and 2000 while energy falls from 4.0% to 2.9% and manufacturing also shows a small decline. In their place, purchases of commercial transportation show a small rise and purchases of services, trade and communications show a substantial increase (from 49 to 54% of total real purchases). The trends in current dollar final demand, however, are somewhat different, reflecting these

Table 14.2
Prices and final demand spending

	1977	1985	1990	2000
Growth rate in output prices (average percent per annum)				
Agriculture, nonfuel mining, construction	7.9	5.9	5.9	
Manufacturing	5.5	3.8	3.7	
Commercial transportation	5.1	3.1	3.4	
Services, trade, communication	7.8	5.6	5.7	
Energy	9.4	7.0	7.0	
Total gross output	6.9	4.9	5.0	
Composition of real final demand spending (percent)				
Agriculture, nonfuel mining, construction	12.1	10.5	9.5	8.7
Manufacturing	32.1	31.7	30.9	30.7
Commercial transportation	2.8	3.1	3.3	3.4
Services, trade, communication	49.0	51.5	53.3	54.3
Energy	4.0	3.2	3.0	2.9
Total	100.00	100.00	100.00	100.00
Composition of current dollar final demand spending (percent)				
Agriculture, nonfuel mining, construction	2.4	11.5	10.7	10.5
Manufacturing	29.6	25.6	23.2	19.5
Commercial transportation	2.5	2.4	2.3	1.9
Services, trade, communication	50.3	55.3	58.7	62.4
Energy	5.2	5.0	5.1	5.6
Total	100.0	100.0	100.0	100.0

quantity changes as well as changes in relative prices. In terms of current dollar expenditures, energy purchases rise in relative importance, manufacturing shows a large decline (from 30 to 20% of total purchases), and there is a large rise in relative spending on services, trade and communications (from 50 to 62% of the total). In sum, final demand shows steady and significant restructuring, in both quantity and expenditure terms, with the main changes being away from manufactured goods towards services.

14.2.4 Patterns of Energy Growth

Energy use is projected to grow less rapidly than the economy and less rapidly than in the pre-1973 period. The reasons for this are the rising real price of energy, leading to conservation in energy use, and the gradual shift of production away from energy-intensive activities.

Within the energy sector there is, at the primary input level, a change away from oil and gas towards coal and nuclear fuels. The associated change at the delivered energy level is the continuing trend towards greater electrification, although the rate of growth of the electric power industry is substantially below historical trends.

These broad developments in the energy system are summarized in table 14.3. There petroleum and natural gas decline markedly in relative importance. Petroleum provided 49% of all energy input in 1977 but by 1990 this share is down to 41% and by 2000 it is under 36%. Natural gas shows an even more drastic decline, from accounting for 26% of energy in 1977 to only 14% in 2000. These shifts are primarily due to the rising prices of oil and gas which lead to substantial conservation in the use of these fuels. Even so, there is a continuing rise in the volume of petroleum used and a slight increase in consumption of natural gas. A large part of oil and gas supplies comes from imports with, in particular, supply expansion being largely provided by imports. This results in the share of imports in total oil and gas consumption rising from 34% in 1977 to 55% by 2000. The declining share of oil and gas in total energy use moderates the overall level of import dependence but some increase still occurs: imports as a fraction of total energy input rise from 24% in 1977 to 28% in 2000. Thus, the heavy reliance upon imported energy, particularly for petroleum supply, which characterizes the U.S. energy system at present, is projected to continue for the rest of the century.

Petroleum and natural gas satisfy only a small part of the increase in demand for energy; coal and nuclear are the fuels that provide the greater part of the increase. Oil and gas account for only 21% of the projected primary energy input between 1977 and 2000, while coal provides 35% and nuclear and other nonfossil energy forms account for 44%. Coal use is projected to grow substantially more rapidly than total energy input until about 1990—its share in total input rises from 19% in 1977 to 25% in 1990. After 1990, coal growth decelerates so that coal maintains about a constant share of total input. Most of this increase is in the use of coal for electricity generation although some demand for coal as an input to synthetic fuel (coal liquefaction and coal gasification) also arises. The final broad category of input is the nuclear, hydro, and other input into electricity generation. This shows rapid expansion, in particular in the period after 1985. By the end of the century, coal and nonfossil are about the same magnitude, each supplying one quarter of U.S. energy use.

Table 14.3
The energy system, 1977–2000

	1977	1985	1990	2000
Energy input (quadrillion Btu)				
Coal	14.1	20.5	28.2	36.5
Petroleum	37.0	42.9	46.0	49.9
Natural gas	19.6	20.5	19.0	20.0
Hydro, nuclear, other	5.1	13.5	18.8	33.1
Total primary input	75.8	97.4	112.0	139.5
Energy input (percent)				
Coal	18.6	21.0	25.2	26.2
Petroleum	48.7	44.1	44.1	35.8
Natural gas	25.9	21.0	17.0	14.3
Hydro, nuclear, other	6.8	13.9	16.8	23.7
Total primary input	100.0	100.0	100.0	100.0
Growth rates of input[a] (average percent per annum)				
Coal	2.1	4.8	6.6	2.6
Petroleum	4.3	1.9	1.4	0.8
Natural gas	4.6	0.6	−1.5	0.5
Hydro, nuclear, other	6.5	12.9	6.9	5.8
Total primary input	4.1	3.2	2.8	2.2
Some key measures				
Fossil input in total (%)	93.3	86.1	83.2	76.3
Imports in total oil and gas (%)	33.7	40.1	45.3	55.1
Imports in total input (%)	23.6	26.1	26.3	27.6
Electricity input in total (%)	29.7	33.2	35.7	45.6

[a] Growth rates in the 1977 column refer to the 1960–1973 period.

The structure of energy use shifts drastically away from oil and gas and, to a smaller extent, away from fossil fuels. Coal and nuclear input grow rapidly with most of the growth occurring in input to electricity generation. Therefore, a central feature of the restructuring of the energy system is an increase in the relative importance of electricity. This percentage rises from 30% in 1977 to 36% in 1990 and 46% in 2000. Thus, the fuels that the United States has in relatively plentiful supply—coal and uranium—are well matched to generate electricity, the delivered energy form that has in the past, and will continue in the future, to show the greatest growth potential.

14.2.5   The Electric Power Industry

Electricity is projected to become increasingly important within the
energy system and within the economy over the rest of the century.[11]
Electricity consumption in the Reference Case rises at about 4.9%
annually, compared to 2.7% for total energy input and 3.1% for real
GNP. Thus, electricity output continues the trend observed in the past
of growing faster than total energy input and GNP. However, the
actual rates of growth of electricity are substantially below those experienced prior to 1973. The previous 7% annual growth rates are
replaced by rates of increase of the order of 4 or 5%, so whereas the
industry in the past doubled in size every 10 years, a doubling is now
projected to take about 15 years or longer.

Table 14.4 shows the principal indicators of the size and output of
the electric power industry in the Reference projection. Electricity
consumption increases at an average of about 4.8% annually during
the 1980s and 1990s. Electricity consumption per capita rises steadily,
from 9.9 kWh in 1977 to 24.4 in 2000, an average annual growth rate of
4.9%. Similarly, the intensity of reliance on electricity in the economy
as a whole steadily increases. In 1977, 1.61 kWh were used, on average, per (1972) dollar of real GNP whereas the 2000 figure is 2.35, corresponding to an annual rate of increase of 1.7%.

The pattern of fuel inputs into electricity generation is projected to
change substantially from present-day patterns. Table 14.5 shows the
trends in fuel inputs. Coal and nuclear fuels, along with a small
increase in hydro input, provide the entire increase in input over the
rest of the century; input of oil and gas declines from present levels.
(In 1977, fuels other than oil and gas accounted for 74% of total input;
by 2000 they are estimated to account for 98%.) This expansion is
characterized by approximately equal growth of coal input and of
nuclear input to generation and by 2000. By 2000, coal and nuclear
each provide about 45% of energy input. This split between coal and
nuclear reflects both existing capacity and the pattern of new investment. The present mix of plants includes much more coal than
nuclear capacity. New investment, however, is projected to include a
greater proportion of nuclear capacity. (This is projected on the basis
of relative cost and does not take account of noncost considerations
which might limit the construction of nuclear capacity. These possible
constraints on nuclear power are explicitly analyzed in the alternative
projections rather than the Reference Case.) Petroleum and gas use

Table 14.4
Growth of the electric power industry

	1977[a]	1985	1990	2000
Electricity generated				
Quadrillion Btu	7.35	10.93	13.59	31.96
Billion kWhr	2153	3187	3961	6404
Peak power demand (GW)	405	605	751	1214
Installed capacity (GW)	551	758	965	1410
Rate of growth (average percent per annum)				
Electricity generated		5.0	4.4	4.9
Installed capacity		4.1	4.9	3.9
Degree of electrification[b]	29.7	33.2	35.7	45.6
Electricity consumption per capita[c]	9.93	13.62	16.16	24.40
Electricity: GNP ratio[d]	1.61	1.76	1.89	2.35

[a] The 1977 numbers are those simulated by the model. There is a small difference between the simulated and actual figures for 1977: electricity generated is estimated to be 2153 billion kWhr whereas actual generation by the electric power industry was 2124 billion kWhr plus imports and purchases from industrial sources of 24 billion kWhr for total commercial generation of 2148 billion kWhr.
[b] Energy inputs into electricity generation as a percentage of total U.S. primary energy input.
[c] Electricity used per person in the population, in kilowatt hours.
[d] Electricity used per dollar of real GNP, kilowatt hours per 1972 dollar.

for electricity generation declines in both relative and absolute terms (from 6 quadrillion Btu in 1977 to 2 in 2000). This reflects both the trends in the prices of these fuels and, in particular, government regulations concerning their use. Also, there is no new construction of base or cycling gas plants and, particularly as existing capacity begins to be retired after the early 1980s, use of gas for electricity generation declines rapidly.

Installed capacity for each fuel type is given in table 14.6. Coal shows a rapid increase in capacity. Between 1977 and 1985, existing projects coming on line increase capacity from 143 to 240 GW, an average rate of expansion of 6.7% annually. In the late 1980s, coal capacity rises still more rapidly, at an average annual rate of 8.5%, reflecting investment decisions made around 1980 to provide additional capacity in the period when the excess capacity inherited from the 1970s becomes fully used. Then in the 1990s, the growth of coal capacity slows, to an average 3.7% annually, as more new investment is directed towards nuclear. Nuclear capacity increases to 150 GW in 1985, as plants currently under construction come into operation.

Table 14.5
Fuel inputs into electricity generation

	1977	1985	1990	2000
Fuel inputs (quadrillion Btu)				
Coal	9.4	13.8	19.4	29.1
Petroleum	0.4	0.8	0.3	0.1
Natural gas	5.1	4.3	1.4	1.2
Nuclear	3.2	9.2	14.1	27.9
Hydro	3.4	4.1	4.5	5.1
Other	0.1	0.1	0.2	0.2
Total	21.7	32.3	39.9	63.6
Composition of fuel inputs (%)				
Coal	43.3	42.7	48.6	45.8
Petroleum	2.3	2.5	0.8	0.2
Natural gas	23.3	13.3	3.5	1.9
Nuclear	14.7	28.5	35.3	43.9
Hydro	15.7	12.7	11.3	8.0
Other	0.5	0.3	0.5	0.3
Total	100.0	100.0	100.0	100.0

Nuclear is then projected to rise to 229 GW by 1990 and to 453 GW in 2000. At this time, nuclear represents 32% of total installed capacity and coal 37%, compared to 9% and 26% in 1977.

Petroleum generating capacity, other than peaking capacity, remains constant at its 1980 level of 145 GW. This represents a small increase over 1977 capacity but, once plants currently being constructed come on line, it corresponds to investment in petroleum capacity being limited to replacement. This specification is imposed on the projections to incorporate the effect of government policy on construction of petroleum capacity. For natural gas even more stringent restrictions were imposed, preventing any new construction so that the level of gas generating capacity steadily declines as older plants are retired. Thus, installed gas capacity declines from 111 GW in 1977 to 53 GW in 2000. Hydro generating capacity grows steadily, but not rapidly, due to the strictly limited number of sites that are suitable for hydro generation at competitive costs. The amount of hydro capacity is projected to rise from 73 GW in 1977 to 117 GW in 2000. (These figures are introduced exogenously; they are not determined by the model.) The final major type of capacity is combustion turbines and internal combustion generators, normally used only for peaking. This is projected to grow approximately in line with total capacity and

Table 14.6
Generating capacities and usage factors

	1977	1985	1990	2000
Generating capacity (GW)				
Coal	142.6	239.7	359.7	517.2
Petroleum[a]	126.2	145.3	145.3	145.3
Natural gas[b]	110.7	90.8	77.7	53.4
Nuclear	51.8	150.0	228.9	452.7
Hydro	73.3	89.0	99.0	117.3
Other[b]	42.4	42.9	54.2	123.9
Total	546.9	757.7	964.8	1409.8
Usage factors (%)				
Coal	0.750	0.658	0.625	0.675
Petroleum	0.048	0.060	0.027	0.008
Natural gas	0.529	0.537	0.219	0.277
Nuclear	0.669	0.669	0.669	0.669
Hydro	0.531	0.530	0.526	0.518
Other	0.017	0.028	0.025	0.018
Total	0.450	0.480	0.469	0.519

[a] This is petroleum and natural gas base and cycling capacity.
[b] This includes all peaking capacity.

total generation. Peaking capacity in 1977 is 42 GW, or 7.8% of total capacity, and in 2000 is projected to be 124 GW, or 8.8% of the total.

Usage factors for each type of capacity are also given in table 14.6. Coal plants, estimated to be operated at an average 75% usage factor in 1977, are operated at an average usage factor between 60% and 70% over the projection period. The usage factor for nuclear plant is assumed to remain at 67%. Petroleum capacity has a low overall usage factor, averaging only about 5%. This corresponds to most petroleum capacity not being used at all and to small volumes of petroleum capacity being used more intensively. The most significant change in usage occurs for natural gas plants. In 1977, these plants are estimated to have a usage factor of 53%. In the future, the usage factor is projected to remain steady until 1985, then to decline drastically to a 20% average by 1990. The decline is in response to rising fuel prices and to government regulation and is offset by new coal and nuclear capacity coming on line to permit reduced reliance on natural gas.

The input cost structure of electricity supply is presented in table 14.7. This shows fuel input prices and capital costs in constant dollars of 1977. The prices of fuel inputs are assumed to increase steadily. The average annual rate of increase of prices is about 2.5% in real

Table 14.7
Input costs to electric power industry

	1977	1985	1990	2000
Fuel input prices, real[a]				
Coal ($(1977)/ton)	23.93	29.16	32.99	42.23
Oil ($(1977)/barrel)	11.11	13.54	15.32	19.60
Gas ($(1977)/MCF)	1.52	1.85	2.10	2.68
Uranium ($(1977)/lb)	23.50	28.42	32.00	40.57
Capital costs, real ($(1977)/KW)				
Coal[b]	695	695	695	695
Oil	436	436	436	436
Gas	436	436	436	436
Nuclear (LWR)	825	825	825	825
Peaking	158	158	158	158
Hydro	596	596	596	596

[a] Coal prices do not include transportation costs; oil prices are for crude petroleum; natural gas prices are for new well-head supplies; uranium oxide prices do not include enrichment and fabrication.
[b] Capital costs for coal plants include the cost of fuel gas desulfurization equipment.

terms. This rise takes the price of coal input from $(1977)24/ton in 1977 to $(1977)42/ton in 2000. Nuclear fuel rises in price from $(1977)24/lb. to $(1977)41/lb. over this same period. The capital cost figures are, in real terms, assumed to be constant over time, i.e., they are assumed to increase at the same rate as general inflation. The cost per installed kilowatt of coal capacity is 695 and of nuclear capacity is 825 (in constant 1977 dollars).

Output prices for electricity are projected to show a continuing rise. In current dollar terms, the price rise over the 1977 to 2000 period averages 7.5% annually. Most of this increase, however, is due to general inflation. When inflation is taken into account and real prices computed, the rate of increase in prices is much smaller, but is nonetheless positive. (This is a reversal of the trend in the years prior to 1973 when real electricity prices showed a steady decline.) The average price of electricity, in constant dollars of 1977, is projected to be 36 mills/kWh in 1977 rising to 42 in 1985 and to 53 in 2000. These imply growth rates of 2.2% annually between 1977 and 1985 and of 1.4% annually over the 1985 to 2000 period. These increases in real prices are due, to some extent, to new capacity being more costly than that already installed but it is mainly due to increasing real costs for operation and maintenance and for fuel.

14.3   The Impact of Capacity Restrictions

14.3.1   Introduction

The first set of issues to be analyzed centers on restrictions on the ability of the electric power industry to expand generating capacity. The central contingency considered is a restriction on the expansion of nuclear generating capacity. This is represented as a prohibition of construction of new nuclear plants, i.e., no new construction could be started although plants already in the construction phase could be completed and brought into operation.[12] This construction prohibition is comparable to the *de facto* nuclear moratoria now in effect in several states.

The same set of pressures, operating through the legislative, regulatory and judicial processes, that led to nuclear restrictions could also lead to pressures against new coal-generation plants. In addition, elimination of nuclear expansion would force investment in base load plants into coal stations which would accentuate the role of coal and could invite increased attention by citizen groups toward restricting the use or impact of coal. In either event, a situation could emerge in which there are restrictions on new coal plants. There does not appear to be pressure for a complete ban on construction of new coal plants so the coal restriction is represented by a partial ban in which new construction of coal-steam plants is limited to half the rate in the Reference Case. Although the one-half figure is arbitrary it is used in an attempt to provide a lower bound to the severity of any coal restrictions that might be expected to accompany nuclear restrictions.

Cost increases are also likely in the event of nuclear and/or coal capacity restrictions. Safety and environmental concerns underlying the pressure that resulted in limitations on new construction might well also result in the imposition of more stringent emission and safety standards at those plants which can be built. Any such increase in environmental and safety standards is likely to require new or additional capital equipment, raising the total cost of each unit of new generating capacity.

Fuel costs may also increase as part of the chain of events initiated by capacity restrictions. A nuclear moratorium would, in the absence of restrictions on new coal capacity, result in the diversion of almost all base-load capacity growth into coal. This would cause a rapid increase in the demand for coal. In market terms, this would greatly increase the potential power of those controlling coal supply. This could result in induced rises in the delivered price of coal. For example, coal companies might take advantage of this market power by acting together to raise prices; the few states that would supply the increased output of coal could turn the market power to their own advantage by the imposition of substantial severance taxes on coal; or railroads and others in strategic areas in the transportation industry might use the rapid demand growth as a basis for raising transportation charges. As well as possible rises in coal prices there would be the potential for increases in oil and gas prices as demand for energy, by utilities and by other users, is partially redirected away from more expensive coal and more expensive electricity.

What emerges from these considerations is an interdependence between restrictions and other external developments affecting the electric power industry and the energy system. An initial restriction on nuclear expansion could set in train a sequence of events resulting in restrictions in coal capacity, higher capacity costs and higher fuel prices. Thus, a nuclear moratorium might occur in isolation or might occur in combination with higher capacity and fuel costs. By the same reasoning, restrictions on coal capacity could occur in isolation or could occur as part of a broader set of energy developments.

It is of practical concern, therefore, to assess the effects of capacity restrictions both individually and in combination with capital and cost changes. Evaluation of different combinations of events is also of interest in determining whether or not the effects of any one restriction are dependent on the existence of restrictions affecting other parts of the energy system. In particular, the effects of a nuclear restriction alone may be less severe than if there is a simultaneous restriction on coal-generating plants. There is the need, therefore, to analyze the effects and interactions of capacity. capital cost and fuel cost changes. A systematic and comprehensive way of organizing these analyses is by the use of the tree structure given in figure 14.1. From the three underlying sets of contingencies—a prohibition of new nuclear construction, a restriction on new coal plan construction, and higher costs for capacity and fuel—this tree structure sets out all possible combinations of events. Eight possible combinations emerge from the three basic contingencies, each of which can be in either of two states—restricted/high cost or unrestricted/lower cost.

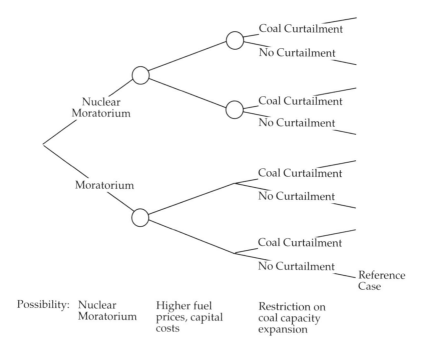

Figure 14.1
Specification of scenarios in Capacity Restriction Case.

In specific terms, the three underlying contingencies are defined as follows:

1. *Nuclear restrictions*: no new nuclear plants can move into the construction phase; plants on which construction began in 1977 or earlier could be completed and brought into operation; existing operating plants would not be restricted.

2. *Higher costs*: fuel prices would increase and tighter environmental restrictions, leading to higher capital costs, would be imposed on new coal and nuclear plants. Beginning in 1978, oil and gas prices would be 20 percent higher than in the Reference Case, coal prices would be double their levels in the Reference Case, and coal and nuclear capacity would increase in cost by $(1977)100 per kilowatt.

3. *Coal curtailment*: restrictions would be imposed on the rate of expansion of coal-fired generating capacity. Plants due to completion by 1983 would be permitted to continue but the rate of increase of installed coal capacity from 1983 onwards would be limited to one half of the rate in the Reference Case.

The eight possible outcomes involving these events are as follows:

Reference Case: no nuclear restriction, reference costs, no coal curtailment.

A1. No nuclear restriction, reference fuel and capital costs, curtailment of coal capacity expansion.

A2. No nuclear restriction, higher fuel and coal capital costs, no coal curtailment.

A3. No nuclear restriction, higher fuel and coal capital costs, curtailment of coal capacity expansion.

A4. Restriction of nuclear construction, reference fuel and capital costs, no coal curtailment.

A5. Restriction of nuclear construction, reference fuel and capital costs, curtailment of coal capacity expansion.

A6. Restriction of nuclear construction, higher fuel and coal capital costs, no coal curtailment.

A7. Restriction of nuclear construction, higher fuel and coal capital costs, curtailment of coal capacity expansion.

To illustrate the general nature of these restrictions, the Reference Case generating capacities can be noted. Table 14.8 gives the Reference Case installed capacities, by fuel type, in 1983 and in 2000. Since each capacity restriction affects plants coming on line after 1983, the 1983 capacities indicate what would be available in the event of a complete ban on new construction. For a nuclear moratorium, nuclear capacity will be 114.4 GW in 1983 and will then decline slightly as older plants are retired. This compares with the 453 GW of nuclear capacity in 2000 under Reference Case conditions. For the coal curtailment possibility, installed coal capacity would be 220 GW in 1983 and would be limited to no more than 369 GW in 2000, rather than the 517 GW figure of the Reference Case.[13]

14.3.2   Case A1: Coal Capacity Restrictions

Case A1 involves restrictions on the construction of new coal-fired electricity generation plants. The restriction is defined as limiting new construction to no more than half the rate of increase observed in the Reference Case. In effect this means that coal-fired capacity, including plants already in existence, cannot exceed 277 GW in 1990 to 306 GW in 2000. The initial impact of this restriction is to force the electric

Table 14.8
Reference case generating capacity in 1983 and 2000 installed capacity (GW)

Fuel	1983	2000
Coal	220.3	517.2
Nuclear	114.4	452.7
Oil, gas[a]	241.4	198.7
Turbines@[b]	44.8	123.9
Other	85.0	117.3
TOTAL	705.8	1409.8

[a] Oil and gas base load and cycling capacity. Turbines and other peaking capacity is not included.
[b] Combustion turbines and other peaking capacity.

power industry to build additional nuclear plants and to increase use of oil and gas in order to meet demand. This shift causes an increase in the price of electricity, which not only affects electricity consumers but also leads to adjustments and costs throughout the economy.

Because the restriction on new coal capacity is defined in terms of the growth rate the effect compounds over time; by 2000 the permitted

Table A1.1
Summary

Macroeconomic summary ($1972 billion)

	1977	1990	2000
Consumption	858.5	1350.9	1759.9
		(−0.1)	(−0.2)
Investment	200.6	315.3	400.5
		(—)	(−0.1)
Government and net exports	278.2	427.2	561.2
		(—)	(—)
GNP	1337.3	2093.4	2721.6
		(−0.1)	(−0.2)

Impacts on electric power industry

	1977	1990	2000
Average price (mills/KWH)	35.7	47.6	54.4
(constant dollars)		(1.8)	(3.9)
Generation (bn KWH)	2153.0	3943.3	6140.8
		(−0.5)	(−4.1)
Capacity (GW)	551.0	963.7	1389.4
		(−0.1)	(−1.4)

Numbers in parentheses represent percent change from the Reference Case.

Table A1.2
Energy

Electric generating capacities and fuel inputs in 2000

	Capacity (GW)	Fuel input (quadrillion Btu)
Coal	305.8	15.3
	(−40.9)	(−47.4)
Oil and gas		2.2
		(37.3)
(Steam)	198.7	
	(—)	
(Turbine)	123.5	
	(−0.3)	
Nuclear	644.1	39.6
	(42.3)	(42.3)
Other	117.3	5.1
	(—)	(—)
Total	1389.4	62.2
	(−1.4)	(−2.2)

Primary energy inputs (quadrillion Btu)

	1977	1990	2000
Coal	14.1	22.9	22.9
		(−18.8)	(−37.3)
Petroleum	37.0	46.6	50.8
		(1.4)	(1.7)
Natural gas	19.6	19.1	20.3
		(0.7)	(1.7)
Nuclear	2.7	19.0	39.6
		(34.5)	(42.3)
Other	2.4	4.7	5.3
		(—)	(—)
Total input	75.8	112.3	138.9
		(−0.3)	(−0.5)
Gas and petroleum imports	17.9	30.2	39.7
		(2.6)	(3.1)

Numbers in parentheses represent percent changes from the Reference Case.

level of coal capacity is 41 percent below the Reference Case level. Although the coal option is partially restricted, utilities are still permitted to expand nuclear capacity to satisfy the growing demand for electricity. In fact, nuclear is the only option to make up this base load capacity and, as a result of increased levels of investment, nuclear capacity is 41 percent higher than the Reference Case by 2000. (Growth in oil- and gas-fired steam plant capacity is assumed to be prevented by government action, and while combustion turbine capacity is not limited, generation by turbines is in most cases a much more expensive substitute for coal generation than is generation by nuclear power.) The sum of coal capacity and nuclear capacity is only 2 percent lower than the Reference Case in 2000, indicating a direct substitution of nuclear capacity for coal capacity. Further, most of the change in the total of coal and nuclear capacity is due to the lower level of demand for electricity caused by the more rapid growth in prices.

While the shift to nuclear capacity makes it possible for utilities to continue to meet the growing demand for electricity it does involve a cost penalty relative to conditions in the Reference Case, causing the price of electricity to increase more rapidly. Because the cost assumptions make coal and nuclear generation fairly similar in cost, for most regions the increase in the price of electricity is small—only 4 percent in 2000 relative to the Reference Case. The increased price does cause a drop in demand for electricity, and as a result total plant capacity and total fuel inputs to electricity fall below the Reference Case level.

Primary inputs of energy are affected by the restructuring of fuel inputs to electricity: total consumption of coal drops sharply, and total input of nuclear increases. At the higher price for electricity some consumers switch to direct use of oil or gas as a less expensive alternative, so total consumption of both oil and gas rises relative to the Reference Case. However, the net effect is for a reduction in the level of total primary energy input. This new pattern of energy use is relatively less intensive in fossil fuels (which provide 68 percent of total input in 2000 compared to 76 percent in the Reference Case). The shift away from fossil fuels is of some importance in terms of the environmental effects of the energy system. A further important consequence concerns imports. As imports satisfy the excess of U.S. demand over supply of oil and gas, and increase in demand for these fuels leads directly to higher imports. The increased level of imports in this case has political and economic costs in addition to those incorporated in the national income effects.

The rise in electricity prices also has some effect on the economy. Higher prices induce producers and consumers to shift purchases away from electricity. This shift involves some efficiency cost and also, by increasing the capital and labor intensity of production, slows productivity growth. The result is that future levels of real output and income are reduced, e.g., real GNP in 2000 is $(1972)4.1 billion less than in the Reference Case. Over the whole 1978–2000 period, the present value of the GNP loss is $(1972)15.9 billion.

14.3.3 Case A2: High Fuel Prices and Capacity Costs

Case A2 involves higher costs for most of the major methods of generating electricity, relative to the Reference Case the price of coal is double, the delivered prices of oil and gas are 20 percent higher, and the capital cost of nuclear and coal plants increase by $(1977)100 per installed kilowatt capacity. The capital cost increases represent a 14 percent increase for coal plants and a 12 percent increase for nuclear plants.

The attractiveness of nuclear investment on relative cost grounds is increased because generation costs for coal plants are increased by a greater proportion. And oil and gas steam plants, hydroelectric plants and geothermal plants are already restricted or limited. Therefore, capacity expansion is redirected toward nuclear: by 2000 nuclear capacity is 42 percent above the Reference Case while coal capacity is 42 percent less. In some cases, it becomes relatively economic to increase the usage factors on existing oil and gas steam plants rather than to add new nuclear or coal capacity. Consequently, oil and gas input to utilities is higher, by 165 percent in 2000, than in the Reference Case.

Table A2.1
Summary

Macroeconomic summary ($1972 billion)			
	1977	1990	2000
Consumption	858.5	1310.2	1694.6
		(−3.2)	(−3.9)
Investment	200.6	296.8	372.6
		(−5.9)	(−7.1)
Government and net exports	278.2	427.2	561.2
		(—)	(—)
GNP	1337.3	2034.1	2628.4
		(−2.9)	(−3.6)
Impacts on electric power industry			
	1977	1990	2000
Average price (mills/KWH)	35.7	55.3	60.9
(constant dollars)		(18.3)	(16.0)
Generation (bn KWH)	2153.0	3383.6	5453.0
		(−14.6)	(−14.9)
Capacity (GW)	551.0	930.6	1332.4
		(−3.5)	(−5.5)

Numbers in parentheses represent percent changes from the Reference Case.

Table A2.2
Energy

Electric generating capacities and fuel inputs in 2000

	Capacity (GW)	Fuel input (quadrillion Btu)
Coal	300.2	6.8
	(−42.0)	(−76.6)
Oil and gas		4.2
		(164.6)
(Steam)	198.7	
	(—)	
(Turbine)	73.3	
	(−40.8)	
Nuclear	642.9	39.6
	(42.0)	(42.0)
Other	117.3	5.1
	(—)	(—)
Total	1332.4	55.6
	(−5.5)	(−12.5)

Primary energy inputs (quadrillion Btu)

	1977	1990	2000
Coal	14.1	12.5	12.9
		(−55.5)	(−64.6)
Petroleum	37.0	39.3	42.7
		(−14.5)	(−14.4)
Natural gas	19.6	16.6	17.9
		(−12.4)	(−10.7)
Nuclear	2.7	17.4	39.6
		(23.2)	(42.0)
Other	2.4	4.5	5.3
		(—)	(—)
Total input	75.8	90.6	118.3
		(−19.1)	(−15.2)
Gas and petroleum imports	17.9	20.4	29.2
		(−30.6)	(−24.2)

Numbers in parentheses represent percent change from the Reference Case.

The mix of fuel to generation can shift from coal toward oil and gas soon after the cost increases, but it is not until the 1990s that the additional nuclear capacity, ordered in response to the cost changes, begins to come on line. Generation costs and electricity prices, therefore, follow a distinctive time pattern: by 1990, when additional nuclear capacity is just beginning to alter the capacity mix in the industry, the price of electricity is 18 percent above the Reference level but ten years later, in 2000, the cost advantages in increased nuclear capacity mean that average prices are only 16 percent higher.

Demand for electricity drops because of the higher price, and remains on a lower growth path throughout the rest of the century. In 2000 demand for electricity is 15 percent lower than the Reference value, which means that demand grows at an average annual rate of 4.1 percent rather than the 4.9 percent of the Reference Case. Slower growth of electricity demand means a slower growth in demand for fuel inputs to electricity. By itself this would mean a drop in the growth of primary energy inputs. In addition, the 20 percent increase in the price of oil and gas causes direct demand for those fuels to drop far enough that, even with an increase in oil and gas use by electric utilities, the total primary inputs of oil and gas fall. The aggregate result is that primary input in 2000 is 15 percent below the Reference Case level, with only inputs of nuclear fuel showing an increase.

One advantage of decreased levels of energy consumption, in particular of oil and gas, is that energy imports decline—in 2000, oil and gas imports are 24 percent less than in the Reference Case. But because of higher delivered energy costs—for oil, gas, and electricity—consumers substitute away from energy, with an associated impact in slower growth of capital and labor productivity. The loss in economic efficiency is substantial—in 2000, real GNP is $(1972)97 billion less than in the Reference Case. The present value of the total real GNP loss over the 1978–2000 period is $(1972)607 billion.

14.3.4   Case A3: Restrictions on Coal Capacity and Higher Prices

Case A3 combines the changes covered separately in Cases A1 and A2—a restriction on coal capacity limiting growth to half the Reference Case rate, together with increases in the price of coal, oil and gas

Table A3.1
Summary

Macroeconomic summary ($1972 billion)			
	1977	1990	2000
Consumption	858.5	1310.4	1693.2
		(−3.1)	(−4.0)
Investment	200.6	296.7	371.7
		(−5.9)	(−7.3)
Government and net exports	278.2	427.2	561.2
		(—)	(—)
GNP	1337.3	2034.3	2626.1
		(−2.9)	(−3.7)

Table A3.1 (continued)

	Impacts on electric power industry		
	1977	1990	2000
Average price (mills/KWH)	35.7	56.3	61.1
(constant dollars)		(20.5)	(16.5)
Generation (bn KWH)	2153.0	3368.8	5451.2
		(−15.0)	(−14.9)
Capacity (GW)	551.0	943.4	1349.6
		(−2.2)	(−4.3)

Numbers in parentheses represent percent change from the Reference Case.

Table A3.2
Energy

Electric generating capacities and fuel inputs in 2000

	Capacity (GW)	Fuel input (quadrillion Btu)
Coal	300.0	6.8
	(−42.0)	(−76.6)
Oil and gas		4.2
		(167.7)
(Steam)	198.7	
	(—)	
(Turbine)	91.9	
	(−25.8)	
Nuclear	641.7	39.6
	(41.8)	(41.8)
Other	117.3	5.1
	(—)	(—)
Total	1349.6	55.6
	(−4.3)	(−12.5)

Primary energy inputs (quadrillion Btu)

	1977	1990	2000
Coal	14.1	12.5	12.9
		(−55.6)	(−64.6)
Petroleum	37.0	39.0	42.7
		(−15.1)	(−14.4)
Natural gas	19.6	16.4	17.9
		(−13.5)	(−10.7)
Nuclear	2.7	18.1	39.6
		(28.2)	(41.8)
Other	2.4	4.5	5.3
		(—)	(—)
Total input	75.8	90.6	118.3
		(−19.1)	(−15.2)
Gas and petroleum imports	17.9	19.9	29.2
		(−32.2)	(−24.2)

Numbers in parentheses represent percent change from the Reference Case.

and higher coal an nuclear capacity costs. The results are almost identical with Case A2, because the combination of higher coal prices and increased capital costs for coal plants brings capacity down almost to the restricted level. By 2000 coal plant capacity in Case A2 is only 0.2 GW above the restricted level, so the additional effect of the coal capacity restriction is very small. Case A3 has electricity prices slightly higher than A2 with generation lower and real GNP lower.

Although the coal capacity constraint has little additional effect in 2000 (electricity price is up by 17 percent compared to 16 percent in A2) it does make a more noticeable difference in the earlier years. For example, in 1990 the higher fuel prices and capital costs alone mean that the most economic level of coal capacity is 287 GW, which is 9 GW greater than allowed under the capacity restriction. The restriction of coal capacity to 277 GW, with the move towards oil and gas generation, causes some increase in costs and in electricity prices—prices are up by 21 percent compared to 18 percent in A2. The slightly more restrictive electricity conditions in A3 than A2 do impose an additional economic cost—real GNP in 2000, compared to the Reference Case, is $(1972)1000 billion less in A3 and $(1972)97 billion down in A2 while the present value of the GNP loss is $(1972)610 bn as opposed to $(1972)607 billion.

14.3.5   Case A4: Nuclear Moratorium

In Case A4 all new construction of nuclear plants is prevented although plants on which construction has already commenced can be completed. Accordingly, nuclear capacity reaches a peak in the early 1980s then gradually declines as older plants are retired. Compared to the Reference Case this implies a very large drop in the use of nuclear power—a decline of more than 80 percent from the projection for 2000. This restriction hits the major part of utilities' expansion plans, forcing them instead to greatly increased investment in coal plants. The detailed economics of the two types of plants differ greatly, but in terms of average generation cost coal and nuclear plants are similar, so although there is a large future shift to coal, there is not such a large resulting increase in costs or electricity prices. By 2000, coal capacity is 69 percent higher than the Reference level (and nuclear capacity is 84 percent lower) while the price of electricity is up by 11 percent. Demand for electricity is 10 percent down in 2000, reflecting not only the higher price structure but also the slower rate of economic growth.

Table A4.1
Summary

Macroeconomic summary ($1972 billion)

	1977	1990	2000
Consumption	858.5	1350.3	1743.4
		(−0.2)	(−1.1)
Investment	200.6	313.0	389.6
		(−0.8)	(−2.9)
Government and net exports	278.2	427.2	561.2
		(—)	(—)
GNP	1337.3	2090.4	2694.2
		(−0.2)	(−1.2)

Impacts on electric power industry

	1977	1990	2000
Average price (mills/KWH)	35.7	48.1	58.3
(constant dollars)		(3.0)	(11.1)
Generation (bn KWH)	2153.0	3870.0	5763.6
		(−2.3)	(−10.0)
Capacity (GW)	551.0	959.5	1395.6
		(−0.5)	(−1.0)

Numbers in parentheses represent percent change from the Reference Case.

Table A4.2
Energy

Electric generating capacities and fuel inputs in 2000

	Capacity (GW)	Fuel input (quadrillion Btu)
Coal	875.2	42.9
	(69.2)	(47.8)
Oil and gas		1.8
		(12.7)
(Steam)	198.7	
	(—)	
(Turbine)	120.6	
	(−2.7)	
Nuclear	83.8	5.2
	(−81.5)	(−81.5)
Other	117.3	5.1
	(—)	(—)
Total	1395.6	54.9
	(−1.0)	(−13.6)

Table A4.2 (continued)

Primary energy inputs (quadrillion Btu)

	1977	1990	2000
Coal	14.1	35.1	48.4
		(24.3)	(32.5)
Petroleum	37.0	46.2	50.9
		(0.3)	(2.0)
Natural gas	19.6	19.0	20.4
		(0.1)	(2.1)
Nuclear	2.7	5.7	5.2
		(−59.9)	(−81.5)
Other	2.4	4.7	5.3
		(—)	(—)
Total input	75.8	110.6	130.1
		(−1.3)	(−6.8)
Gas and petroleum imports	17.9	29.6	39.9
		(0.4)	(3.6)

Numbers in parentheses represent percent changes from the Reference Case.

The increase in the price of electricity causes a reduction in the growth in demand, and therefore in fuel inputs to electricity. The net result is a decline, relative to the Reference Case, in total primary inputs of energy by 7 percent. This decline comprises a large drop in nuclear inputs to electricity, a smaller increase in coal inputs to electricity, and small increases in primary inputs of oil and gas use in electricity and as substitutes for electricity. The substitution of oil and gas which, in turn, leads to higher energy imports—imports in 2000 are 4 percent higher than in the Reference Case.

As long as coal plants can be built in place of nuclear plants the overall effect of the nuclear moratorium can be limited, although changes in the composition of energy inputs and in the capacity and fuel mix in electricity generation are large. Even so, the capacity restriction does lead to costs imposed on the economy as a whole. The efficiency and productivity effects of the shift from electricity to other inputs results in some retardation of economic growth. By 2000, total income or product, as measured by real GNP, is $(1972)32 billion less than in the Reference Case. In terms of the present value of GNP losses over the projection period, the nuclear moratorium causes a difference of $(1972)94 billion, which is more than is caused by less stringent limits on coal capacity (Case A1), but much less than is caused by an increase in fossil fuel prices and capital costs (Case A2).

14.3.6   Case A5: Restrictions on Coal and Nuclear Capacity

In Case A5, the nuclear moratorium is in effect and, in addition, coal capacity growth is limited to half the Reference Case rate. This is an important combination of restrictions because the impact of the nuclear moratorium alone is to cause electric utilities to meet future demand with an accelerated growth in coal capacity; with the coal option partially closed utilities must turn to other types of generation to meet rising demand.

For the short term there exists excess capacity within the electric power industry in the form of oil- and gas-fired steam plants, many of which are either not used or not being fully used, and coal plants which are not being run at full capacity. The period until the late 1980s can be characterized as a period in which nuclear capacity grows to the maximum level permitted under the moratorium, and the excess capacity within the industry is managed so that existing plants are used at a higher level of capacity. This process involves an increase in production costs because of the fuel mix shifts relative to the Reference Case, with utilities using much more oil and gas. At

Table A5.1
Summary

Macroeconomic summary ($1972 billion)			
	1977	1990	2000
Consumption	858.5	1348.5	1718.6
		(−0.3)	(−2.5)
Investment	200.6	312.7	385.6
		(−0.8)	(−3.8)
Government and net exports	278.2	427.2	561.2
		(—)	(—)
GNP	1337.3	2088.4	2665.4
		(−0.3)	(−2.2)
Impacts on electric power industry			
	1977	1990	2000
Average price (mills/KWH)	35.7	48.6	64.0
(constant dollars)		(3.9)	(22.0)
Generation (bn KWH)	2153.0	3862.0	5315.3
		(−2.5)	(−17.0)
Capacity (GW)	551.0	854.0	1187.2
		(−11.5)	(−15.8)

Numbers in parentheses represent percent change from the Reference Case.

Table A5.2
Energy

Electric generating capacities and fuel inputs in 2000

	Capacity (GW)	Fuel input (quadrillion Btu)
Coal	305.8	19.5
	(−40.9)	(−32.9)
Oil and gas		23.9
		(1414.6)
(Steam)	198.7	
	(—)	
(Turbine)	481.6	
	(310.6)	
Nuclear	83.8	5.2
	(−81.5)	(−81.5)
Other	117.3	5.1
	(—)	(—)
Total	1187.2	53.6
	(−15.8)	(−15.6)

Primary energy inputs (quadrillion Btu)

	1977	1990	2000
Coal	14.1	27.2	28.0
		(−3.5)	(−23.3)
Petroleum	37.0	51.4	66.9
		(11.7)	(34.1)
Natural gas	19.6	20.9	24.5
		(10.2)	(22.7)
Nuclear	2.7	5.7	5.2
		(−59.9)	(−81.5)
Other	2.4	4.6	5.3
		(—)	(—)
Total input	75.8	109.9	129.9
		(−1.9)	(−6.9)
Gas and petroleum imports	17.9	36.7	60.1
		(24.8)	(56.1)

Numbers in parentheses represent percent change from the Reference Case.

projected price levels oil and gas will be significantly more expensive than either coal or nuclear fuel as inputs to electricity generation.

By the end of the 1980s the electric power industry will reach the limits of growth in traditional forms of generation because of the coal capacity limit and nuclear moratorium. It is assumed for this case that, as in the Reference Case, that government restrictions on the construction of new oil and gas fired steam plants continue, and that hydroelectric and nontraditional generation methods cannot expand faster than in the Reference Case. The only remaining types of generating plant unrestricted and potentially available to meet continued demand growth are combustion turbines and internal combustion plants.

Turbines and internal combustion facilities require less capital and less construction time than other types of plants, but are relatively expensive in terms of the quantity and price of their fuel inputs and in terms of maintenance. At current and probable future oil prices the average cost of electricity generated by combustion turbines is higher than the average cost for generation from coal, nuclear, hydro, or oil or gas steam plants. Nevertheless, since they are the only plant type available for growth to keep up with demand, construction of combustion turbines is projected to accelerate rapidly. By 2000, the capacity of such plants is more than four times the Reference level. This capacity configuration is sufficient to meet demand without shortages, but doing so will require that combustion turbines be used to meet cycling loads and perhaps even base load demands, rather than being held in readiness to help meet peak demand, as is the current practice.

The shifts from coal and nuclear toward oil and gas in electricity generation lead to a very large rise in utility use of these fuels—utility use of oil and gas increases from 1.6 quads in the Reference Case in 2000, to 23.9 quads in Case A5. Although construction costs are lower than for steam plants, the higher fuel and operating costs lead to a marked rise in overall generating costs and in electricity prices; by 2000, prices are 22 percent higher than in the Reference Case. Electricity demand grows less rapidly as a result of the higher prices (and slower economic growth) so by 2000 it is 17 percent lower than the Reference level. (It should be noted, though, that this demand can be satisfied by available capacity, there are no shortages.)

The increase in the price of electricity causes demand for electricity to fall, and for some of this demand to be shifted to increased use of oil and gas. The lower level of electricity demand is reflected in lower total energy input to utilities, and in lower total U.S. primary energy input. Because the nuclear and coal restrictions cause a major restructuring of energy consumption, the overall fall in energy inputs is the aggregate effect of many changes: coal inputs drop as demand from the electric utilities falls, nuclear inputs drop for the same reason, and oil and gas inputs rise both because of increased use by utilities and because of increased direct use.

The relative decline in the use of coal and nuclear energy provides a reduction in many indicators of environmental health and safety damage or risk. At the same time, these energy changes have significant costs, quite apart from the direct impact on the electric power industry. The rise in oil and gas use must be accommodated by increased imports; in fact, energy imports in 2000 are projected to be 56 percent higher than in the Reference Case, a rise of about 10 million barrels a day oil equivalent. This rise in the degree of import reliance in itself involves significant political costs and increased risk of economic cost. These major energy restructurings also exact an economic cost. The slower productivity growth leads to real GNP in 2000 being $(1972)60 billion less than in the Reference Case. The present value of the loss in real income over the 1978–2000 period due to the coal and nuclear restrictions is $(1972)171 billion.

14.3.7 Case A6: Nuclear Moratorium and Higher Prices and Costs

In Case A6, there is a nuclear moratorium as well as higher prices of coal, oil and gas and higher capital costs for new coal and nuclear plants. In the Reference Case, nuclear plants provide a large part of

Table A6.1
Summary

Macroeconomic summary ($1972 billion)			
	1977	1990	2000
Consumption	858.5	1303.4	1667.9
		(−3.7)	(−5.4)
Investment	200.6	293.6	363.0
		(−6.9)	(−9.5)
Government and net exports	278.2	427.2	561.2
		(—)	(—)
GNP	1337.3	2024.2	2592.1
		(−3.4)	(−4.9)
Impacts on electric power industry			
	1977	1990	2000
Average price (mills/KWH)	35.7	60.0	67.1
(constant dollars)		(28.4)	(27.8)
Generation (bn KWH)	2153.0	3076.8	4797.7
		(−22.3)	(−25.1)
Capacity (GW)	551.0	830.1	1157.0
		(−14.0)	(−17.9)

Numbers in parentheses represent percent change from the Reference Case.

Table A6.2
Energy

Electric generating capacities and fuel inputs in 2000

	Capacity (GW)	Fuel input (quadrillion Btu)
Coal	651.9	30.5
	(26.0)	(5.0)
Oil and gas		5.4
		(241.8)
(Steam)	198.7	
	(—)	
(Turbine)	105.3	
	(−15.0)	
Nuclear	83.8	5.2
	(−81.5)	(−81.5)
Other	117.3	5.1
	(—)	(—)
Total	1157.0	46.2
	(17.9)	(−27.3)

Primary energy inputs (quadrillion Btu)

	1977	1990	2000
Coal	14.1	20.5	35.9
		(−27.3)	(−1.7)
Petroleum	37.0	40.3	45.3
		(−12.4)	(−9.2)
Natural gas	19.6	17.2	18.4
		(−9.6)	(−8.0)
Nuclear	2.7	5.7	5.2
		(−59.9)	(−81.5)
Other	2.4	4.7	5.3
		(—)	(—)
Total input	75.8	88.3	110.0
		(−21.1)	(−21.2)
Gas and petroleum imports	17.9	21.9	32.3
		(−25.2)	(−16.1)

Numbers in parentheses represent percent change from the Reference Case.

capacity expansion through the rest of the century, so the nuclear moratorium forces utilities to expand in other types of plants to meet demand. If prices and costs were at the Reference Case level almost all of the shift would be into coal plants, which are only slightly more expensive than nuclear plants in terms of average generation costs. But one of the effects of the introduction of higher fuel and capital costs is that the relative economics of different types of plants changes so that in some areas oil and gas steam plants are preferred to coal.

The other major effect of the higher costs is that they accentuate the impact of the nuclear moratorium on the price of electricity by increasing the difference between the cost of nuclear generation and the cost of generation by plants that are used in place of nuclear plants. The greater increase in the price of electricity then causes demand for electricity to drop even farther.

By 2000 the combination of the nuclear moratorium forcing a shift to other methods of generation and the higher fuel and capacity costs lead to noticeable increases in generation costs so that the price of electricity is 28 percent higher than the Reference Case. At the higher price, and with the associated slowing of economic growth, demand is 25 percent lower than in the Reference Case. This demand can be satisfied from available capacity; there are no shortages. Coal becomes the primary fuel input to electric utilities, although the use of oil and gas also increases over the Reference level. The increased use of oil and gas is in the form of higher usage factors for existing oil and gas steam plants. The large demand reduction means that energy inputs into electricity generation are well below the Reference Case levels.

The combined effect of higher prices in all forms of delivered energy means that less final energy is consumed. This, together with the electricity restrictions, leads to a reduction in each type of primary energy input. The decrease in fuel inputs to electricity is composed of a large decrease in nuclear inputs, and small increases in fossil fuels—coal, oil, and gas. However, this small increase in coal input is offset by a decline in the direct use of coal and the same is true for oil and gas. Total U.S. primary energy input in 2000 is 21 percent less than in the Reference Case. One important consequence of these energy changes is that the lower levels of oil and gas use translate into comparable reductions in imports; in 2000 total imports of oil and gas are 16 percent below the Reference level.

The economic impact of higher energy prices is heightened in this case by the fact that all forms of delivered energy increase in price. There are widespread substitutions away from energy in input and spending patterns. One aspect of these substitutions is an increase in capital and labor input per unit of output. This input restructuring is equivalent to a slowing in the growth of capital and labor productivity. Given the limited supply of these factors, the productivity slowdown leads to a slowing of economic growth. In 2000, this growth effect results in real GNP being $(1972)134 billion less than in the Reference Case. For the whole 1978 to 2000 period, the present value of the loss in real income is $(1972)724 billion. By either measure of economic impact the combination of the nuclear moratorium and higher fuel and capital costs leads to a greater economic cost than the nuclear moratorium alone, higher costs alone, the coal restriction alone, or any other combination of two of these three changes.

14.3.8   Case A7: Coal Restrictions, Nuclear Moratorium, and High Costs

Case A7 includes all three sets of changes: (a) construction of nuclear plants is limited to those already under construction, (b) construction of coal plants is limited to half the Reference Case rate, and (c) the price of coal is double the Reference Case levels, the price of oil and gas is up 20 percent, and the capital cost for new coal plants and new nuclear plants is increased by $(1977)100 per kilowatt.

The restrictions on plant capacity and the higher fuel prices alter the construction plans and fuel use policies of the electric utilities, with the final result being large-scale use of oil and gas, even at the higher price. There is currently excess capacity within the industry in

Table A7.1
Summary

Macroeconomic summary ($1972 billion)			
	1977	1990	2000
Consumption	858.5	1296.3	1657.0
		(−4.2)	(−6.0)
Investment	200.6	292.6	360.3
		(−7.2)	(−10.2)
Government and net exports	278.2	427.2	561.2
		(—)	(—)
GNP	1337.3	2016.1	2578.5
		(−3.8)	(−5.4)
Impacts on electric power industry			
	1977	1990	2000
Average price (mills/KWH)	35.7	59.9	69.8
(constant dollars)		(28.0)	(33.1)
Generation (bn KWH)	2153.0	3070.2	4598.7
		(−22.5)	(−28.2)
Capacity (GW)	551.0	763.1	1088.7
		(−20.9)	(−22.8)

Numbers in parentheses represent percent change from the Reference Case.

Table A7.2
Energy

Electric generating capacities and fuel inputs in 2000

	Capacity (GW)	Fuel input (quadrillion Btu)
Coal	305.8	19.4
	(−40.9)	(−33.3)
Oil and gas		15.7
		(895.6)
(Steam)	198.7	
	(—)	
(Turbine)	383.1	
	(209.2)	
Nuclear	83.8	5.2
	(−81.5)	(−81.5)
Other	117.3	5.1
	(—)	(—)
Total	1088.7	45.3
	(−22.8)	(−28.7)

Primary energy inputs (quadrillion Btu)

	1977	1990	2000
Coal	14.1	17.4	24.8
		(−38.3)	(−32.2)
Petroleum	37.0	42.8	52.2
		(−6.9)	(6.7)
Natural gas	19.6	17.8	21.0
		(−6.2)	(5.1)
Nuclear	2.7	5.7	5.2
		(−59.9)	(−81.5)
Other	2.4	4.6	5.3
		(—)	(—)
Total input	75.8	88.4	109.4
		(−21.1)	(−21.6)
Gas and petroleum imports	17.9	25.0	42.3
		(−15.0)	(9.9)

Numbers in parentheses represent percent change from the Reference Case.

the form of underutilized oil and gas steam plants. By using these plants more intensely, and using the nuclear plants already under construction and coming on line in the 1980s, the industry is able to meet demand without major shifts until the late 1980s. Even by 1985, however, the price of electricity climbs above the Reference growth path particularly because of increased use of oil and gas, which are relatively expensive fuels even without the 20 percent increase in price, and even more expensive with this price rise. In addition, coal consumption continues to increase but the fuel cost doubles, further contributing to the rise in generation costs and electricity prices.

By the end of the 1980s the supply situation is highly constrained—nuclear capacity has reached a ceiling and is even declining as some of the early plants are retired, coal capacity is growing but slowly, and oil and gas steam plants are already used to capacity and utilities are not permitted to build more. Because of higher fuel prices and greater use of oil and gas the price of electricity is projected to be 28 percent above the Reference Case (in 1990) and this price rise does slow the growth in demand, somewhat easing the pressure of demand against supply capacity. Utilities at this point have only one option available for large-scale expansion of capacity to meet a growing electricity demand; this option is capacity expansion in the form of combustion turbines and internal combustion plants. These plants are normally restricted to peaking use on cost considerations, but with other base and cycling capacity restricted, they are systematically used for both peak and off-peak generation. This strategy permits demand to be accommodated but the high costs, particularly the fuel costs, of this type of generation forces up generations costs and electricity prices. Thus, shortages are avoided but at the expense of high electricity prices—average prices in 2000 are 33 percent above the Reference Case level.

All forms of delivered energy—electricity, oil, gas and coal—are more expensive than in the Reference Case. The higher prices by themselves cause a drop in demand for all forms of delivered energy. However, within the electric power industry, even though total demand is down, and total fuel inputs are down, the use of coal and nuclear energy is so limited that oil and gas consumption is far above Reference Case levels, ten times above in 2000. In addition, the price of electricity increases by an even greater percentage than the price of oil and gas and there is some substitution of oil or gas for electricity. The result is a substantial realignment of the pattern of primary fuel inputs—coal and nuclear are greatly reduced while oil and gas are increased. The rise in oil and gas use is of significance because it is supplied through increasing the level of oil and gas imports; imports rise to 10 percent above the Reference level by 2000. This increase in total oil and gas use, and in imports, is a phenomenon of the 1990s: it is only after 1990 that supply constraints force utilities into rapid expansion of oil and gas use. Further, it is significant the increase in oil and gas use and imports occurs despite the demand reducing effects of a 20 percent increase in oil and gas prices.

The high cost of energy in all forms has serious economic consequences. Although extensive use of combustion turbines, along with
increased imports of oil and gas, make it possible to avoid shortages,
energy becomes a much more expensive input to production and consumption. The resulting input restructuring, and associated productivity penalties, force economic growth onto a lower path. In every
future year, productivity potential, real income and production are
reduced below those obtaining under Reference Case conditions. In
2000 the projected GNP in Case A7 is $(1972)147 billion less than in
the Reference Case, representing a loss of 5.4 percent. The cumulative
effect, over the rest of the century, has a present value of $(1972)791
billion, equivalent to approximately 60 percent of the Gross National
product in 1978.

14.4   Summary and Conclusion

14.4.1   Nuclear Moratorium

The nuclear moratorium comprises a prohibition of the beginning of
any new construction of nuclear electricity generating plants in 1977
or beyond. Plants under construction in 1977 are permitted to be completed and brought into operation and plants already in operation in
1977 are permitted to continue in normal operation. The effects of this
capacity restriction in terms of impacts on the electricity sector, the
energy system and the economy were reviewed in the previous section. The effect of restrictions on new nuclear generating capacity can
be presented in four points:

a. The nuclear restrictions are sustainable in that the electric power
industry is still able to satisfy demand for electricity and economic
growth can continue at an appreciable positive rate.

b. At the same time, the moratorium does involve significant costs in
terms of its electricity, energy and economic impacts. The electricity
costs involve consumers paying higher prices for electricity and making do with reduced quantities. The energy costs involve greater use
of coal and other fossil fuels, with attendant environmental problems,
and potentially much higher levels of imports of oil and gas, with
associated costs in terms of economic and political stability and security. The economic costs involve reduced future levels of income, production and purchasing power.

c. The costs of the moratorium can be greatly affected by other policies and changes; if the moratorium is introduced on top of other restrictions, in particular any restrictions on coal use, then the costs rapidly rise above those for a moratorium introduced in isolation.

d. Although the costs of a nuclear moratorium are sustainable they may be large and are certainly significant relative to any benefits that might be expected from the moratorium.

14.4.2   Restrictions on Coal-Fired Generating Capacity

The restrictions on expansion of coal-fired electricity generating capacity involve the limitation of the rate of capacity expansion to one-half the rate projected for the Reference Case. The effects of such restrictions can be summarized in four points.

a. The coal restrictions can be sustained by the electric power industry by shifting towards other fuels, although there is some resulting increase in costs and prices and a slight slowing of electricity demand growth.

b. The coal restrictions do have effects beyond the electric power industry—growth of coal production is slowed, growth of substitute fuels is accelerated, in some circumstances imports of oil and gas are significantly increased, and there is some slowing of growth of incomes and production throughout the economy.

c. The effects of the coal restrictions depend greatly on other energy policies and developments; prior changes which increase the relative prices of coal fuel and equipment tend to reduce the cost of coal restrictions while prior nuclear restrictions greatly increase the costs.

d. The coal capacity restrictions bring both benefits and costs. The benefits arise from reduced extraction and burning of coal with corresponding improvements for the environment, work safety and air quality, although it can be noted that capacity restrictions are not the only way of pursuing these benefits, other approaches include land reclamation laws, and increased use of low sulfur coal. The costs take the form of disruption to the electric power industry, increased prices to electricity consumers, less use of electricity by consumers, some loss of future incomes and production, and increased reliance on imported oil and gas.

14.4.3   Higher Fossil Fuel Prices and Capacity Costs

These changes do not involve quantitative limitations on capacity or fuel use but cover higher prices for coal, oil and gas together with increased capacity costs for the construction of new coal-fired electricity generating equipment. The effects of higher fossil fuel prices and higher coal-fired electricity generating capacity costs can be summarized:

a. Higher fossil fuel costs have a substantial and widespread impact—energy use is greatly curtailed and economic growth is noticeably slowed.

b. Some benefits are obtained from the increase in fossil fuel costs: imports of oil and gas are reduced and less use of fossil fuels implies some environmental improvement.

c. These changes involve sizeable costs—electricity consumers face higher prices and make do with less electricity, users of coal, oil and gas also face large increases in their costs, and there are costs imposed throughout the economy in terms of reduced incomes, production and purchasing power. While these costs are sustainable, for example real GNP continues to increase at an appreciable rate, the fact remains that these costs are significant in both absolute and relative magnitude.

14.4.4   Interactions Among Energy Restrictions

Each of the energy changes considered—nuclear moratorium, coal restrictions, higher fossil fuel and capacity costs—has a substantial impact on the energy system and the economy. The impacts compound, however, when one change is introduced into conditions in which other energy restrictions are already in force. In almost all cases, the effect of an energy change superimposed upon another restriction is more severe than the effect of that change when introduced in isolation. Two areas of impact in which this interaction is particularly pronounced are oil and gas imports and the general economic costs in terms of real GNP reduction.

Consider first the introduction of a nuclear moratorium. When introduced in isolation or when superimposed on higher fossil fuel costs, the nuclear restriction results in a rise of about 11 percent in electricity prices and an increase of about 2 quads in oil and gas imports. However, when introduced into an energy system already subject to coal capacity restrictions, the nuclear moratorium results in electricity price rises of about 18 percent and in increases of up to 20 quads in oil and gas imports. The reason for the difference in effects is that, if coal restrictions are in operation, a nuclear moratorium forces utilities to use oil and gas for generation growth as all other large-scale fuel sources are closed off. Increased oil and gas use, in turn, leads directly to higher prices and higher energy import levels. Correspondingly, the economic impacts are greater for nuclear restrictions when superimposed on coal restrictions than for nuclear restrictions in isolation—the present value of real GNP loss is $(1972)155 bn compared to $(1972)94 billion.

Significant interdependence also emerges in the case of coal capacity restrictions. Coal restrictions introduced in conditions of higher fossil fuel prices and coal capacity costs have minimal effects since cost considerations have already induced utilities to move away from coal in their expansion plans so the coal constraint is almost satisfied anyway. The coal restrictions by themselves have somewhat greater impact—oil and gas imports increase by about 1 quad and the present value of the real GNP loss is $(1972)16 billion. However, when the coal restrictions are superimposed on the nuclear moratorium, the effects are several times greater—oil and gas imports rise by 22 quads and the present value of the real GNP loss is 171 in $(1972)billion. The reason for the greater effect is that coal restrictions force utilities towards oil and gas when the nuclear option is not available. The increased reliance on oil and gas raises costs and electricity prices, imposing economic costs, and at the same time drawing in much larger quantities of oil and gas imports.

These interactions concern the differential effect of introducing an energy restriction when other restrictions are already in force—this differential impact varies according to the preexisting conditions. A different type of interdependence involves the introduction of multiple restrictions and whether or not joint restrictions have an impact greater than the sum of their separate effects. In this dimension it also turns out that there can be significant interaction between restrictions so that the joint impact exceeds the sum of the parts. Table 14.9 summarizes the effects of restrictions in terms of their impacts on energy imports and on the economy.

The sum of the separate effects of a coal restriction and a nuclear restriction is an economic cost with present value of $(1972)110 billion. Jointly, these restrictions impose an economic cost of $(1972)171

Table 14.9
Reference Case Generating Capacity in 1983 and 2000

	Change in oil and gas imports in 2000 (quadrillion Btu)	Change in present value of real economic cost ($(1972)bn)
Coal	1	−16
Nuclear	1	−94
Sum	2	−110
Coal, nuclear	22	−171
Coal	1	−16
Costs	−9	−607
Sum	−8	−623
Coal, costs	−9	−610
Costs	−9	−607
Nuclear	1	−94
Sum	−8	−701
Costs, nuclear	−6	−724
Coal	1	−16
Costs	−9	−607
Nuclear	1	−94
Sum	−7	−717
Coal, costs, nuclear	4	−791

billion. Similarly, oil and gas imports rise by 2 quads for the separate effects compared to 22 quads for simultaneous restrictions. These figures show a highly interactive relationship between coal and nuclear restrictions. The consequences of changes that include higher costs for fossil fuels and coal capacity involve, in contrast, a much smaller degree of interaction. Coal restrictions and cost increases together have about the same impact as the sum of their separate effects; the same is true for nuclear restrictions and cost increases. But, when the cost changes are combined with both nuclear and coal restrictions a strong interaction again appears. Both oil and gas imports and economic costs are appreciably higher for the three changes together than the sum of their separate effects.

There is, then, a consistent feature running through the results of all these cases in terms of interactions between restrictions. This is that nuclear restrictions and coal restrictions together compound the costs imposed by either one; their joint impact is much greater than the sum of their separate effects. This is true for nuclear and coal restrictions with or without any of the other restrictions considered, including higher fossil fuel and capacity costs. Thus, while restrictions on coal-fired generated capacity or on nuclear capacity each impose a significant cost on the energy and economic systems, the effect of simultaneous coal and nuclear restrictions is much more severe than either of their separate effects would suggest.

Notes

1. The Long-term Inter-industry Transaction Model is a general equilibrium model of the U.S. economy, based on the energy-economy model originally developed by Hudson and Jorgenson (1974a). Recent applications of the Long-term Industry Transactions Model are discussed by Hudson and Jorgenson (1978a,b,c).

2. The Regionalized Electricity Models a partial equilibrium model of the electric utility industry originally developed by Baughman and Joskow (1974). The model and its applications are discussed by Baughman, Joskow, and Kamat (1979).

3. Methodology for model integration presented by Hogan and Weyant (1980). Applications of integrated models are discussed by Baughman, Cazalet, Hudson, Jorgenson, Kresge, Kuh, and North (1978).

4. A brief survey of models of the U.S. electric utility industry is given by Baughman, Joskow, and Kamat (1979), pp. 10–17.

5. Surveys of models of the U.S. energy sector are given by Brock and Nesbitt (1977), by Charles River Associates (1977), by Hogan and Weyant (1980), and by Manne, Richels, and Weyant (1979).

6. Integration of the Hudson-Jorgenson model with models of the energy sector is discussed by Bernanke and Jorgenson (1975) and by Hoffman and Jorgenson (1977). For a detailed comparison of the linkage between Hudson-Jorgenson and Baughman-Joskow models with other model integration efforts, see Hogan and Weyant (1980), pp. 88–98.

7. A survey of studies of the demand for electricity is given by Taylor (1975).

8. A survey of studies of the demand for energy is given by Taylor (1977).

9. Alternative population projections for the United States are given by Bureau of the Census (1977).

10. More detailed projections of U.S. economic growth and energy utilization on the basis of the Hudson-Jorgenson model are presented by Hudson and Jorgenson (1974a). These projections were incorporated into a study of future U.S. economic growth by Edison Electric Institute (1976). A new study of future U.S. economic growth employing the combined Hudson-Jorgenson and Baughman-Joskow models is currently under way by the Edison Electric Institute.

11. More detailed projections of the future growth of the electric power industry on the basis of the Baughman-Joskow model are presented by Baughman, Joskow, and Kamat (1979), pp. 122–156.

12. The impact of a nuclear moratorium on the electric utility industry has been analyzed by Weinberg (1979).

13. Baughman, Joskow, and Kamat (1979), pp. 158–178, have analyzed the impact of the following restrictions on the electric utility industry within a partial equilibrium framework:

1. Air quality restrictions
2. Peak load pricing
3. Decreased nuclear lead times
4. Nuclear moratorium
5. High cost of capital
6. Reprocessing and plutonium recycle.

We present an analysis of nuclear moratorium higher fuel and coal expansion, and all possible combinations of these restrictions within a general equilibrium framework. Baughman, Joskow, and Kamat (1979), pp. 12 and 207, provide a brief discussion of partial and general equilibrium approaches.

References

Allen, Roy G.D. 1956. *Mathematical Economics*. New York: St. Martin's Press.

———. 1960. The Structure of Macro-Economic Models. *Economic Journal* 70 (March): 38–56.

Almon, C., M.R. Buckler, L.M. Horowitz, and T.C. Reimbold. 1974. *Interindustry Forecasts of the American Economy*. Lexington, VA: Heath.

Arrow, Kenneth J. 1960. Price-Quantity Adjustments in Multiple Markets with Rising Demands. In *Mathematical Methods in the Social Sciences, 1959*, eds. Kenneth J. Arrow, Samuel Karlin, and Patrick Suppes, 3–15. Stanford, CA: Stanford University Press.

Bain, Joe S. 1956. *Barriers to New Competition*, Chapter 3, pp. 53–113. Cambridge, MA: Harvard.

Balestra, Pietro. 1967. *The Demand for Natural Gas in the United States*. Amsterdam: North-Holland.

Balestra, Pietro, and Marc Nerlove. 1966. Pooling Cross Section and Time Series Data in the Estimation of a Dynamic Model: The Demand for Natural Gas. *Econometrica* 34, no. 3 (July): 585–612.

Barouch E., and George Kaufman. 1974. *Sampling Without Replacement and Proportional to Random Size*. Cambridge, MA: Massachusetts Institute of Technology.

Baughman, M.L., E.G. Cazalet, Edward A. Hudson, Dale W. Jorgenson, D.T. Kresge, E. Thomas Kuh, and D.W. North. 1978. *Initiation of Integration*, Final Report EA-837, July. Palo Alto, CA: Electric Power Research Institute.

Baughman, M.L., and Paul L. Joskow. 1974. *A Regionalized Electricity Model*, Energy Laboratory Report No. MIT-EL-75-005, December. Cambridge, MA: MIT.

Baughman, M.L., Paul L. Joskow, and D.P. Kamat. 1979. *Electric Power in the United States: Models and Policy Analysis*. Cambridge, MA: MIT Press.

Baumol, William. 1959. *Economic Dynamics*. London: Macmillan, 2nd. ed.

Behling, D.J., R. Dullien, and Edward A. Hudson. 1976. *The Relationship of Energy Growth to Economic Growth Under Alternative Energy Prices*, BNL 50500. Upton, NY: Brookhaven National Laboratory.

Behling, D.J., W. Marcuse, M. Swift, and R.G. Tessmer. 1975. *A Two-Level Iterative Model for Estimating Inter-Fuel Substitution Effects*, BNL 19863. Upton, NY: Brookhaven National Laboratory.

Beller, M., ed. 1975. *Sourcebook for Energy Assessment*, BNL 50483. Upton, NY: Brookhaven National Laboratory.

Bellman, Richard. 1960. *Introduction to Matrix Analysis*. New York: McGraw-Hill.

Bergson, Abram. 1938. A Reformulation of Certain Aspects of Welfare Economics. *Quarterly Journal of Economics* 52, no. 2 (February): 310–334.

Bernanke, Ben, and Dale W. Jorgenson. 1975. The Integration of Energy Policy Models. *Computers and Operations Research* 2, no. 3 (September): 225–249.

Berndt, Ernst R. 1990. *The Practice of Econometrics: Classic and Contemporary*, Reading, MA: Addison-Wesley.

Berndt, Ernst R., and Laurits R. Christensen. 1973a. The Translog Function and Substitution of Equipment, Structures, and Labor in U.S. Manufacturing, 1929–1968. *Journal of Econometrics* 1, no. 1 (March): 81–114.

———. 1973b. The Specification of Technology in U.S. Manufacturing. University of British Columbia Discussion Paper 73–17, November.

———. 1974. Testing for the Existence of a Consistent Aggregate Index of Labor Inputs. *American Economic Review* 64, no. 3 (June): 391–404.

Berndt, Ernst R., and Dale W. Jorgenson. 1973. Production Structure. In *U.S. Energy Resources and Economic Growth*, eds. Dale W. Jorgenson and Hendrik S. Houthakker, ch. 3. Washington, DC: Energy Policy Project.

Berndt, Ernst R., and David O. Wood. 1979. Engineering and Econometric Interpretations of Energy-Capital Complementarity: A Reconciliation. *American Economic Review* 69, no. 3 (June): 342–354.

Boeke, Julius Herman. 1953. *Economics and Economic Policy of Dual Societies*. Haarlem: Tjeenk Willnik (earlier edition in two vols. 1942, 1946).

Breyer, Steven G., and Paul W. MacAvoy. 1974. Regulating Natural Gas Producers. In *Energy Regulation by the Federal Power Commission*, ch. 3, 56–88. Washington, DC: The Brookings Institution.

Brock, Horace W., and Dale M. Nesbitt. 1977. *Large-Scale Energy Planning Models: A Methodological Analysis*, Report to the National Science Foundation. Menlo Park, CA: Stanford Research Institute.

Buck, John Lossing. 1930. *Chinese Farm Economy*. Chicago, IL: University of Chicago Press.

Bullard, Clark W., and R. Herendeen. 1973a. *Energy Cost of Consumption Decisions*, Document 135. Urbana, IL: Center for Advanced Computation, University of Illinois at Urbana-Champaign.

———. 1973b. *Energy Cost of Consumer Goods 1963–1967*, Document 140. Urbana, IL: Center for Advanced Computations, University of Illinois at Urbana-Champaign.

Bureau of the Census. Various annual issues, 1973–1983. Pollution Abatement Costs and Expenditures. Washington, DC: U.S. Department of Commerce.

———. 1977. Projections of the Population of the United States: 1977–2050. *Current Population Reports*, Population Estimates and Projections, ser. P-25, no. 704 (July).

Bureau of Economic Analysis. Various monthly issues. *Survey of Current Business*.

Bureau of Economic Analysis. 1977. *The National Income and Product Accounts of the United States, 1929–1974: Statistical Tables*. Washington, DC: U.S. Government Printing Office.

Burmeister, Edwin, and A. Rodney Dobell. 1970. *Mathematical Theories of Economic Growth*. New York: Macmillan.

Burrows J.C., and Thomas A. Domencich. 1970. *An Analysis of the Oil Import Quota*. Lexington, VA: Heath.

Carter, Anne P. 1970. *Structural Change in the American Economy*. Cambridge, MA: Harvard University Press.

Carter, Anne P., and Andrew Brody. 1970. *Contributions to Input-Output Analysis*, vols. I and II. Amsterdam: North-Holland.

Central Intelligence Agency. 1977. The International Energy Situation: Outlook to 1985 (April).

Centre for Industrial Development, Department of Social and Economic Affairs. 1965. *A Study of Industrial Growth*. New York: United Nations.

Chambers, Jonathan David. 1953. Enclosure and Labour Supply in the Industrial Revolution. *Economic History Review* 5: 319–343.

Champernowne, David Gawen. 1958. Capital Accumulation and Full Employment. *Economic Journal* 68: 218–244.

Chapman Duane, T.D. Mount, and T.J. Tyrrell. 1972. Electricity Growth: Implications for Research and Development. Testimony before the Committee on Science and Astronautics, U.S. House of Representatives, June 16.

Charles River Associates. 1977. *Review and Evaluation of Selected Large-Scale Energy Models*, Report to the Electric Power Research Institute, June. Cambridge, MA: Charles River Associates.

Chenery, Hollis B. 1960. Patterns of Industrial Growth. *American Economic Review* 50: 624–654.

Cherniavsky, E.A. 1974. *Brookhaven Energy System Optimization Model*, BNL 19569. Upton, NY: Brookhaven National Laboratory.

———. 1975. *Linear Programming and Technology Assessment*, BNL 20053. Upton, NY: Brookhaven National Laboratory.

Chipman, John Somerset. 1951. *The Theory of Inter-Sectoral Money Flows and Income Formation*. Baltimore: Johns Hopkins Press.

———. 1954. A Note on Stability, Workability, and Duality in Linear Economic Models. *Metroeconomica* 6 (April): 1–10.

Christensen, Laurits R., Dianne Cummings, and Dale W. Jorgenson. 1978. Productivity Growth, 1947–1973: An International Comparison. In *The Impact of International Trade and Investment on Employment*, ed. W. Dewald, 211–233. Washington, DC: U.S. Government Printing Office.

Christensen, Laurits R., and Dale W. Jorgenson. 1969. The Measurement of U.S. Real Capital Input, 1929–1967. *Review of Income and Wealth*, ser. 15, no. 4 (December): 293–320.

———. 1970. U.S. Real Product and Real Factor Input, 1929–1967. *Review of Income and Wealth*, ser. 16, no. 1 (March): 19–50.

———. 1973a. U.S. Income, Saving and Wealth, 1929–1969. *Review of Income and Wealth*, ser. 19, no. 4 (December): 329–362.

———. 1973b. Measuring Economic Performance in the Private Sector. In *The Measurement of Economic and Social Performance*, ed. Milton Moss, 233–251. NBER Studies in Income and Wealth, vol. 37. New York: Columbia University Press.

Christensen, Laurits R., Dale W. Jorgenson, and Lawrence J. Lau. 1971. Conjugate Duality and the Transcendental Logarithmic Production Function. *Econometrica* 39, no. 4 (July): 255–256.

———. 1973. Transcendental Logarithmic Production Frontiers. *Review of Economics and Statistics* 55, no. 1 (February): 28–45.

———. 1975. Transcendental Logarithmic Utility Functions. *American Economic Review* 65, no. 3 (June): 367–383.

Clark, Collin. 1957. *The Conditions of Economic Progress*, 3rd. ed. London: Macmillan.

Congressional Research Service. 1978. *U.S. Energy Demands and Supply, 1976–1985*. Final Report to the Subcommittee on Energy and Power, Committee on Interstate and Foreign Commerce, House of Representatives, 95th Congress, First Session (March). Washington, DC: U.S. Government Printing Office.

Darmstadter, Joel, Jay Dunkerley, and Jack Alterman. 1977. *How Industrial Societies Use Energy: A Comparative Analysis*. Baltimore, MD: Johns Hopkins Press.

Debreu, Gerard, and I. N. Herstein. 1953. Nonnegative Matrices. *Econometrica* 21 (October): 597–607.

Domar, Evsey D. 1946. Capital Expansion, Rate of Growth, and Employment. *Econometrica* 14 (April): 137–147.

––––––. 1957. *Essays in the Theory of Economic Growth*. New York: Oxford University Press.

Dorfman, Robert, Paul A. Samuelson, and Robert M. Solow. 1958. *Linear Programming and Economic Analysis*. New York: McGraw-Hill.

Douglas, Paul H. 1948. Are There Laws of Production? *American Economic Review* 38, no. 1 (March): 1–41.

Dovring, Folke. 1959. The Share of Agriculture in a Growing Population. *Bulletin of Agricultral Economic Statistics* 8: 1–11; reprinted in Carl K. Eicher and Lawrence W. Witt (eds.). 1964. *Agriculture in Economic Development*, pp. 78–98. New York: McGraw-Hill.

Duesenberry, James S. 1958. *Business Cycles and Economic Growth*. New York: McGraw-Hill.

––––––. 1950. Hicks on the Trade Cycle. *Quarterly Journal of Economics* 64 (August): 464–476.

Dullien, R., ed. 1976. *User's Guide to the DRI Long-Term Interindustry Transactions Model*. Interim Report to the U.S. Department of the Interior. Washington, DC: U.S. Government Printing Office.

Dupree W., and R. West. 1972. *United States Energy Through 2000*. U.S. Department of the Interior Report, December.

Eckstein, Otto. 1978. *The Great Recession*. Amsterdam: North-Holland.

Edison Electric Institute. 1976. *Economic Growth in the Future.* New York: McGraw-Hill.

Electric Power Research Institute. 1977a. *Technical Assessment Guide*. Palo Alto, CA.

––––––. 1977b. *Supply 77*. Palo Alto, CA.

Ellis, Howard S. 1961. Las economías duales y el progreso. *Revista de Economía Latinoamericana* 1: 3–17.

Energy Information Administration. 1977. *Annual Report to Congress*, vol. III.

––––––. 1978. *Annual Report to Congress*, vol. II.

Energy Research and Development Administration. 1975. *A National Plan for Energy Research and Development, and Demonstration: Creating Energy Choices for the Future*, ERDA 48. Washington, DC: U.S. Government Printing Office.

––––––. 1976. *A National Plan for Energy Research and Development, and Demonstration: Creating Energy Choices for the Future, 1976*, ERDA 76–1. Washington, DC: U.S. Government Printing Office.

Erickson, Edward W. 1970. Crude Oil Prices, Drilling Incentives, and the Supply of New Discoveries. *Natural Resource Journal* 10, no. 1: 27–52.

Erickson, Edward W., and Robert M. Spann. 1971. Supply Response in a Regulated Industry. *Bell Journal of Economics and Management Science* 2: 94–121.

Executive Office of the President. 1977. *The National Energy Plan*, Office Energy Policy and Planning. Washington, DC: U.S. Government Printing Office.

Federal Energy Administration. 1976. *1976 National Energy Outlook*. Washington, DC: U.S. Government Printing Office.

Fei, John C., and Gustav Ranis. 1961a. A Theory of Economic Development. *American Economic Review* 51: 533–534.

———. 1961b. Unlimited Supply of Labor and the Concept of Balanced Growth. *Pakistan Development Review* 1: 30.

———. 1963. Capital Accumulation and Economic Development. *American Economic Review* 53: 288.

———. 1964. *Development of the Labor Surplus Economy*. Homewood, IL: Irwin.

Firth, Raymond William. 1946. *Malay Fisherman*. London: Paul, Trench, Trubner.

Firth, Raymond William, and B.S. Yames, eds. 1964. *Capital, Saving and Credit in Peasant Societies*. Chicago, IL: Aldine.

Fisher, Franklin M. 1964. *Supply and Costs in the United States Petroleum Industry: Two Econometric Studies*. Baltimore, MD: Johns Hopkins Press.

Friedman, B. 1956. *Principles of Applied Mathematics*. New York: Wiley.

Frisch, Ragnar. 1933. Propagation Problems and Impulse Problems in Dynamic Economics. In *Economic Essays in Honor of Gustav Cassel*, 171–206. London: G. Allen and Unwin Ltd.

Gantmacher, F.R. 1959. *Applications of the Theory of Matrices*, trans. J.L. Brenner. New York: Interscience (1st ed., Russian, 1954).

Georgescu-Roegen, Nicholas. 1951. Relaxation Phenomena in Linear Dynamic Models. In *Activity Analysis of Production and Allocation*, ed. Tjalling C. Koopmans, 116–131. New York: Wiley.

Goldberger, A.J. 1959. *Impact Multipliers and Dynamic Properties of the Klein-Goldberger Model*. Amsterdam: North-Holland.

Goldman, Marshall I. 1977. Some Critical Observations about the CIA Analysis of the Need for Soviet Oil Imports, mimeographed.

Goodwin, R.M. 1948. *Towards a Dynamic Economics*. London: Macmillan.

———. 1949. The Multiplier as a Matrix. *Economic Journal* 69 (December): 537–555.

———. 1950. Does the Matrix Multiplier Oscillate? *Economic Journal* 60 (December), 764–770.

———. 1951. The Nonlinear Accelerator and the Persistence of Business Cycles. *Econometrica* 19 (January): 1–17.

———. 1952. Econometrics in Business Cycle Analysis, In *Business Cycles and National Income*, ed. A.H. Hanson, 417–468, Chapter 22. New York: Norton.

———. 1955. A Model of Cyclical Growth. In *The Business Cycle in the Post-war World*, ed. E. Lundberg, 203–221. New York: St. Martin's Press.

Gordon, Roger, and Dale W. Jorgenson. 1976 The Investment Tax Credit and Counter-Cyclical Policy. In *Parameters and Policies in the U.S. Economy*, ed. O. Eckstein, 275–314. Amsterdam: North-Holland.

Griliches, Zvi. 1957. Hybrid Corn: An Exploration in the Economics of Technical Change. *Econometrica* 25: 501–522.

Gutman, G.O. 1957. A Note on Economic Development with Subsistence Agriculture. *Oxford Economic Papers* 9: 323–329.

Hall, Robert E. 1978. Stochastic Implications of the Life Cycle-Permanent Income Hypothesis: Theory and Evidence. *Journal of Political Economy* 86: 971–987.

Hall, Robert E., and Dale W. Jorgenson. 1971. Application of the Theory of Optimum Capital Accumulation. In *Tax Incentives and Capital Spending*, ed. Gary Fromm, 9–60. Washington, DC: The Brookings Institution.

Hall, Robert E., and Robert S. Pindyck. 1977. The Conflicting Goals of National Energy Policy. *The Public Interest* 47 (Spring): 3–15.

Hansen, Lars P. 1982. Large Sample Properties of Generalized Method of Moments Estimators. *Econometrica* 50, no. 6 (November): 1029–1054.

Harrod, Roy F. 1939. An Essay in Dynamic Theory. *Economic Journal* 49 (March): 14–33.

———. 1948. *Towards a Dynamic Economics*. London: Macmillan.

Hawkins, David. 1948. Some Conditions of Macro-Economic Stability. *Econometrica* 16 (July): 309–322.

Hawkins, David, and Herbert A. Simon. 1949. Note: Some Conditions of Macro-Economic Stability. *Econometrica* 27 (July-October): 245–248.

Hickman B, ed. 1972. *Econometric Models of Cyclical Behavior*, vols. I and II. NBER Studies in Income and Wealth, vol. 36. New York: Columbia University Press.

Hicks, John R. 1942. Consumers' Surplus and Index Numbers. *Review of Economic Studies* 9, no. 2 (Summer): 126–137.

———. 1950. *A Contribution to the Theory of the Trade Cycle*. London: Oxford University Press.

Higgins, Benjamin. 1956. The 'Dualistic Theory' of Underdeveloped Areas. In *Economic Development and Cultural Change* 4: 99–115.

Hoffman, Kenneth C. 1973. A Unified Framework for Energy System Planning. In *Energy Modeling*, ed. M.F. Searl. Washington, DC: Resources for the Future.

Hoffman, Kenneth C., and E.A. Cherniavsky. 1974. *Interfuel Substitution and Technological Change*, BNL 18919. Upton, NY: Brookhaven National Laboratory.

Hoffman, Kenneth C., and Dale W. Jorgenson. 1977. Economic and Technological Models for Evaluation of Energy Policy. *Bell Journal of Economics* 8, no. 2 (Autumn): 444–466.

Hoffman, Kenneth C., P.F. Palmedo, W. Marcuse, and M.D. Goldman. 1973. *Coupled Energy Systems—Economic Models*, BNL 19293. Upton, NY: Brookhaven National Laboratory.

Hogan, William W. 1977a. Capital Energy Complementarity in Aggregate Energy Economic Analysis. Unpublished paper, Energy Modeling Forum, Institute of Energy Studies, Stanford University (September).

———. 1977b. Energy and the Economy. Unpublished paper, Energy Modeling Forum, Institute of Energy Studies, Stanford University (September).

Hogan, W.W., and J.P. Weyant. 1980. *Combined Energy Models*. Report to the Electric Power Research Institute, Energy and Environmental Policy Center. Cambridge, MA: Harvard University.

Hsieh, C. 1952. The Nature and Extent of Underemployment in Asia. *International Labor Review* 55: 703–725.

Hudson, Edward A., and Dale W. Jorgenson. 1973. Interindustry Transactions. In *U.S. Energy Resources and Economic Growth*, eds. Dale W. Jorgenson and Hendrik S. Houthakker, ch. 5. Washington, DC: Energy Policy Project.

———. 1974a. U.S. Energy Policy and Economic Growth, 1975–2000. *Bell Journal of Economics and Management Science* 5, no. 2 (Autumn): 461–514.

———. 1974b. Tax Policy and Energy Use. In Committee on Finance, United States Senate, *Fiscal Policy and the Energy Crisis*, 1681–1694. Washington, DC: Ninety-Third Congress, First and Second Sessions.

———. 1974c. Economic Analysis of Alternative Energy Growth Patterns, Report to the Energy Policy Project, Ford Foundation. In *A Time to Choose*, eds. D. Freeman *et al*, 493–511. Cambridge, MA: Ballinger.

———. 1975a. Tax Policy and Energy Conservation. In *Econometric Studies of U.S. Energy Policy*, ed. Dale W. Jorgenson. Amsterdam: North-Holland.

———. 1975b. Projections of U.S. Economic Growth and Energy Demand, Report to the Edison Electric Institute, September. In *Structural Change and Current Problems Facing Regulated Public Utilities*, ed. R.W. Greenleaf, 75–128. Indianapolis, IN: Graduate School of Business, Indiana University.

————. 1977. *The Long-Term Interindustry Transactions Model: A Simulation for Energy and Economic Analysis*. Final report to the Applied Economics Division, Federal Preparedness Agency, General Services Administration, Washington, DC (September).

————. 1978a. Energy Policy and U.S. Economic Growth. *American Economic Review* 68, no. 2 (May): 118–123.

————. 1978b. Energy Prices and the U.S. Economy, 1972–1976. *Natural Resources Journal* 18, no. 4 (October): 877–897.

————. 1978c. The Economic Impact of Policies to Reduce U.S. Energy Growth. *Resources and Energy* 1, no. 3 (November): 205–230.

Ichimura, Shinichi. 1954. Toward a General Nonlinear Macrodynamic Theory of Economic Fluctuations. In *Post-Keynesian Economics*, ed. K. Kurihara, 192–226. New Brunswick: Rutgers University Press.

Ishiwata, S. 1957. Estimation of Capital Stocks in Prewar Japan (1868–1940). Unpublished Paper D27, Institute of Economic Research, Hitotsubashi University, Tokyo, in Japanese.

Iversen, K. 1954. Machine Solutions of Linear Differential Equations: Applications to a Dynamic Economic Model, unpublished Ph.D. thesis, Harvard University, January.

Jack Faucett Associates. 1973. *Data Development for the Input-Output Energy Model*. Final Report to the Energy Project. Washington, DC.

————. 1975. *Historical Energy Flow Accounts*. Final Report to the Federal Energy Administration. Washington, DC.

Johnson, Harry. 1954. Increasing Productivity, Income-Price Trends and the Trade Balance. *Economic Journal* 64: 462–485; Reprinted in *International Trade and Economic Growth*, 94–119. London: Allen and Unwin, 1958.

Johnston, B.F. 1962. Agricultural Development and Economic Transformation: A Comparative Study of the Japanese Experience. *Food Research Institute Studies* 3: 223–275.

Jorgenson, Dale W. 1960. On a Dual Stability Theorem. *Econometrica* 28 (October): 892–899.

————. 1961a. The Structure of Multi-Sector Dynamic Models. *International Economic Review* 2, no. 3 (September): 276–291.

————. 1961b. The Development of a Dual Economy. *Economic Journal* 71: 309–311.

————. 1965. Subsistence Agriculture and Economic Growth. Paper presented to the Conference on Subsistence and Peasant Economics, Honolulu, Hawaii, March 5, 1965.

————. 1975. Consumer Demand for Energy. In *Proceedings of the Workshop on Energy Demand*, ed. W.D. Nordhaus, 765–802. Laxenburg, Austria: IIASA.

———. 1976. Energy and the U.S. Economy: Present and Future. In *A Challenge for the Materials Industry: Changing Energy Economics*, ed. John H. DeYoung, Jr., 3–16. Washington, DC: American Institute of Mining, Metallurgical, and Petroleum Engineers.

———. 1977. Energy and the Outlook for U.S. Economic Growth. *Data Resources Review* 6, no. 12 (December): 1.10–1.19.

———. 1978. The Role of Energy in the U.S. Economy *National Tax Journal* 31, no. 3 (September): 209–220.

———. 1989. Capital as a Factor of Production. In *Technology and Capital Formation*, eds. Dale W. Jorgenson and R. Landau, 1–36. Cambridge, MA: MIT Press.

———. 1995. *Postwar U.S. Economic Growth.* Cambridge: The MIT Press.

———. 1996a. *Capital Theory and Investment Behavior.* Cambridge: The MIT Press.

———. 1996b. *Tax Policy and the Cost of Capital.* Cambridge: The MIT Press.

———. 1997a. *Aggregate Consumer Behavior.* Cambridge: The MIT Press.

———. 1997b. *Measuring Social Welfare.* Cambridge: The MIT Press.

———. Forthcoming. *Econometrics and Producer Behavior.* Cambridge: The MIT Press.

Jorgenson, Dale W., and Lawrence J. Lau. 1975. The Structure of Consumer Preferences. *Annals of Social and Economic Measurement* 4, no. 1 (January): 49–101.

Jorgenson, Dale W., and Brian D. Wright. 1975. The Impact of Alternative Policies to Reduce Oil Imports. *Data Resources Review* 4, no. 6 (June).

Kahn, Alfred E. 1960. Econoimc Issues in Regulating the Field Price of Natural Gas. *American Economic Review* 50: 506–517.

Kahn, Richard F. 1931. Home Investment and Unemployment. *Economic Journal* 41 (June): 173–198.

Kaldor, Nicholas. 1934. The Equilibrium of the Firm. *Economic Journal* 44: 60–76.

———. 1955–1956. Alternative Theories of Distribution. *Review of Economic Studies* 23: 83–100. Reprinted in *Essays on Value and Distribution.* London: Duckworth, 1960.

———. 1957. A Model of Economic Growth. *Economic Journal* 67: 591–624. Reprinted in *Essays in Economic Stability and Growth*, 259–300. Glencoe: Free Press.

———. 1960. Characteristics of Economic Development. In *Essays in Economic Stability and Growth*, 233–242. London: Duckworth.

————. 1961. Captial Accumulation and Economic Growth. In *The Theory of Captial*, eds. Friedrich A. Lutz and Douglas C. Hague, 171–222. London: Macmillan.

Kaldor, N., and James A. Mirrlees. 1962. A New Model of Economic Growth. *Review of Economic Studies* 29: 172–192.

Kantorovich, Leonid, and Tjalling C. Koopmans. 1976. Problems of Application of Optimization Methods in Industry. Federation of Swedish Industries, Stockholm (November).

Kao, C.H.C., K.R. Anschel, and Carl K. Eicher. 1964. Disguised Unemployment in Agriculture: A Survey. In *Agriculture in Economic Development*, eds. Carl K. Eicher and Lawrence W. Witt, 129–143. New York: McGraw-Hill.

Karlin, Samuel. 1959. Positive Operators. *Journal of Mathematics and Mechanics* 8 (November): 907–937.

Kaufman, George. 1973. *Sampling Without Replacement and Proportional to Random Size*. Cambridge, MA: Massachusetts Institute of Technology. This is also listed in ch. 8 as Barouch and Kaufman (1974).

Kaufman, George, Y. Baker, and D. Kruyt. 1974. Model of the Oil and Gas Discovery Process—Part I. Unpublished Memorandum. Cambridge, MA: Sloan School of Management, MIT. March.

Kemeny, J.G., Oskar Morgenstern, and G.L. Thompson. 1956. A Generalization of the von Neumann Model of an Expanding Economy. *Econometrica* 24 (April): 115–35.

Kenadjian, B. 1961. Disguised Unemployment in Underdeveloped Countries. *Zeitschrift für Nationalökonomie* 9: 216–223.

Khazzoom, J. Daniel. 1973. The FPC Staff's Econometric Model of Natural Gas Supply in the U.S. *Bell Journal of Economics and Management Science* 2, 51–93.

Klein, Lawrence, and Arthur S. Goldberger. 1955. *An Econometric Model of the United States, 1929–1952*. Amsterdam: North-Holland.

Koopmans, Tjalling C. 1951a. Analysis of Production as an Efficient Combination of Activities. In *Activity Analysis of Production and Allocation*, ed. Tjalling C. Koopmans, 33–97, Chapter 2. New York: Wiley.

————. 1951b. Introduction. In *Activity Analysis of Production and Allocation*, ed. Tjalling C. Koopmans. New York: Wiley.

————. 1957. Allocation of Resources and the Price System. In *Three Essays on the State of Economic Science*, 1–126. New York: McGraw-Hill.

Krein, Mark G., and M.A. Rutman. 1948. Linear Operators Leaving Invariant a Cone in Banach Space. *Uspekhi Matematischeskikh Nauk*, N. S. III (1948): 3–95 (American Mathematical Society, Translations, no. 26, 1950).

Kuznets, Simon. 1957. Quantitative Aspects of the Economic Growth of Nations, II. Industrial Distribution of National Product and Labor Force. *Economic Development and Cultural Change* 5, supplement.

Lau, Lawrence J. 1974. *Econometrics of Monotonicity, Convexity, and Quasiconvexity.* Institute for Mathematical Studies in the Social Sciences, Stanford University Technical Report no. 123, March.

Leibenstein, Harvey. 1954. *A Theory of Economic-Demographic Development.* Princeton, NJ: Princeton University Press.

——. 1957. *Economic Backwardness and Economic Growth.* New York: Wiley.

Leibenstein, Harvey, and W. Galenson. 1955. Investment Criteria, Productivity and Economic Development. *Quarterly Journal of Economics* 70: 343–370.

Leontief, Wassily W. 1947. Introduction to a Theory of the Internal Structure of Functional Relationships. *Econometrica* 157, no. 4 (October): 361–373.

——. 1951. *The Structure of the American Economy, 1919–1939,* 2nd ed. (1st ed. 1941). New York: Oxford University Press.

——. 1953. Dynamic Analysis. In *Studies in the Structure of the American Economy,* ed. Wassily Leontief, 53–90. New York: Oxford University Press.

Lewis, William A. 1954. Economic Development with Unlimited Supplies of Labour. *Manchester School* 22: 139–191.

——. 1955. *The Theory of Economic Growth.* London: Allen and Unwin.

——. 1958. Unlimited Labour: Further Notes. *Manchester School* 26: 1–32.

Lovell, M.C. 1963. A Comment on the Viability of Multi-Sector Dynamics Model. *International Review* 4, no. 1 (January).

MacAvoy, Paul W. 1962. *Price Formation in Natural Gas Fields.* New Haven, CT: Yale University Press.

——. 1974. *The Separate Control of Quantity and Price in the Energy Industries.* Cambridge, MA: Massachusetts Institute of Technology.

MacAvoy, Paul W., and Robert S. Pindyck. 1973. Alternative Regulatory Policies for Dealing with the Natural Gas Shortage. *Bell Journal of Economics and Management Science* 4, 454–498.

——. 1975. *The Economics of Natural Gas Shortage, 1960–1980.* Amsterdam: North-Holland.

MacDuffee, D. 1933. Theory of Matrices. In *Ergebnisse der Mathematik und ihrer Grenzgebiete.* Zweite Bank, 5, Berlin: Verlag von Julius Springer.

Malinvaud, Edmond. 1970. *Statistical Methods of Econometrics.* Amsterdam: North-Holland.

Mandelbaum, K. 1945. *The Industrialization of Backward Areas.* Oxford.

Manne, Alan Sussman, R.G. Richels, and J.P. Weyant. 1979. Energy Policy Modeling: A Survey. *Operations Research* 27, no. 1 (January): 1–36.

Marcuse, W., L. Bodin, E.A. Cherniavsky, and Y. Sanborn. 1975. *A Dynamic Time Dependent Model for the Analysis of Alternative Energy Policies*, BNL 19406. Upton, NY: Brookhaven National Laboratory.

McKenzie, Lionel. 1960. Matrices with Dominant Diagonals and Economic Theory. In *Mathematical Methods in the Social Sciences, 1959*. ed. Kenneth J. Arrow, Samuel Karlin, and Patrick Suppes, 47–62. Stanford, CA: Stanford University Press.

McManus, Maurice. 1957. Self-contradiction in Leontief's Dynamic Model. *Yorkshire Bulletin of Economic and Social Research* 9 (May): 1–21.

Mellor John W., and Robert D. Stevens. 1956. The Average and Marginal Product of Farm Labor in Underdeveloped Economies. *Journal of Farm Economics* 38: 780–791

Meier, Gerald M., and Robert E. Baldwin. 1957. *Economic Development*, Part II. New York: Wiley.

Morishima, Michio. 1958. A Contribution to the Nonlinear Theory of the Trade Cycle. *Zeitschrift für Nationalökonomie* 18: 165–174.

———. 1958. Prices, Interest, and Profits in a Dynamic Leontief System. *Econometrica* 26 (July): 358–380.

———. 1960. A Reconsideration of the Walras-Cassel-Leontief Model of General Equilibrium. In *Mathematical Methods in the Social Sciences, 1959*. ed. Kenneth J. Arrow, Samuel Karlin, and Patrick Suppes, 63–76. Stanford, CA: Stanford University Press.

———. 1964. *A Dynamic Leontief System with Neoclassical Production Functions, Equilibrium Stability and Growth*. Oxford: Oxford University Press.

Mount, T.D., Duane Chapman, and T.J. Tyrrell. 1973. *Elasticity Demand in the United States*. Oak Ridge National Laboatory Report, June.

National Petroleum Council. 1971. *U.S. Energy Outlook: An Initial Appraisal, 1971–1985*. Washington, July.

———. 1972. *U.S. Energy Outlook*. Washington, December.

Nicholls, William H. 1964. The Place of Agriculture in Economic Development. In *Agriculture in Economic Development*, eds. Carl K. Eicher and Lawrence W. Witt, 11–14. New York: McGraw-Hill.

———. 1963. An Agricultural Surplus as a Factor in Economic Development. *Journal of Political Economy* 71: 1–29.

Nikaido, Hukukane, and Hirofumi Uzawa. 1960. Stability and Nonnegativity in a Walrasian Tatonnement Process. *International Economic Review* 1 (January): 50–59.

Nordhaus, William D. 1976. The Allocation of Energy Resources. *Brookings Papers on Economic Activity* 3: 529–570.

Ohkawa, Kazushi. 1957. *The Growth Rate of the Japanese Economy since 1878.* Tokyo.

Ohkawa, Kazushi, and R. Minami. 1964. The Phase of Unlimited Supplies of Labor. *Hitotsubashi Journal of Economics* 6: 1–15.

Ohkawa, Kazushi, and Henry Rosovsky. 1964. The Role of Agriculture in Modern Japanese Economic Development. In *Agriculture in Economic Development*, eds. Carl K. Eicher and Lawrence W. Witt, p. 52. New York: McGraw-Hill.

Ortega, J.M., and Werner C. Rheinboldt. 1970. *Iterative Solution of Nonlinear Equations in Several Variables.* New York: Academic Press.

Oshima, Herbert. 1958. Underemployment in Backward Economies: An Empirical Comment. *Journal of Political Economy* 66: 259–263.

Pindyck, Robert S. 1978. *OPEC, Oil Prices, and the Western Economies.* Cambridge, MA: Energy Laboratory, MIT.

Quesnay, François. 1894. *Tableau Oeconomique.* London: British Economic Association (1st ed. 1758).

Ricardo, David. 1911. *Principles*, p. 35 (1st ed. 1817). London: Dent.

Robinson, Joan. 1953–1954. The Production Function and the Theory of Capital. *Review of Economic Studies* 21: 81–106.

———. 1955–1956. Reply. *Review of Economic Studies* 23: 247.

———. 1958. *The Accumulation of Capital.* London: Macmillan.

———. 1959. Some Problems of Definition and Measurement of Capital. *Oxford Economic Papers* 11: 157–166.

Rosenstein-Rodan, Paul N. 1943. Problems of Industrialization of Eastern and South-Eastern Europe. *Economic Journal*, 53: 202–211.

———. 1957. Disguised Unemployment and Underemployment in Agriculture. *Monthly Bulletin of Agricultural Economics and Statistics* 6: 1–7.

Samuelson, Paul A. 1939a. Interactions Between the Multiplier Analysis and the Principle of Acceleration. *Review of Economic Statistics* 21 (May): 75–78.

———. 1939b. A Synthesis of the Principle of Acceleration and the Multiplier. *Journal of Political Economy* 47 (December): 786–797.

———. 1966. Nonsubstitution Theorems. In *The Collected Scientific Papers of Paul A. Samuelson*, ed. J. Stiglitz. Cambridge, MA: Massachusetts Institute of Technology.

Samuelson, Paul A., and Robert M. Solow. 1953. Balanced Growth under Constant Returns to Scale. *Econometrica* 21 (July): 412–424.

Sargan, John D. 1958. The Instability of the Leontief Dynamic Model, *Econometrica* 26 (July): 381–392.

Schultz, Theodore W. 1956. The Role of the Government in Promoting Economic Growth. In *The State of Social Sciences*, ed. Leonard D. White. Chicago, IL.

———. 1964. *Transforming Traditional Agriculture*. New Haven, CT: Yale University Press.

Smithies, Arthur. 1957. Economic Fluctuations and Growth. *Econometrica* 25 (January): 1–52.

Solow, Robert M. 1952. On the Structure of Linear Models. *Econometrica* 20 (January): 29–46.

———. 1955. The Production Function and the Theory of Capital. *Review of Economic Studies* 23(2), no. 61: 101–8.

———. 1956. A Contribution to the Theory of Economic Growth. *Quarterly Journal of Economics* 70: 65–94.

———. 1957. Technical Change and the Aggregate Production Function. *Review of Economics and Statistics* 39: 312–320.

———. 1959. Competitive Valuation in a Dynamic Input-Output System. *Econometrica* 27 (January): 30–53.

Spaventa, Luigi. 1959. Dualism in Economic Growth. *Banca Nazionale Del Lavoro, Quarterly Review*, 51: 386–390.

Statistical Office of the United Nations, Department of Economic and Social Affairs. 1965. *The Growth of World Industry, 1938–1961, International Analyses and Tables*, 194–195. New York: United Nations.

Suits, Daniel B. 1962. Forecasting and Analysis with an Econometric Model. *American Economic Review* 52, no. 1 (March): 104–132.

Sussman, P.N. 1974. *Supply and Production of Offshore Gas under Alternative Leasing Policies*. Cambridge, MA: Massachusetts Institute of Technology.

Taylor, Lester D. 1975. The Demand for Electricity: A Survey. *Bell Journal of Economics* 6, no. 1 (Spring): 74–110.

———. 1977. The Demand for Energy: A Survey. In *International Studies of the Demand for Energy*, ed. William D. Nordhaus. Amsterdam: North-Holland.

Tinbergen, Jan. 1942. Zur Theorie der langfristigen Wirtschaftsentwicklung, *Weltwirtschaftliches Archiv*, Band 55, no. 1, pp. 511–549; translated and reprinted as (1959), "On the Theory of Trend Movements," in *Jan Tinbergen, Selected Papers*, eds. Leo H. Klaasen, Leendert M. Koyck, and Hendrikus J. Witteveen, 182–221. Amsterdam: North-Holland.

Tobin, James. 1952. A Survey of Rationing. *Econometrica* 4: 521–553.

————. 1955. A Dynamic Aggregative Model. *Journal of Polictical Economy* 63: 103–115.

Uhler, Robert S., and Paul G. Bradley. 1970. A Stochastic Model for Determining the Economic Prospects of Petroleum Exploration Over a Large Region. *Journal of the American Statistical Association* 65: 623–630.

United Nations. 1968. *A System of National Accounts.* New York: Department of Economic and Social Affairs, United Nations.

Uzawa, Hirofumi. 1956. Note on Leontief's Dynamic Input-Output System. *Proceedings of the Japan Academy* 32 (February): 79–82.

Vaccara, Beatrice N. 1970. Changes Over Time in Input-Output Coefficients for the United States. In *Contributions to Input-Output Analysis,* eds. Anne P. Carter and Andrew Brody, 238–260. Amsterdam: North-Holland.

Walras. 1954. *Elements of Pure Economics,* transl. W. Jaffé. Homewood, IL: Irwin.

Warriner, Doreen. 1939. *Economics of Peasant Farming.* London: Oxford University Press.

————. 1948. *Land and Poverty in the Middle East.* London: Royal Institute of International Affairs.

————. 1955. Land Reform and Economic Development. In *Fiftieth Anniversary Commemoration Lectures,* p. 26. Cairo.

Weinberg, A.M., ed. 1979. *Economic and Environmental Impacts of a U.S. Nuclear Moratorium 1985–2010.* 2nd edition. Cambridge, MA: MIT Press.

Wicksell, Knut. 1923. A Mathematical Analysis of Dr. Åkerman's Problem. *Ekonomisk Tidskrift* 25: 157–180. Reprinted in *Lectures on Political Economy,* vol. 1, trans. E. Classen. London: Routledge and Kegan Paul, 1934.

Wielandt, Helmut. 1950. Unzerlegbare nicht-negative Matrizen, *Mathematische Zeitschrift* 52.

Wiles, W. 1956. *Price, Cost and Output,* chapter 12 and appendix, pp. 202–251. Oxford: Blackwell.

Index